T0201486

Retooling Politics

Donald Trump, the Arab Spring, Brexit: digital media have provided political actors and citizens with new tools to engage in politics. These tools are now routinely used by activists, candidates, nongovernmental organizations, and parties to inform, mobilize, and persuade people. But what are the effects of this retooling of politics? Do digital media empower the powerless or are they breaking democracy? Have these new tools and practices fundamentally changed politics or is their impact just a matter of degree?

This clear-eyed guide steps back from hyperbolic hopes and fears to offer a balanced account of what aspects of politics are being shaped by digital media and what remains unchanged. The authors discuss data-driven politics, the flow and reach of political information, the effects of communication interventions through digital tools, their use by citizens in coordinating political action, and what their impact is on political organizations and on democracy at large.

ANDREAS JUNGHERR is Assistant Professor in Political Science at the University of Konstanz, Germany. His research addresses strategic adaptation to digital technology by organizations, political actors, and citizens in international comparison; he also focuses on harnessing the potential of computational social science. He is author of the books *Analyzing Political Communication with Digital Trace Data* (2015) and *Das Internet in Wahlkämpfen* (with Harald Schoen, 2013).

GONZALO RIVERO is a research data scientist at the Statistics and Evaluation Sciences Unit at Westat, USA. His research focuses on political representation, electoral behavior, and quantitative methods for public opinion research.

DANIEL GAYO-AVELLO is an associate professor in the Department of Computer Science at the University of Oviedo, Spain. His main area of interest is web mining with a focus on social media. He has published in venues such as *Communications of the ACM, IEEE Internet Computing*, and *IEEE Multimedia*. He coedited a special issue of *Internet Research* on the predictive power of social media, and contributed a chapter on political opinion to the book *Twitter: A Digital Socioscope* (2015)

Retooling Politics

How Digital Media Are Shaping Democracy

ANDREAS JUNGHERR

University of Konstanz

GONZALO RIVERO

Westat

DANIEL GAYO-AVELLO

University of Oviedo

CAMBRIDGE
UNIVERSITY PRESS

CAMBRIDGE
UNIVERSITY PRESS

University Printing House, Cambridge CB2 8BS, United Kingdom

One Liberty Plaza, 20th Floor, New York, NY 10006, USA

477 Williamstown Road, Port Melbourne, VIC 3207, Australia

314–321, 3rd Floor, Plot 3, Splendor Forum, Jasola District Centre,
New Delhi – 110025, India

79 Anson Road, #06–04/06, Singapore 079906

Cambridge University Press is part of the University of Cambridge.

It furthers the University's mission by disseminating knowledge in the pursuit of
education, learning, and research at the highest international levels of excellence.

www.cambridge.org
Information on this title: www.cambridge.org/9781108419406
DOI: 10.1017/9781108297820

© Andreas Jungherr, Gonzalo Rivero, and Daniel Gayo-Avello 2020

First published 2020

Printed in the United Kingdom by TJ International, Padstow Cornwall

A catalogue record for this publication is available from the British Library.

Library of Congress Cataloging-in-Publication Data
Names: Jungherr, Andreas, author. | Rivero Rodríguez, Gonzalo, author. |
Gayo-Avello, Daniel, 1975- author.
Title: Retooling politics : how digital media are shaping democracy / Andreas Jungherr,
Gonzalo Rivero, Daniel Gayo-Avello.
Description: Cambridge ; New York, NY : Cambridge University Press, 2020. | Includes
bibliographical references and index.
Identifiers: LCCN 2019051270 (print) | LCCN 2019051271 (ebook) | ISBN 9781108419406 (hardback) |
ISBN 9781108297820 (epub)
Subjects: LCSH: Communication in politics–Technological innovations. | Political participation–
Technological innovations. | Digital media–Political aspects. | Big data–Political aspects. |
Technology and democracy
Classification: LCC JA85 .J86 2020 (print) | LCC JA85 (ebook) | DDC 320.01/4–dc23
LC record available at https://lccn.loc.gov/2019051270
LC ebook record available at https://lccn.loc.gov/2019051271

ISBN 978-1-108-41940-6 Hardback

Contents

Acknowledgments

We started this book in early 2017, at a time when the literature on digital media and politics was undergoing a deep transformation, trying to make sense of the unexpected events that had happened the year before. The landscape was very exciting and intimidating as we set out to structure academic debates that were quickly evolving. It also meant that the always exhausting and absorbing process of writing a book was even more demanding. We feel very lucky to have been able to rely on our friends and family, who patiently offered us unconditional support during this journey. Our deepest gratitude goes to Hortensia Fernández, Valeska Gerstung Lucía Leal, Haley Miller, and Víctor Sancho. The book would have been impossible without you.

Although three of us appear on the cover, this book has been a shared journey with many other colleagues who were always ready to offer their time to provide feedback and encouragement. We owe a special debt of gratitude to the participants in a workshop held at the University of Konstanz (Germany) in spring of 2018, who were kind enough to spend two days working with us on an early version of the manuscript. We thank Shelley Boulianne, Sara Colella, Jan Dix, Fabrizio Gilardi, Max Heermann, David Karpf, Steffen Kramer, Shannon McGregor, Ralph Schroeder, and Jasmin Siri for their participation, insightful comments, and generous advice. The workshop was made possible by the generous funding from the Cluster of Excellence "Kulturelle Grundlagen von Integration" at the University of Konstanz.

Many colleagues read different versions of the chapters and provided us with invaluable comments. We thank Berta Barbet Porta, Oliver Posegga, Harald Schoen, and Yannis Theocharis who read parts of the manuscript and gave us detailed feedback. In addition, Marco T. Bastos, Pablo Fernández-Vázquez, Pascal Jürgens, Rasmus Kleis Nielsen, Adrian Rauchfleisch, and Alexander Wuttke were always only one quick email away and provided us with rapid feedback and advice every time the road did not seem clear to us anymore.

We are thankful for the expert guidance by the team at Cambridge University Press. Lauren Cowles and Amy He steered us through the intimidating process of making this book a reality and showed remarkable patience and understanding as the work extended for much longer than any of us would have anticipated. We also thank Lauren for her comments to an early draft that helped us convey our ideas more effectively.

Thank you for all your help and support. The book and the experience of writing it would have been poorer without you.

*****

Disclaimer: The opinions expressed in this book are our own and are not intended to reflect the views and positions of our employers (University of Konstanz, Westat, and University of Oviedo) or their clients.

1

The Rise of Digital Media and the Retooling of Politics

It is June 2015 and the famous American reality-TV personality Donald Trump announces his bid for the Republican nomination to the 2016 race for the US presidency. Journalists, Republican donors, and prospective voters now have to decide if they should take his bid seriously. The history of American presidential campaigns is littered with celebrities and third-party candidates who tried to capitalize on their fame or success by entering politics. While some like Ronald Reagan, Arnold Schwarzenegger, or Michael Bloomberg proved to be successful, most celebrity candidacies turned out to be mere blips in the history of American politics. How should observers decide on whether Donald Trump's bid fell into the first or the second category? The Trump campaign portrayed their candidate as being in touch with the long-forgotten people lacking a voice in US politics (Green 2017), a group that the campaign of the Democratic frontrunner Hillary Clinton helpfully labeled "deplorables" (Chozick 2016). To assess the validity of Trump's claims, journalists decided to take to social media as a source of how well his message resonated with the public.

True to his past as a controversial reality-TV star, Trump regularly posted highly controversial and provocative messages on Twitter, agitating against immigrants, denigrating opponents, and taunting the media (Barbaro 2015). This meant breaking protocol with established campaigning styles and contradicting expectations of appropriate behavior for presidential candidates. But publicly visible interactions with tweets in the form of retweets, likes, or mentions allowed the campaigns and onlookers to assess the relative popularity of the claims. Reportedly, this made Trump's tweets a weather gauge for the campaign to assess the fit of messages for their intended audience (Green 2017, 128). Journalists read these publicly visible metrics as signs of Trump being in touch with Americans. Let us for the moment ignore whether social media metrics indeed offer a true reflection of public opinion; in 2015 their use

1

as such helped transform a reality-TV personality into the Republican presidential candidate and ultimately into the US President.

*****

It is spring 2016, but in Britain politicos of all stripes are not enjoying the first sunny days on the sceptered isle. Instead, they are hard at work. On June 23, British voters are called to decide in a referendum on Britain's status in the EU. Loose coalitions across party lines work overtime trying to convince Britons of "Britain Stronger in Europe" or that they should "Vote Leave" (Shipman 2016). Although both campaigns were well funded, could rely on seasoned campaigners, and were aligned with powerful political parties and factions, they still faced a common challenge: How to contact voters? Established parties and other political organizations, such as labor unions and nongovernmental organizations (NGOs), spend years on building contact lists. They collect names and contact information of members, sympathizers, and people who get in touch with the organizations. These lists allow an organization to contact people directly at a later point, to mobilize them to vote, to protest, or to provide them with pertinent information on current events. In the past, the power of established parties and political organizations has in no small part rested on their being the only actors who were able to quickly reach a significant subset of the population (Bimber 2003). But how should an organization such as "Vote Leave," that was founded only a few months earlier, develop a list of people and establish how to contact them?

"Vote Leave" ended up using two different approaches. For one, the campaign went to where likeminded people already interacted: the Facebook pages of eurosceptics. By running targeted ads to people who had liked well-known eurosceptic Facebook pages, "Vote Leave" reached users sympathetic to their message and tried to have them register in the campaign's database. Facebook's ad manager tool even allowed the campaign to identify users who shared characteristics with users who had liked eurosceptic pages but had not liked these pages themselves, thereby allowing "Vote Leave" to move beyond the eurosceptic core (Shipman 2016, 416f.). In addition, on May 27, four weeks before the referendum, the "Vote Leave" campaign announced a prize of 50 million pounds to everyone who correctly predicted the winner of all 51 matches in the Euro 2016, an international soccer tournament held in France that summer. Participants were asked for their names and contact information. Some 120,000 people responded. The contact list of "Vote Leave" had just grown significantly at no cost to the campaign as the odds of winning this bet were tiny and nobody won the prize. The list was later put to use by the campaign in an intensive outreach blast over the last 24 hours of the campaign, when half a million text messages were sent reminding people to vote (Shipman

2016, 407; Cummings 2017). We can debate the question of how significant this effort was in face of 17.4 million votes in favor of Britain leaving the EU (Editorital Team 2016). But given that only 1.3 million fewer voters favored remaining in the Union, any small edge could have been decisive.

*****

We could have chosen similar examples from many other countries. The actors and causes may have been less prominent, but the challenges actors faced and the way they addressed them by using digital tools would have corresponded strikingly with these examples. All over the world, politicians, campaigns, NGOs, activists, and citizens are using digital tools in politics. They use them to pursue needs that are as old as politics: How do I get the media to pay attention to me and what I say? How do I get my message out? How do I get people mobilized when it counts? How do I coordinate my team in order to reach as many people as possible? How do I build an organization? How do I decide whom to contact and whom to ignore? All these needs have existed and have been met countless times well before the introduction of digital media. But digital media have changed the way political actors pursue such needs. Digital media have provided political actors with new tools and in turn changed the way some of politics is done: They have retooled politics and through this continue to shape the practice of democracy. This book is about these universal political needs of participants in politics, the way they are pursued by the use of digital media, and the way digital media are retooling the practice of politics in contemporary democracies.

We believe the available evidence does not point to a fundamental trans-formation of politics through digital technology. Instead, we believe digital media play an essential role in fulfilling a series of universal needs for political actors in the pursuit of their goals in democracies. Digital media change politics, but not necessarily in a fundamental way, overturning established power structures. Instead, change happens in democracies within established institutional frameworks. This first leads to changes in political practices, moving on to processes, and might even result in the emergence of new voices. Yet, as such changes are gradual and embedded in existing power structures and institutions, they will not transform politics fundamentally. They do, however, retool politics, as described in what follows.

Digital media have changed the character and business model of news organizations; many actors have turned into active participants in political communication spaces and are able to push content or commentary in infor-mation flows, while audiences have an increasingly active role in determining which stories and perspectives rise to prominence and travel widely. This has led to the erosion of power and authority of traditional media organizations, allowed for a much more active contestation of political facts, and contributes to the emergence of new voices in political discourse.

This process has changed the channels and routes through which political information reaches people. Political actors have to adapt to the new dynamics of information spaces by establishing new channels to reach people directly, develop relationships with new allies that allow them to reach people indirectly, and to adapt to new rhythms and communicative conventions in these environments. This results in the emergence of new intermediaries in public discourse who until now had no business or institutional dealings with politics, such as providers of digital platforms, while at the same time weakening the influence of traditional intermediaries, such as media companies.

The move into new communicative environments and use of new technologies has impacted the type and strength of effects political information has on recipients. Depending on your point of view, this might lead to a growing divide between politically interested and uninterested audiences, political polarization, or strong persuasive effects of information shared by friends online. Yet any discussion of effects has to remain conscious of the social and motivational embeddings of digital media that might weaken or offset any direct effects. Moreover, technological change in digital media makes establishing cumulative evidence over time difficult as different developmental stages of digital technology differ in likely effect patterns.

Digital tools have changed the way political actors coordinate supporters and collective action. Allowing people to coordinate quickly and at low cost has been seen as an important element in strengthening democratic movements in autocracies and vitalizing Western democracies in giving protest movements voice and presence in public discourse. While true, this optimistic view tends to emphasize the role of digital media in collective action, allowing the coordination of people already willing to participate. While important, this is only one element in collective action. Often the more difficult part is getting people to cooperate in the first place, and here digital media's contribution is limited.

Digital media have been also charged with deep impact on political organization. By taking over central functions of organizations in politics – such as the keeping of membership lists thus allowing for the coordination of collective action and the publication and dissemination of information – digital media are seen by some as making political organizations superfluous. Success stories of decentralized issue-driven protest movements, such as #MeToo or #Occupy, are often raised to illustrate the potential for politics without central organizations. Yet these accounts often skip over the short duration of these movements, their difficulty in exerting political change beyond an initial capturing of the public agenda, and the troubles that come with informal hierarchies. So, while digital media probably will not lead to the end of formal political organizations, they initiate adaptation processes with regard to funding, membership types, and networks of allied organizations and groups for traditional political organizations.

Finally, through new measurement opportunities and metrics, digital media have changed the way political actors are seeing the world. By increasing data storage and computing power and by collecting ever more data on people's interactions with digital tools and sensors, digital technology has significantly extended the data available to political actors, journalists, and the public. Correspondingly, the hopes and fears associated with data-driven practices in politics have skyrocketed. While some have hoped for an increasing role for data-driven practices, making politics more evidence-based and efficient, others point to the well-known dangers of management-by-metrics, losing sight of what actually matters in favor of what happens to be easy to measure. Yet others point to the dangers of rampant surveillance. While neither hopes nor fears are likely to materialize in full, this is an important area, shifting the way politicians, bureaucrats, journalists, and the public make sense of the world, thus highlighting the need to figure out which part of political reality tends to be emphasized or neglected by digital metrics.

This, in turn, has shaped the way contemporary democracy is practiced all over the world and has given rise to new expectations as to how and what democracy is supposed to deliver. While a radical deepening of democracy with regard to its reach in societal areas and breadth of participation is unlikely to materialize, the impact of digital media on democracies is clearly felt. This impact can be felt in the monitoring of politicians by individuals or institutions, the mediating or unmediating of the relationship between political elites and the public, the reshaping of relationships in the political representation of citizens through politicians and parties, and the fragility of political information environments. This impact is pervasive, albeit not necessarily transformative in changing fundamental characteristics in practiced democracy.

In light of the apparent role of digital media in getting Donald Trump elected, as well as their supposed role in shifting the British electorate toward Brexit and inciting democratic revolutions in autocracies, our claim of a non-transformative impact might feel like a callous provocation. Yet a closer look reveals that although the role of digital media in these events was highly visible and without a doubt instrumental, it was far from decisive in causing the outcome. But we have to be careful. Just because digital media might not have shifted the balance of political power decisively does not mean they did not have an impact on politics.

To generally declare digital media to have transformed politics is highly simplistic and risks mistaking the presentation of politics for its substance. On the other hand, declaring that digital media have not touched politics at all means being willfully blind to weak or indirect effects of digital media on politics, such as, for example, changing the institutional and organizational foundations of public discourse or collective action. In fact, the practice of contemporary politics is deeply shaped by the use of digital media. They have retooled politics by providing political actors with new ways to pursue their political needs and changed how some of politics is done. Yet, in assessing the role of digital media, we have to take care not to over- or underestimate their impact. This might make for slightly less exciting reading than an inspirational tale of empowering change. It has the benefit, though, of providing an accurate account of the multifaceted and pervasive impact of digital media on politics.

1.1 What to Expect?

We aim to provide a fresh perspective on the role of digital media in politics. We do so by taking a needs-oriented perspective. We start by asking what needs political actors share in the pursuit of political goals in democracies and how they have used digital media to help them. This allows us to examine the role of digital media in politics by focusing on the specific needs faced by political actors and organizations. This needs-oriented discussion allows us to identify areas in politics impacted by digital media and areas remaining more or less untouched. We thus transcend a false dichotomy between transform-ation and stasis and are able to identify effects in unexpected areas and in varying degrees of impact.

We mainly discuss democracies. While we also discuss the role of digital media in the transition from autocratic systems into democracies, we will touch on this fleetingly. In autocratic political systems, politics and communication have a lower impact and do not necessarily follow the same dynamics as in democracies. An additional challenge is that the literature on digital media in politics is very thin on cases from Africa, Asia, Latin America, Russia, and South America (for welcome exceptions see Oates 2013; Livingston and Walter-Drop 2014; F. L. Lee and Chan 2018; Nyabola 2018). This is deeply problematic as digital media are, of course, pervasively used in these regions, which offer different institutional and political settings from those in Western democracies. This makes them very interesting cases for the uses and effects of digital media under alternative institutional and cultural contexts. Given the underdeveloped state of the literature, this discussion will have to wait for the future.

We will rely heavily on cases and findings from the United States. This forces the question of what we can learn from US-based findings. The crux of the matter is that the United States is the democracy in which digital media have developed the furthest, are adopted most widely, and have shown the most obvious effects in politics. Consequently, it is also the country where digital media and their role in politics have been examined most closely. Accordingly, this makes the United States the environment for which we have the broadest collection of well-understood cases. Furthermore, for better or worse, US politics is followed closely internationally. This allows us to refer to cases that most readers of this book can be expected to be familiar with.

And yet the United States is also very different from any other democracy. For one, elections are a multi-million-dollar industry. This has led to the emergence of a rich ecosystem of consultancies willing and able to invest in the development of digital tools and services supporting candidates on any level of politics. Over the last twenty years political discourse in the country has degenerated into a veritable blood sport, with the two sides of the aisle pummeling each other mercilessly. This has led to a weakening of political institutions, rendering them highly vulnerable to challenges by digital media.

Any uncritical generalizations on the role of digital media in politics based on cases and findings from the United States is obviously deeply naive. Yet nor should we ignore what we can learn about the role of digital in politics from US-based studies. Instead, when we discuss US cases and findings we provide the respective context. This allows readers to draw their own conclusions and assess whether or not the cases and findings discussed here travel successfully to other contexts of interest.

1.2 Digital Media and the Needs of Political Actors

When we use the term *digital media*, we combine a broad concept of media as found in sociology and communication research with a technology-centric perspective as found in computer and information science. We refer to institutions and infrastructures that produce and distribute information encoded in binary code. On the one hand, this anchors us with uses of a specific technology: the production, encoding, storing, distributing, decoding, and consumption of information in binary code. On the other hand, it allows us to broadly discuss institutions, organizations, and practices associated with the use of this specific technology. Thus, in our discussion of the role of digital media in politics, we can address political uses of specific technologies, such as email for political organization and coordination or weblogs as hosts for politically relevant information. We can also address the institutional and organizational settings this technology is embedded in and respective changes – for example, the impact of the widespread use of online ads by sellers and buyers of goods on the newspaper industry, or the consequences of ad hoc issue-based mobilization on the political economy of political organizations.[1]

We also use the terms *digital tools* and *digital services*. By digital tools we mean specific instances of digital technology that, in principle, could be used in the pursuit of specific political needs or goals. This could be websites, e-mail, or social networking sites. With digital services, we refer to processes that enable the embedding of digital tools in structural or organizational environments. Digital services thus allow for the strategic uses of digital tools by political actors. Providers of digital services can be political organizations themselves, for example by way of dedicated divisions, or third-party vendors specialized for political customers, or providers of general-purpose services, such as Facebook, Twitter, or Google. For example, in our terminology databases are a digital tool for political parties and candidates to store and access information on potential voters. The process of conceptualizing populations of interest, translating this into statistical models, identifying corresponding individuals in the database, and making their contact information available to local campaigners on the ground who can then knock on doors is an example of a digital service. This allows us to differentiate between digital technology and the institutional processes governing the actual use of the said technology in politics.

In order to characterize the political effects of digital media we have to differentiate between three elements of the political system: polity, policy, and politics (Heidenheimer 1986). *Polity* refers to the institutional and normative foundations of political systems. Here, the impact of digital media is indirect. If we find polity change associated with digital media – such as a very

---

[1] Our definition is a combination of definitions of *media* by Couldry (2012) and *digitality* by Boast (2017). Couldry defines media as "the institutional dimensions of communication, whether as infrastructure or content, production or circulation" (Couldry 2012, 2). In his history of digital technology, Boast emphasizes the nature of digital as encoding wide varieties of information in a uniform format: "what makes the digital, as we use it today, *digital* is that the combination of ons and offs, in very specific albeit complex ways, encodes information. Over the past 150 years these codes have encoded all types of information, including all of our media. Translating or encoding something, a mediation, into a code of ons and offs – this is digital, and this is the foundation of all digital technology" (Boast 2017, 10). Combining both perspectives allows us to account for the social and institutional embedding of digital media as well as the characteristics of digital technology and its role in encoding information.

optimistic reading of the events around the Arab Spring – then it will be realized through politics and changes in the power dynamic between societal interests. *Policy* is the content of rules and decisions of institutions in societies that are collectively binding for each member of society. Here, the impact of digital media can be expected to be felt on the establishment of guidelines for institutions and state organizations on how to use digital media and rules and regulations concerning the public use and provision of digital technology and services. These changes are likely to be gradual and within an existing framework of institutional governance and regulation of technology and services. They are not the subject of this book. Finally, *politics* is the process in which societal interests compete in order to influence the content of policy or to gain representation in institutions of the state which develop, implement, or adjudicate the application of policy. In this competition the impact of digital media on politics should become visible most clearly.

In political competition for positions, influence, or policies actors and organizations have a series of needs:

• they need access to the flow of political information in mass media, online communication, and political talk;
• they need to reach people with their message either directly or indirectly through collaboration with other societal actors;
• they need to change minds in order to convince people of their position or to mobilize them into action;
• they need to coordinate others sharing the same interests or concerns into public expression or into collective action;
• they need to form and maintain organizations; and
• they need to collect data about the world and then interpret and assess that data.

In the pursuit of these needs, digital media provide communicative environments and the degree to which digital media structure communicative environments in politics and allow actors and organizations to systematically improve their relative position shows us the influence of digital media on politics.

Access to the Flow of Political Information

Political information flows through societies like water flowing from a spring into a river, broadening into a delta before spilling into the sea. Information starts at the source by someone covering an event, leaking a story, launching a press release, etc. Most of these initial information inputs evaporate quickly as they fail to attract amplification, whether through prolonged talk or through media coverage. Amplification through media coverage is crucial for any piece of information to travel far and wide through societies. Without it, information remains limited to a small community of interest without developing larger societal impact. Political actors and activists must find access to this flow of political information, otherwise their public visibility and that of their causes and concerns remains low, making it unlikely that they will be able to mobilize public opinion successfully for their political goals.

In the past, gaining access to the flow of political information meant attracting or influencing mass media coverage. In the age of broadcast television, this meant designing events based on their appeal to television cameras, producing short, catchy soundbites sure to make it into news coverage, or staging a series of events lending themselves to an attractive narrative. On a more mundane level, this could also mean having dedicated staff acting as media liaisons, keeping in continuous contact with journalists or designated talking heads. Attracting media coverage also required adapting to the temporal rhythms of news production, for example by timing one's press conferences, releases, rebuttals, or high points during partially televised speeches exactly in accordance with the production schedules of news programs or newspapers. In this process, a balance between political actors and organizations, journalists and media organizations, and consultants emerged that contributed to and shaped the flow of political information. Digital media have shaken this balance to the core.

Digital media have extended the number of outlets covering politics as well as increased the variance of production modes, coverage guidelines, and business models of political news production and consumption. Gone are the days when only a handful of media organizations decided on what is news and agreed on a set of editorial standards in the coverage of politics. The contemporary media system encompasses any number of outlets covering politics, from lowbrow muckraking to highbrow investigative journalism. The discerning reader can choose freely among many online political news outlets according to her tastes. On the one hand, this means access to information is harder to contain for political elites, so transparency might increase. On the other hand, this also means that journalistic standards are tougher to uphold as sensationalist coverage is only one click away. *In extremis*, the abundance of voices and the difficulty in agreeing on common points of view might lead to epistemic crises over what version of political events or even which facts the public can agree on. Current concerns about purposeful disinformation or so-called fake news are very much a consequence of this development.

The abundant amount of free coverage online makes it harder for news organizations to charge for coverage. Why pay for information that others cover for free? This leads to the erosion of established business models of news production and endangers the long-term persistence of established news organizations. It remains unclear whether new news providers can find sustainable business models themselves. Digital media thus deeply impact the established structure of organizations shaping the flow of political information, with potentially far-reaching consequences for the quality of publicly available information on politics and subsequent discourse.

Digital media have also led to heightened visibility of audience reactions. By posting information, comments, or public exchanges on personalized websites or blogs and (semi-)public profiles on social networking platforms, such as Facebook or Twitter, individual users are clearly part of the flow of political information. They pick up on news coverage and elite communication, or actively point out stories that in their view have been underreported. Where once these reactions were restricted to around the water cooler at work, the living room, or the pub around the corner, digital media makes the topics, content, and perhaps even the sentiment of audience reactions broadly visible and countable. Audience reactions manifest in clicks, shares, likes, or comments become measurable and start to influence the flow of political information. What audiences react to travels widely and gets covered more intensely. What audiences ignore floats out of sight. Digital media thus increase the number of actors injecting and amplifying items in the flow of political information (Chadwick 2017) and "tether" political elites, journalists, and audience much more closely to one another (Schroeder 2018).

Today it is as important as ever for political actors to gain access to the flow of political information. Yet participants, rhythms, and dynamics of this flow have changed through digital media. This means political actors have to adjust their tactics for how to attract or influence coverage in this new environment. We will discuss these changes and consequences for politics in Chapter 2.

Reaching People

It is not enough for political actors to be part of the flow of political information; they also need to reach specific people with specific information. Supporters have to be alerted to a group's position on current events, undecideds have to be contacted to tip the electoral balance, and members of issue publics have to be activated in order to support contested causes. Political actors can achieve reach either directly or indirectly. In achieving reach, we find significant changes in opportunities and practices by political actors driven by the use of digital media.

In the recent past, directly reaching people involved political actors contacting them by mail or in conversation in canvassing drives in shopping malls, at voters' doorsteps, or in personal appearances. In practice this meant maintaining extensive lists of contact information of members or supporters, as well as large volunteer forces in order to be able to mount large-scale canvassing operations. Both mail and canvassing are highly resource-intensive, limiting their use to campaign seasons.

Today, digital media extend the opportunities for direct contact by political actors. Email allows for repeated contact at negligible costs. The publication of websites, short messages, images, or videos on hosted sites or branded profiles on third-party platforms such as Facebook, Twitter, or YouTube allows for the production and unfiltered distribution of text and multimedia content to a self-selected audience independent of editorial decisions of media organizations. While costs in the production of this content might still be high, distribution costs are lower and the flexibility with regard to chosen content is higher than before. Moreover, these opportunities allow parties to communicate directly with members, supporters, and the public without being subject to the editorial decisions of journalists. This can be seen as a severe weakening of the traditional gatekeeping power of media organizations: their role in deciding which events and topics become news, which speakers to allow to voice their position on their programs, and in which light to present political actors. That being said, it has become increasingly clear that what appears to be direct reach on websites and branded profiles on third-party platforms is probably best thought of as a new form of indirect reach made possible through the services of new intermediaries in political discourse – online platforms.

Political actors also rely on intermediaries to reach people indirectly. In the past, this generally meant that media organizations had to carry the message to their audiences. Political actors or their representatives were featured in regular coverage or purchased exposure through ads. Political actors also relied on allied organizations, such as churches or labor unions, to carry their message to their members or, even better, mobilize their membership to carry the message of selected political actors further into society. The fracturing of mass audiences and the weakening of traditional organizations in social life have made these outreach practices less practicable and effective.

Today, indirect reach is strongly shaped by digital media. In the past, political actors who had the necessary budget depended on media organizations to carry ads or soundbites to reach their audiences. Today, this role is increasingly supplemented if not replaced by online platforms. Political actors depend on online platforms such as Facebook, Twitter, or YouTube to enable their content to reach people. While highly effective in reaching predefined sections of the public, political actors have to submit to governance rules of platforms that are often nontransparent and constantly shifting. Digital media have thus introduced a new set of powerful intermediaries between political actors and the public whose role in the process is nontransparent and ill-understood.

Thus it is far from clear that digital media necessarily lead to an increase in direct communication between political actors and the public. Intermediaries between political actors and the public are not disappearing but changing. We will address these and other questions of how digital media have changed the way political actors are reaching people in Chapter 3.

Effects of Information

Communication is not only about providing information; it is also about convincing people and changing minds. Political actors need to convince people of a position, try to increase the salience of a topic, build the public recognition of a candidate, or mobilize supporters to show up at a protest or turn out to vote. Also, with regard to the effects of information, digital media have impacted politics.

We have nearly a hundred years of communication research available, conceptualizing and testing the uses and effects of media coverage and communicative interventions by political elites. The state of the art of communication and persuasion research holds that isolated communicative interventions by political actors have limited effects on recipients, with some more elaborate interventions apparently having greater chances of success while less obtrusive ones have rather weak effects. While this literature is helpful, we should be aware that digital media come with specific usage, exposure, and technological conditions that might change the way information effects occur. These conditions include unbundling, social sharing, algorithmic confinement, informational abundance, and the drastic lowering of information costs.

These differences have to be considered if we want to use previous findings and conceptualize information effects on digital media. For example, one important characteristic of digital media that potentially impacts the effects of communicative interventions is the social sharing of information. On digital media people will not necessarily directly encounter political information published by political actors or media organizations. At least as often, they will encounter this information indirectly because one of their contacts shared content on their (semi-)public profile or in a directed message. This adds a social element to the reception of information. It is not only the originator of the information or a professional communicator guiding your attention to content, it is someone from your social circle that is forwarding you a message. This opens the possibility that the nature of the relationship with that person, e.g., friendship or trust, influences the way a user processes political information, thereby increasing the likelihood for information transmitted this way to developed persuasive effects.

A series of claims have been raised with regard to the change of information effects through digital media. On the individual level, digital media might bring new people into politics by lowering the costs of political information or participation. It has also been argued that by providing people with an abundance of information, digital media might contribute to political polarization or a divide between politically interested and disinterested people as they become able to select information and interaction partners online that conform with their existing interests or political opinions. This might lead to a sorting of people into echo chambers based on partisanship or interests. Somewhat contradictorily, others have argued that algorithmic selection of information and log-in to apps limits the informational choices available to people. This then contributes to accidental exposure to political information by people independent of their prior political interests.

This quick overview has already illustrated that the field is far from being settled. We find various, sometimes contradictory expectations that tend to shift according to technological changes in the development of digital media. While it is thus important to keep an open mind regarding potential shifts in effects of information in digital media, the breadth of prior research on the effects of information points to effects being somewhat limited. This is often forgotten when the assumed communicative effects of information in digital media are discussed. Most of the time, the misplaced expectations of strong or even transformative information effects online might do little harm beyond their impact on the campaign budgets of eager politicians. Yet, in the current debate about the dangers of political manipulation or disinformation on digital media, mistaken beliefs in the power of digital media might indeed end up damaging public trust in elections or the soundness of political discourse. Remaining realistic with regard to the effects of communication on digital media is thus more than just an academic concern. We discuss these and related ideas in Chapter 4.

Collective Action

In order to achieve their goals, political actors need to coordinate supporters and issue publics. While this is true for all political actors, it is of particular importance to those outside the established power structures or outside the current political consensus. The role of digital media in serving this need has been at the forefront of public debate, especially with regard to their perceived role in enabling anti-establishment protest movements in Western democracies, such as #Occupy, as well as protest movements against autocracies, as seen during the so-called Arab Spring. Yet upon closer examination this might not be a simple story of digital media transforming political power after all.

Activists can use digital tools successfully to activate grievances and to manage the operational aspects of protests. This has led some to expect political systems to destabilize as issue- or event-driven contestation can materialize quickly and lead to significant society-wide mobilization. This is even true in environments traditionally hostile to collective action, such as autocracies. But governments have learned to counteract digitally supported challenges to their authority by shutting down the internet or by countering and disrupting activists' information flows on online platforms. This is especially true in autocracies, where governments are less dependent on public opinion. Thus, while digital media help challengers to the political status quo pursue their goals, established political forces can use digital media as well to suppress them. This increases the importance of looking closely at the mechanisms by which digital media can serve as a coordination platforms for political actors.

In thinking about collective action, political actors face challenges along two lines: they need to *coordinate* people and they need to get them to *cooperate*. Coordination problems are largely about getting the word out to supporters and issue publics about the when, where, and what of collective action. When will there be a protest? Where will there be a protest? And what will be done at that protest? These are predominantly questions of information transmission. By lowering the costs of information publication, transmission, and reception for political actors, digital media are of great use in serving these needs. But transmitting information is only part of the challenge.

To mobilize people, political actors need to create among them a willingness to cooperate. In autocracies with potentially harsh government sanctions against protesters, this is of paramount importance. Yet creating a willingness to cooperate is also important for political mobilization in democracies. These challenges are harder than challenges of information transmission. Consequently, digital media do not necessarily transform this dimension of politics. Yet even here the indirect effects of digital media can be felt, for example by creating the impression of success and immediacy of political mobilization in the direct social environment of members of the public, or by deepening people's social ties with their geographic or ideational community online. Considering these indirect contributions of digital media in subsequent successful political mobilization is an important element of assessing their role in contemporary politics.

So, while at first it appears that digital media's role in mobilizing people for political action makes a clear-cut case for their transformative power in politics, closer examination paints a much more complicated picture. While digital media are powerful tools to get the word out about collective action and to coordinate events, the role of digital media in creating willingness among people to participate is more muted and indirect. This does not mean the contribution of digital media is negligible, as some critics of "clicktivism" or "hashtag activism" like to insinuate; it is just much more conditional than a deterministic story of technology-driven political transformation. Moreover, we must not neglect the power of governments to offset the opportunities digital media provide to activists. This power ranges from outright shutdowns of digital media, to interference in the flow of information online, to actual physical harassment of activists identified through their activity on digital media. Those cases in which the strongest transformative potential was originally ascribed to digital media may turn out to be the cases in which the powers of the status quo have the best chance to offset digital media's opportunities for activists. We will discuss these questions more extensively in Chapter 5.

Organizations

Organizations serve political actors' need for sustained coordination of people sharing the same interests, the persistent articulation and pursuit of these interests in the democratic process and institutions, and a continued presence in politics over time. Yet political organizations are routinely challenged over whether they legitimately represent the true interests of individual members and their tendency to create power imbalances and hierarchies. The rise of digital tools and services has given hope to some that there might be an opportunity for politics without, or at least with severely weakened, organizations. This makes the future of political organizations an important further element in the effects of digital media in politics.

In the past, political organizations coordinated politics by keeping dedicated lists of members, supporters, or people interested in specific topics. These lists served as the foundation of event- or issue-driven mobilization. Without organizations, there is no list of likeminded people. Without a list of likeminded people, there is no mobilization. This link contributed to the strength of organizations in politics and made it difficult for political ad hoc collaboration to emerge without the support of existing organizations, such as parties, interest groups, labor unions, or NGOs. Digital media has changed this.

Digital media has changed the political economy of organizing politics by lowering the costs of establishing and keeping lists of likeminded people, allowing issue publics to find each other quickly, even with regard to newly emerging topics, and by drastically lowering the costs of contacting people. Today's organizers do not have to rely on a top-down hierarchical organization stepping in and doing the heavy lifting. It is now possible for coordinating structures to emerge quickly on an ad hoc basis in order to address specific issues or react to given events.

Some hope that by lowering the costs for individuals to connect and to coordinate, digital media will make political organizations superfluous. This has become known by the catchy phrase "organizing without organizations" (Shirky 2008). The early success of digitally enabled activism in predominantly short-lived, single-event, or single-issue campaigns has illustrated the power of this idea. Yet these examples have also pointed to the limits of this approach to organizing in politics. The resulting movements showed themselves to be short-lived, their supporter groups significantly diminished over time, and they proved to be massively challenged in translating initial grievances into inputs into the policy-making process. So, instead of looking for digital media to replace traditional forms of political organizations, we should think of them as providing new forms of organizing politics that might offer powerful opportunities in selected cases. In other cases, it might not be so much about organizing politics *without* organizations but instead about organizing politics with *different* organizations (Karpf 2012b).

Active adaptation processes will bring about different political organizations. To assess the effect of digital media on politics, we therefore also have to look at the internal structures and processes of contemporary political organizations. Probably the two most decisive areas of the adaptation process are rethinking membership and rethinking the financing of organizations.

Political organizations have started to experiment with membership rights and dues. This has given rise to much more flexible and low-effort membership models that allow people with only a fleeting interest in the organization to exert influence and stay informed without having to commit too firmly to an organization. This extends the reach and the finances of organizations by including people who might be put off by traditional membership models. On the flipside, when done wrong this risks devaluing what it means to be a member of a political organization and weakens their influence and power to act.

There has also been a shift in financing patterns of organizations away from a limited number of big, steadily giving donors to an event- or issue-driven crowdfunding model. These changes directly impact the work of organizations. Working with a limited number of big donors allows organizations to invest in long-term development and long-term goals. Organizations depending on crowdfunding will necessarily have to follow current trends in order to attract donations. This increases the danger of funding being diverted from issues not currently at the top of the agenda or from long-term investment into staff through trainings, or even less staff to begin with. These developments might then impact the ability of an organization to pursue long-term goals and to interface with the policy process. In this way digital media might indirectly weaken the role of organizations in politics by taking away the foundation on which they have achieved their tasks.

The impact of digital media on political organizations is thus split. Depending on your point of view, they might weaken the role of organizations in politics by allowing people to perform some of the tasks in politics that were originally fulfilled by organizations. Alternatively, organizations might lose their monopoly on some political tasks, such as coordination and mobilization, but gain others. The role of organizations might thus shift but not weaken. In addition, digital media are changing internal processes and practices in organizations. These changes might include active adaptation by organizations in order to realize the potential of digital media in their work. Other changes might be imposed on organizations as digital media change the political economy of politics and thereby the financing model of organizations, which in turn might impact the character and resilience of political organizations. We will discuss these developments in detail in Chapter 6.

Seeing the World

In order to engage in politics, actors and organizations have to form assessments about the world. For example, they have to find ways to assess public opinion, to measure the impact of their interventions, and to incorporate information they have on individuals in strategic action. Digital media have extended the opportunities for political actors and organizations to measure what is happening in the world and to intervene in politics.

Take public opinion as an example. Political actors and organizations constantly assess public opinion and adjust their actions accordingly. Politicians and parties keep a close eye on the movement of opinion polls, interest groups watch and try to influence the topics people deem important at any time, and even individuals try to assess the opinions of those around them before voicing their own opinions on politics. In the past, assessing public opinion depended strongly on media coverage and the polling industry. Today, these sources of information on public opinion are still highly influential, but in addition political professionals and journalists are increasingly taking to digital media to infer public opinion. Journalists look for attention spikes on Twitter in deciding what topic to cover in order to attract eyeballs to their sites, politicians pay attention to the varied reactions on their social media profiles in order to assess the popularity of a given stance or policy, and supporters of parties or social movements refer to the strength of their share in political online communication to illustrate the legitimacy of their group. Yet while public expressions on digital media are easy and quick to measure, they might be misleading. The political use of digital media is highly skewed to specific slices of the population. Voiced expression online is thus unlikely to be representative of the opinions of the general population. Moreover, the form this expression takes is different from traditional opinion polls and thus it is unclear how these expressions can be meaningfully interpreted. Finally, the volume of online expression is comparatively easy to manipulate by interested parties. Actors overly reliant on digital media to assess public opinion are thus trading speed and apparent precision for the very serious risk of severely mismeasuring public opinion.

This simple example illustrates some of the underlying challenges facing political actors to incorporate digital data in their established ways of making sense of the world. Digital data might be seemingly ubiquitous and easy to use, but it is unclear what precisely it measures. Do its insights pertain to the general population or just those people using digital services? Do its metrics correspond to what is of interest in politics, or do digital metrics mainly pertain to digital phenomena? In short, does digital data document politics at large or does it instead start to shape politics in its image by enticing those in politics to predominantly focus on phenomena and groups visible in digital metrics? These are fundamental questions that arise any time new data sources and metrics become available in social life. In this, digital data sources and metrics are no different. Yet as of now the apparent exceptionalism and perpetual novelty of digital media have pushed these questions somewhat to the background of the debate.

More generally, digital media have increased the amount of information available to political actors, companies, and governments about each individual. This allows actors and organizations to fine-tune their interactions with the public. For example, in electoral politics information available on US voters allows parties to identify people of interest to them, measure the impact of specific interventions, and model the likely effects of similar interventions on other people with shared characteristics. This data-driven approach to campaigning reportedly had a big impact on Barack Obama's success in 2008 and 2012 in actively extending the voter pool by specifically targeting and mobilizing hard-to-reach and low-propensity voters. Yet in this and other cases we have to be careful to differentiate between knowledge of the use of data-driven procedures and their actual effects on the success of a campaign or organization. Currently, we know a lot about when data-driven techniques have been used but very little about their effects. This makes it difficult to differentiate between instrumental uses of data-driven procedures in order to achieve operational goals and rhetorical uses in which the use of data-driven procedures serves to signal an organization's prowess to the public and competitors.

By providing new data sources in politics, digital media thus contribute to shaping the assessment of the world by politicians, campaigners, journalists, and the public. This makes this process an important element if we want to understand their impact on politics. We offer a broad account of what it means to assess the political world using digital media and digital metrics in Chapter 7.

Serving or Breaking Democracy?

Looking at the changes we just charted, a larger question starts to move into view: What do these various changes mean for the state of democracy? Do the various footprints of digital media in different areas of politics and the political communication environment strengthen or weaken democracy? To this question, there are two answers regularly advanced whose relative prominence depends on their resonance with external events.

Optimists expect that digital media and digital tools will make it possible to successfully solve challenges of collective action and organization. By doing so, they will empower challengers to the political status quo and will give people marginalized in contemporary politics access to power. This is seen as invigorating politics by broadening its base and making it more reactive. Pessimists, on the other hand, fear that digital media and digital tools can be used by entrenched societal elites to modulate the reach of new voices and restrain dissidents. In this view digital media serve the powerful by allowing them to better control or manipulate the public. Recently, pessimists have also pointed out that digital media might serve challengers to the political status quo who challenge democracies as a whole instead of challenging their current incarnations. Digital media might thus contribute to a weakening of democracy and control by established elites by allowing challengers to rise to power.

Both types of expectations can be found in the literature going back to the early days of the internet. Their prominence waxes and wanes with techno-logical developments and events seemingly favoring the one or the other. The events of the Arab Spring and international anti-globalization protests gave rise to many optimists emphasizing the role of digital media in enabling democratic transformation in autocracies and strengthening bottom-up participation in Western democracies. The election of Donald Trump a few years later shifted public debate and expectations. Now, digital media are seen as manipulating publics at will, and social media companies appear to represent entities beyond democratic control whose internal decisions threaten Western democracies. These shifting narratives point to the importance of grounding an assessment of the effects of digital media on democracies not exclusively on external events and their perceived role in them.

In this attempt, we need to pay attention to two different goals that point to democratic areas and functions shaped by digital media. First, we need to inquire about their effects on the ability of the public to control and select political elites.

Second, digital media might also be seen as the kick-starter of a deeper transformation of democratic practices and opportunities. By promising to solve classic problems in political coordination, digital media might offer a technological foundation to allow for more direct and more far-reaching participatory opportunities for the public, leading to an extension of democratic participation. To examine the role of digital media in the deepening of democracy we need to focus on their contributions to public deliberation, their role in allowing and extending participatory opportunities and their realization, and their contribution in the amelioration of political and social inequalities in participation and representation.

This brief account has already shown that the discussion on the consequences of digital media for democracy grounded in competing theories of democracy offers promising starting points that allow for a balanced and evidence-driven discussion. This might take away some of the clarity of digital media either serving or breaking democracy, but it allows for a more balanced assessment of their impact on different democratic elements and functions. We provide such an assessment in Chapter 8.

1.3 What Are the Drivers of Digital Media's Impact on Politics?

Stepping back from the contribution of digital media to specific political needs, we can identify two general mechanisms underlying the preceding accounts. By encoding information independent of its original format – such as text, audio, or video – in binary code, digital media make information of any origin, size, and complexity instantly accessible, transmittable, reproducible, and machine readable. This impacts various areas of politics through two general mechanisms:

- lowering the costs of information production, dissemination, retrieval, and access; and
- connecting individuals, groups, actors, and devices in close networks.

These mechanisms have impacted politics by altering the relative power balance between people and elites and challengers and incumbents. They have also challenged established political institutions, such as news media or political parties, by weakening their economic, organizational, and ideational foundations. It thus pays to take a closer look at them.

Lowering Information Costs

Digital media are relatively cheap to produce, publish, copy, store, and retrieve. They are not free, but their costs beat those of any other form of information production, distribution, or storage. They make any kind of digitalized information instantly abundant and non-exclusive. In fact, keeping digital information from spreading, for example through paywalled access or dedicated copy protection schemes, is surprisingly hard. This lies at the heart of the challenges faced by content providers whose previous business model was the tight control of access to information goods, such as news, music, or films. In politics, the lowering of the cost of publishing and retrieving information has led to a massive increase of political information (Bimber 2003). Initially this was seen as an opportunity for positive change in politics, as it would provide a check to the power of mass media organizations in deciding which news to cover and which to ignore. Alternative news sources were expected to pick up the slack and pressure established news organizations to cover what the public saw as important. Moreover, internet users were expected to double-check news coverage by accessing original sources online and searching for alternative coverage. This early optimistic view has given way to a much more pessimistic assessment. Now, public debate is dominated by worries about people using the freedom to access a multitude of news sources online in order to follow their own interests and preconceptions, thereby potentially insulating themselves from factual information and losing sight of the breadth of pluralistic positions in public discourse.

The transformation of information into digital form has also increased the speed of its distribution and expanded the number of available distribution channels. Once information is published it can travel in seconds around the world and reach people on a multitude of ubiquitous devices. In the age of television or radio, people had to gather at specified times of the day in front of dedicated devices in order to receive current information. Today's devices allow users to choose how they receive information and to directly interact with it. Information reaches users, for example, as push messages on their devices from sources they have consciously decided to subscribe to, via directed messages from friends and contacts who actively want to share information, via updates of information on friends and contacts interacted with on social networking sites, or through online ads on various sites. This multitude of channels contributes further to the increased speed with which digital information flows through networks of people and devices.

Social and other network connections have also contributed to a lowering of the costs of coordinating people, thereby enabling the ad hoc issue-based organization of collective action (Bimber 2003). In the past, the political coordination of people depended on long-standing bureaucracies administrating contact information for people who held vested interests in a specific topic, and mobilizing them around specific events, topics, or causes. This led to the entrenchment of political organizations, such as parties, interest groups, labor unions, and NGOs, at the heart of collective action. The high speed at which digital information travels, the low costs in spreading messages, and the quick formation of issue publics online have created an environment allowing for much more flexible coordination and issue-driven mobilization without the support of existing political organizations – in the words of Clay Shirky, "organizing without organizations" (Shirky 2008). Again, in the beginning this was seen as enabling much broader participation in politics than previously, when this depended on the interests and activities of existing political organizations. However, digitally enabled movements have proved to be highly fragile over time once public interest in the inciting event or issue declines. Even the most popular examples of digitally enabled political participation, such as the Arab Spring or #Occupy, have fallen short once they had to translate enthusiasm and contention into successfully contributing to the policy process. In fact, by shifting the focus to more short-term, issue-driven activities while neglecting the development and financing of long-term structures, digital media might introduce a significant degree of fragility in organized politics.

Networked Communication

Digital media contribute to connecting individuals, groups, actors, and devices to ever denser networks. This impacts the speed and breadth of information flow, organizational structures, and social relationships and interactions. Connections in digital media manifest themselves in data traces on platforms enabling the networking of people, actors, and devices. The power inherent in using the knowledge of network structures and algorithmically shaping connections and providing services has brought the role of digital media companies to the fore of public debate.

Digital media have allowed users to form and maintain networks across multiple dimensions. Traditionally social networks were limited to people sharing space, activity, or affiliations. Physical and temporal constraints meant that networks were generally of limited size and updating these networks with new information occurred infrequently. Digital media did away with these limitations. Users with (semi-)public profiles can connect with others based on a variety of dimensions, be it a shared past, shared space, shared interest, shared friends, or shared activities. There is little decay of network connections in digital media. Once connected, users normally stay connected. This increases the extent of social network connections considerably. Moreover, digital media allow for the instant updating of all connections with new information, thereby contributing massively to the speed of distribution of information relevant to the network (Rainie and Wellman 2012).

Networks shape the flow of information among individuals and between groups. By extending and broadening the number of network ties of which individuals remain aware, information can travel much more quickly and broadly among communities of interest. The technological representation of the links allows the systematic mapping of these flows and over time allows the identification of individuals or organizations important to the flow of information. This knowledge allows the development of a much deeper understanding of the structure and power relationships in the flow of information through societies.

Once networks become more pertinent in social relations, they also start to impact organizational structures. Network structures are perceived as providing powerful alternatives to hierarchical or centralized structures, be they organizational or social (Raymond 1999; Castells 2001). Increased visibility, technological manifestation, and manageability of network structures thus also have consequences for the design and governance of organizations and institutions.

The power of networks manifests itself increasingly on privately provided platforms, such as Facebook, Twitter, Google, or YouTube. This makes the companies running these platforms increasingly important shapers of social structures. Network effects drive the emergence of platforms as powerful new intermediaries. Platforms such as Facebook or Twitter provide their users with the opportunity to interact through personalized profiles. The use of a platform for any user increases exponentially with the number of all available users on the platform. Linear user growth on a platform thus still leads to exponential growth in the use that users are expected to make of the platform. Platforms have strong log-in effects for their users that make it hard for competitors to emerge in market segments where there are strong incumbents. This has contributed to a tendency for mono- or oligopolies to emerge and raises challenges with regard to the regulation of these platforms. Usually we find one platform provider dominating a specific market segment: Amazon is the platform of choice for selling and buying of goods; Google is the platform of choice for online ads; Facebook is the social networking site of choice to keep in contact with friends, family, and neighbors. At the same time, some of these platforms have emerged as important spaces for political information and political talk. Google provides an important gateway to political information, while Facebook and Twitter are important spaces for political information to reach users. This makes platform providers important intermediaries for political discourse; it also means that their internal governance decisions potentially impact politics in unforeseen ways.

An important and predominantly opaque element in the governance of platforms is algorithmic decision-making and shaping of users' opportunity spaces. The machine-readable format of digital media allows the use of automated analysis and decision rules. These algorithms form the backbone of digital services. They form the basis of what information users see, what offers they are made on commercial platforms, and which ads are targeted to them. This raises serious issues with regard to differential informational or participatory opportunities users have, given their individual characteristics or behavioral traits. Unobserved and unregulated discriminatory practices with regard to political information, mobilization, and participation raise serious issues that are much deeper than those arising from the use of the same practices in commercial contexts. As most algorithms remain proprietary information of platform providers, their exact specification and effects remain ill-understood but are increasingly the focus of critical debate and study.

1.4 Retooling Politics: Providing New Tools in the Pursuit of Political Goals

The roots of digital technology and digital services in the counterculture and outside of established industries have always connected them with narratives of challenging the status quo in society, business, and politics. Digital technology was seen as "disrupting" business models and industries (Christensen 1997), liberating the individual on society's fringes from anomie and suppression (Rheingold 1993; Barlow 1996), and allowing ordinary citizens to have their voices heard and to challenge party structures and political elites (Grossman 1995; Trippi 2004). These early accounts have set the stage for transformative societal changes across the board, and many examples illustrate the transformative potential of digital technology.

Apple's iPhone and the AppStore changed fundamentally what people expected from their mobile phones and left former market leaders Nokia and Blackberry crumbling (Merchant 2017). Napster irrevocably changed the way people access music, critically cutting into the revenue streams of major music labels (Knopper 2009). Craigslist and Google Online Ads provided new and more efficient ways for ad providers and customers to find each other, thus all but crippling traditional ad-based business models, such as newspapers (Auletta 2018). Examples like these have created the expectation that digital technology allows challengers to radically shift what it means to be active in a field and also radically change the power balance directly, threatening even well-established incumbents. It is only natural that these expectations should also run through much of the current debate on the role of digital media in politics.

There are a series of examples that people list when they point to the transformative power of digital media in politics. In electoral politics, the most prominent are the US presidential campaigns of Barack Obama. By extensively collecting data and incorporating data analysis in its decision process, the Obama campaigns are seen as having transformed the practice of election campaigning. Sophisticated use of data-driven decision-making is seen as allowing a campaign to more efficiently choose whom to contact, where to place ads, and how to spend money internally. In short, Obama was seen as having transformed the gut-based business of electoral politics into a data-driven enterprise, enabled by smart uses of digital data (Issenberg 2012c; Kreiss 2016).

Moreover, protest politics is seemingly transformed by smart actors using digital media. Probably the most prominent example in this field is the Arab Spring of 2010. At the time, a series of prolonged protests erupted in various Arab countries and led to changes in government in some Arab autocracies. Proponents of the transformation thesis see digital media as instrumental in these changes. Digital media were perceived as allowing protesters to coordinate protests and to communicate their grievances, goals, and cases of police oppression and as having shifted the scales of political power toward decentralized movements of citizens coordinating around shared grievances, severely limiting the oppressive power of centralized autocratic governments (Castells 2012).

While catchy, these examples – and others like them – turn out to represent not so much transformation as adaptation. While the available evidence points to data-driven practices playing an important role in multiple aspects of the Obama campaigns, it is far from clear that this transformed the practice of electoral campaigning significantly (Baldwin-Philippi 2017). There is little evidence of pervasive uses of these techniques in international campaigns beyond press releases and opinion pieces. Instead of transforming electoral politics, the Obama campaigns predominantly changed the narrative of what successful campaigning had to look like. This might have been transformative for the sales pitches of various political consultancies, but not for campaigning as such. The next successful US presidential candidate, Donald Trump, ran a campaign that showed no interest in using the Obama playbook. Instead of data-driven voter outreach based on statistical models developed in-house, the Trump campaign bet on free media coverage generated by the controversial nature of their candidate and followed the recommendations on ad placement from outside vendors, such as Facebook, Twitter, and Google (Kreiss and McGregor 2018). His campaign involved buying digital services, not developing them. This treats digital campaigning as an area of fully commodified services that are available off the shelf to any campaign (Vaccari 2010).

Thus, instead of changing the game of electoral campaigning by providing a new unbeatable template of how successful campaigns are run, the campaigns of both Obama and Trump look like successful adaptation processes by organizations with specific goals to the opportunities provided by digital media. For the Obama campaigns this meant incorporating data-driven processes and expertise deeply in their organizational structure. For the Trump campaign, this meant outsourcing this work to market leaders and contracting them if needed. Neither campaign changed the fundamentals of political campaigning. Both decided who their likely supporters were and how best to reach them – Obama through data analysis, Trump through gut feeling and the services of third parties. Digital media played a role in both campaigns, but only as a tool to facilitate campaign strategy and organizational culture.

If we closely examine examples of supposed transformation in protest politics, similar patterns appear. The uses of digital media by protesters in the Arab Spring were not as pervasive as claimed, nor did they fundamentally transform protests. Instead, the classical functions of protesting – such as coordination, getting the message out, and associating with sympathizers not directly present – were fulfilled by using digital media (Howard and Hussain 2013). As such, digital media were not transformative. Instead, you had an actor – the protest-ers – who managed to incorporate digital media in their action repertoires, providing them with an advantage over their opponents. This corresponds much more with adaptation processes than with transformation. Once we extend our view temporally beyond the immediate protests, we also see that digital media were not transforming the power dynamics sustainably. In Egypt, for example, digitally enabled protesters were able to force President Hosni Mubarak into retirement, but they were not successful in gaining power themselves. Instead, during the first open election, the Muslim Brotherhood won, not by digital activism, but instead through traditional organizing and campaigning. Protesters were able to marshal attention only for a short time.

Political actors, organizations, and the public use digital media in pursuit of their goals. Doing so successfully means adapting practices, structures, and processes to best make use of the affordances provided by digital media. This changes the way politics is engaged in and presented. It retools politics. But it does not necessarily lead to changes in the fundamentals of politics; it merely shapes how they are pursued. Political actors and organizations still pursue the same goals and use communication to fulfill the same needs as they did before the advent of digital media:

• they still try to get their message injected in media and popular discourse;
• they still try to reach people either directly or indirectly;
• they still try to change minds and to mobilize people;
• they still face challenges in the coordination of supporters;
• political organizations remain important in translating attention and engage-ment in sustainable political action and change; and
• political actors still try to orient themselves in the world through quantifica-tion and metrics.

These needs have not changed; what has changed is the way they are pursued. Focusing on the use of digital media by political actors in fulfilling their needs in the pursuit of politics allows us to assess the actual impact of digital media on politics without falling for catchy narratives.

Once we adopt a needs-oriented, procedural perspective on the role of digital media in politics, we find few signs of transformative change. Instead, we find digital media embedded in the pursuit of various tasks for political actors and organizations. Here, digital media do not necessarily lead to trans-formative change, fundamentally changing the nature of politics or its power dynamics. Instead, we witness gradual change in various aspects of politics, such as the practices of individuals and organizations, the structures of organ-izations, and the emergence of new actors.

These developments change politics gradually but might be overlooked if everything short of the transformation of politics is seen as evidence for no substantial change. Our procedural perspective avoids this pitfall and instead allows for the identification of small but meaningful changes in politics against the backdrop of large continuities. This allows for a pragmatic assessment of the role of digital media in politics and associated changes without either unduly exaggerating or belittling them.

2

The Flow of Political Information

Where did you last encounter a piece of political information? Chances are, you clicked on a link a friend sent you on a messaging app, read the preview to a piece on the Facebook wall of a colleague, or followed a retweet posted by an acquaintance on Twitter. Depending on your predilections for the ways of the ancients, you might also have picked up a printed newspaper or watched the news on a television set.

And what source did you find this information on? Was it a partisan blog you keep reading to remind yourself of the wrongheadedness of political opponents? Was it a news aggregator that sifts through the daily headlines and promises to show you only those that matter? Was it a podcast catering to your wonky interests? Or was it a news organization or public broadcaster?

Most of the time, we do not think about the routes by which political information reaches us or the sources they come from. After all, information is information and news is news. Yet, looking closely, routes and sources matter a great deal. The speed at which news breaks, is reported, and is commented on matters with regard to the quality of coverage, and can contribute to a sense of breathlessness and shape the rhythm of unfolding political events (Chadwick 2017). The nature of organizations covering news matters as well. Public broadcasters might follow transparent rules for quality control and fact checking. In contrast, commercially funded news organizations can be expected to follow the old adage "if it bleeds, it leads" in an effort to keep audiences glued to their coverage. How news is financed will impact what news is covered and how (Nielsen 2012b).

Rhythms and sources in the flow of political information have changed dramatically under the influence of digitalization. The current power balance between news organizations, political actors, and civil society has developed under the conditions of twentieth-century mass communication technology (Bimber 2003). But digitalization has changed core aspects of communication technology, changes that deeply impact the structure and flow of political information in societies (Williams and Carpini 2011; Bennett and Pfetsch 2018; Jungherr, Posegga, and An 2019a; Whibey 2019). These changes find expression in various contemporary phenomena in political communication, be it the hijacking of the news through controversy by political challengers like Donald Trump or a seeming deterioration in the standards of news production as expressed by the apparent prominence of so-called fake news. The current moment of collective concern about the quality of public discourse in democracies or the future of news as a democratic institution points to the changes to the established power balance that are under way and whose consequences are far from clear.

2.1 The Role of Organizations in the Flow of Political Information

The flow of information is important in politics. Citizens depend on information about society, the plans and activities of their government, and alternative options to exert democratic control (Keane 2013); politicians depend on information about their constituents, supporters, and critics (Dahl 1989); while governments depend on information about the states they govern and their population (Scott 1998). In order to shape the information available, politicians and parties try to put out statements on their positions and policies to the public, activists try to focus attention on contentious issues, governments try to control and limit the flow of information to the public, while journalists and editors try to navigate competing interests in reporting news. Political actors and news organizations thus compete for control over the flow of political information (Schudson 2008, 2017).

This complex system of interactions has been called an "interorganizational field" (Sparrow 2006), in which individual actors and organizations compete for the attention of the public and for dominance of their issues of interest, frames of reference, and narratives by producing, distributing, filtering, and commenting on information (Gitlin 1980; Entman 2004; Benson 2006; Entman and Usher 2018; Schroeder 2018). In this competition, equilibria of influence tend to emerge only to be disrupted by shifts in the resources to which competing actors have access, for example economical, ideational, or technological resources (Fligstein and McAdam 2012). Accordingly, the shift to digital media has severe consequences for the established political information systems.

News organizations and political organizations – such as parties, interest groups, and nongovernmental organizations (NGOs) – have traditionally been at the center of the flow of political information, which they produce, filter, distribute, and annotate (Bimber 2003). News organizations decide what news to cover, which actors to give voice to, and which topics to emphasize. This creates a deep interconnection between news organizations and democratic systems (Schudson 2008, 2017; Shoemaker and Reese 2014).

This supports a view of political organizations where the control of information is a political power source administered by specialized bureaucracies (Scott 1998; Bimber 2003). News organizations are sometimes allies picking up and amplifying the information given by powerful political actors (Bennett 1990; Entman 2004; Cook 2005), sometimes vigilant watchmen checking the narratives of powerful political actors while providing counter-narratives, thereby providing the basis for monitory democracy (Keane 2009; Graves 2016), or muckrakers waging campaigns bent on destabilizing the powerful through the coverage or incitement of scandals (Bennett 2005a, 2005b, 2016). Especially consequential in this is news organizations' power as gatekeepers of what information reaches the public (Shoemaker and Vos 2009) and as arbiters of politics, deciding which political actor to penalize for perceived rule breaking and which narrative or agenda to publicly contest (Fligstein and McAdam 2012).

This political role of news organizations is shaped by explicit legal and tacit regulations, which determine their influence. Political news can thus be thought of as part of a set of political institutions determining the practice of politics in democracies (Ryfe 2012; McChesney and Pickard 2017). Changes in the structural determinants of political news thus also impact other political institutions.

News organizations are also dependent on the public accepting their role in the flow of information. In the United States, this acceptance appears increasingly fraught in the face of public distrust in political elites in general (Doherty, Kiley, and Johnson 2017; van der Meer 2017) and the media in particular (Ladd 2012). This erosion of trust coincides with, or might be driven by, challenges to the role of news organizations emerging from digitalization. The question remains open whether these trends remain specific to the United States or whether the country is simply foreshadowing what will also materialize in other Western democracies.

As long as technology favors de facto control by a small set of important actors over what information gets out to mass audiences, erosion of public trust might not matter much because there is no alternative way to produce or distribute information. Digitalization has changed this condition by deeply affecting – if not destroying – traditional business models for news coverage, and changing the way audiences access and interact with information

(Williams and Carpini 2011; Keane 2013). These challenges to the power of
political and news organizations to control the flow of information might even
challenge political systems, be they democratic (Keane 2013) or autocratic
(Castells 2012; Howard and Hussain 2013; Weidmann and Rød 2019).

Technological innovation might thus lead to a shift in power dynamics
between different organizational types and actors. This potential shift promises
to emerge most clearly if we examine the interdependent relationships of the
contributors to the flow of political information from a systems perspective.

2.2 Media Systems

We anchor the discussion of digital media's effects on the flow of political
information in our understanding of the interdependent relationship between
news organizations, news audiences, and political actors. This systems perspective allows us to focus on the actions and practices of actors, their
incentives, their embeddedness with other social subsystems, and their inter-
dependence (Easton 1965).

We define a media system as

- a set of actors contributing to the production of media content, of which
  political news is an important subset;
- audiences consuming this content;
- institutions implicitly or explicitly governing these activities; and
- practices.

The actions and practices of actors in the media system are enabled or
restricted by economic incentives, norms of behavior shared by specific groups
of actors, legal regulation, and the affordances of contemporary media technology. Actors' strategic choices are based on their level of discursive power,
or in other words, their relative influence in the media system, its interconnected social subsystems and the choices by other actors (Jungherr et al.
2019a). We understand media systems as inherently open to the influence of
other social subsystems, with the political system being of special relevance in
a media system concerned with political news.

The specific setup and balance of media systems varies between political,
legal, and cultural units. These might coincide with country borders but do not
necessarily have to (Hallin and Mancini 2004, 2012). Media systems also vary
over time given the evolution of interconnected social subsystems and the
development of media technology. These variations affect the flow of political
information and the influence of specific actors and organizations in it.

The technological change represented by digital media can impact any of the elements of media systems. By changing economic incentives and affordances, the power structure of actors in the media system and interconnected social subsystems might shift. Established actors might lose influence while new actors might arise. This in turn is likely to impact norms and practices of contributors and consumers in media systems (Chadwick 2017; Schroeder 2018; Jungherr et al. 2019a).

Our use of the term "media system" goes beyond the scope of the term as predominantly used in comparative communication research. For one, we avoid the narrowing of the term "media" by equating it with political news. More importantly, while previous accounts have differentiated media systems according to diverging normative foundations of news (Siebert, Peterson, and Schramm 1963) or different configurations of media, economics, politics, and regulation (Hallin and Mancini 2004, 2012), we do not focus on identifying specific media system types. Instead, we use the concept to identify specific actors, influences on their actions, and practices that might be influenced by digital media.

Our use of the term "media systems" is related to what some have called media or information ecologies (Davenport and Prusak 1997; Nardi and O'Day 1999; Fuller 2005). While the use of these terms shares our focus on actors, incentives, practices, and their interdependency, they remain somewhat loosely defined and open to often contrasting uses. Our explicit anchoring of the concepts in systems theory allows for a richer and more precise vocabulary.

The term "information regime" also encompasses economic and technological influences on the ways in which news organizations cover politics and influence public opinion formation and democratic practice (Williams and Carpini 2011). Yet its use usually gives the misleading impression of clearly defined stages in which specifically configured "regimes" follow each other in neat sequence, suggesting an evolutionary or maybe even intentional progression. In practice, we suspect that various regimes can and do coexist. Our use of the term media system allows for this.

Also related but distinct is the term "information environment." This term has been used in the past to identify the information that respondents likely have had available in forming political preferences and coming to decisions (Carpini 2000; Jerit, Barabas, and Bolsen 2006; Aalberg, Aelst, and Curran 2010; Jungherr, Mader, et al. 2018). In our conception, information environments emerge given specific configurations of media systems. They are clearly important but to us form an outcome of media systems.

Our conception of media systems owes most to the use of the term "hybrid media system" (Chadwick 2017), which offers a powerful account of a specific configuration of contemporary media systems. With Chadwick (2017) and Couldry (2012), we share a concern for the importance of practices, actors, and organizations in the setup of media systems. Yet we still feel that the organizational and institutional elements of a media system offer promising leverage for the analysis of the working, determinants, and effects of contemporary news media (Jungherr et al. 2019a). For the purposes of our analysis of the influence of digital media on politics, we feel it best to take a more general stance, allowing us to identify determinants of the emergence or configuration of contemporary media systems. Strategic choices by actors in our system of interest, as well as shifts in their influence given shifts in interconnected social subsystems driven by technological innovation, could lead to disruptions in the setup of media systems (Fligstein and McAdam 2012).

2.3 Controlling Access and Flow of Political Information

Before digitalization, political news came primarily in physical form, on paper, radio waves, or television signals. These manifestations made political news a scarce good. There was a limited number of newspaper copies, and once bought a copy would typically be read only by a comparatively small number of audience members. This made it easy for producers to control and charge for access. Radio and television news was scarce two times over. For one, the radio and television spectrum is limited and owned by only a small number of people who can use it for broadcasts. In addition, radio and television news was temporally scarce. Because broadcasts occurred at given intervals, audience members had to arrange their schedules to accommodate the broadcast schedule. While recording programs was an option, large-scale archiving was prohibitively cumbersome. Again, producers of political news had close control over the presentation of and access to information. These characteristics led to regular patterns in the use of political information. Political news was used predominantly routinely, either by reading the same newspapers every day or regularly switching on the television set during the time of prominent newscasts. Maintaining comprehensive archives of news and information was restricted to specialized institutions or organizations. Contextualizing current affairs through information from the past or sources underlying reports was cumbersome and usually restricted to professionals. Over time, individual habits and social structures developed to cope with these characteristics and limitations of information communication technology (ICT). All this changed once information became digitalized (Tewksbury and Rittberg 2012; Webster 2014).

Once information of any kind becomes digitalized, its economics fundamentally change. Digital information can be copied, stored, and provided at next to no cost. This makes it much harder for information producers and distributors to control and monetize access (Shapiro and Varian 1999). With regard to political news and information, this change could lead to a heralded age of "information abundance" (Bimber 2003): free access to political news and information for everyone. At the same time this puts an axe to the economic and social foundations of organizations and institutions producing and providing access to political news and information in the first place (Levy and Nielsen 2010).

Changes in the economy of news are closely related to changes in the way political news and information are accessed now. To access newspapers one had to either buy them directly, access publicly shared issues (e.g., in libraries or coffee houses), or share an issue with family, neighbors, colleagues, or friends. So, while social sharing of newspapers was a reality, it was limited. Similarly, news in broadcast media (such as television and radio) had to be accessed at times determined by the news producer through the appropriated devices. Thus news producers controlled physical and temporal access to news. This allowed publishers to create a second customer base by selling ads to parties interested in reaching news audiences (Picard 2011).

This also led to a highly structured rhythm of political news production. Broadcast and publication schedules, with their fixed deadlines after which no news could be included in the upcoming show or edition, structured political life into "news cycles" (Molotch and Lester 1974; Schlesinger 1977; Tuchman 1978; Gans 1979). With the emergence of 24-hour-news channels, established patterns changed. With no fixed deadlines for news to "break," the speed at which news was disseminated and reacted to rose significantly (Kovach and Rosenstiel 1999; Rosenberg and Feldman 2008; Young 2009; Sellers 2010). But although temporally the news cycle accelerated, by and large it was still dominated by the same contributors and sources.

Control of the temporal flow and physical access to news allowed news organizations to be de facto gatekeepers to public discourse. They decided what events and stories to cover and which actors to give voice to (Bennett 2004; Shoemaker and Vos 2009; Shoemaker and Reese 2014). These decisions are not necessarily unbiased or impartial. For example, studies consistently show that newspapers and broadcast media tend to recognize official sources, i.e., governmental organizations, politicians, and established political elites, over new actors or organizations, thereby reinforcing established political power structures (Molotch and Lester 1974; Bennett 1990; Livingston and Bennett 2003; Boykoff 2012).

Digitalization has introduced a series of changes in media systems that challenge these established ways of controlling access and flow. These lead to systematic shifts in media systems shaping the flow of information.

2.4 Challenges

A Multitude of Voices

Two important characteristics of digital media have challenged and transformed the political information production and consumption systems that developed during the twentieth century. First, digital media lowered the costs of information publication and distribution considerably. Second, the internet replaced a one-to-many communication system with a many-to-many communication environment.

The drastically lowered cost of production and distribution of information (Shapiro and Varian 1999) is of crucial importance if we want to understand the contemporary political communication environment. Nearly everyone is able to publish political information, analysis, or commentary online at little cost, for example on personally hosted websites, commercially provided sites, or online platforms. Once published, this information is available to almost everyone with an internet connection.

Digitalization has thus brought an age of information abundance with regard to availability and accessibility (Neuman 1991; Bimber 2003). One consequence of this is a rapid increase in the number of voices covering and commenting on politics. If the mass media once held a monopoly on deciding "what is news" (Gans 1979), today their power as sole providers and thereby gatekeepers (Shoemaker and Vos 2009) of political information is significantly reduced (Shoemaker and Reese 2014). This partial reduction of mass media's political power was originally seen as a way of providing balance to some of the biases in mass media coverage, for example in favoring established political elites (Chadwick 2017). At this point, centralized structures establishing political agendas were predominantly viewed critically by commentators and academics. This changed with the 2016 election of Donald Trump as US President and the seemingly widespread presence of disinformation or so-called fake news during the campaign. The astounding amount of political information not vetted by professional and unpartisan journalists or editors has led to a renewed prominence of voices more critical of the loss of political gatekeepers and their structuring influence on political news (Ball 2017; D'Ancona 2017). This shift in the debate on the role of institutions structuring political information flows is telling. While mass media of the past might not always have lived up to their promise as nonpartisan arbiters of political discourse, they might still have had a beneficial stabilizing influence on society. Their editorial processes, financial independence, and societal governance contributed to excluding extreme voices from public discourse and ensured a – however limited – quality of public debate by enforcing a requirement for at least some degree of factualness for political information to enter public discourse (Jungherr, Schroeder, and Stier 2019). One interesting question for the years to come is what types of institutions will emerge to take over these functions with the lessening of the influence of mass media.

In classic communication models, mass media are understood as forming a one-to-many broadcast communication system (Laswell 1948; Katz and Lazarsfeld 1955). At the center of this model lie specific instances of mass media, e.g., a newspaper, that through their political, economic, and institutional control of distribution technology communicate with a mass audience. Other examples would include an email newsletter or a website. These communication systems enable a group of senders to communicate with many audience members at the same time. Yet they do not enable audience members, the many, to speak back to the senders. Thus, political, economic, and social power structures are seen as being reinforced by one-to-many communication systems.

Many-to-many communication systems provide a potential alternative to this concentration of power (Hoffman and Novak 1996). Users of digital media have the opportunity to communicate with each other. Examples of this from the early days of digitalization are bulletin boards or websites allowing visitor comments. While many-to-many communication is a technological standard implemented into digital communication technology from the start, for regular users it came to the fore with the emergence of Web 2.0 technology (Jensen 2010; Jensen and Helles 2017). The label Web 2.0 covers a set of technological advancements, user-centric practices, and business models that shifted internet use from information publishing, finding, and consuming toward engagement between users and authors (O'Reilly 2005). This enabled real-time exchanges on websites and platforms, thereby opening up the range of active participation for internet users. This technological shift was accompanied with a burst of think pieces on the new "interactive" nature of digital technology allowing for true dialogue between internet users and political, economic, or social elites (Levine et al. 2000; O'Reilly 2005).

As a consequence of this combination of technological and ideological shifts, everyone could post and comment on political information on sites provided by individuals, new media organizations, political actors, and traditional news organizations. In these comments, users and authors started to interact. Increasingly, this accessibility was also demanded from political elites, such as candidates for office (Stromer-Galley 2000; Stromer-Galley and Baker 2006). Formerly inaccessible elites, such as authors, editors, or politicians, thus became accessible to their audiences. This meant that their version of events and selection choices became objects of public critique and contention. This further weakened the power of traditional gatekeepers of political information and strengthened users who were no longer simply consuming political information but whose reactions, positive or negative, became part of the public negotiation of meaning. The American journalism scholar Jay Rosen calls these users "people formerly known as audience" (Rosen 2006). Accordingly, journalists, politicians, and researchers increasingly started to conceptualize and treat audiences not so much as passive receivers but much more as active participants in the construction of information flows.

Digital media – in the form of blogs, Twitter feeds, Facebook pages, or comment sections on news sites – have provided a forum for citizens, activists, interested parties, and challengers to the status quo to comment on current events or introduce new perspectives not covered by broadcast or print media. The media scholar Andrew Chadwick has introduced the term "information cycle" to conceptualize these developments:

> Political information cycles may involve greater numbers and a more diverse range of actors and interactions than news cycles as they are traditionally understood. They are not simply about an acceleration of pace nor merely the reduction of time devoted to an issue ... Rather, they are characterized by more complex temporal structures. They include many non-elite participants, most of whom now interact exclusively online in order to advance or contest specific news frames or even entire stories ... Political information cycles work on the basis of cross-platform iterations and recursion. This serves to loosen the grip of journalistic and political elites through the creation of fluid opportunity structures with greater scope for timely interventions by online citizen activists ... The combination of news professionals' dominance and the integration of non-elite actors in the construction and contestation of news at multiple points in a political information cycle's lifespan are important characteristics of contemporary political communication.
>
> (Chadwick 2017, 64)

As Chadwick points out, information cycles are not deterministic disruptors completely offsetting the power of news organizations (Jungherr et al. 2019a). While there are indeed cases in which non-elite actors managed to enter, disrupt, or initiate coverage of current events or political scandal, their reach ultimately depended on mass media to incorporate their contribution in their coverage (Karpf 2010a; Chadwick 2011a, 2011b). This indicates that while digital media certainly have infringed on the near monopoly on the construction of political reality through mass media organizations, these organizations still play a very important role (Williams and Carpini 2011). The audience for political niche news in the United States is rising, for instance, but most people still encounter news through the major networks (Webster 2014). Moreover, temporal patterns in political Twitter communication have been shown to follow patterns set by mass media coverage (Jungherr 2014). So, instead of supplanting old logics of media selection, distribution, and power relationships with the new logics of information flow on digital media, Chadwick speaks of a "hybrid media system" in which old and new actors and logics interact (Chadwick 2017).

Closely connected to the increase in available sources providing political information is a loss of authority of established media organizations. In the age of mass media, traditional news organizations held vast authority as impartial providers of news. Prominent brands and their anchor personalities were trusted arbiters of political competition whose coverage and commentary reached large audiences. Today, the authority of traditional news organizations is heavily contested (Schieffer and Schwartz 2017; Bennett and Livingston 2018; Gurri 2018; Kurtz 2018). Commercial broadcasters face new and aggressive competition from digital-born news outlets (Nicholls, Shbbir, and Nielsen 2016), while publicly funded broadcasters face political challenges contesting their impartiality and attacking their public funding. Here, we often find surprising alliances between commercial news organizations and challengers of the political status quo. Commercial news organizations have always perceived public broadcasters as unfair competition in the business of news. Political challengers who attack the political status quo often agitate heavily against public broadcasters as they perceive them to support the status quo while discriminating against the political fringes (Sehl, Simon, and Schroeder 2019). This and the ready availability of alternative and often free information sources provides a formidable challenge to the authority of individual news brands but also the foundation of publicly funded broadcast media.

The extension of available sources of political information thus brings positive aspects in democracies by providing more room for pluralist voices in public discourse. At the same time, the widening of sources brings challenges by eroding the influence and legitimacy of traditional news organizations in filtering and structuring the flow of political information. This poses the challenge of determining what institutions will fulfill this democratic function in the future or whether discourse in Western democracies becomes less focused and noisier.

Unbundling and Atomization

The flow of information is further complicated by the "bite-sized" format of digital political information. Newspapers and news programs forced media organizations to bundle information. This technology-driven bundling brought consequences for the political information environment, the financing, and the branding of news organizations. For example, audience members of television news programs interested in sports or the weather were being forced to stay tuned through the political news section, thereby picking up information along the way – so-called accidental or incidental exposure (Krugman and Hartley 1970; Prior 2007).

Digital technology unbundled political news (Bakos and Brynjolfsson 2000; Carr 2008; Hermida 2014). Users find and point each other to content of interest, be it through blogposts, email, social networking sites, or microblogs (Purcell et al. 2010; Hermida et al. 2012; Mitchell et al. 2013, 2016). This has made users important contributors and arbiters in the flow of information by actively selecting varied content from various sources and pointing others to it. While established news brands have web presences on which they present news content, the unbundling of news means that users do not necessarily encounter content there. Instead, the distribution of content by users on their personal web presences and social media profiles means that decentralized blogs and centralized social media platforms have emerged as prominent places where users encounter news and political information. This started with bulletin boards, web forums, and blogs and proceeded to the decisive influence that social networking sites like Facebook or Twitter have today in the allocation of public attention toward news content. This has made popular internet platforms into frenemies of news organizations. On the one hand, news organizations depend on online platforms to distribute their content, but on the other hand, it is far from clear how to monetize this attention.

Since online platforms have become important distribution channels for news organizations to reach their audiences, they have started to adapt to their selection and distribution logics. Traditional news organizations try to use online platforms to benefit from attention and prominent placement of their content. News organizations have incentives to prepare news content to benefit its placement and interaction rates on online platforms. This can even take the form of privileged partnerships between online platforms and media organizations (Benton 2015a, 2015b; Stelter 2015; Newton 2017). A drawback to this is that media organizations potentially lose influence by giving up their function as a central destination for news, thereby losing the opportunity to monetize audience attention, cross-promote content on their platforms, and gain insight on audience behavior and interests. They thus risk losing influence and knowledge over central elements of the information economy (Shapiro and Varian 1999; Bakos and Brynjolfsson 2000). This increase in the importance of online platforms for the publication and distribution of news, commentary, and political information has been met with increased regulatory attention and growing controversy about monetizing of content and the role of algorithms and editorial rules in deciding on prominent display of content (Napoli 2014, 2015; Mullany 2015; Napoli and Caplan 2017; Nielsen and Ganter 2018).

In addition to the unbundling of content, there is also a development toward the atomization of political information. In the past, television news was heavily criticized for creating a soundbite culture of political coverage by reducing politicians' statements to second-long clips, so-called soundbites (Hallin 1992; Esser 2008). Moreover, critics found that television news followed aesthetic conventions developed in entertainment formats or movies, thereby introducing frames from entertainment television into news coverage (Bennett 2005a, 2005b). These critiques are part of the mediatization debate in communication science, which is defined by two strands: one that tries to identify regularities and determinants in the way media cover politics, and the other focusing on how media conventions in turn shape politics. The first strand focuses on the influence of media structures, practices, and aesthetic conventions on the selection and shaping of political coverage (Shoemaker and Reese 2014). The second strand examines the impact of these processes on the shaping of social and political processes and events in order to generate coverage (Mazzoleni and Schulz 1999; Schulz 2004; Strömbäck 2008).

Analogous to the emergence of the soundbite, the growing importance of digital media in political communication has led to the emergence of new stylistic features of political information. Increasingly, political information comes in bit-size bites. Be it a tweet pointing to an article, a central quote featuring an image of the candidate in a sharepic, a YouTube clipping from a larger program segment, or even a seconds-long clip featuring one central statement in the form of an animated gif, media organizations and campaigns increasingly package political information in a format corresponding with usage conventions of popular platforms and allowing for easy sharing between users (Jenkins 2006). This potentially allows politicians access to large audiences who are not directly interested in politics but are exposed to these information snippets through sharing by their friends or their trending on platforms. This might thus offer a new pathway to accidental learning online (Tewksbury, Weaver, and Maddex 2001; Y. Kim, Chen, and Gil de Zúñiga 2013; Valeriani and Vaccari 2016). But the uncritical adoption of cultural conventions of online discourse and adjustment to the technological demands of platforms might bring unforeseen negative consequences for democratic discourse by further favoring the short snappy soundbite and further empowering the online platforms on which content is shared (Weisenthal 2016). This new stage of mediatization has only recently become the focus of researchers, and therefore the extent of this phenomenon and its impact on politics can currently only be guessed at.

The Business of News

While publicly funded media organizations such as the United Kingdom's BBC or Germany's ARD and ZDF do not rely on ad revenue to finance their news programs, commercial news organizations do so heavily. For them, the business of news has two sides: selling news to audiences and selling advertisers access to audiences (Picard 2011). Both sides of this business model are severely challenged by the extension of specialized and often free content offerings online and the unbundling of content (Grueskin, Seave, and Graves 2011).

The first side of the classic business model of news is selling access to content to audience members. Some news organizations, such as for sale newspapers, magazines, or pay per view channels, sell their product to audience members. To get access to content, audience members have to pay. As shown previously, in the past this was easy to enforce as access to content could easily be controlled. The current lack of access control makes it harder to enforce payment for content. Additionally, news organizations face challenges from online news organizations that offer content free of charge. In the early 2000s established news organizations started to react to this challenge by offering their content free of charge in the hope of monetizing content through ads (Ananny and Bighash 2016). Once these hopes failed to materialize, news organizations introduced paywalls that limited access to content for paying customers. While this model has been successful for big established news brands such as the New York Times, Financial Times, and The Economist, it is far from certain this model can successfully sustain other lesser national brands or local news organizations (Pickard and Williams 2014). Additionally, news organizations fear that paywalls limit the spread of their contributions and therefore limit their social and political influence (Oh, Animesh, and Pinsonneault 2015).

The second side of news as a business model, providing ad customers access to news audiences, is usually more important for the bottom line of commercial news organizations. News organizations sell advertisers or sponsors space among their content to present ads or sponsored stories. Here, advertisers big and small get access to the audience of a specific news organization. In this case, the news organizations serve as platforms (Evans and Schmalensee 2016; Parker, Alstyne, and Choudary 2016) or, in more formal terms, a multi-sided market (Evans and Schmalensee 2007; Tirole 2016). They connect advertisers with potential customers. Content produced by news organizations serves as the glue selecting and connecting these two sides. By providing catch-all or specialized content attracting specific audiences, news organizations shape audiences that advertisers can then address given the target audiences of their products. For example, running ads in a newspaper providing high-quality financial information might attract audience members for whom this information is important to their jobs and worth money. Advertising in such a medium makes sense for luxury brands or businesses catering to this clientele. Alternatively, a local news organization, such as a local radio station, caters to a very specific local subset of the population. Here, it makes sense for advertisers of local goods, such as apartments, local business, or secondhand goods, to advertise. In a time before the internet, buying a local newspaper might thus not necessarily speak of direct interest in the local news. Instead, buying the newspaper might be driven by the need for an apartment or a cheap local secondhand furniture item ready for pickup. News organizations thus earn money not only by directly selling news but also by offering a platform for advertisers and audience members to find each other.

This side of the news business model has been severely disrupted by the internet (Nielsen 2012b; Bell and Owen 2017). The role of news organizations as platforms was taken over first by dedicated online ad platforms, such as Craigslist, and later through Google and Facebook (Evans, Hagiu, and Schmalensee 2006; Evans and Schmalensee 2007, 2016; Parker et al. 2016). Through their reach and finely tuned options for whom to display ads to, Google and Facebook have developed into much more promising platforms for ad customers than news organizations. This ate severely into the revenue stream of news organizations and contributed significantly to the crisis in the financing of political journalism. To be sure, news organizations display ads on their online presences and in their apps. Yet the crucial difference compared with the past is that these ads are predominantly placed by other companies running ads across multiple sources. These dedicated online ad placement companies thus come to know more about the audiences of news organizations and monetization opportunities than any isolated news organization on whose presence the ads are placed.

For example, you might visit the online store of your favorite brand looking for a shirt. You browse but decide not to buy just yet. You then check your profile on your social networking site of choice and click on an article a friend recommended to you. On the site of the news organization, you are shown an ad for the item you previously considered buying on the online shop. In this example, the news organization allows another company to run ads that are responsive to your prior behavior on other sites online, be it for example through cookies or fingerprinting your browser. In this example, neither the online shop nor the news organizations knows much about your online interactions and behavior. Only the company charged by the online shop to run ads knows why you are shown which ad alongside which content. News organizations only open up their space to allow for these ads, but do not decide on what to show to whom. In this world, news organizations run the risk of merely providing the digital real estate for the display of ads while losing the capability and insights necessary to decide on whom to show ads to and for what reason. By losing insights into which ad customer wants to reach which part of their audience, news organizations lose the ability to provide crucial matching services to ad customers. This part of the business moves from them to online platform providers and centralized online ad agencies.

At this point it seems like wishful thinking for news organizations to develop into dominant platforms between audiences and businesses again. This means news organizations have to figure out if they can run their business based on subscriber counts, sponsored content, and the money redistributed to them for ad displays (Rusbridger 2018). The answer to this question matters. Once news stops being a viable business for media organizations, a series of democratic functions are at risk. Democracies depend on institutions continuously monitoring the activities of politicians on national and local levels. Most of the time, this will result in the coverage of the mundane goings on of politics. Without this continuous coverage and the institutional development and maintenance of political expertise specific to locales or topics, political corruption, mismanagement, and other wrongdoing will remain hidden from public sight (Schudson 2008, 2017; Bennett 2016). While there is plenty of evidence that media organizations struggled with this "watchdog" (Norris 2014) function even before their business models were challenged by digitalization, these fresh economic pressures have increased the urgency to determine if and how news organizations can still fulfill this function.

2.5 Consequences

These challenges directly impact the role of news organizations in the flow of political information. They threaten the business model of news organizations and lead to the emergence of new entrants in media systems, contributing to and filtering the flow of political information. As a consequence, the gatekeeping function of news organizations, with their explicit and tacit rules and norms of political news coverage, is challenged and with it news organizations' role as arbiters and enablers of monitory democracy. In turn, it is much harder for societies to agree on political facts, leading to a crisis of legitimacy of political information, exemplified by the terms "post truth" and "fake news." Finally, these challenges drive change in the nature, institutional setup, and relative power of news and political organizations, thereby potentially deeply impacting the channeling of political information, preferences, and interests.

New News Organizations

The challenges to the business model of news (Nielsen 2012b) deeply impact the ability of news organizations to fulfill their role in exerting control in the flow of political information (McChesney and Pickard 2017). In a selected case, observers have noted that the current economic crisis of news production has led to a decrease in original news stories with an increase in dissemination and commentary. Moreover, they have noted an increase in stories in which journalists simply took cues from government officials and political elites, with a parallel decrease in stories driven by journalists identifying and pursuing stories of their own volition, thereby giving rise to concerns of an increasing replacement of news with public relations (Project for Excellence in Journalism 2010). These findings document one specific case, but they point to the fact that journalism successfully fulfilling its political role is dependent on its sufficient funding.

This situation is more complicated still as the economic decline of traditional news organizations is met with a steady increase in new digital-born (Nicholls et al. 2016) news organizations pushing into the business of news. Over the short span of a few years, various online sources developed into powerful players rivaling traditional news organizations for scoops and public attention. For example, the Reuters Institute Digital News Report 2018 puts the weekly reach of the Huffington Post at 18 percent of all US news consumers and Buzzfeed News at 14 percent. This compares with 17 percent for the New York Times Online, 16 percent for CNN.com, 16 percent for Fox News Online, and 15 percent for the Washington Post Online (Newman et al. 2018). This goes to show that new news organizations have a comparable online reach to some of the most dominant traditional providers of political news. Some of these new news organizations, such as the Huffington Post (founded in 2005) (Cohan 2011, 2016a, 2016b) or Breitbart News (founded in 2007) (J. Green 2015; Stern 2016), have their roots firmly in the political blogosphere. Others, like Buzzfeed News (its parent site Buzzfeed was founded in 2006), are news divisions embedded in organizations that provide a broad menu of cultural, humorous, gossipy, and playful content, all put together to be easily shared across social networking platforms and to drive click rates (Lafrance and Meyer 2015). Others, yet again, like Politico (founded in 2007), specialize in detailed political coverage combined with the speed and love for controversy, gossip, and muckraking of other online publications (Sherman 2009; Filloux 2011).

The story of the extension of sources of political information starts with the rise of political blogs. On December 20, 2002, the then US Senate majority leader, the Republican Trent Lott, resigned from his position. This followed a controversy about Lott's remarks, a few days earlier, at the 100th birthday of Republican US Senator Strom Thurmond that critics had taken as "an implicit endorsement of segregation" (Stolberg 2002). In mass media coverage of the event, Lott's statement did not feature strongly. Only after political blogs focused on the statement and provided historical information on Thurmond establishing the context for Lott's statements did mass media start to pay attention. The ensuing public controversy eventually led to Lott's resignation (Davis 2009, 22f.). This brief episode was the first prominent case in which political bloggers established their political power by covering aspects of political events overseen or ignored in political coverage of mass media and engendering heavy debate in politically vocal online communities, in turn attracting the attention of traditional media, which originally had ignored a given story (Lessig 2004; Perlmutter 2008; Davis 2009).

In the early 2000s, technologically weblogs represented a significant reduction in the complexities of publishing and the maintaining of personal websites. Services like Blogger or WordPress allowed users to register and publish their thoughts on personalized weblogs without having to master the intricacies of HTML coding. This was a significant lowering of the technological barrier and allowed even technologically unskilled users to regularly publish posts on personalized sites. Unsurprisingly, this proved to be very popular and extended the active participatory uses of the web to new demographics. A central feature to weblogs is the chronological ordering of posts, with the newest post standing on the top of the page. This gave blogs the appearance of public diaries or chronicles of events and emphasized the temporal structuring of information, just like in the display of news. This made weblogs a natural tool for people interested in providing an alternative outlook on the news from the one provided by traditional mass media.

Early examples of alternative news organizations gaining popularity by adopting the weblog format on the conservative side of the American political spectrum are the Drudge Report (founded 1995) and Breitbart News (founded 2007). On the left side, we find Talking Points Memo (founded 2000), Daily Kos (founded 2002), and Huffington Post (founded 2005). Common to these sites is their stated goal to provide political coverage alternative to political coverage in mass media, which often is perceived to be politically biased and commercially driven. Often the founding of these sites coincides with their favored party losing the race for the US presidency. For example, the conservative-leaning Drudge Report was founded during the Clinton presidency, Breitbart News was founded at the advent of the Obama presidency, while the liberal Talking Points Memo, Daily Kos, and Huffington Post were founded or rose to prominence during the second Bush presidency. Political blogging thus emerges as a powerful alternative source of news in a political system where traditional news organizations are perceived as being particularly close to the government (Bennett 1990; Entman 2004). It is important to note that this appears to be true for US conservatives (Drudge 2000; Breitbart 2011) and liberals (Armstrong and Moulitsas Zúniga 2006; Kerbel 2009) alike, depending on which party is occupying the White House. But not only openly partisan news organizations have emerged from the political blogosphere. In the late 2000s, as the economic crisis deepened, various new news organizations emerged that subscribed to the ideals of nonpartisan, critical investigative reporting. Examples include but are not limited to Politico and ProPublica in the United States, and Krautreporter in Germany.

Just as important as the emergence of new news organizations is their fragility. The most famous story of a digitally born news organization that shone brightly for a while only to disappear soon thereafter is that of the new media company Gawker (founded 2002, closed down 2016) (Holiday 2018). Given its famously muckraking reputation, Gawker might be a surprising candidate for a discussion of new news organizations. But its rise and fall are in fact very instructive for the supposed power and actual fragility of new news organizations. In the early 2000s, Gawker was an immensely successful new media company that ran a series of tech, gossip, and lifestyle blogs. Gawker blogs followed a template for creating salacious headlines with an eye to attracting consistently high traffic counts as well as playing fast and loose with the privacy rights of the subjects of their stories. While there were many cases in which Gawker attracted the ire of the subjects of its coverage, for our purposes two of these episodes are important. In 2007 Valleywag, a blog in Gawker's media network, outed Silicon Valley investor Peter Thiel as homosexual, followed by a comment of Gawker founder Nick Denton speculating on the reasons why Thiel might have tried to keep his sexual orientation a secret (Thomas 2007). This story that came to haunt Valleywag's parent company Gawker in the coming years and directly contributed to its bankruptcy in 2016 (Holiday 2018). Five years later, in 2012, Gawker published a clip of a sex tape of wrestler Terrence Gene Bollea, better known under his stage name Hulk Hogan. This led to a lawsuit by Hogan, partially funded by Peter Thiel, the subject of the aforementioned Valleywag story. Gawker lost this suit. After a settlement with the aggrieved Hogan, Gawker filed for bankruptcy (Margolick 2016). This episode is instructive as it powerfully illustrates the fragility of even the most powerful of online media companies. It is also perceived to have had a chilling effect on the publication of potentially damaging material on celebrities on online sites. For example, this "Gawker effect" has been cited as one reason for publications being wary of publishing material about allegations of sexual misconduct of then Amazon Studios chief Roy Price (Masters 2017).

This episode is important for two reasons. First, it shows that new news organizations are highly fragile to outside forces even when at the height of their perceived influence as measured through click counts. Thus what might constitute a new news organization of high influence today might be gone tomorrow. Moreover, and probably more importantly, the proliferation of online news platforms does not necessarily mean that each and every news item will find its way to the public. The perceived influence and litigiousness of story subjects has a powerful chilling effect on editors of online news platforms, who are increasingly aware of their sometimes very fragile position. So, instead of transparency for all, the proliferation of online news platforms might have to led to transparency for some.

Parallel to these developments, traditional newspapers and television news programs started to rethink their formats and business models, and developed into news organizations trying to extend their established brands into news platforms across multiple communication channels (Usher 2014; Küng 2015; Rusbridger 2018; Dunaway et al. 2019). For publishers of newspapers, this meant increasingly producing content in other formats. For example, the New York Times not only produces articles published in the paper edition, it also produces videos, podcasts, and visually stunning data journalism that is only truly accessible through its digital editions. These and other content formats do not live only on the dedicated website or the official app of the New York Times. This content is published on and optimized for various third-party platforms, such as Facebook. This is not only true for the New York Times; any successful news organization has to figure out how to position itself in this new environment. The specific answers to this challenge differ, with various news brands choosing different strategies (Küng 2015). Even traditional news organizations thus become multi-channel, multi-content information providers, with all that this shift entails. At the same time, new news organizations are not necessarily staying exclusively in the digital realm. Many news organizations that started online quickly tried to establish print editions, for example Politico. The reason for this can be seen in the perceived prestige associated with having a print edition and also the opportunity to sell ad space and sponsored content for higher rates compared with online (Edmonds 2017). We, therefore, should be careful to not simply equate these new news organizations with their physical representation in either digital or analogue media formats.

It is also important to keep a sense of perspective. Just because there is the potential for new news outlets to arise online does not necessarily mean they are destined to take over media systems. For one, most of the successful examples of digital-born news outlets are based in the United States. This is no accident. It is much harder for digital-born news organizations to develop viable business models or significant audience reach in European media systems than it is in the United States (Nicholls et al. 2016). Possible reasons for this could be the stronger position of publicly funded broadcasters and therefore a generally less competitive environment for the production of political news, or the segmentation of European news markets along languages and borders, again severely limiting the market for news. The disruptive potential of new news organizations might thus depend strongly on the regulatory environment in which news organizations find themselves competing. Moreover, just because there is a mass of new information out there does not necessarily mean it is also read. Various studies have shown that even in the United States, traditional media are still the most widely used source of political information (Webster 2014) and that even among online news sources there are only a few central sources that reliably command the attention of large audiences (Hindman 2009, 2018b). Add to this the fragility of new news organizations discussed previously, and the relationship between old and new news organizations emerges as more complicated than a simple story of replacement.

We thus find a truly diverse mix of organizations providing news in a variety of content formats across a wide mix of channels. This dilutes the borders between traditional news media, originally anchored in specific distribution channels such as newspapers or television, and digital-born news media. In essence, no matter their origin, today news organizations are in the business of producing and distributing news content in various formats and across various distributions channels. This also means business models and economic incentives align. New outlets like Buzzfeed and traditional news organizations like the Washington Post both look to click counts and interaction metrics of their articles with a view to optimizing them in order to sell more ads (Wu 2016). And yet, given their brands, traditional news organizations would be well advised to refrain from the worst excesses of clickbait headlines and coverage associated with online journalism. So, while economic incentives align, reactions to them might differ.

Combining Old and New

This emergence of new news organizations contributing to the flow of political information introduces a new set of actors with potentially diverging norms, institutional goals, and economic incentives to the coverage of politics. The sociology of news has long emphasized the importance of internalized norms, journalistic self-image, and their expression in tacit newsroom norms and practices for the structure and self-regulation of political journalism (Schudson 2011; McQuail 2013; Shoemaker and Reese 2014). While there is a valid argument to be made that these shared norms, tacit rules, and practices were honored as least as much in the breach as in their observance (Bennett 2016), a predominant homogeneity in the social backgrounds of journalists, newsroom compositions, business models, and organizational structures allowed for the identification of a "journalistic field" (Benson 2006) in which participants shared an implicit understanding of what constituted good or at least legitimate political journalism – a shared understanding that the contemporary observer will be hard pressed to identify among the current contributors to the flow of political information.

Not surprisingly, new news organizations have been heavily critiqued for their perceived break with established norms of political journalism. The founder and long-time editor of the Huffington Post, Arianna Huffington, has been repeatedly and heavily criticized for editorial practice and interventions that some have seen as favoritism for personal friends and business contacts (Cohan 2016a). Breitbart News is routinely challenged for its political coverage, which is openly partisan and is seen by some as bordering on the provision of politically motivated conscious disinformation to its readers (J. Green 2015). Furthermore, Politico is routinely criticized for its boulevardization of news coverage, with a continuous focus on scoops, gossip, and controversy (Sherman 2009), and its highly competitive newsroom culture (Abad-Santos 2013). Overall, the online presences of news organizations have to contend with the challenge of turning political coverage into clickbait and thereby contributing to the trivialization of news and the pollution of the flow of political information (Hamblin 2014; Wu 2016).

For example, in early 2017, CNN published a story on the existence of a secret intelligence report alleging Russian agents had compromising information on then President-elect Donald Trump (Perez et al. 2017). This led to a frenzy in the news media and social media as to the presumed contents of this dossier (Graham 2017b). Hours later, the news and curiosity site Buzzfeed published said document on its website "so that Americans can make up their own minds about allegations about the president-elect that have circulated at the highest levels of the US government" (Bensinger, Elder, and Schoofs 2017). This is an interesting case. At that time, the dossier seems to have been available to a number of American news outlets, yet most of them held back on either reporting on or publishing it because they were unsure of the veracity of its claims (Graham 2017a). A mixture of newsroom practices on how to ascertain the credibility of sources and internalized responsibility for the democratic process led them to hold back, where a new news outlet mainly driven by the need for attention pushed forward. One could see this as a triumph for transparency, potentially heralding an age when there are no secrets or privileged information for the political cognoscenti. Or one could see this as a deeply troubling sign that the need for attention fueled by controversy and speed will lead news outlets to ultimately discard norms and practices of self-control and, therefore, contribute to a destabilization of political systems. In fact, this ability to set news agendas and thereby fracture public discourse in countries by using alternative news sources and manipulating social media is a central feature of so-called cyberwar, the goal of which is to create doubt and division in target countries through weakening trust in central organs of public discourse (Arquilla and Ronfeldt 2001; Farrell and Schneier 2018; Singer and Brooking 2018).

While it is easy to judge some of the shrill and crass manifestations emerging from new news organizations, one should be careful not to unduly overestimate the perceived purity of political journalism in earlier days. Not surprisingly, these challenges are usually put forward by direct competitors of digitally born news organizations, and as such we should be careful not to mistake a publicly conducted struggle about the legitimacy of participants in contributing to the media system as unbiased analyses of the current state of political news. With new actors come new norms, expressions, and practices. Some of them might be harmful to the flow of political information through a society, yet some might simply seem shrill and unfamiliar now while they are new and commentators and the public have not yet learned to anticipate and place them in what we have come to expect from political news.

Furthermore, the rules and newsroom practices might converge. While traditional newsrooms come with outlet-specific rules and practices to ensure a degree of quality control, these practices might change given the speed and metric-dependency of online journalism. For example, while in the past an editor would decide what was newsworthy given her experiences, professional norms, and her perception of her outlet's audience, today a quick glance at the dashboard of a social media monitoring tool of choice reveals the current distribution of public attention online between a given set of topics, which in turn provide the anchor for new coverage trying to capture a share of this attention on one's own platform. Various studies document the increasing influence of social media monitoring and user behavior analysis in newsrooms (Hamby 2013; Anstead and O'Loughlin 2015; Webster 2014; Christin 2018). Consequences of this practice can already be identified in the coverage patterns of political topics and their prominence on social media. For example, Wells et al. (2016) showed that during the Republican primaries for the US presidential election in 2016, mentions of Donald Trump on Twitter were a reliable predictor of the intensity of subsequent media coverage. While the actual driver of this statistical relationship remains hidden in their analysis, this pattern corresponds well with a model of editors using social media monitoring to identify objects of public attention and commissioning their writers to produce content addressing that issue, thereby directing some of that public attention to their own platforms and providing additional eyeballs for their ad customers.

The growing prominence of digital media as carriers for political information forced traditional news organizations to shift their production models to accommodate digital technology. This also means abandoning content models focused on one carrier medium exclusively. In this we see a characteristic of digital media. Convergence is a tendency toward a growing mix of different media types, channels, rhetorical conventions, audiences, and usage practices (Jenkins 2006). This convergence also finds expression in traditional news organizations collaborating with new news organizations in an attempt to reach new audiences and to learn about the dynamics of digital news consumption. For example, in 2012 the New York Times and Buzzfeed collaborated in their coverage of the conventions during the 2012 US presidential race (Garber 2012). This growing link also finds expression in the hiring practices of digitally born news organizations keen on hiring experienced personnel from traditional news organizations and vice versa, and even extends to tech billionaires buying established news outlets. For example, in 2013 internet entrepreneur and Amazon founder Jeff Bezos bought the Washington Post (Isaac 2014), adapting practices and processes of the technology company to the news sector in the process (Bond 2014; Rosoff 2017). Other high-profile acquisitions of traditional news organizations by figures from the digital economy include the sale of the New Republic in 2012 to Facebook cofounder Chris Hughes (Lizza 2014) and of The Atlantic in 2017 to Laurene

Powell Jobs, widow of Apple founder Steve Jobs (Frankel and Heath 2017). These developments are interesting as they show that traditional news organizations are increasingly run the way technology companies are run, while entrepreneurs coming from the digital tech sector very consciously set their sights on important brands of traditional news organizations in order to benefit from the symbolic power and the political legitimacy associated with the history of traditional news organizations.

Increasingly with regard to content, collaborations, personnel, and ownership, boundaries between traditional and digitally born news organizations tend to blur. This can be seen as a further element of the hybridity in the contemporary media system conceptualized by Chadwick (2017). Given this increasing interlinkage across various areas, it is not surprising to find the economics of the two converging. Centrally, digitally born and traditional news organizations share a dependency on eyeballs and clicks on their content. If both rely heavily on the reach they can offer ad customers, they rely heavily on extending their audience. While part of this can be achieved by growing a stable audience base, currently news organizations depend on their content traveling widely through social networking platforms or social recommendations such as email or chat programs. Here we can differentiate between purchased reach, for example through ads or sponsored posts, and reach earned through social recommendations and people sharing the content provided by news organizations. Especially the second part of this has received considerable public attention under the term attention economy (Wu 2016; Thompson 2017) with a specific focus on which type of content would create "viral" sharing patterns (Jenkins, Ford, and Green 2013; Nahon and Hemsley 2013; Goel et al. 2016). In practice, it seems that after a first stage in which social networking platforms illustrated to news organizations their perceived power to shift audiences in their direction (Warzel 2013), they increasingly let them pay for the privilege (Ingram 2016; Peterson 2016; Peston 2017). This is another area in which specifics are very much in flux and where power dynamics are continuously renegotiated.

Online platforms provided by technology companies have become important distribution channels for content provided by news organizations. This makes them and the algorithms governing the display of content very important determinants in the flow of political information. In the context of the fascination with the perceived role of disinformation or so-called fake news during the US election campaign of 2016, the role of algorithms in the selection, display, and emphasis of news items has jumped to the forefront of public debate (Diakopoulos and Koliska 2017). While the question of the actual determinants and effect of these algorithmic selection processes is probably still best thought of as undecided, the centrality of online platforms as a distribution belt for attention toward the output of news organizations makes them, their organizational decision-making, the setup and governance process of algorithmic selection processes, and potential auditing mechanisms of central importance for public debate and academic attention.

In combination, we thus can diagnose a growing convergence between different economic incentives, internalized norms and ideals, newsroom practices, and coverage patterns across news organizations:

> The hybrid media system is built upon interactions among older and newer media logics – where logics are defined as technologies, genres, norms, behaviors, and organizational forms – in the reflexively connected fields of media and politics. Actors in this system are articulated by complex and ever-evolving relationships based upon adaptation and interdependence and simultaneous concentrations and diffusions of power. Actors create, tap, or steer information flows in ways that suit their goals and in ways that modify, enable, or disable the agency of others, across and between a range of older and newer media settings.
>
> (Chadwick 2017, 4)

This high degree of interdependency between different types of news organizations following different economic incentives, newsroom practices, and ideational foundations makes the whole system highly vulnerable to agenda hacking. In this system, it only takes one important actor to jump on a story for the others to follow. It even suffices if the appearance of sufficient levels of public attention is generated, for example through comparatively high levels of public attention expressed in social media metrics (Azari 2016; Wells et al. 2016; Chadwick 2017). Objects of attention and controversy online – even if only directly visible to a small section of a population, journalists, political elites, and social media monitoring tools – might successfully translate into broad news coverage, which in turn has the potential to reach large parts of the population. Surgically placed provocations online, even if only directly visible to a select few, can, through the conveyor belt of social media monitoring tools and consonant news coverage across various news organizations, potentially reach large audiences.

Currently we do not know the degree to which this growing interdependency between traditional and new news organizations, digital platforms, and audiences leads to a loss of influence of traditional news organizations. While we find a multitude of actors and voices contributing to contemporary information flows in political communication spaces, this does not necessarily mean traditional news organizations and brands lose their ability to select topics and voices that will be heard. In fact, in many accounts they emerge as important transmission belts for stories and voices originally reported or found online to reach large audiences. Identifying the dynamics, degrees, and determinants of discursive power in these relationships emerging from this new interdependency is one of the immensely promising empirical questions of contemporary research (Jungherr et al. 2019a).

While this development should in principle hold internationally, it is important to note that the account given here nearly exclusively relies on findings and episodes from the United States. While there are some studies illustrating the role of digitally born news organizations in other media systems and the transformation of traditional news organizations induced by digitalization (Nicholls et al. 2016; Cornia, Sehl, and Nielsen 2017), predominantly the academic debate focuses on US-based accounts. This is understandable as the United States is at the center of the digital transformation of media systems and politics, but it is also severely limiting if we want to understand what is general about this development and what is specific to the unique contexts of US politics and its media system. Moreover, we know embarrassingly little about the dynamics of large non-Western media systems, whether in Asia (Stockman 2013; Aneez et al. 2016; Sen and Nielsen 2016; Repnikova 2017), Latin and South America (Albuquerque 2005, 2019), the Near East (Hassan 2015), or Africa (Albuquerque 2016; Nyabola 2018). This also limits our understanding of the impact of digital media on media systems and the flow of political information in autocracies, transitional democracies, or non-OECD countries (Bailard 2014). This is all the more troubling since, as we have shown, the impact of these developments on the flow of political information and therefore on political power and the monitorial capabilities of a population is severely felt in established Western democracies. This makes this a topic of vital concern in systems that are much more in flux and where information is subject to much more direct control by the state.

All this goes to show that digital media significantly changed the nature of news organizations contributing to media systems. For the analysis of political information flows, this means accounting for potential shifts in the norms of individuals participating in the media system, shifts in the economics of news production and distribution, and also shifts in the rhetoric of news content. It remains an open question how long it is useful to differentiate between traditional news organizations and those born digital.

Who Watches the Gates?

One of the central roles of news organizations with regard to the flow of political information is their decision on what news to cover and what to ignore. In this, they decide which events, topics, actors, and perspectives to put before the public and which to further emphasize. They also become de facto referees of the political competition between parties, candidates, interest groups, activists, and the public by explicitly commenting on politics but also by the implicit evaluations inherent in their decisions on what news to cover and what to ignore. They are gatekeepers in the flow of political information (Shoemaker and Vos 2009).

The role of news organizations as gatekeepers has featured prominently in communication research. At the heart of these studies lie individual-level factors focusing on characteristics of news items and the decision-making process of journalists and editors, the role of routines in determining which stories even rise to the attention of news organizations, and organizational factors accounting for the influence of newsrooms and the organizations running them (Shoemaker and Cohen 2006; Pressman 2018). In this debate, researchers are trying to establish what a legitimate practice of this gatekeeping function would look like. In the more optimistic accounts, news organizations, through internalized democratic norms, established practices of quality control in news validation and content production, economic independence, and political impartiality, would present the public with a filtered but balanced view of the news (Schulz 1989). This selection of news would allow citizens to evaluate political actors and take positions on the issues of the day. It is no surprise that most empirical studies found that traditional news organizations failed in the face of these lofty expectations. For example, in focusing on biases in news selection and their role as gatekeepers, US researchers routinely found that traditional news organizations, even before the advent of the internet, had a worrying closeness to government, a tendency toward framing news along the lines of entertainment and scandal, and economically driven biases in favor of the interests of their ad buyers (Bennett 2016).

For many authors critical of the established structures and process for managing the flow of political information, the internet, with its lowering of the costs of publishing and finding information and the increase in sources of political information, provided a chance to counter the influence of news organizations and to offer a counterbalance to the established biases in news selection, commenting, and emphasis. For example, William Dutton saw in the internet the emergence of a new institution that challenged the established press in their role as gatekeepers in the flow of political information. Riffing off Edmund Burke's calling the press the "Fourth Estate," Dutton speaks of the internet-enabled rise of a "Fifth Estate":

> In the twenty-first century, a new institution is emerging with some characteristics similar to the Fourth Estate, but with sufficiently distinctive and important features to warrant its recognition as a new Fifth Estate. This is being built on the growing

use of the Internet and related information and communication technologies (ICTs) in ways that are enabling "networked individuals" to reconfigure access to alternative sources of information, people and other resources. Such "networks of networks" enable the networked individuals to move across, undermine and go beyond the boundaries of existing institutions, thereby opening new ways of increasing the accountability of politicians, press, experts and other loci of power and influence.

(Dutton 2009, 2)

Internet users, so-called citizen journalists (Allen and Thorsen 2009), would research and break stories independent of traditional news organizations. By publishing news items on their own web presences or on alternative news sites, they were expected to break the monopoly of news organizations to put information in front of the public. This was seen as part of the internet breaking the technologically introduced scarcity of space for information that characterized former news media like newspapers or television. As the internet had no space restrictions, everybody was seen as being able to put information in front of people. In this new world, even if traditional media might decide not to cover an event or to ignore political factions or speakers, political coverage on digital media would give them a space. While traditional media organizations are still selecting what to cover and what to ignore, their decisions will be supplemented or contested by the selection decisions of a myriad of alternative news sources online. Whether this actually correctly describes coverage dynamics between traditional and alternative media is best thought of as an open question (Jungherr et al. 2019a).

If gatekeeping was a necessity for journalists to decide which information was worth publishing and which could be neglected, depending on the scarcity of the news medium in question, the internet made this superfluous. The practice of gatekeeping would be replaced by a practice of gatewatching by internet users, who would

observe what material is available and interesting, and identify useful new information with a view of channeling this material into structured and up-to-date news reports which may include guides to relevant content and excerpts from the selected material. . . . news Websites based upon gatewatching frequently engage less in the publishing of complete, finalized news reports than in the *publicizing* of the news stories which have become newly available in other information sources; their own news items often take the form of brief summaries or digests which combine pointers to a number of such reports and discuss their relevance, identify different angles for evaluating the same event, or make connections to other related issues.

(Bruns 2005, 18f.)

Mark how both Dutton and Bruns put the emphasis very much on the curating of available information and not on the creation of new information or news stories. If anything, the role of users as curators of the flow of information online has become even more central with the growing importance of social networking platforms in the work of news organizations (Bastos, Raimundo, and Travitzki 2013; Meraz and Papacharissi 2013; Jungherr and Jürgens 2014b; Anstead and O'Loughlin 2015). This points to one of the central vulnerabilities of the new communication environment introduced by challenges to the business of news. What information is there to be curated if news organizations are not able to finance the process of creating new stories? What kind of control of political and economic actors is truly possible if nobody is able to dedicate resources into investigative reporting? Are the odd citizen journalists and whistleblowers enough to fill a structural gap emerging in the political information space by the economically motivated withdrawal of news organizations as originators of news stories and information? And does the new dependency on content open the door for the skillful manipulation of media by political actors willing to spend the necessary resources to produce investigative reports on opponents, channeling this information to audiences through traditional news organizations hungry for content?

An example of the latter case could be witnessed during the Democratic primaries for the US presidential race in 2016. Republican donors financed a seemingly independent research group, the Government Accountability Institute, investigating the finances of the Clinton Foundation. The resulting dossier, "Clinton Cash," was published to wide reactions in book form (Schweizer 2015) and featured strongly, among other outlets, in the pages of the New York Times (Chozick 2015). At the time, the dossier was widely seen as strengthening Hillary Clinton's competitor in the primaries, Bernie Sanders, and ended up framing her public image well into the actual race against the Republican candidate Donald Trump. By financing the dossier and launching it early in the campaign cycle, Republican partisans succeeded in capturing the political agenda and defining a political opponent early in the race (J. Green 2015). The role of the New York Times in this episode powerfully illustrates the vulnerability of even the strongest of traditional news organizations to the capturing of their agenda through the provision of skillfully produced content. The power to influence the coverage of other, less prominent news organization through similar means or directly sponsored content should be correspondingly high.

Common to early accounts of this process is the underlying feeling that established news organizations and institutions managing and filtering the flow of political information are biased and that a decentralized citizen-driven alternative to their dominant role might be a welcome corrective. In these accounts citizens emerge as active participants in managing the flow of political information through their public interactions in comment sections, blogs, and social media, as correctives actively challenging potentially biased accounts of events in political coverage by news organizations, and as "citizen journalists" actively following and filing stories of public relevance that traditional media missed (Bruns 2005; Rosen 2006; Allen and Thorsen 2009). They thereby emerge as equal partners and arbiters in a concert of voices providing, filtering, and guiding the flow of political information, contributing to an increasingly complex political information cycle (Chadwick 2017). In these early accounts the rise of the political blogosphere, the increasing prominence of social media in political debate, and the emergence of alternative news organizations was seen as a largely positive influence on the state of the political information flow. Since then, more critical voices have emerged.

For one, it seems far from certain that new contributors to the political communication space are able to fill the hole ripped into the political communication space by the withdrawal of traditional news outlets. This is especially true for news on the local or state level (Project for Excellence in Journalism 2010). Consequently, the Fifth Estate might end up curating an ever smaller amount of information as the volume of original content drops. It is far from clear whether this will be enough to lead to greater control of political and economic elites. These doubts are further reinforced since as of now we know little about the actual dynamics of the collective curating process of political information online. What we do know paints a far less optimistic picture than the one provided in early accounts. For example, a closer look at the political blogosphere in the United States showed that public attention was predominantly focused on a small selection of central blogs while most received next to no attention at all (Hindman 2009). This leaves open the question whether the new dynamics of the political communication space truly favor outsiders or whether existing political hierarchies are merely mirrored and reinforced (Davis 1999; Margolis and Resnick 2000). Furthermore, the collective curating process of political information on social networking sites, such as Facebook or Twitter, has been shown to be highly vulnerable to manipulation attempts (Mustafaraj and Metaxas 2010), thereby raising the question of how robust this new element in the flow of political information is, and whether news organizations' reliance on it renders them more at risk for manipulation than their old practices and routines. Finally, we have to ask the question whether it is truly enough for political information to be published on blogs or alternative news sites to reach a larger audience. Various close examinations of scandals and the flow of political information show that while alternative sites might break a story, these stories have to be picked up by major news organizations to reach a large audience and in turn lead to political consequences (Karpf 2010a; Chadwick 2011b). Major news organizations thus remain central to the flow of political information.

These are only a few observations that show that while we know quite a bit about the role and biases of traditional news organizations in their function as gatekeepers, the role of the new multi-channel, multi-content news organizations and their interplay with "citizen journalists" and interested political actors or internet users is far from understood. There is a consensus, though, that through the entrance of new players as news providers and the increasing ability of individuals to enter the information cycle through communicative interventions on blogs or social media, the strong gatekeeping function of news organizations in the flow of political information by deciding what is news has been challenged. The exact consequences of this challenge are the subject of controversial scientific and public debate. Yet one of the most recent expressions of this challenge can be found in the public debate about disinformation and so-called fake news, or the public negotiation about what facts should actually be considered as true.

Who Determines What Is True?

In recent years, public concern about commonly agreed upon facts in the political information flow have grown. Terms such as "post truth," "post-factual," or "fake news" are labels of contestation that commentators, journalists, politicians, and partisans are combatively assigning to competitors. The goal of this labeling and counter-labeling of claims and actors is to delegitimize competitors and adversaries. Examples of this are the New York Times columnist Paul Krugman diagnosing the Republican presidential candidate in 2012, Mitt Romney, as running a "post-truth campaign" (Krugman 2011), or the Financial Times identifying Britain after Brexit as a "post-factual democracy" (Barrett 2016), or US President Donald Trump cutting off journalists working for the television network CNN with the words: "I am not giving you a question. You are fake news" (Snider 2017). The weakening of the power and legitimacy of gatekeepers in the flow of political information described previously, growing distrust in public authority figures and the media, and increasing political tribalism have created a void in which communicative legitimacy is up for grabs – a void in which disagreement reigns about what constitutes political fact and who legitimately is expected to arbitrate among social and political factions in the competition about facts, remedies, and political power (Ball 2017; D'Ancona 2017; Davis 2017). The role of technology, enabling the rise of alternative sources of news and voices directly challenging established authorities and news media, plays a central if not the exclusive role in this development (Gurri 2018).

The political blogosphere in the United States emerged as a direct challenge to political coverage of the Clinton–Lewinski scandal, the Bush presidency, and the Iraq War by the mass media. Central to these challenges was the perception that mass media were unduly fixated on the salacious details of the Clinton–Lewinski affair, or were too closely associated with the US government to provide critical coverage of the Iraq War (Bennett, Lawrence, and Livingston 2007; Perlmutter 2008). Given perceived biases in the coverage of mainstream media, explicitly partisan alternative news sources emerged. Overall, this challenge to established news organizations was seen as an enrichment of the political information space. Alternative perspectives and speakers underrepresented in traditional mainstream media coverage were seen as gaining visibility and voice. This challenge to established structures of the political information space enabled by digital technology and social media was widely seen as normatively desirable (Chadwick 2006).

While during the late 1990s and early 2000s alternative voices in the political information space emerged on the political left, the late 2000s and 2010s saw challengers emerge on the right. Those voices were closely linked with populist parties and candidates of the far right. While these parties and candidates challenged the political consensus, for example in the UK referendum to exit the European Union or in the candidacy of Donald Trump for the US presidency, alternative right-wing news sources, such as Breitbart, rendered support in actively challenging the coverage of "mainstream media" and their perceived slights of populist voices and the "censorship" of the true voice of the people.

Soon this challenge not only extended to the coverage or neglect of specific angles in stories but started to concern the veracity of accounts and facts. Politicians and alternative news sources combined forces to challenge the authority of established mass media to legitimately and impartially cover politics, be it the continuous needling of "mainstream media" and "gotcha coverage" by the US Tea Party (Tracinski 2008), the continuous challenge of the publicly funded BBC by politicians and partisans from either political side in the United Kingdom (FT View 2015; Robinson 2017; Ruddick and Khomami 2017), or the ongoing challenge of publicly funded broadcasters in Germany by private media and right-wing populists (Meier 2016; Döpfner 2017). Over time, partisans in these countries started to disagree about which central media organizations were in actual fact impartial gatekeepers in the political information space but started to stick to news sources with explicit political allegiances. Soon, journalists working for these outlets, politicians, and mainstream journalism started to challenge each other with regard to the veracity of their claims, giving rise to the terms "post truth" and "fake news." In practice, these terms tend not to be clearly defined but work as labels to challenge the legitimacy of specific actors and sources in the political information space.

This process received its preliminary high-water mark during the campaign for the Brexit referendum in the United Kingdom and the campaign for the 2016 presidential election in the United States. Supporters of the Brexit referendum were seen by the established media in the United Kingdom as playing fast and loose with the facts, such as the claim that Brexit would bring savings of 350 million pounds weekly to Britain's budget, which would then be available for reallocation to the National Health Service (Peston 2017). Yet these rhetorical choices pale in the face of the outright falsehoods that candidate and later US President Donald Trump spun during the campaign and in government (for an exhaustive list see Leonhardt and Thompson (2017)). In lockstep with the candidates, alternative news sources attacked opposing candidates, news sources, or established elites in their coverage; news sites of dubious origin suddenly appeared for a few stories, only to fall silent soon thereafter; and wild stories of dubious veracity and obvious falsehoods circulated on social media, apparently reaching wide audiences (Ball 2017; D'Ancona 2017; Bennett and Livingston 2018).

Not all originators of published falsehoods reaching wide audiences during the US campaign cycle are known, but those who are include Macedonian teenagers (Subramanian 2017), Russian propagandists (Pomerantsev 2015; MacFarquhar 2016; Confessore and Wakabayashi 2017), Republican political action committees (PACs) (Silverman and Parti 2017), perpetrators of hoaxes (Silverman and Singer-Vine 2016), and conspiracy theorists (Silverman 2016). The actual effects of these false stories introduced into the flow of political information during the campaign are highly contested, and will be addressed by us in greater detail in Chapters 3 and 4. Yet already the presence and broad visibility of these items constitutes a change to previous times, when established news organizations had greater power as gatekeepers over which information or which speaker was allowed access to the flow of political information. A growing distrust in institutions of political and media systems thus contributed to growing distrust in facts or truths in general.

During the 2016 campaign cycle, the main distribution channel of purposeful disinformation and accidental misinformation seems to have been social networking platforms like Facebook and Twitter (Lazer et al. 2018). The reasons for this are multiple. For one, controversial or fake items were skillfully designed to "hack the attention economy" (boyd 2017) by using humorous memes and clickbait headlines, and eliciting strong emotions of anger and outrage among their readers. Once exposed to these items, users on social networking platforms readily shared, liked, or commented on them, not necessarily because of their belief in the veracity of their claims but as an expression of political tribal loyalties. The use of these items thus might have been at least as much expressive or identity-protective as informative (Kahan 2017a).

Online platforms were also instrumental in putting contested information in front of users in the first place. On platforms like Facebook, Twitter, or YouTube, contested items could reach high visibility through automated display of "trending topics," items that achieved high interactions among users during given time windows, or algorithmically identified related content to that originally selected by users. Through these features, social networking platforms can point users' attention to information of apparent public interest documented through high interactions by other users. The flip side to this is that these metrics are easily hackable through automated interactions with content (Mustafaraj and Metaxas 2010). Buying clicks on items thus might lead to exposure to actual eyeballs courtesy of the facade of popularity and the "trending topic" and "related content" features of social networking platforms. Another distributive mechanism is ads. Ads allow the originators of information to get their content in front of users corresponding with their audience goals. This feature, for example, has given rise to the speculation that the Trump campaign explicitly targeted weak Clinton supporters on social networking platforms with content designed to have them abstain from the vote come election day (Green and Issenberg 2016).

While the actual effects of these distribution patterns are impossible to determine after the fact, they have given rise to the sneaking suspicion that the internet, social media, and social networking platforms might have damaged US democracy (Persily 2017). While this is ultimately a normative judgment, without a doubt social networking platforms have allowed new distribution patterns for political information to emerge that favor malicious hit-and-run actors. In the past, it was much harder for malicious actors to get their information in front of many readers. Through social networking platforms, this has changed.

Yet this is not so much a natural feature of social networking platforms as it represents a conscious hacking of specific functionality and features of these sites current as of 2016. We thus should be careful not to simply extrapolate from the 2016 US presidential election to the future of information flows in international campaigns. For one, the specific laws and regulations of elections vary considerably internationally, thereby leading to different political information environments. Second, and probably more importantly, social networking platforms have come under increased public scrutiny with regard to their role in the flow of political information (Foroohad 2017; Lynch 2017). More likely than not, this will lead them to adapt their publicly available features, reporting practices, and underlying algorithms, negatively impacting the potential for misleading political information to spread among users.

This, in turn, points to an interesting question: In the contemporary media system, who are legitimate arbiters of the veracity of political information and claims by political actors? Should this truly be private companies (Nyhan 2017), fact checkers with varying credentials, financial sources, or partisan alignments (Graves 2016), or can the traditional media organizations use the growing uncertainty to reassert their role as honest gatekeepers (Robinson 2017)? These are questions very much at the center of the current debate, with far from obvious answers. The mapping of these characteristics of contemporary information flows is far from solved and a very promising research area.

In the final account, the label "fake news" is highly problematic as it is part of a struggle for legitimacy in a world of weakened gatekeepers to the flow of political information. Prominent gatekeepers of the status quo, such as well-known journalists and newspapers, challenge new entrants, such as alternative news sites or bloggers, as peddlers of "post truths." At the same time, prominent incumbents of the status quo, such as political or economic elites, try to do the same with actors or media challenging them by labeling them "fake news." Conversely, new entrants to the flow of political information try to do the same to established gatekeepers and political actors. This finds expression in the turn against "mainstream media" or in challenging the legitimacy of public broadcasting media as "censors" or "state propaganda." In public discourse, labels such as "fake news," "populist," or "demagogue" do not serve primarily as neutral identifiers of clearly defined concepts. Instead, they are part of a political and institutional struggle for legitimacy and dominance. In scientific discourse, these terms should be used sparingly and only in the context of clear conceptualizations, being careful not to accidentally replicate the agendas of the combatants in the public sphere.

For some, the "post-factual" age and the apparent prominence of "fake news" in public discourse is a consequence of social media. As has been shown, the driver of this debate is much more likely to be found in the erosion of trust in established organizations and institutions structuring the flow of political information, and the emergence of competitors and challengers of the political status quo. In this, technology surely plays an enabling and accelerating role. Yet it is only one contributing factor among many deeper social developments contributing to the weakening of social structures and institutions (Davis 2017). Central in this are changes in the roles and constitutions of news organizations and political organizations, such as parties and interest groups.

2.6 Retooling the Flow of Political Information

By changing the economics of publishing and accessing political information, digital technology and social media have deeply impacted the established institutional, organizational, and normative structure of media systems. Established structures that emerged during the twentieth century in the context of mass media technology and mass audiences are changing and adapting to new technological affordances and economic models for audiences and producers of political information. This has led to the emergence of a new set of alternative and often partisan news sources, a widespread culture of challenging the accounts of central actors in established media systems by "the people formerly known as the audience" (Rosen 2006), the weakening of the gatekeeping function in the flow of political information by traditional media organizations, the contentious public negotiation of "facts" or "fake news," and a challenge to the setup, practices, and hierarchies of traditional political organizations, such as parties and interest groups.

These patterns have become most visible in the United States and the United Kingdom. In other countries, similar patterns have been identified but their effects have, until now, remained less severe, thereby pointing to potentially powerful boundary conditions for the transformative power of digital technology and social media in established political systems and subsequent consequences for political discourse, public opinion formation, and potentially election results.

Currently, we do not understand these boundary conditions sufficiently. This is due to a combination of factors. For one, most research and public debate is focused on the United States. The reasons for this are obvious. The United States offers a highly visible, most likely case for the transformative power of digital technology: Silicon Valley is the birthplace and incubator for much of the technological, ideological, and economic innovation underlying the services challenging the established media system; the use of social media is widespread among the population; the strongly market-driven incentives of the established media system and the highly partisan nature of contemporary politics rendered established news and political organizations extremely vulnerable to the challenge emerging from digital technology; and finally, the pure spectacle of US politics and the widespread international consequences of the outcomes of its political decisions make it a highly attractive case for international commentators and scholars to discuss. This has given us very perceptive and insightful accounts of the transformative potential and impact of digital technology and social media in the United States. Yet the same factors that make the United States such a promising case make US findings deeply contingent and of dubious generalizability.

This challenge is reinforced by a tendency to neglect contextual conditions of the effects of digital technology in favor of what are perceived to be universal laws or trends and a near exclusive focus on its impact in OECD countries. To move beyond this stage, research has to adopt a comparative framework identifying contextual conditions for the role and impact of digital technology and social media in established political information systems through careful case selection. This includes extending our understanding by careful case work on the role of digital technologies in underexamined countries, including its role in information systems of autocracies (Hassan 2015), transitional democracies, places of emergent statehood (Livingston and Walter-Drop 2014), countries with a deep tradition of publicly funded information systems (Küng 2015; Nicholls et al. 2016), and Asian countries with exceptionally high technological adoption and non-Silicon Valley services (Stockman 2013; Repnikova 2017). Only through deeper knowledge of these cases will we be able to identify what is universal about what we have seen in the United States and what is limited to its very specific contemporary conditions.

This also includes greater attention being paid to the role of information systems in politics by political science and sociology. Currently, communication research is the scientific field most active in examining the role and impact of shifts in information systems on public discourse, political systems, and outcomes. While highly instructive, communication research generally tends to put limited emphasis on boundary conditions of effects and disruptive patterns, seeking the root causes and determinants in communication. Political science and sociology, with their interest in and tradition of looking at a variety of potential influencing factors, promise a rich understanding of the role of digital technology and social media for information systems embedded in structures, institutions, and behavior. For this to happen, though, these fields first need to develop a sustained interest in communicative institutions, organizations, and practices.

This also means a shift in methods. While the rise of readily available digital data sources has led to much interest in their incorporation into social science (Lazer et al. 2009; Jungherr 2015; Salganik 2018), they only offer partial insights into the full range of the transformation of information systems. To be sure, these data and methods have been highly instructive with regard to the reach and flow of information through contemporary media systems. But they only offer limited insights into institutional, organizational, and normative changes as well as impacts on the economics of news and newsroom practices. For this, qualitative methods of organizational and institutional research offer obvious potential.

Central to identifying the role of digital media in political information systems is the identification of contingencies. Their transformative potential for the economics of news organizations might depend significantly on the dependency of news organizations on market forces, with market-driven news systems being highly vulnerable to shocks and publicly funded news systems being more resistant to change. Moreover, we have to examine what determines the professional norms and practices of established and new entrants into media systems. Are new entrants necessarily clickbait-driven disruptors of the status quo or do they share norms with journalists working for established news organizations? Are there determinants consistently leading to the emergence of one or the other? Finally, how can we explain levels of trust and distrust in established contributors and arbiters in information flows across countries, cultures, and media systems? Is distrust a necessary feature of contemporary societies and digitally driven change, or is it driven by contextual factors, for example the nature and intensity of partisan political discourse?

Currently these are open questions, with the United States providing a case illustrating the high transformative potential of digital technology and social media on information flows. The question whether this influence is stable across countries and time is far from answered, offering a promising area of future comparative research.

3

Reaching People

Imagine for a moment that you are a member of a local group of activists. Your group found out that the recently proposed zoning regulation threatens to cut off vital channels of airflow into your city with unforeseen consequences. At the next meeting of the city council, you want to demonstrate the strength your concerns have with the general public. But how do you get the word out?

Do you organize a canvassing stand at a municipal hot spot to raise awareness? But how to staff the stand and how to finance the materials? Do you try to get the local paper to run a story about the consequences of the new zoning proposition? But who still reads the paper? Do you start a Facebook group? But can you expect to reach the age group in your city concerned with airflows and zoning regulations there? In short, how do you reach the right people when it matters?

Now put yourself in the shoes of the head of communication of a politician's campaign for national office. Your goal is voter mobilization. But how to reach potential voters? Do you book your candidate on a national news program? But who except for political junkies watches those today? Do you run Facebook or Google ads? But who clicks on those anyway? Do you produce "viral" content in the hope your target audience catches the bug and distributes it further on messenger apps or social media? But how to control your message and image this way? Or do you send volunteers door to door to directly reach out to potential voters? But how do you determine which door is worth knocking on?

Figuring out how to reach the right people at the right time is one of the crucial tasks of anyone working in politics. It is also one of the tasks in politics that has been impacted the most by digital media. By weakening traditional media and political organizations, digital media have also weakened their contribution to political actors achieving reach. At the same time, digital media have introduced new ways and opportunities to reach people. In this chapter we will sketch the challenges and opportunities of achieving reach through digital media.

3.1 Three Dimensions of Reach

Parties, candidates, governments, nongovernmental organizations (NGOs), interest groups, and social movements all face the same challenge: how to reach the right people at the right time to further their political goals. The specifics of what exactly constitutes the "right people," the "right time," the political goals, and the communicative content and intent vary across actors and political contexts. Strategies to achieve reach and the need to adapt to shifts in media systems, described in Chapter 2, vary accordingly.

For example, political membership organizations – such as parties, unions, NGOs, or interest groups – and social movements may want to distribute information in a timely fashion to their members and supporters. Candidates might want to engage in communication with sections of the public likely to be receptive to their position. Contacting these people brings the challenge of figuring out how to reach them in the first place. Reach can be achieved by political actors either directly or indirectly. Direct reach allows political actors to contact people without a mediating other. Indirect reach, conversely, means that political actors use others to contact people on their behalf. This might be, for example, a news organization or other allied political actor, such as unions campaigning for progressive candidates.

These approaches are not mutually exclusive and none is inherently better. Both direct and indirect reach have benefits and drawbacks that each organization has to strategically weigh in light of their specific goals and circumstances. The same organization may rely on different approaches under different circumstances, while the same approach may fail to materialize the same benefits at different points in time or for different actors.

On the one hand, direct reach offers organizations control of the message and delivery but might limit the total number of contacts. On the other hand, indirect reach allows actors to increase their reach to people while piggybacking on the relationship of trust between their partners and people contacted by them. In this process, they also transfer the costs of contact to the mediator. Examples of this are unions engaging in outreach for parties and candidates aligned with the labor movement or churches supporting conservative candidates. In a more nefarious case, political actors can also pose as groups they suspect might find it easier to convince people. One example of this is the Russian disinformation campaigns during the 2016 US presidential election that targeted African Americans while posing as activist groups associated with the Black Lives Matter movement (Levin 2017). They did so expecting that these supposedly allied activist groups might carry more weight as the sender of a message than anonymous accounts or groups openly aligned with Russia.

But indirect contact also means a loss of control of one's message to the mediating other. Relying on mass media to transmit one's message in regular coverage means giving up control of the context in which one's statements are presented or commented on. Loss of message control might even happen when parties send out members or volunteers for voter outreach (Enos and Hersh 2015). So, while indirect reach has significant benefits with regard to costs and audience size, it also brings challenges that might induce political actors to increase their capabilities of reaching people directly without having the message filtered, even if this means incurring the sometimes significant costs of buying ad space with news organizations or online platforms or developing their own lists of potential recipients of information. Digital media have increased the capabilities of political actors to directly reach people while at the same time making it more complicated and costly to reach people through news media or traditional allies.

We differentiate between three dimensions of reach: breadth, precision, and speed.

By *breadth*, we refer to how many people are potentially reached through communication on a given channel. Traditionally, mass media have had very broad reach. The second dimension of reach is the *precision* with which political actors can choose whom to contact. This might be achieved by using a very specific membership list or by appearing or advertising in niche media to target specific subsets of the population. The third dimension is the *speed* with which people can be reached. Each of these dimensions is affected in a different way by digital media.

Mass media have been a dominant and important tool in campaigns over the last 50 years, but the effects of digitalization on media systems described in Chapter 2 threaten to limit the total breadth of reach likely to be achieved for political actors by sticking to mass media. Here the question is how political actors can achieve broad reach under these new conditions of fragmented audiences.

With digitalization, precision may be increased. While it was always possible to identify a publication venue catering for specific subgroups of the population, the rise of openly partisan outlets online has made this form of indirect reach even easier. Online marketing also makes possible the identification of individuals who are promising targets for selected messages and the tailoring of messages to the specific tastes of individuals (Nickerson and Rogers 2014; Hersh 2015). Additionally, online marketers have access to the contact information of ever more people, allowing their customers direct access to promising contacts through online ads or targeted messages. This increased precision in direct and indirect reach of political actors has raised warning signs for some who expect a further fragmentation of the public sphere through increased politically narrow casting of carefully selected messages for potentially receptive audiences (Bennett and Manheim 2006).

Digitalization also allows people to be reached much more quickly. The current onslaught of news arriving every moment from a myriad of outlets breaks what was left of the temporal structure of political communication (Chadwick 2017). This increase in speed also increases demands for timely communication by political actors. Be it the email blast to party members or supporters in reaction to breaking news, instant ad buys on search engines of search terms associated with unfolding televised candidate debates, or the posting of pithy messages or images on online platforms in response to surprising developments to capture the spirit of the moment, these are all tactics used by contemporary political actors to utilize the new affordances of digital technology and react to its challenges.

3.2 Reaching People Directly and through Partners

The most immediate way for political organizations and political actors to reach people is to contact them directly. To do so they depend on lists of people sympathetic to the cause with information on how to contact them. These lists could be membership files, lists of people previously in contact with the organization, lists of people who previously supported a similar cause, or lists of promising contacts provided by third parties. The effectiveness of the first three types of lists depends on the strength of political organizations and movements. The reach of the third type depends strongly on technology, the strength of identification approaches of promising contacts, data protection laws, and the belief of political parties in their efficiency. As we will discuss in Chapter 7, digital media strongly impact the production and use of third-party lists by political actors, especially in the United States.

The strength of political organizations varies between countries. This can be seen most clearly in comparing the role of political parties. In the United States, party organizations are comparatively weak, with campaign organizations bearing the major share of organizing and campaigning work. Direct voter contact is handled predominantly by volunteers and paid staffers

(Nielsen 2012a; Enos and Hersh 2015; McKenna and Han 2015). In countries with stronger party membership, such as Germany or the United Kingdom, direct voter outreach is driven by party members themselves (Scarrow 1996). In these countries direct contact has long been a fixture of campaigning, mainly because parties and candidates never switched as decisively to televised campaign spots as their US counterparts did in the 1980s and 1990s. But even in countries with traditionally strong party organizations, parties are increasingly challenged by declining membership numbers, raising the question of how to organize direct voter contact.

A host of other political actors and organizations also reach out to voters – some clearly allied with specific parties, some with shifting allegiances, and some only focused on specific issues. Traditional examples are unions supporting progressive parties (Berry and Wilcox 2018). These allegiances feature most strongly in configurations of political systems in which social cleavages still align strongly with party lines (Riedl 2016). With the weakening of these traditional alignments and the decline in membership and influence of these traditional socio-political organizations, the ability of parties to reach individuals indirectly through these partner organizations weakens (Berry and Wilcox 2018), while new organizations emerge to capitalize on the affordances of digital media (Karpf 2012b). We will come back to this point in Chapter 6 when we discuss the role of digital media in the work and transformation of political organizations.

These developments do not mean that partner organizations play no role in extending the reach of political parties and candidates. For example, in the United States, political action committees (PACs) often run significant ad campaigns in support of or opposition to political candidates, while NGOs focused on specific policy areas also support candidates by running ad campaigns and even through direct voter outreach (Rozell, Wilcox, and Franz 2012). Thus, while the social influence of traditional partners of parties might have decreased over time, their place has been taken by new organizations and other partners. This has led researchers to conceptualize political organizations as increasingly complex "assemblages" of actors and organizations with sometimes overlapping and sometimes divergent interests (Nielsen 2012a; Kreiss 2016).

Direct outreach can happen in the form of direct mail, hand-delivered flyers, calls, or personal visits. While always a staple of local campaigns, these approaches have recently experienced a renaissance in campaigns on the national level, mostly due to increased precision of reach through data-driven practices (Issenberg 2012c; Nielsen 2012a).

Overall, the decline in membership of political organizations makes it more difficult for them to reach people directly. This increases the importance of focusing one's contact attempts on promising targets. Fewer membership numbers mean fewer resources, which in turn also means that fewer contacts can be made overall. The choice of whom to contact thus becomes more important. Moreover, higher mobility of people and the associated rapid turnover of addresses and decrease of telephone landlines means that political actors face increasing difficulties in reaching people they have selected as promising contacts. This increases the importance of regular list maintenance and the establishment of alternative contact channels. As we will show, digital media exacerbate these challenges but also offer promising opportunities for political actors to face them successfully and gain advantages over less adaptive competitors.

3.3 Reaching People through News Media

In the recent past, the most effective way for political actors to reach people was by getting news media to cover them. Ideally this would happen by news media offering them airtime or news columns in which they could present their views in unfiltered statements, guest editorials, or sound bites. Recognition by news media might also happen in general coverage. Importantly, though, in general coverage the message of a political actor can be expected to be filtered and contextualized by the editorializing of journalists or by contrasting it with positions of political competitors. In addition, or as alternative to this "free" media coverage, political actors also use paid ads to gain access to the audiences of news media.

For recognition by the media, political actors adapt their tactics and practices in order to create more coverage. This has been called adapting to the "media logic" of political coverage (Altheide and Snow 1979). Political events are staged in order to provide impressive images for television coverage (Bennett 2005a, 2005b), complicated policy positions are broken down to fit into ever shorter sound bites (Hallin 1992), and even candidate selection factors in the supposed mass media appeal of competitors (Jamieson 1996). This tendency for politics and even policy to conform with media logics has been heavily critiqued as corrupting politics and diluting political discourse (Entman 1989; Jamieson 1992; Patterson 1993). Some scholars even see political and social phenomena as being driven predominantly by the demands and incentives of media systems and logics (Schulz 2004; Lundby 2009).

The reasons for this dependence on news media are obvious. In mass societies, news media with access to mass audiences allow political actors access to the broadest publics for their messages, making them crucial channels for political actors in their efforts to appeal to voters, to set issues on the political agenda, or to signal their positions to supporters.

3.4 Mass Media's Declining Reach

Well before the rise of the internet and digital media, mass media had taken a hit concerning the size of their audiences. The growing spread of cable and satellite television in the United States from the late 1970s onwards transformed a media environment with limited choice in available channels to an environment where choice was abundant (Rogers 1986; Neuman 1991; Prior 2007; Williams and Carpini 2011).

This matters with regard to politics. In a media environment with little choice, potentially diverging preferences of audience members do not matter much. Once audience members choose to watch television, they are locked into the programming choices of a strictly limited set of television channels. This makes political content hard to avoid even for those in the audience disinterested in politics. As a consequence, political information also reaches audience members who are watching television for very different reasons than watching the news. This has become known as accidental exposure (Krugman and Hartley 1970), incidental (Guo and Moy 1998) or passive learning (Krugman and Hartley 1970), or – even more evocatively – as a "trap effect" (Schoenbach and Lauf 2002) in which audience members with little preferential inclination are "trapped" into learning about politics. Additionally, a media environment with little choice is expected to lead to the emergence of mass audiences whose members are largely exposed to the same information and, therefore, share a common informational background.

A media environment with higher choice, in contrast, allows audience members to sort themselves according to their preferences for content. Audience members interested in sports would predominantly watch the sports channel instead of watching a general news program and waiting for the sports segment. Opportunities for choice thus create highly fragmented audiences along the lines of their preferences, thereby reducing the chance for incidental learning about politics (Prior 2007). Additionally, this might also lead to a fracturing along topical preferences into issue publics (Kim 2009) or along partisan lines (Stroud 2011). On the one hand, this development might lead to a fracturing of the stabilizing role of mass media in providing a majority of the population with common information about politics and the issues of the day. This might even contribute to political polarization. On the other hand, this development also may potentially have dramatic effects with regard to the degree to which news organizations can help political actors to reach their audience. At a time when news programs or newspapers command large audiences, they are of crucial importance to political actors. But once audience numbers shrink, political actors have to start thinking about alternative ways to reach people who opted out of news coverage.

But what do we mean when we talk about mass media losing reach? Let us take a look at the reach of selected mainstream news sources in Germany, the United Kingdom, and the United States between 1995 and 2016/2017.

In Table 3.1, we show the reach of prominent television news programs, newspapers, and their respective websites in Germany, the United Kingdom, and the United States. Between these three countries, we have three different media systems with differing degrees of public versus commercial financing of news. Here, the United States represents the country with the strongest dependency on private financing of news, while Germany represents the other end of the spectrum, with the strongest role of publicly funded news. The United Kingdom falls between these extremes (Hallin and Mancini 2004).[1]

[1] In assessing the reach of television news programs, we rely on audience ratings. In assessing newspaper reach, we rely on circulation numbers of workday editions. Finally, in assessing the reach of websites, we rely on publicly reported monthly visitor counts. While each of these metrics is problematic in establishing the total reach or influence of these news sources (Webster, Phalen, and Lichty 2014), the comparison of these metrics between 1995 and 2016/2017 is informative with regard to the development of their reach over time.

To determine audience ratings, we rely on the following sources:
USA Television: Nielsen Ratings 1995 (Pew Research Center 2006; Brooks and Marsh 2007, 1694); 2017 (The Associated Press 2017).
UK Television: Broadcasters Audience Research Board (BARB) Ratings, 1998 average ratings for June 26–30; 2017 average ratings for June 29–July 2; available online at www.barb.co.uk/viewing-data/weekly-top-30/.
German Television: Gesellschaft für Konsumforschung (GfK), 1995 (Darschin and Frank 1997, 181); 2016 (Zubayr and Gerhard 2017, 136).
For newspaper circulation, we rely on the following sources:
Circulation New York Times: Alliance for Audited Media (AAM), 1997 (Glaberson 1995); 2016 (The New York Times Company 2017, 3).
Circulation The Daily Telegraph: Audit Bureau of Circulations Ltd (ABC), 1995 ("List of Newspapers in the United Kingdom by Circulation" 2017); 2017, October, available online at www.abc.org.uk/product/2323.
Circulation Süddeutsche Zeitung: Informationsgemeinschaft zur Feststellung der Verbreitung von Werbeträgern e.V. (IVW), 1998/Q1, 2017/Q3, available online at www.ivw.eu/aw/print/qa/titel/1986.
Circulation Frankfurter Allgemeine Zeitung: IVW 1998/Q1, 2017/Q3, available online at www.ivw.eu/aw/print/qa/titel/1827.
To determine unique visitors to websites, we rely on the following sources:
Unique Visitors Websites USA: Comscore 2017, June (Acquire Media 2017).
Unique Visitors Platforms UK: Comscore 2017, January (Ponsford 2017).
Unique Visitors Websites DE: Tagesschau.de: INFOnline 2017, October, available online www.ard.de/home/die-ard/fakten/ard-mediendaten/ARD_Reichweitendaten/409224/index.html; heute.de: na FAZ.net: IVW 2017, November, available online at http://ausweisung.ivw-online.de/index.php?i=1161&a=o54433; Süddeutsche.de: IVW 2017, November, available online at http://ausweisung.ivw-online.de/index.php?i=1161&a=o53703.

Table 3.1 *Development of media usage figures between 1995 and 2017*

	1995	1998	2016/2017	Change (%)	Country
Television News					
(Viewers, in million)					
CBS 60 Minutes	13.54		12.23	−10	US
(Households)					
ABC World News Tonight	9.35		8.56	−8	US
(Households)					
NBC Nightly News	8.30		8.08	−3	US
(Households)					
CBS Evening News	7.54		6.42	−15	US
(Households)					
BBC Six O'Clock News		5.61	4.27	−24	UK
(Households)					
Tagesschau, 20h (Viewers)	8.36		9.12	9	DE
heute, 19h (Viewers)	5.38		3.84	−29	DE
Newspapers					
(Circulation, incl. e-paper, in million)					
New York Times (Workday)	1.08		0.57	−47	US
Daily Telegraph	1.13		0.47	−58	UK
Süddeutsche (Workday)		0.47	0.37	−21	DE
Frankfurter Allgemeine (Workday)		0.48	0.27	−44	DE
Websites					
(Unique monthly visitors, in million)					
Comcast NBCUniversal			155.30		US
CBS Interactive			148.04		US
New York Times (Site)			85.06		US
ABC-Freeform Media Group			54.42		US
BBC Websites			39.90		UK
Daily Telegraph (Site)			25.40		UK
tagesschau.de			69.90		DE
Süddeutsche (Site)			29.05		DE
Frankfurter Allgemeine (Site)			28.77		DE
heute.de			na		DE

Trends in these audience metrics largely point in a similar direction across all countries. Major news programs in the United States show a decline in viewers between 1995 and 2016/2017 between 3 and 15 percentage points. In Germany and the United Kingdom the decline is even steeper, between 24 and 29 percentage points. Only the 8 PM edition of Germany's *Tagesschau* breaks this pattern by showing an increase of 9 percentage points in viewership. For prominent newspapers, this picture of declining reach is even more drastic. The circulation of four prominent newspapers in Germany, the United Kingdom, and the United States dropped by between 58 and 21 percentage points. While the impression of relative decline in reach is hard to shake, we should be careful not to neglect the influence of news programs (Webster 2014). The total reach of prominent news programs in television and newspapers might have declined but is still significant as shown by these metrics. Moreover, the available information on the unique monthly visitors on websites of various news organizations complicates the simple account of declining reach of news organizations. The unique monthly visitor counts on all websites exceeds by far viewer and circulation metrics even in the golden past of mass audiences.

This points to an important distinction already mentioned in Chapter 2, that is, the difference between the reach of a bundled news object – such as a newspaper or a news program – and the reach of news content produced by news organizations but accessible independently from content bundles. While the total reach of content bundles provided by news organizations thus decreases, isolated content snippets produced by news organizations might today actually have a reach much larger than ever before. In other words, a complete news program with all segments and editorial comments today might be watched by fewer people than twenty years ago. Yet one segment or sound bite from the program might reach more people than the number of people who would have watched the program even at its height. This is possible through amplification on digital media and the distribution of content snippets by audience members on their social media profiles or through messenger services. The prominence of these content snippets on digital media might be related to the strength of the news organization providing the content. Content from a prominent program on a prominent channel can be expected to be shared widely. But a just as important driver might be the content or the item itself. A juicy clip from an otherwise obscure television program can also reach large audiences independent of the prominence of the program it was first screened on. Thus, controversy or surprise stimulated by a news item can give it broad reach independent of the overall reach of the bundled news content of the respective news organization (Jungherr, Posegga, and An 2019a).

Political actors thus cannot expect that their presence in content bundles – such as newspapers and television news programs – necessarily reaches broad audiences. Established news organizations might help in reaching audiences but not to the same degree as in the past. Instead, the reach of isolated items today via digital media is much more likely driven by the content characteristics impacting the number of clicks or shares on online platforms (Jenkins, Ford, and Green 2013; Nahon and Hemsley 2013; Goel et al. 2016). This might lead political actors to adapt to this new logic of reach, focusing more on controversial, emotional, or surprising contributions. In addition, this might lead to a shift in paid advertising. If traditional content bundles, such as newspapers and television programs, provide a lowered overall reach, political actors might shift their ad buys toward websites or platforms. This raises significant challenges with regard to the regulation of online ads and their transparency (Barnard and Kreiss 2013; Kreiss and McGregor 2018; Kim et al. 2018).

Overall, the developments of increasing media choice and associated audience fragmentation, lowered audience numbers for leading news outlets, and the unbundling of content raise the central question of how important news organizations still are in providing political actors with reach. Directly related to this is the question of how political actors adapt to this new media environment and what potential alternatives they pursue in reaching people.

3.5 Determining Reach

So far, we have talked about reach as if it were a clearly established metric that would allow comparison across media types and time. While in general the concept of reach allows for meaningful discussion of how digital media impact a specific area of politics, this is of course a simplification. Already in the golden age of mass media there were controversies over how to establish the true reach of mass media. Should you focus on the total count of copies printed, distributed, or paid for? Or should you try to establish how many people actually read copies of the newspaper, paid for or not? Similarly, how should you establish the viewing figures of television programs? Should you rely on measuring what selected audience members were actually watching on TV or should you ask them in surveys of their viewing habits? The observational approach of having sensors tell you what selected people were actually watching allows researchers to speak with confidence of viewing habits. Yet how representative are people who choose to comply with this type of observation in the first place, and how representative is their behavior once they know they are being watched? The alternative is little better. Relying on self-reported behavior of media usage is a highly problematic metric as it is doubtful that people can remember their media use correctly, and even if they do, it is unclear whether they are actually interested in telling the truth about it. Establishing the reach of media by measuring audiences is thus complicated and was so even back in the comparatively uncomplicated age of mass media (McQuail 1997; Webster and Phalen 1997; Prior 2009; Webster, Phalen, and Lichty 2014). This task has grown more complicated still in contemporary media systems.

Measuring the reach of political information on digital media by surveys is a prominent approach. For example, the Pew Research Center and the Reuters Institute for the Study of Journalism regularly publish survey results on the use of digital media for political information (Duggan and Smith 2016; Newman et al. 2018). Similarly, academic studies such as the American National Election Study, the British Election Study, or the German Longitudinal Election Study query respondents in varying levels of detail about their use of digital media in the context of electoral behavior. While these datasets offer insights into aspects of the reach of political information on digital media, they also illustrate the challenges of relying on self-reported behavior.

For one, the measurements underlying this type of research are likely to suffer from the same over-reporting of political information use driven by social desirability as research on news audiences of traditional news (Prior 2009). This is likely to lead to an overestimation of the reach of political information online. Even worse, it is unclear which questions to ask. In the past, if you were interested in the reach of traditional media, such as newspaper or television, you could ask respondents simply whether they had encountered political news in the newspaper or on television. The reach of the medium of interest was easily distinguishable because newspapers and television news came in clearly different formats that were consumed on different devices. While not ruling out respondents confusing whether they received information through the newspaper or the television set, in principle there was a difference. With regard to the reach of political information on digital media, the meaning of this distinction is lost. People tend to consume information stemming from different sources on the same device, be it a computer, mobile device, or internet-enabled smart TV. On these devices content from legacy news organizations, television channels, and digital-born outlets is accessible. Simply querying respondents whether they have used the internet in the recent past to access political information or news tells us very little. For example, if we are interested in the reach of television news, we cannot simply ask whether respondents have watched the news on television. Instead, we have to query whether they have watched specific programs irrespective of the channel they encountered them on. Watching a clip of a news program on YouTube matters in assessing the reach and potential influence of this program as much as knowing how many people watched it while it ran in its scheduled time slot on television. Yet doing so means asking ever more detailed questions and consequently means inflating survey length and putting considerable trust in the precision of a respondent's memory.

Similarly, survey research is challenged by the fact that exposure to political information and news online happens in varying contexts and environments that bring potentially divergent usage practices and effects. For example, a user might purposefully access her favorite news program on the website of the news organization of her choice. While she is consuming political information online, this suggests purposeful and selective behavior, which in turn suggests regular news consumption, general political interest, high political sophistication, and consequently the likelihood of rather small persuasive media effects. In contrast, another user might encounter the same information on a social networking platform through the recommendation of one of her contacts. Here, political interest and sophistication are not a given and the encounter with the political information was probably not the primary motive for logging onto said social networking site. This makes accidental exposure to political information more likely. Moreover, by receiving the clip through the recommendation of a contact, the user encounters information endorsed by a person she trusts. All this makes the persuasive effects of information more likely than for the user encountering the same information through regular and purposeful exposure. We will discuss this further in Chapter 4.

While this example focused only on two different ways to consume information online, there are many more. This makes it impossible to query for all of them in surveys and raises considerable challenges of comparing usage responses over time. Through their specific modes of information display, newspapers and television both forced users into specific consumption behaviors that were themselves comparable. This is completely different online. The question "have you used the internet to consume political information or news?" groups together widely diverging usage patterns and behaviors, while analogous questions for political information use in newspapers or on television queried for much more consistent phenomena. So again, researchers relying on surveys must depend on precise questions if they do not want to be stranded with a bucket category containing widely divergent usage patterns and behaviors and thus allowing only weak inferences to be made.

One alternative is the analysis of actual browsing behavior. Companies like ComScore, YouGov, or the Gesellschaft für Konsumforschung (GFK) sell access to browsing data that was collected through browser plug-ins on the machines of selected participants. While many expect this tracking data to offer a remedy for some of the well-known issues associated with the measurement of audience behavior based on self-reporting (Prior 2009), in truth there are a number of new issues associated with this data source.

Most importantly, researchers using this data have to reflect on whether, for their research topic, a set of users willingly installing a plug-in to monitor their browsing behavior online can be deemed representative of a population of interest (Jürgens, Stark, and Magin 2019). At least with regard to questions regarding the use of political information and news, this seems somewhat doubtful. Social desirability is likely to kick in once users know that they are being watched. This might make users more likely to seek out specific content while avoiding other deviant, radical, or less wholesome content, leading in turn to an underestimation of the reach of content and sources deemed radical or deviant. Yet it might well be that this feeling of being watched diminishes over time and users revert back to their normal behavior. The breadth of devices used to access political information online could also allow for evasive behavior of panelists, using unmonitored devices for specific uses while using their monitored devices only for those deemed safe for monitoring. While this purposeful evasion might be limited, it has been shown that tracking apps vary with regard to the breadth of data they have access to depending on devices' operating systems (Kreuter et al. 2018). This again introduces measurement biases. Finally, the fundamental question remains if the choice to install such a monitoring browser plug-in in the first place does not create a systematically skewed sample in favor of users with low privacy preferences and potentially low political interest or sophistication. These concerns do not of course invalidate work based on tracking data. Instead, they point to inherent challenges with this measurement approach that researchers have to address.

There is also the option to infer the reach of political information online through publicly available interaction metrics, such as clicks, likes, or shares. Various social media services display these metrics prominently and offer the opportunity for data vendors and providers of audience analytics to develop proprietary metrics and solutions. As discussed in Chapter 2, these metrics are routinely used in newsrooms or by politicians to assess the reach of their content and contributions and thereby influence program planning and messaging choices (Anstead and O'Loughlin 2015; Webster 2014). While thus clearly of relevance, researchers still have to apply caution in relying on these metrics. For one, it is not necessarily clear what these metrics actually document (Jungherr 2015; Jungherr, Schoen, and Jürgens 2016), nor how robust these metrics are against concerted attempts at coordinated manipulation. So, instead of measuring actual reach of information, they instead might simply measure attempts at making specific content visible or to hijack the media agenda. Again, this does not necessarily argue against using these metrics in principle. Instead, these observations emphasize the need to contextualize these metrics and employ transparent judgment in their use.

No single measurement approach allows for an unproblematic and reliable assessment of the reach of political information on digital media. One solution to this challenge might lie in the combination of different data sources, for example individuals' survey responses, browsing data, and digital trace data of user behavior on social media channels (Vaccari, Chadwick, and O'Loughlin 2015; Guess, Nyhan, and Reifler 2018b). While this sounds sensible, in practice it raises a series of non-trivial challenges with regard to the selection of participants willing to agree to this rather comprehensive behavioral and attitudinal monitoring, the protection of their privacy, and informed consent.

3.6 Mass Audience versus Niche Audiences

A focus point in the discussion of informational reach through digital technology is the conflict between reaching people in scale and breadth and reaching small subsections of the population. Here the terms "echo chamber" and "filter bubble" feature heavily. Both point to a perceived feature of digital technology leading to increased political polarization and social fragmentation by allowing individual audience members to interact predominantly in largely politically homogeneous communication environments, thereby reducing exposure or interaction with politically divergent others. Both concepts are heavily contested, not least since empirical evidence for them is thin. Yet this has not impacted their widespread acceptance. To better understand this divergence, we have to go back to democratic expectations connected with mass and fragmented audiences.

The breadth of reach by mass media has received much attention from communication research (for a comprehensive overview see McQuail 2010, 51–110). Researchers reacted to the emergence of totalitarian regimes in Germany and Soviet Russia during the 1940s and the perceived interconnection between mass societies and mass media. Building on these early efforts, the widespread diffusion of television sets from the 1960s onwards, with limited channel choice, led researchers to turn their focus to the consequences of the fact that, in the words of Ithiel de Sola Pool, "two-thirds of the population of the United States was exposed for two to four hours a day to the same messages – or at least one out of three or four limited alternatives" (Pool 1983b, 258f.).

Expectations diverged about the effects on democracy of this exceptionally high reach of only a few media organizations. Some saw mass media as an important factor in socializing audiences, forming coherent publics, and, by providing a common focus, enabling public discourse (Janowitz 1952; Stamm 1985; Jankowski 2002). Others emphasized the tendency of mass media to reduce individuals to members of an anonymous audience and expected this to lead to deteriorating social links in communities (McCormack 1961; Putnam 2000; Sunstein 2001). Another group focused on the power suspected to sit with the owners of media organizations achieving this broad reach and the commodification of audiences through selling advertisers access to them (Dahlgren 1995; Murdock and Golding 2005; Fuchs 2009). Broad reach to large sections of the population thus has been associated with traits that strengthen democracy as well as undermine it. Similarly contradictory expectations persist with regard to the democratic consequences of fragmented audiences facing overwhelming opportunities for informational choice.

There has been much hope put into electronic and digital media to open up public discourse to new voices and perspectives by drastically lowering the costs of communication. This increase in the diversity of information and sources has been widely seen as enabling cultural and political pluralism, which mass media were seen as hindering (Pool 1983a; Neuman 1991). Digital media in particular were seen as a remedy to the perceived deterioration of social ties between individuals in mass society. By allowing members of issue publics underserved by mass media coverage to find specific information relevant to their interests and by enabling meaningful interactions between them, digital media were seen as providing the basis for a renewed sense of community (Rheingold 1993). In both views the fragmentation of mass audiences is thus perceived as beneficial. Digital media potentially provide a broader and more diverse set of information for public discourse, thereby contributing to a more pluralistic democratic culture., Furthermore, digital media allow members of issue publics to find relevant information, to get in touch with each other, and to provide the environment for meaningful social interaction, thereby potentially leading to a renewed sense of community in subgroups of the population. Fragmentation, therefore, emerges as a potentially positive force for democracy.

In contrast, others have argued that digital technology contributes to increased control by central actors in society. In principle, digital technology documents every interaction and page view, thereby allowing the development of detailed user profiles. These profiles can then be used for marketing and persuasion purposes aimed at increasingly differentiated subgroups of a population, allowing advertisers and political actors ever more precise access to subgroups of interest. The commodification of fragmented audiences might thus actually be greater than the commodification of mass audiences (Dahlgren 2013; Fuchs 2017). Moreover, there is the question of surveillance with regard to the use of political information, political expression, or interactions online. Even in Western democracies, the awareness that one's political behavior is continuously being watched might have a chilling effect. This is doubly true for autocratic regimes (Morozov 2011). This worry might not matter much if political activity on digital media remains distributed across many different providers of services, apps, or platforms. Yet in the aftermath of the US National Security Agency (NSA) spying scandal and with increasing awareness of the power of a few central platforms as access points to political information, the worry about who might be watching and collecting data on political behavior online seems increasingly relevant (Schneier 2015). Potential shifts and international variations in ideas of what constitute legitimate claims for individual privacy are important to observe, as these ideas and their public acceptance have always been fluid (Igo 2018). This opens up another field in which the growing uses of digital media might develop strong social effects. In any case, the fragmentation of audiences alone does not seem to offer respite from the commodification or control of audiences, already diagnosed for mass audiences.

There are also negative expectations connected with an expected fragmentation of mass audiences based on suspected user behaviors and motives. By allowing people to choose information sources, digital media give audiences the opportunity to fragment based on their interests. As discussed, optimists focused on associated potentials of a more pluralistic public sphere with a richer and more diverse set of voices and perspectives. In contrast, pessimists were quick to point out that this might actually lead to a split between politically interested people and those less interested and less involved. In the past, people who were not interested in politics had no opportunity to avoid political media coverage completely. Consequently they were exposed to at least a minimum of political news. In contrast, the informational abundance provided by first electronic and later digital media means that there was no necessity for people to expose themselves to politics if they did not really want to (Prior 2007). After all, once you had completed the sports section in your paper, you might switch to the politics section for want of anything better to do. Yet in the sports section of the internet, you will never run out of fresh material to read. Following this account, audience fragmentation, driven by allowing audiences more choice in media consumption, might thus erode some of the educational functions provided by mass media. Consequently, instead of leading to a pluralistic democracy, it might lead to the depoliticization of large parts of the population. Even more prominent are expectations that digital media might lead to political polarization.

3.7 Echo Chambers and Filter Bubbles

The legal scholar Cass Sunstein argued that opportunities of media choice would lead people to predominantly consume information reconfirming their originally held political beliefs and to predominantly interact with others holding the same beliefs. This, over time, would lead to increasing political polarization among the public, with members of opposing sides having no information about and empathy for political opponents (Sunstein 2001). In this account, informational choice would not lead to fragmentation along issue publics, potentially leading to a more pluralistic democratic discourse, nor along the line of politics versus non-politics, thereby leading to a depoliticization of large parts of the population. Instead, Sunstein's expected divide runs along partisan lines, leading to political polarization and the subsequent deterioration of political discourse. Sunstein coined for this expectation the evocative term "echo chamber," which he elaborated and updated in several subsequent publications (e.g., Sunstein 2007, 2017).

In 2011, the political activist Eli Pariser built on this. In his original statement, Sunstein saw the users and their preferences as the drivers of political segregation once they were given choice in abundant information environments. Pariser pointed out that in algorithmically selected information environments, like Facebook, the opportunity for choice was actually long gone. Instead, algorithms were selecting information items likely to create interactions and presenting them to users based on their past behavior or that of their friends. An initial preference for information with a specific political slant would be reinforced by algorithms prioritizing information with exactly that slant while excluding others. Over time, users were thus expected to move into "filter bubbles" hermetically excluding opposing partisan views (Pariser 2011).

In combination, "echo chambers" and "filter bubbles" have developed into two of the most widely held beliefs in public discourse with regard to the effects of digital media on democracy. For example, *New York* magazine declared that "The 'Filter Bubble' Explains Why Trump Won and You Didn't See It Coming" (Bear 2016); *Wired* proclaimed confidently, "Your Filter Bubble Is Destroying Democracy" (El-Bermawy 2016); while the New York Times diligently listed a number of services that present people with content supposedly in opposition to their political views in their guide on "How to Escape Your Political Bubble for a Clearer View" (Hess 2017). But the certainty with which the belief in "echo chambers" and "filter bubbles" is held in public meets with skepticism among scientists. Time and again empirical evidence has not shown patterns and outcomes coherent with the expectations proposed so evocatively by Sunstein and Pariser. Given the prominence of both concepts despite contested empirical evidence, it pays to examine the literature a little more closely.

Both concepts combine claims regarding the structure of human interaction, supposed psychological mechanisms driving these structural patterns, and sweeping expectations of societal change resulting from these interaction structures. This makes for exciting editorials but not necessarily for successful scientific concepts. This mélange of elements and expectations is problematic as it has led people to point to evidence of either element and confidently exclaim the presence of "echo chambers" or "filter bubbles." This is not helpful. Find a homogeneous communication space online? Echo chambers. Get the impression you see predominantly news coming from a familiar political slant? Filter bubbles. This seems too cavalier an approach for us to accept the far-reaching claims associated with both concepts. Remember: driven by a psychological preference for information confirming one's previously held beliefs, people, if given the choice, are expected to consciously choose news sources, items, or interaction partners in accordance with their current beliefs and partisan affiliation while avoiding contradicting sources, items, or partners. Over time this would lead people online, either by choice or by an algorithmic cage, to mainly see information in line with their political views and also for them to mainly interact with people holding the same beliefs. This will lead to in-group polarization and runs the risk of destabilizing democracy. This is a demanding set of expectations with wide-reaching claims with regard to the political effects of digital media. Let us examine the different elements of both concepts closely.

It is far from clear that psychological mechanisms will always lead people to prefer information in line with their political attitudes, much less to actively avoid contradicting information. Instead, this pattern seems to depend on the motivations leading people to consume information and also on their predispositions. For people to prefer information in line with their partisan identities, they first have to have partisan identities or coherent ideologies allowing them to identify supporting or opposing information and sources. This is doubtful for the majority of people (Converse 1964; Fiorina, Abrams, and Pope 2010; Achen and Bartels 2016). Yet even for the minority of media consumers with strong partisan affiliations or coherent ideologies, it is far from certain that they will actively avoid information and interactions contradicting their beliefs (Garrett 2009a, 2009b). People have different goals for their information use and online interactions. For example, they might consume media for entertainment purposes or in search of specific information helping them to achieve a goal or find a solution to a problem (Kunda 1990). There is evidence that for media use following non-accuracy motives – such as entertainment, habitual, or expressive uses – psychological mechanisms might lead people to prefer information supporting their prior beliefs and discard other information (Jost, Hennes, and Lavine 2013; Kahan 2016a, 2016b). This being said, media use following accuracy goals appears to be more robust against these biases (Evans 2008; Petty, Briñol, and Priester 2009). The confidently proclaimed global preference or even need for supporting information seems thus only to be of relevance for a minority of media users, namely those with strong partisan affiliations, and even for those this might be largely dependent on contextual conditions. But what can we say about the expectation of predominantly homogeneous news exposure online?

Using web-browsing data, Flaxman, Goel, and Rao (2016) show contradicting evidence. Overall, for regular users of online news the authors found a moderate degree of ideological segregation. The degree of segregation increases somewhat for opinion pieces linked to from social media. Overall this type of news constituted only a tiny fraction of news traffic – in this study only 6 percent of political news traffic. While these findings are consistent with the "echo chamber" idea, they also indicate that this is far from a dominant phenomenon on social media. The authors also find evidence contradicting the idea that users of online news predominantly see information confirming their previously held political beliefs. Instead, they show that use of social networking platforms and search engines increases the exposure to news from the opposite partisan spectrum.

Underlying the "echo chamber" and "filter bubble" theses is an unspoken expectation that political information use and user interactions follow similar patterns across platforms. For example, audience members of clearly partisan news outlets like Fox News or MSNBC are thus expected to not use mainstream media without clear partisan affiliation. Or, to build on an example for digital media use, users who are active in politically homogeneous subreddits should avoid politically cross-cutting subreddits. As various studies show, this is not the case. For example, users active in homogeneous subreddits were also very active in cross-cutting subreddits exposing them to information challenging their views (An et al. 2019). There is even more evidence that audiences of partisan news outlets also follow the news on mainstream nonpartisan outlets.

Webster (2014) shows a surprising degree of overlap between the audiences of partisan news channels and nonpartisan mainstream news programs in the United States. Thus, audience members interested in partisan news do not avoid more balanced news programs. This finding significantly weakens a central proposition of the "echo chamber" theory. Using an updated method, Mukerjee, Majó-Vázquez, and González-Bailón (2018) come to the same conclusion. Additionally, Fletcher and Nielsen (2017a) show that news audiences in Denmark, France, Germany, Spain, the United Kingdom, and the United States were not fragmented along partisan lines. Instead, there was evidence of higher fragmentation in Denmark and the United Kingdom driven by the prominence of a few publicly funded news sources with exceptionally high reach across the population, leading to less audience duplication across sources. Similarly, Dubois and Blank (2018) show that in the United Kingdom, only a small segment of the population was likely to communicate in echo chambers, and media users with strong political interests especially avoided echo chambers. Overall, these studies show that exclusive echo chamber communication is rare even for audience members of highly partisan media. Even these audience members additionally consume news from politically unaffiliated mainstream outlets. Yet this pattern only emerges once we move from the analysis of individual media sources to an analysis of media repertoires, that is, the whole set of media sources individuals use (Hasebrink and Popp 2006; Hasebrink and Domeyer 2012). A central claim of both the "echo chamber" and the "filter bubble" discourse, that political partisans would lose sight of the position of political others, is thus not met.

With regard to social media providing a highly likely environment for echo chambers and filter bubbles to emerge, Alcott and Gentzkow (2017) show that during the 2016 US presidential election only 14 percent of Americans named social media as their main source of political information. Pointing in a similar direction, Stark, Magin, and Jürgens (2017) show that for German users in 2016 Facebook was only a minor gateway to news, thereby qualifying the influence of any potential "filter bubble" significantly. Looking at sources linked to on Twitter, Shore, Baek, and Dellarocas (2018) show that a large majority of users linked to political content that was more moderate than the content they received in their feed. Bakshy, Messing, and Adamic (2015) compared the ideological slant of content shared socially by users on Facebook and content chosen by the News Feed algorithm. They report that individual choices limited exposure to cross-cutting information more than algorithmic decisions on Facebook. Correspondingly, Möller et al. (2018) show that algorithmic content curation offered users articles with a similar degree of diversity as human editors. Additionally, Geiß et al. (2018) show that social media use for news did not lead users to retreat into politically segregated groups with regard to their perceptions of important political issues. For the news forum Reddit, An et al. (2019) show that users active in politically homogeneous environments supporting Donald Trump or Hillary Clinton tended also to be active in cross-cutting environments where they directly engaged with supporters of the opposing candidate. Similarly, Conover, Ratkiewicz, et al. (2011) show that Twitter users tend to interact actively across partisan lines. In combination, it does not appear as if social media would be a communication environment dominated by homogeneous interactions along partisan lines. These findings are supported by literature reviews in which the authors also could not identify convincing evidence for "filter bubbles" emerging from personalization and algorithmic recommendations (Borgesius et al. 2016; Guess et al. 2018a). Overall, empirical studies do not offer strong evidence for news exposure on news sites or social media to be more strongly divided along partisan lines than offline communication.

This being said, recently researchers have turned to testing the workings of algorithms recommending content to users of online platforms depending on their previous browsing patterns. For example, using data collected on YouTube, Rauchfleisch and Kaiser (2019b) show that in 2018 recommended channels indeed fell into politically distinct groupings. In other words, users who were watching videos on far-right channels on YouTube could expect to be recommended further far-right content instead of channels challenging said views. This points to an interesting challenge. Although in general there appears to be little evidence for users moving in political "echo chambers" or "filter bubbles" online, current implementations of recommendation algorithms indeed seem to preferentially present politically homogeneous content. This alone might not support the far-reaching consequences associated with "filter bubbles" and might shift in future revisions of recommendation algorithms for political content. Yet it shows the importance of analyzing the inner workings and outputs of algorithmic governance of online platforms with regard to their consequences for the preselected slice of reality users encounter there. To account for the impact of algorithmically selected news on personalized websites or apps, Jürgens and Stark (2017) recently provided a promising framework for future work.

What about the final piece in the puzzle, the expectation of increased political polarization for internet users? Also in this regard, the available evidence does not support the fears associated with "echo chambers" or "filter bubbles." Using survey and individual-level browsing data, Gentzkow and Shapiro (2011) show that for 2009, the ideological segregation in online news consumption in the United States was low in absolute terms while being slightly higher than for offline news consumption and significantly lower than for face-to-face communication. If we want to speak of "echo chambers," we must look for them in face-to-face exchanges between people.

The available evidence seems to indicate that there might indeed be politically homogeneous spaces online in which people sharing the same political opinions tend to interact. Yet these politically homogeneous interactions seem not to extend across a majority of digital communication environments. Instead, they appear to be limited to specific services or spaces on services. Moreover, it does not appear as if activities in politically homogeneous interactions or communication environments extend to a majority of online users. They seem to be especially relevant for users of high political interest and partisans who tend to seek out these spaces. At the same time, for this group the persuasive effects of information online are unlikely anyway given their previously held partisan opinions. Furthermore, there appears to be little evidence of the more far-reaching expectations for political discourse at large. An important problem with the concepts "echo chamber" and "filter bubble" is their linking of a set of isolated empirical observations with far-reaching social consequences. This has given license to many commentators to extrapolate from simple observations to far-reaching and dire consequences for public discourse and democracy without providing adequate evidence of any such link.

But why are both claims so prominent in public debate? For one, "echo chambers" and "filter bubbles" are very evocative concepts and intuitive metaphors. In addition, most people worrying about the influence of digital media on politics are strongly politically involved – either as direct participants, such as journalists or politicians, or indirectly, such as politically interested internet users. These are very specific subgroups who, given their political interests and very active media use, might subjectively experience "echo chambers" or "filter bubbles" in their own media use and from this erroneously extrapolate to the experiences of all other users.[2] Finally, currently there is a fight for ideational power between social media companies and established media organizations. Here, perceived negative effects on democracy by digital media play into the hands of traditional news organizations fighting for influence and political and public support.

The discussion about "echo chambers" and "filter bubbles" is instructive for examining the role of digital media in politics. The power of evocative metaphors in the marketplace of ideas, generalizations from one's own usage experiences to those of others, and political and economic interest make powerful drivers of a concept's popularity. In these contexts, scientists have to be especially careful in theorizing and developing empirical findings.

Unfortunately, the debate about whether there is evidence supporting or refuting "echo chambers" or "filter bubbles" stands in the way of addressing related questions of high importance: Does abundant informational choice actually lead to a fragmentation of audiences for political news? Is the consequence of this that people drop out completely from receiving political news or news from an opposing partisan perspective? Or are we instead witnessing an extension of people's media repertoires in which traditional, politically

---

[2] For a similar argument see this tweet by Cristian Vaccari: https://twitter.com/25lettori/status/957175925325680641.

cross-cutting news sources are combined with new additional information sources that report the news from a partisan or specialist perspective? Are social structures emerging that are counteracting potential tendencies toward fragmentation, and do they vary between different media systems? What are the dynamics and effects of algorithms recommending news content on online platforms, what goes into the decisions underlying their design, and how are they audited? On these questions, the jury is still out and the potential for comparative empirical research is evident.

3.8 Cutting Out the Middlemen

Digital media allow political actors to cut out the middlemen, traditional news media, and reach their constituency directly or through new mediators. This shifts the power dynamics in one of the most important relationships in political communication, the one between political elites and journalists. After all, why rely on journalists if one can reach members of the public directly? Databases with comprehensive contact information for people, advanced and detailed opportunities to run ads directed at specific subgroups of a population provided by digital platforms such as Google or Facebook, and the willingness of people to connect with political organizations directly and provide them with their contact information have significantly extended the opportunities for political actors to communicate directly with selected subgroups, be they supporters or likely voters. While some have described this trend as beneficial in reinvigorating public discourse and enabling the rise of new and alternative political actors unduly disadvantaged by the filtering process of traditional media organizations, others have emphasized the dangers of these opportunities in fracturing democratic discourse.

Traditionally, parties and candidates largely depended on news media and partner organizations to reach the public. Parties held contact information on their members, which in political systems with strong party organizations could be sizable. For example, in its heyday in 1976 the German Social Democrats (SPD) could reach over one million members while the German conservatives (CDU) could reach well over half a million members in the same year (Niedermayer 2017). Still, even then reaching beyond the core of party members meant relying on intermediaries, such as media organizations or allied organizations, for example unions, churches, or interest groups. But doing so was either expensive, as with ad buys, or was accompanied by a severe lack of message control by having partner organizations take over the communication. Furthermore, by relying on others for reach, parties and politicians never gained direct access to the members of the public contacted on their behalf and therefore remained dependent on intermediaries. This also meant they were only rudimentarily able to evaluate the effects of their interventions. From the perspective of political actors, this situation was far from optimal.

Digital media opened new opportunities for parties and candidates to directly reach people. But more often than not this introduced a new set of intermediaries in the process. At the heart of this promise lies the combination of contact information for people and various additional bits of information about them, for example socio-demographic characteristics or behavioral data documenting their use of digital platforms. Digitalization of information has made the combination of different data sources trivially easy and comparatively cheap. It is no surprise to find various companies providing tailor-made solutions for political actors to reach specific subsets of the population directly. This can happen either as an offshoot of a larger online ad business, as in the cases of targeted advertising opportunities on Google or Facebook, or in the provision of dedicated services and solutions customized for politics, such as NGP VAN or the GOP Data Center.

These offerings contain two promises. The first promise is to reach people otherwise not reachable for political parties. The second promise is to reach people specifically selected as being susceptible to a communicative intervention by the political actor in question. We will discuss the data-driven approaches underlying the second promise in detail in Chapter 7. For now, let it suffice to say that reach through digital media is about both breadth and precision.

The growing role of new intermediaries between political actors and the public raises a series of issues regarding their role in public discourse. The big online platforms Facebook, Google, and Twitter in particular currently face increased scrutiny as their importance in the flow of political information rises. What principles govern their display of political content (Zittrain 2014)? How do they regulate political ads (Kim et al. 2018)? Under what conditions do they give out data or support selected political actors (Cadwalladr and Graham-Harrison 2018; Kreiss and McGregor 2018)? These are only a few of the emerging questions regarding the governance structure of online platforms in the context of their role in politics. The often nontransparent and shifting governance structures and rules of online platforms thus increasingly become subject to academic, public, and regulatory attention (Gillespie 2010; Kreiss and McGregor 2019).

While data-driven contacts through new intermediaries are currently very prominent cases of how campaigns and parties try to cut out traditional media organizations as middlemen, they are not the only way. Media fragmentation into ever smaller audience segments brings the challenge for political actors of how to ensure that relevant information reaches its designated audiences. In the past, it may have been enough to take out an ad or place an interview in a major newspaper or newscast to reach one's designated audience. Today it is doubtful that these tactics suffice. One example for reaching people outside the realm of traditional media is the communication strategy chosen by the Obama White House to advertise health care reform. Instead of exclusively relying on traditional media to carry the news and point to the registration platform, the White House chose to make the President available for niche programs, such as popular political satire programs such as the *Colbert Report*, or alternative formats such as the comedic YouTube format "Between Two Ferns." Some commentators derided this as a degradation of the office of President, while the White House defended it as a conscious choice to reach young people who had the most to gain from health care reform but were at the same time least likely to be reached through traditional news programs (Eilperin 2015; Hirschfeld Davis 2015; Shear 2015). While this approach might not cut out the middlemen completely, it changes their nature. The few highly important media venues of the past are bypassed in favor of small niche venues that command specific audience subsets. In practice, this leads political actors to use a diverse portfolio of venues to reach specific audience subsets instead of relying on a few sources to reach mass audiences uniformly. Consequently, this leads to loss of influence for these catch-all middlemen.

Additionally, political actors have to rely much more on audiences sharing information themselves. Social sharing of information has become an important source of traffic for news outlets online (Newman et al. 2018). People do not necessarily find an article or video by routinely browsing the source it is published on. Instead, they increasingly find it through social sharing. Celebrities or so-called influencers might post videos on their Instagram feeds, a colleague might post a link to a news item on their LinkedIn profile, friends might comment on a comment by a politician on Twitter, and family members send out links to articles on messenger apps. These are different but increasingly important ways for people to find stories or to find out about political events or contestation (Barberá et al. 2015; Thorson and Wells 2016; Valeriani and Vaccari 2018). For political actors this creates a challenging new set of intermediaries that collectively contribute to the reach their messages receive. In the process, the publics sharing information and news are also negotiating its meaning (Meraz and Papacharissi 2013; Bennett, Segerberg, and Yang 2018). This public negotiation of meaning and the often invisible nature of exactly what content was shared on which channel makes this a very challenging element of achieving reach by political actors and further contributes to the weakening of more centralized middlemen.

Either by choice or by necessity, political actors thus turn to new intermediaries in their attempts to reach people. Correspondingly, traditional intermediaries, such as former mass media or allied organizations, lose influence. While traditional middlemen thus run the risk of being cut out of the information flow, a new set emerges whose role and influence in the flow of political information is ill-understood and offers rich research potential as their influence in politics rises.

3.9 The Reach of Disinformation

In the aftermath of Donald Trump's US presidential campaign in 2016, the role of disinformation on digital media has featured prominently. Websites publishing purposefully misleading information, political ads targeted to supposedly politically insecure users, coordinated groups of users paid to impersonate members of the American public online, and automated accounts actively pushing selected content and interacting with users engaging in political discourse form a complicated web of interconnected tactics that various actors, foreign and domestic, used in order to influence the outcome of the 2016 US presidential election (Persily 2017). This has given rise to prominent pundits declaring digital media a danger for democracy (Soros 2018), an assessment that seems doubtful at best once we examine the available evidence.

One element of this set of disinformation tactics is websites posting purposefully misleading information. This has been prominently discussed under the problematic term "fake news" that we already encountered in Chapter 2. These sites spring up in reaction to events during political campaigns or events of high political controversy (Popken 2018a). They post purposefully misleading information about candidates or participants in these events (Popken 2017). For example, during the presidential contest between Hillary Clinton and Donald Trump, websites started to claim that Clinton was running a child-trafficking ring from a Washington pizzeria. This hoax traveled far and wide online under the term #pizzagate and led a disturbed individual to conduct an armed attack against said pizzeria to liberate supposedly imprisoned children (Aisch, Huang, and Kang 2016; Metaxas and Finn 2017).

For reach, these sites depend crucially on distribution on social networking sites, as they emerge and disappear spontaneously and thus do not develop loyal audiences. Fringe and partisan media organizations are another important element in the distribution of misleading information from these sources, by picking them up and thus distributing them further (Benkler, Faris, and Roberts 2018; Marwick and Lewis 2017). Media organizations, especially those with a partisan focus, were thus important multiplicators of information purposefully introduced into the information cycle to mislead the public (Benkler et al. 2018). Similar tactics have been found in countries as different from the United States as Brazil (Leahy and Schipani 2018; Schipani 2018), Cambodia (Rajagopalan 2018), India (Murgia, Findlay, and Schipani 2019), Myanmar (Frenkel 2016), and South Sudan (Patinkin 2017). Germany even introduced far-reaching legislation – the network enforcement act – to try to hold online platforms accountable for the veracity of information published on them (Eddy and Scott 2017).

While purposeful disinformation undoubtedly was a part of the 2016 US presidential race (Jamieson 2018), its actual impact is doubtful. It is estimated that 27 percent of the American adult population had visited "fake news" websites (Guess et al. 2018b). On the face of it, this sounds like a significant share of the population, but as people being exposed to this content tended to be highly partisan with a strong leaning toward the Republican political spectrum (Alcott and Gentzkow 2017; Guess et al. 2018b), the persuasive impact of this purposely misleading content is probably limited. In addition, while metrics of interaction with misleading content on social networking sites seem at first glance to be very high, in comparison with the total volume of content rolled out and interactions performed, these numbers quickly lose relevance (Watts and Rothschild 2017; Lazer et al. 2018). For example, Guess, Nagler, and Tucker (2019) show that 8.5 percent of respondents in a representative survey in the United States for whom the authors had access to their Facebook profiles during the 2016 US presidential campaign had shared on their Facebook profiles at least one link to domains known for publishing disinformation. Another study showed that during the same campaign, only about 1 percent of Twitter accounts that could be matched with registered voters accounted for 80 percent of exposure to known sources of misinformation, while only 0.1 percent accounted for 80 percent of sharing. As in other studies, accounts associated with known sources of disinformation tended to be associated with partisan and highly politically engaged users. Again, this raises doubts with regard to the persuasive effects of disinformation given the prior political involvement of its audience (Grinberg et al. 2019). In combination, these findings raise doubts with regard to the actual reach these sites achieved as well as their persuasive potential. Their use might thus have followed predominantly performative or entertainment usage motives instead of informative ones.

Given this evidence, it seems unlikely that these sites and the amplification of their content on social networking sites played a major role in influencing the vote during the 2016 presidential election (Nyhan 2018). For other countries, information on the reach of purposefully misleading information is largely lacking. But early studies indicate, at least for Europe, even lower prevalence of "fake news" in the online news consumption than was seen in the United States (Fletcher et al. 2018), indicating the need for a qualified debate about the role and impact of purposeful misinformation online. This gap between causal attribution and actually empirically identified usage patterns has given rise to warnings against rushing through far-reaching regulations. These might have unforeseen consequences for the overall media system and the flow of political information motivated by what in reality might be a fringe phenomenon without far-reaching consequences (Nielsen 2018).

While this might hold for Western democracies with established party systems, public trust in political institutions, and stable media systems, disinformation campaigns might prove much more disruptive in the context of developing or transitioning democracies (Silver 2019). But as of now systematic accounts of tactics used in these disinformation campaigns and their effects are lacking.

Disinformation campaigns not only post purposefully misleading information on dedicated sites or online platforms, they also run sock-puppet accounts on social networking platforms. These accounts are used to push content, simulate support for or opposition to politicians, and reinforce and silence other users. The goal of these activities is the disruption of public discourse online. This can happen through the employment of dedicated personnel who coordinate in running large numbers of social media accounts impersonating members of the public of a country whose political discourse they seek to disrupt, and by the use of semi- or fully automated accounts that autonomously push content or interact with selected users (MacFarquhar 2018; Nimmo 2018; Scola 2018; Shane 2018; Kargar and Rauchfleisch 2019). The goals of these activities vary (Kovic et al. 2018).

By posting high volumes of messages mentioning political topics or politicians, the customers of these disinformation services aim to impact the climate of public opinion as shown on social networking platforms, thereby potentially swaying media coverage in their favor (Watts and Rothschild 2017). Another popular tactic is to inflate the follower counts of selected politicians to suggest broad public support and to repost and interact favorably with content posted by them (Confessore et al. 2018; Vynck and Wang 2018). For one, this can impact users of these networking platforms in their perception of issues. More importantly, though, this can impact the assessment of issues through political actors and media organizations using audience metrics on social media.

Pushing content in association with politically relevant keywords or the names of politicians also has spillover effects on other online services. For example, search engines like Google use content on social networking platforms like Twitter or Reddit to establish the connections users make between keywords and underlying concepts in real time. This input is then used to select and weigh search results and to suggest additional phrases once specific keywords are used. Pushing large amounts of content linking the name of a politician with a scandal thus potentially allows operators of botnets to impact the search results for these politicians. The use of this practice has been repeatedly shown, with online platforms being slow to adapt (Mustafaraj and Metaxas 2010, 2017; Lewis 2018; Nicas 2018; Robertson, Lazer, and Wilson 2018).

In combination, the activities of sock-puppet farms can prove disruptive to public discourse. In public debate these dangers have been discussed most prominently in the context of the potential for electoral meddling by Russia in the 2016 US presidential election. But as work by Mustafaraj and Metaxas (2010) and Mustafaraj and Metaxas (2017) shows, these practices and the potential for the manipulation of public discourse were visible long before 2016 and extend to any political actor willing to pay for these services. In the context of the 2016 US presidential election, Twitter identified and deleted at least 200,000 tweets supposedly posted by accounts associated with Russian disinformation efforts (Popken 2018b). Based on Twitter's estimates, roughly 1.4 million users interacted with related accounts (Twitter PublicPolicy 2018). It is unclear, however, if the accounts interacting with misinformation efforts were actual users or other accounts that were themselves part of the disinformation effort. That being said, the impact of these practices depends heavily on the role of online platforms in public discourse and the degree to which traditional media adjust their news coverage based on trends on social media. Here, the United States is undoubtedly an extreme case. Perhaps the weaker role of digital media in public discourse in other countries and news coverage more independent from trends on social media explain why these issues have been predominantly identified in the United States and have proved to be of much less relevance in other electoral contexts. We will come back to targeted efforts at disinformation and censorship in the discussion of collective action and state efforts to stop it in Chapter 5.

A high proportion of related research has focused on the identification of automated accounts, so-called bots, and the mapping of their activity (Shao et al. 2018). Bots are accounts on online platforms, such as Twitter or

Facebook, that automatically post messages without direct human interference (Chu et al. 2010). In their activity bots aim at the same goal as sock-puppet accounts run by humans, namely disinformation. For example, bots can be programmed to post variations of messages containing specific keywords during times of high political attention, such as televised leaders' debates or during ongoing public controversy. Bots can interact with other users, be they human or automated. This allows automated accounts to form bot networks interacting and retweeting content and thereby simulating public interest in selected topics (Ferrara et al. 2016). It has been estimated that between 9 and 15 percent of all Twitter accounts are bots (Varol et al. 2017). Yet this assessment includes all automated accounts, not just those active in politics or disinformation.

No doubt driven by the apparent novelty of colorful associations inspired by imagining autonomous algorithms taking over political discourse, there has been considerable research attention focused on the identification of automated accounts on social media platforms (Bessi and Ferrara 2016; Davis et al. 2016; Subrahmanian et al. 2016; Stukal et al. 2017; Varol et al. 2017; Bastos and Mercea 2019). Here, caution is advised. For one, automated identification of bots is only a probabilistic endeavor. Even if an account scores high on your bot-probability score of choice, this does not necessarily mean that this account is actually a bot. Without knowing the false positive rates of these procedures, that is, the number of accounts falsely identified as bots, their results remain subject to doubt (Rauchfleisch and Kaiser 2019a).

The attempt at automated bot detection is further complicated by the growing sophistication of their operators. Automated accounts are only one tool in the box of actors interested in influencing political media coverage and public discourse (MacFarquhar 2018; Scola 2018; Shane 2018). While much of the current debate has focused on automated accounts, there is no reason to assume that their identification and neutralization guarantees the shutdown of disinformation tactics. Instead, increasingly there is a trend toward bot–human hybrid accounts. These accounts are predominantly used by human users and only in phases of high political interest are they included in automated and coordinated communicative activity (Parlapiano and Lee 2018). These hybrid accounts are much harder to identify automatically than fully automated accounts. Yet they are at least as important for the disruption of political activity online as fully automated ones (Grimme, Assenmacher, and Adam 2018). The same goes for accounts filled by human users who are paid to post coordinated content (Yang, Yang, and Wilson 2015).

It is no surprise to find that with the growing importance of online platforms for political discourse, they have also become arenas of political disinformation tactics (Singer and Brooking 2018). Naturally, research attention has focused on the most novel and easily measurable aspect of these tactics, the role of automated accounts. Yet, as has been discussed, the apparent ease of detection might actually be deceptive and if not used with caution might lead to unjustified delegitimization of fringe positions and partisans. Furthermore, the focus on identifying bots and the documentation of their behavior has not been matched by the analysis of effects of bot activity (for an exception see Munger 2017). Even studies that claim to show effects usually only show activity of accounts designated as bots. Simply identifying some accounts as likely bots and telling stories about supposed effects is not enough. Instead of focusing on bots, it seems more sensible to focus on the practice and effects of political disinformation tactics online in general while treating bots as a special case of this larger phenomenon.

Recently, fears of being manipulated by shady actors online or the power of bots in debilitating public discourse have been transposed to artificial intelligence (Helbing et al. 2017; Brundage et al. 2018). While this debate is largely taking place in an evidence-free zone, we should be careful to hold this emerging discourse to higher standards than previous digital-technology-is-destroying-democracy scares.

3.10 Retooling the Reach of Political Information

The shifts in achieving reach for political information have been wide-ranging. Shifting audience behaviors and technological advances have led to significant changes in the practices of political actors in reaching out to audiences and have also introduced a new set of challenges for societies in figuring out what these new dynamics mean for established structures regulating the flow of political information and political discourse.

Traditional news organizations continue to provide political actors with broad reach (Webster 2014). Still, they have lost the exclusivity of giving voice to actors interested in introducing information or opinion into the political information cycle (Chadwick 2017). In this, the vetting of information seems to take a backseat to criteria influencing shareability or clickworthiness (Jenkins et al. 2013; Nahon and Hemsley 2013). This potentially provides rumor propagation and disinformation campaigns access to audiences irrespective of uptake by traditional media organizations (Bennett and Livingston 2018). While the degree of this might be more limited than expected by some commentators, generally it raises the question of whether there are features rendering media systems more or less robust to this challenge.

Comparative studies on the reach and impact of disinformation across countries are still lacking. Anecdotally it seems as if media systems with strong publicly funded news media, like Germany, are more robust against this challenge, while media systems with predominantly privately funded news, like the United States, appear to be more vulnerable. This would make sense as publicly funded and transparently run news organizations have more incentives to stick with a fact-based mission of news production without having to cater too strongly to shifts in public attention or controversy to generate ratings. Additionally, the regulation of speech in the European Union and in the United States differs strongly with regard to priorities (Jones 2016). The US emphasis on free speech in the context of First Amendment rights makes it much harder to effectively prosecute even blatant cases of disinformation. EU regulation makes conscious disinformation a much riskier endeavor. Simply put, the United States might simply make a commercially and politically more promising target. This would explain the current focus of disinformation campaigns on the US market.

One remedy against the perceived deterioration in the quality of the political information flow could lie in the strengthening of publicly funded news organizations. This matters gravely, as publicly funded media organizations are currently facing significant challenges (Aretz 2018). In Britain, the BBC faces persistent cost-cutting and oversight demands (Bond 2017); in Germany, the public broadcasters are in a continuous battle with privately funded media organizations over their rights to publish content on the internet (Hanfeld 2018) and face challenges from the political right regarding their impartiality (Angelos 2016); and in Switzerland, recently there was an unsuccessful referendum on shutting down public service broadcasting (Atkins 2018). Across various countries, the idea of news as a public good to be funded by taxpayers to offset the market's inability to provide unbiased high-quality news coverage is losing influence just as the fear of uncontrollable political disinformation online rises. This should give even ardent opponents of public service broadcasting at least some pause.

Moreover, the question of political actors shifting their communication tactics from attempting to reach broad sections of the public to ever more narrowly defined subsections might be problematic. For one, if political actors or their allies shift from universally accessible communication campaigns toward those specifically defined subsets, this means that a large part of their campaign remains invisible to most parts of the public and professional observers. This potentially opens the door to dog whistle campaigns in which only a subset of the population receives a message specifically targeted to their needs and interests in order to mobilize them while the rest of the country remains ignorant of that signal. This might allow political actors to engage in more provocative, controversial, or negative communication than in campaigns that have to be rolled out in full visibility to all. In the worst case, this might lead to a radicalization of parts of the public invisible to the rest and to electoral watchdogs like the press (Howard 2005; Bennett and Manheim 2006).

Importantly, we have to pay attention to the rise of new intermediaries in the relationship between political actors and the public. While new intermediaries like online platforms or companies providing data-driven solutions for ad display or voter contact provide powerful services to political actors, their governance structure and practices are currently opaque (Gillespie 2010; Kreiss 2012c). This has given rise to speculation as to their role and influence in politics. Platforms, journalists, and academics alike have to do a better job at making transparent the governance structure, role, and effects of these new intermediaries in allowing political actors to achieve reach.

As with so many of the questions raised in this book, there is not enough evidence to conclusively judge the likely outcome of these challenges. Furthermore, due to the lack of systematic comparative evidence, the dependency of specific outcomes on specific contextual conditions can only be guessed at currently. Yet, as briefly discussed, there seems to be a strong contingency of the transformative influence of digital media on the reach of political information on the degree of openness of media systems to economic pressures on news production. It is also important to keep in mind that one of the most persistent motives in researching political effects of digital media is that empirical findings almost never support the colorful extremist visions of public intellectuals or commentators. This can be seen most clearly in the debate about "echo chambers" and "filter bubbles" and is likely to repeat itself once the debate on "fake news" and disinformation campaigns settles. So, while it is safe to say that digital media changed the media environment in which political actors seek to achieve reach for information and therefore led them to adapt their practices and tactics, it is much harder to find systematic evidence for transformative shifts in politics overall. One reason for this might be that political attitudes and behavior are much harder to shift than some commentators suggest. This is the focus of Chapter 4.

4

The Effects of Political Information

Reaching people is not enough. Communicators want to influence them as well. So, the question becomes what effects digital media have on those exposed to them. Do digital media change the game by rendering people helpless under their spell? Or do they introduce new groups of people to politics who previously abstained? Any new step in the development of media technology raises the same question: Is it business as usual or do we experience a whole new set of effects? In examining the effects of digital media on users, we should at least be conscious of communication research's findings of previous eras. This means focusing on the nature and plurality of different kinds of effects. As Ithiel de Sola Pool wrote back in 1983:

> It is true, of course, that social research dramatically debunked lay generalizations about the enormous controlling effects of the new mass media. Hundreds of studies showed that human beings and societies somehow absorbed these stimuli without being overwhelmed by them. But whether the effects of mass media are "big" or "small" is hardly a serious question for social science. The significant research questions concern the kinds of effects that occur under different circumstances and the processes by which these effects take place.
>
> (Pool 1983b, 259)

Similarly, in examining the effects of digital media, we should not follow naively claims of maximal effects of digital media confidently put forward by pundits, nor should we play the game of merely disproving these adventurous claims. These theories are best understood as gambits at capturing the attention economy of public discourse, instead of meaningful contributions in trying to understand effects of digital media.

Instead of refuting expectations that were not to be taken seriously to begin with, we instead should start by thinking about what we know of communicative effects of other media and take this as a baseline for formulating expectations about likely effects. Following this, we should check these

103

expectations in the context of what makes digital media different from other media technology and identify features that might introduce new or different effects. Following this first step, we will discuss the literature on digital media's effects on individuals, focusing on political activation and participation, the learning of political information through digital media, and the effects of political expression online. Next we will discuss the effects of digital media on a larger scale on society. Here, we will discuss available research on polarization and digital divides. These discussions will show areas of fruitful and differentiated research on the contingency of the effects of digital media.

4.1 What Do We Know?

While digital media are perpetually new media in that they keep reinventing themselves with regard to services carrying information, technology information is accessed on, and usage conditions and conventions, there is no need to start from scratch. For over seventy years, communication research and psychology have provided us with a powerful understanding of the effects of information transmitted in media or through targeted communicative interventions by political actors (Rogers 1994; Neuman and Guggenheim 2011; Oliver, Raney, and Bryant 2019). This cumulative research effort provides us with a strong foundation on which to base our expectations of the effects of political information in digital media.

Exposure to informational content, for example in media coverage or in directed interventions by political actors, can have various different effects on recipients. One potential effect is the changing of attitudes toward issues, actors, or prospective behavior. Falling short of downright attitude change, another potential effect is the transmission of information on issues or actors. This could mean the learning of new aspects of an issue or an actor, learning about connections between issues and actors, or adjusting the perceived importance of an issue (McLeod, Kosicki, and McLeod 2009).

The effects of any one item or intervention are likely to be short-lived. This could be due to recipients simply forgetting the information provided (Hill et al. 2013; Bartels 2014); alternatively, in a noisy communication environment with many stimuli, any initial effect might be offset by the effects of other contradicting items or interventions (Druckman and Lupia 2016).

While there is thus a very real chance for the effects of isolated pieces of information and interventions to be diluted quickly, repeated exposure to content emphasizing the same information and making the same points is likely to cumulatively develop more long-lasting effects (Holbert 2005). In addition, there might be dominant characteristics of media technology, such as newspapers or television, that over time and with repeated use of that medium lead to cultivation effects. One example of this might be an increased feeling of insecurity among television users, not because of any one televised item but instead because of television content across genres predominantly emphasizing threats of violence and crime (Gerbner 1998; Morgan and Shanahan 2010).

Media effects do not appear to work uniformly across all recipients (Oliver and Krakowiak 2009). Instead, the strength of effects seems to vary across recipients given their previous attitudes or knowledge about an issue or actor. A series of psychological mechanisms leads to the qualification of any information received and can even determine the likelihood of exposure in the first place. Of those mechanisms, motivated reasoning is among the most prominently discussed. The expectation is that recipients assess the content of media items or communicative interventions based on its accordance with their previously existing attitudes and social groups with which they feel closely affiliated. Information contradicting previously held attitudes or challenging groups one feels affiliated with tends to be discarded during information processing, and therefore tends not to develop effects (Jost, Hennes, and Lavine 2013; Lodge and Taber 2013; Kahan 2016a, 2016b).

These biases could also come to matter with regard to information exposure. People seem to be systematically more willing to choose information that appears to be in line with previously held attitudes or groups one feels affiliated with (Stroud 2017). The drivers of this choice are disputed. Some think that a psychological need for supporting information lies behind this phenomenon (Festinger 1957). This would express itself by users not only preferring supporting information or media brands but also actively avoiding contradicting information and sources. Others point to empirical evidence inconsistent with these expectations, indicating that active avoidance of potentially contradicting information and sources appears to be rare (Garrett 2009a, 2009b). Consequently, an apparent preference for specific news items or sources could be driven by factors other than psychological need, for example a preference for local news or news specific to a given profession. If political attitudes turn out to be a covariate of these drivers of media selection, it might seem from the outside – erroneously – that politics makes users choose media content or sources. This has been called de facto selectivity (Sears and Freedman 1967; Sears 1968).

The likelihood for any effects to emerge seems to depend on the motives with which recipients consume information (Kunda 1990; Rubin 2009). In communication research, the uses and gratifications approach emphasizes that media effects vary based on the motives with which audience members approach media use (Rubin 2009). If recipients approach media items or communicative interventions with accuracy goals, in other words if they are interested in getting to the bottom of things or have vested interests in having correct information at their disposal, psychological biases and short cuts seem not to impact information processing much. Alternatively, if users approach media items or interventions with entertainment or identity-serving motives, biased processing is much more likely and limits the likelihood of attitude change or the uptake of new information.

In psychology, this has been reflected in various dual-processing models (Evans 2008; Petty, Briñol, and Priester 2009), in which system-one thinking (alternatively called "hot" or "fast" cognition) is associated with superficial, affective, and potentially biased processing while system-two thinking (alternatively called "cool" or "slow" cognition) is associated with more robust, conscious, and reflective thinking (Kahneman 2011; Lodge and Taber 2013). This has led to attempts by communicators to trigger one or the other processing mode depending on which type they deem more likely to serve their goals (Kahan 2016b).

Exposure and processing decisions are also likely to be driven by cues or to be based on heuristics. Most recipients do not engage deeply with media content or communicative interventions. Instead, their exposure decision and processing route is likely to be superficial. In order to still make sense of the world without spending too much effort on the task, people tend to react to cues, such as the identity of a sender or the brand of a news channel, and heuristics – rules of thumb – such as analogies (Mondak 1993; Lau and Redlawsk 2001; Nicholson 2012). As a consequence, people encounter political information very seldom in isolation but perceive a series of contextual information which in turn will influence the effect of new information. In practice this will often lead to a weakening of the effects of information contradicting recipients' sense of self or group belonging while reinforcing information supporting said identities (Jost et al. 2013). This makes it extraordinarily difficult to change the opinions of politically interested and invested audience members.

In general, there seems to be a challenge for political communicators in reaching those recipients most likely to be convinced. While people with an interest in politics might be likely to watch media coverage of politics or read about it, these people are also already likely to hold a political opinion and are likely partisans. So, while they might receive information, this information is unlikely to change their views considerably given the psychological processes discussed previously. At the same time, those recipients with little prior knowledge of politics and only weakly held views on issues or candidates are potentially swayed by new information but unlikely to receive it. In other words, those most likely to be convinced or to learn are also the ones least likely to be exposed in the first place (Zaller 1992). A central challenge of political communication thus lies in reaching people who are uninterested in politics.

Finally, social structures such as media repertoires, information environments, and social networks alter the effects of political information. Information received by the media or through communicative interventions has to compete with other information in recipients' media repertoires and the communication environment (Webster 2014). People do not consume media in isolation. Instead, they consume them across different sources and channels. These individual sets are called media repertoires (Hasebrink and Popp 2006; Hasebrink and Domeyer 2012). If the structure of media repertoires or information environments cumulatively emphasizes a specific set of information, it is likely for it to develop strong and lasting effects. If, on the other hand, the information environment cumulatively focuses on different aspects of reality, any initial effect might dissipate quickly. The same is true for social networks in which individuals are embedded, such as family, friends, or the workplace. If personal conversations in these environments focus on said information, its effect can be expected to persist. If, on the other hand, these environments ignore said information or actively argue against it, effects might dissipate quickly.

The picture that emerges is that media content and communicative interventions can have effects. Yet these effects seem to be strongly bounded by the degree of competitiveness in the information environment, the degree of recipients' cumulative exposure across channels and time, recipients' previously held attitudes and group affiliations, as well as the motives underlying exposure conditions. What does this mean for the effects of political information transmitted in digital media?

4.2 Why Should the Effects of Digital Media Be Different?

In thinking about the likely effects of digital media, we have to remain conscious of the fact that they combine aspects from print and audiovisual media. Digital media content comes in the form of text, images, audio, and video files. In principle, we should thus expect their effect characteristics to also hold for digital media. That being said, digital media share specific characteristics emerging from the underlying technology and cultural usage patterns, which differ from traditional media (Boulianne 2011; Neuman 2016). These differences potentially impact the kinds of effects they have on individual users and society at large.

One of the most important features of digital media for politics is the radical lowering of costs of publication and access to information (Bimber 2003). One consequence is that internet users now have the opportunity to access political information on nearly any topic of their choice at low or no cost or effort (Boulianne 2011). This might lead people formerly not engaged in politics to engage with political information online and in turn to become politically active – provided, of course, that information costs are at the heart of what keeps people from engaging with politics. This point is not uncontested. Since the internet offers low-cost access not only to political information but to information of all kinds, it may well be that existing interests determine what information people consume online. In this reading, the lowering of information costs through digital media would not necessarily translate into the activation of politically disinterested users. Instead, politically interested users are expected to consume more political information than before while politically uninterested users can spend even more time with information not directly touching on politics (Prior 2013). This has led to increased interest in the dynamics and determinants of selective exposure.

An alternative view sees the political communication space online as a communication environment of habitual and algorithmic constraint. For example, habitual users of general-purpose news apps or Facebook users reading their news feed do not actively choose political information but are still likely to see it there. This would open up the chance for accidental exposure to political information for users not directly interested in politics (Bode 2016; Valeriani and Vaccari 2016; Fletcher and Nielsen 2017b; Settle 2018; Vraga et al. 2019).

Informational abundance is also connected with a plurality of voices and sources. While some have seen this as a chance for groups underrepresented in the coverage of traditional media to gain public voice and recognition (Castells 2009), this plurality of voices, content, and tone of political information and discourse online also brings challenges. For example, currently public debate has focused on what is perceived to be an overwhelmingly negative tone of political comments online, vicious trolling of users, and hate speech (Coe, Kenski, and Rains 2014; Phillips 2015; Theocharis et al. 2016). While digital media might thus on the one hand open up political discourse to new perspectives and voices, it might on the other hand also contribute to a deterioration of public discourse into negativity and harassment, thereby potentially leading people to disengage from politics.

Another characteristic that sets digital media apart from older media technology is the element of social exchange of and around political information. Users share and comment on political information on personalized spaces online, for example blogs, Facebook, Twitter, or messenger services. They are also able to comment directly on many online news sources, making reactions to news media coverage public. People thus encounter not only political information online but also direct contextual information, such as who in their social environment supported or opposed a given piece of information. This might change the dynamics of political information acquisition (Chadwick, Vaccari, and O'Loughlin 2018; Settle 2018; Valeriani and Vaccari 2018). Moreover, the opportunity to express political opinions online might get people to engage with politics more actively. These exchanges might also be more deeply embedded in emotional appeals and feature stronger personal storytelling than those encountered in political media coverage (Papacharissi 2010, 2015), again potentially changing effect dynamics.

Another potentially crucial difference between digital media and media technologies like print or television is the exposure condition. Technology dictates the conditions of exposure to political information. While newspaper reading might happen on the go and television watching might happen out of the corner of one's eye, in general these technologies require the dedicated decision to pull out a newspaper or sit before a screen. Compare this with exposure to digital media. You are sitting in front of your computer and should be writing, a book chapter for example, but your mind wanders and you find yourself visiting a news website of choice or checking up on your social media feeds. Or you are out on the town and waiting for a bus and you pull out your phone and read up on news or social media. This makes news exposure online habitual and ubiquitous. Thus, digital media use is much freer from temporal, spatial, and contextual constraints compared with the use of traditional media technology. Again, this might change the types of effects we can expect political information online to achieve.

While there are thus considerable differences in the characteristics of digital media and older media technology, it is far from clear if these differences translate deterministically into systematically divergent effects. In the following, we will discuss empirical findings on a selection of prominently discussed effects of political information on digital media on individual users and society at large.

4.3 Effects on Individuals

Bringing People into Politics

A prominent topic in researching political effects of digital media is their influence on political participation. Do digital media make users more likely to participate politically, be it through traditional means – for example by voting, protesting, or donating money – or new forms of political participation – such as commenting on a politician's Facebook profile, signing online petitions, or retweeting a call to protest. Digital media could thus facilitate traditional modes of political participation or extend them through a new repertoire of politically meaningful actions (Anduiza, Jensen, and Jorba 2012; Bennett and Segerberg 2013; Theocharis 2015; Theocharis and van Deth 2018a; Theocharis and van Deth 2018b).

Some even expect digital media to lead to the political activation of previously uninterested users, such as the complacent, the poor, or the young. By lowering the costs of political information and coordination, people previously disinterested in politics might start to follow political news or engage in politics during election campaigns (Carpini 2000; Krueger 2002; Bimber 2003; Ward, Gibson, and Lusoli 2003). Alternatively, users might encounter political information accidentally in the posts of friends or family or see them participate online and might thus be pulled into participating at a later point (Utz 2009; Bode et al. 2014; Gil de Zúñiga, Molyneux, and Zheng 2014; Valeriani and Vaccari 2016; Wang and Shi 2018). Another potential driver of political participation by digital media could be more indirect. Various authors point to active digital media use being a likely driver of interconnecting people more strongly within their community. This increased interconnection could then later translate into an increased readiness to support said community through political participation (Gil de Zúñiga and Valenzuela 2011; Gil de Zúñiga, Jung, and Valenzuela 2012; Boulianne 2015).

Other authors differ in that they do not necessarily expect digital media to lead to an activation of formerly politically disengaged users. Instead, digital media might serve primarily as a tool for people already likely to be active in politics, thereby adding to their participation repertoires (Bimber 2001; Weber, Loumakis, and Bergman 2003; Xenos and Moy 2007; Bimber and Copeland 2013; Copeland and Bimber 2015). Digital media thus would not necessarily activate politically disengaged users but instead help already politically inclined users to increase their political influence by facilitating participation. In the words of Schlozman, Verba, and Brady (2010), digital media would serve as a "weapon of the strong." In a systematic meta-analysis of 38 topically relevant studies, Boulianne (2009) showed that internet use did not lead to the activation of politically uninvolved respondents. Instead, the internet tended to be used for political participation or information by politically interested users (Boulianne 2009, 205).

Theoretically, the two camps diverge with regard to the suspected foundations of political participation. Proponents of the digital-media-as-activation claim seem to follow a simple model that sees political participation as driven by direct or indirect costs of political information or participation. By reducing these costs, digital media are thus likely to activate people to political participation. This very simple model runs counter to what political behavior and social movement research treat as drivers of participation, such as the influence of social, economic, and ideational resources (Verba and Nie 1987; Verba, Schlozman, and Brady 1995) or opportunity structures (McAdam, Tarrow, and Tilly 2001). According to these richer conceptualizations, reducing costs of political participation or information should only play a minor role in activating politically disinterested people. Following this reading, one should expect information in digital media to have only a very moderate effect, if any, on political participation.

These expectations have also been raised with regard to newer forms of digital media, such as blogs, social networking platforms, or YouTube (Valenzuela, Park, and Kee 2009; Vitak et al. 2011; Bond et al. 2012; Conroy, Feezell, and Guerrero 2012; Gil de Zúñiga et al. 2012; Tang and Lee 2013; Bode et al. 2014; Haenschen 2016). Here, a similar picture emerges as with earlier technological manifestations of the internet. Building on her original meta-analysis, Boulianne shows that also for these new forms of digital media there exists an overall positive connection between use and political participation, but that as before, the causal nature of this link is doubtful (Boulianne 2015). That being said, there is growing evidence that digital media might indeed open up a way into political participation for young people (Boulianne and Theocharis 2018). So, while digital media might not necessarily extend participation among people whose political engagement has already stabilized, they might serve as entry points into political participation for people who are still in their political socialization phase.

One important challenge for researchers looking for cumulative evidence on this question is the perpetual changes in digital media (Karpf 2012a). Our contemporary internet, which users largely access through mobile apps, is significantly different from the internet of social media platforms predominantly accessed through browsers. Moreover, this internet was significantly different from an internet of predominantly unchanging websites, which again was different from an internet of message boards. There is no guarantee that future iterations of digital technology will not lead to qualitative shifts in usage modes and patterns and in turn to different effects on political participation. As we have seen, the available literature has addressed the relationship between political participation and the use of digital media at various stages in the technological development of the internet. While fundamental results seem to hold over time, there is no guarantee they will continue to do so (Boulianne 2009, 2015).

Another challenge is that most studies in this field use cross-sectional data for which the identification of causal relationships between variables is notoriously problematic. The few available panel studies show contradicting results (Holt et al. 2013; Kahne, Lee, and Feezell 2013; Dimitrova et al. 2014; Theocharis and Quintelier 2016), while one of the even fewer experimental studies identified a negative effect of Facebook use on political participation (Theocharis and Lowe 2016).

The question of the impact of digital media on political participation is far from solved. Recently, the debate has started to differentiate between various potential effects, the use of various tools and services, and more precise measurement of specific usage patterns (Shah, Kwak, and Holbert 2001; DiMaggio et al. 2004; Xenos and Moy 2007; Hargittai and Shaw 2013). While promising in principle, this development brings the risk of getting lost in idiosyncratic operationalizations and maybe even effect fishing. Without a strong theoretical foundation, empirical studies can get sidetracked in chasing arbitrary and small effects that might emerge in isolated studies and contexts but are not replicated in other contexts (Wuttke 2019). This danger is heightened once researchers include effects in arbitrarily selected subgroups in their population of interest. This makes the systematic development of theoretical foundations in the choice of variables, subgroups, and operationalizations crucial. It also means not accepting each and every significant result presented in a paper at face value, but also paying attention to effect strengths and the statistical power of studies. After all, not every statistically significant effect is meaningful and not every sample size allows for confident conclusions (Calin-Jageman and Cumming 2019).

While the debate on the activating power of digital media is thus still ongoing, for us the most convincing evidence indicates that digital media might not be a tool for activating disengaged and disadvantaged people. Instead, it appears to us more as a powerful tool for politically interested people and those likely to engage in politics. One exception appears to be young people. Here, digital media might indeed promise to be a gateway into political participation. Yet the question remains if those young people brought into politics by digital media socio-demographically fall into groups unlikely to participate in politics or whether socio-demographically they fall among the usual suspects of politically engaged people. In the first case, digital media would indeed promise to shift the balance of political participation. In the second case, they would provide a new entry point for people of a kind who in the past found their way into politics along different routes.

As so often with politics, the issue appears to us not necessarily to be about reducing costs of engaging in politics but instead creating the inclination to engage with politics in the first place (Prior 2019). If this fails, digital media indeed will be predominantly a weapon of the strong. That being said, in cases and political systems where opportunities for political participation are limited, for example in weak democracies or oppressive or autocratic regimes, digital media might indeed enable participation. Yet even in these cases it is unlikely that digital media are the tools of choice for uneducated and politically disengaged people. Instead, they are likely to be used by resource-endowed if disenfranchised users. We will discuss this challenge in detail when we focus on protests and collective action in Chapter 5.

Informing and Changing Minds

We have seen previously that ever more people encounter news and political information on digital media, where they find a mix of news items from traditional media organizations, partisan outlets, and peddlers of downright disinformation (Jungherr, Posegga, and An 2019a). In a study of the use of online news in 36 countries, the Reuters Digital News Report 2017 showed that 47 percent of respondents across all markets encountered news on Facebook, 22 percent on YouTube, 10 percent on Twitter, and 15 percent on the messaging application WhatsApp (Newman et al. 2017, 11). While there is strong variance in the usage numbers across countries, these figures show the importance of digital media as sources of news and political information. What are the effects of this communication environment and these outlets on the uptake of political information by users?

In principle, content encountered online should show similar effect dynamics as content encountered in other media. Yet as discussed previously, the context of exposure (e.g., purposeful vs. accidental, authoritative sources vs. social endorsement cues) is likely to matter in the type of information acquisition effects we can expect. Of these, the suspected difference between purposeful and accidental exposure to political information online has featured very strongly in previous research.

In the early days of research into the political effects of digital media, the internet was seen as a high-choice media environment in which users purposefully selected and accessed information of interest to them. Politically interested users were expected to visit news sites, political blogs, or websites of political parties or candidates (Bimber and Davis 2003; Lawrence, Sides, and Farrell 2010; Tewksbury and Rittberg 2012). Politically disinterested users would choose different sites with different types of information. Exposure to news or political information online was thus seen as being primarily purposeful. As a consequence, political information would predominantly reach people interested in politics. As established by political communication research, these people, while likely to receive political information, are less inclined to change their minds based on new information. In high-choice media environments, the effects of political information are thus likely to be constrained to reinforcing already held attitudes, agenda setting, or signaling group positions. If correct, this would give digital media a strong role in information transmission within political groups or among partisans but little effect in changing minds.

In Chapter 3, we saw that this suspected feature of digital media led some to expect a gradual political polarization of societies, as people were expected to see only political information supporting already held beliefs, thus reinforcing said beliefs without providing access to opposing viewpoints or information (Sunstein 2001; Pariser 2011). As of now, there has been little if any empirical evidence showing these suspected effects (Borgesius et al. 2016; Guess et al. 2018). One reason for this could be that in high-choice environments a divide in source and content selection by users might not run predominantly along partisan lines but instead along the divide between people generally interested in politics and those who are not (Prior 2007). People interested in politics might show a preference for content and sources in line with their political views (Garrett 2009a, 2009b), yet given their general interests, they are also likely to sample the coverage of other sources, such as mainstream news outlets or even selected content or sources across the partisan divide (Webster 2014). To be sure, this still does not mean that this cross-cutting exposure will make them change their minds on politics, given the likely strength and elaboration of previously held political beliefs. Alternatively, the empirical failure of these conjectures could also lie in the fact that by now digital media resemble far less a high-choice media environment than a low-choice environment.

It was not implausible to characterize early developmental stages of the internet as a high-choice media environment. As long as digital media consisted predominantly of websites that could be accessed either directly, through hyperlinks, or through search engines, exposure to news or political information online followed purposeful and directed behavior. It is doubtful that the current technological incarnation of the internet shares these characteristics. Social networking platforms and messenger services carry ever more traffic to news sites, and dedicated news apps channel user attention on mobile devices. In this environment, exposure to news and political information is not necessarily purpose-driven. Instead, personalized algorithmic content selection and users' social networks are important drivers of exposure to content. Users decide to open an app or to log onto their social media profiles. There, they check the content currently available to them on their personalized profiles. This creates the opportunity for accidental exposure or incidental learning independent of the actual interests of users.

It has long been held that people not interested in politics might be the most promising targets of political information as their political attitudes can be expected to be less strongly settled than those of politically interested people. With this audience, the communicative challenge lies in reaching them with political information. Television was seen as a viable opportunity for unintended – accidental – exposure to political news or information for people not interested in politics and those not looking for news (Blumler 1970). Audience members switched on the television for entertainment purposes and encountered news and political information accidentally (Krugman and Hartley 1970; Robinson 1973; Zukin and Snyder 1984; Schoenbach and Lauf 2002). While this pattern arguably lost influence once television extended its originally limited offering of channels and thus developed into a high-choice media environment (Prior 2007), it might be that parts of the internet have developed into environments of accidental exposure (Boulianne 2011).

For example, the Reuters Digital News Report 2017 showed that 36 percent of respondents reported that they had seen news from sources they would otherwise not have visited on social media. Forty percent of respondents reported that they had seen news stories they were not interested in on social media (Newman et al. 2017, 43). Accidental exposure to sources and content thus seems to be a consistent feature on social media and can thus be expected to become more relevant as these features of digital media grow in importance (Bode 2012, 2016; Dimitrova et al. 2014; Valeriani and Vaccari 2016; Fletcher and Nielsen 2017b; Boczkowski, Mitchelstein, and Matassi 2018; Vraga et al. 2019).

This widespread non-purposive-driven exposure to news through digital media also seems to have given rise to what Gil de Zúñiga, Weeks, and Ardèvol-Abreu (2017) call a news-finds-me perception among online users. People holding this perception do not feel they have to actively search for information. Instead, they expect that if news is of relevance to them it will find them anyway. The authors warn, though, that people sharing this attitude over time tend to rely less on traditional news for information and become less knowledgeable about politics even while respondents are exposed to political information on social media. Exposure to news and political information on social media thus seems to have weaker effects on political knowledge than purposive exposure on traditional media. This finding is also corroborated by work by Shehata and Strömbäck (2018). Additionally, Yamamoto and Kushin (2014) show that the use of social networking platforms in the context of a US presidential election led to an increase in cynicism, apathy, and skepticism. Accidental exposure on digital media thus is far from producing predominantly positive effects.

While social networking sites are an important source of news and political information in the contemporary media environment, they are best seen as one piece in a varied set of information sources (Webster 2014). In 2017, only 2 percent of US respondents reported using only social media as their news source in the week prior to the survey (Newman et al. 2017, 11). In addition, while public debate focuses strongly on political content on social networking sites such as Facebook, political content only makes up a very small share of all information posted there (Wang 2017). Additionally, the political content that makes it onto social media platforms is far from universally popular. For example, in an eye-tracking experiment Bode, Vraga, and Troller-Renfree (2017) showed that in a simulated Facebook news feed, respondents tended to quickly scroll over political content. This tendency grew according to the degree to which the content was clearly identifiable as political and respondents' political interest decreased. Moreover, Settle (2018) has argued in her "END framework" that social media lead their users to become more aware of their own and others' political identities, which in turn leads them to judge their political others much more harshly than nonusers of social media. Getting political information from the social media feeds of personal acquaintances might thus not only provide political information but also lead to a much more acute awareness of dividing lines between political groups and ultimately greater political polarization.

While digital media are thus an important piece in the contemporary political media system, their effects are far from certain. Digital media seem to combine elements of purposeful and accidental exposure to news and political information. In principle, they thus bring the potential of exposure to political information to users not primarily interested in politics who might be more likely to be convinced by information encountered accidentally. Yet exactly these users also appear to avoid political information once exposed, thus lowering the chance for content to develop effects. Once exposed, these effects might lead to further disengagement from politics, be it through loss of political knowledge, increased cynicism, or apathy. Overall, the uses of digital media for news or political information are deeply embedded in the use of other news and information sources, such as traditional news organizations. We can therefore expect the effects of digital media also to be contingent on information encountered in this competitive information environment. As a consequence, one should be careful of having too much hope for political activation or too much fear of political anomie based on informational uses of digital media.

Political Talk

Digital media are not only a channel enabling political participation or a source of political information. Digital media are also a very active space of political talk (Shah et al. 2017). Users post reactions to political events, political media coverage, or politicians' statements. They comment on posts of contacts, engage actively in dedicated groups on political issues, and carry politics into discussion groups concerned with other topics. Political communication research has long recognized the importance of personal exchanges about politics among friends, family, colleagues, and loose acquaintances (Gamson 1992; Cramer Walsh 2004; McClurg, Klofstad, and Sokhey 2017). The primacy of enabling and encouraging social exchange in the design of digital media, and especially social networking platforms, also makes this an important research topic. Research has focused on identifying the patterns of political talk online, characterizing speech situations online, identifying their effects on participants, and using the associated digital traces for a better understanding of the events referred to in political talk.

One feature of digital media is the ability for people interested in the same topic to quickly form exchange networks. This can happen, for example, around topical hashtags on Twitter or in dedicated groups or fan pages on Facebook. These "networked publics" (Varnelis 2008; boyd 2011; Gurri 2018) can emerge and dissolve quickly, offering the opportunity for political talk among previously unacquainted people sharing the same topical interests. Another important feature of political talk on social media is that political posts and comments appear in the flow of users' mundane activities and messages. Thus, contacts who know a user from work or from leisure activities see her updates on volunteering at a food bank or protesting. This potentially makes politics into a more visible feature of a user's identity to her contacts across different social contexts and thus inspires political talk beyond her immediate circle of politically active contacts. This "context collapse" (Marwick and boyd 2011) allows political expression, exchange, and talk to travel into previously non-political contexts and circles.

These characteristics of digital media as communication environments means that political talk online diverges strongly from communication environments of deliberative exchange (Neuman, Bimber, and Hindman 2011). Political talk online is emotional, phatic, humorous, and personal. Papacharissi and Fatima Oliveira (2012, 12) have characterized these exchanges accordingly as "affective news":

> [contributions] blended emotion with opinion, and drama with fact, reflecting deeply subjective accounts and interpretations of events, as they unfolded.

This goes to show that not all political talk on digital media takes the form of constructive or tolerant exchange. While phatic communication can take the form of public expressions of caring, support, public mourning, or love, phatic communication also encompasses the other side of the spectrum of human emotions (Jungherr, Posegga, and An 2019b). It can contain sarcastic and hurtful humor, verbal aggression, insults, and systematic harassment (Phillips 2015; Nagle 2017). Accordingly, the effects of this impoliteness or downright incivility in political talk on participants has developed into a vibrant research area (Coe et al. 2014; Theocharis et al. 2016; Rainie, Anderson, and Albright 2017; Rains et al. 2017; Su et al. 2018). This research has shown that impoliteness in political talk online can lead to audience members falling back on previously held opinions and discarding new information presented in the discussion or media coverage that comments are reacting to (Anderson et al. 2014; A. A. Anderson et al. 2018). Impoliteness in follow-up communication to media coverage would thus limit the informational effects of this content. These perceived consequences have given rise to research testing the potential of dedicated interventions directed at users posting impolite, threatening, or harassing comments (Munger 2017).

A corollary to this research is the question of how the conditions in online communication spaces impact the willingness of people to engage publicly in political talk online. Building on the "spiral of silence" theory (Noelle-Neumann 1974), researchers have examined how the perceived climate of opinion in communication spaces, such as Facebook or comment sections of websites, impacts the propensity of users to post comments (Gearhart and Zhang 2015, 2018; Kwon, Moon, and Stefanone 2015; Hoffmann and Lutz 2017; Chan 2018; Chen 2018). The original theory stated that people assess the climate of opinion in any situation before deciding to publicly express their political opinion. If they feel their opinion is shared by a majority of participants in a communication space, they are seen as likely to state their own opinion publicly. If, on the other hand, they assess their opinion to be in the minority, they are expected to tend to stay silent, due to a deeply ingrained fear of social isolation. Over time, apparent majority opinions are thus expected to be voiced more often and thus become more dominant while apparent minority opinions are voiced infrequently and disappear over time (Matthes 2015). One consistent finding in this literature is that across contexts communication environments with heterogeneous political opinions lead to generally lower propensity for political talk online among participants (Gearhart and Zhang 2015; Hampton, Shin, and Lu 2017; Hoffmann and Lutz 2017; Wells et al. 2017; Chan 2018).

Another prominent area of research into political talk online looks at comments and public exchanges in the context of political television coverage.

Live coverage of important political events in particular, such as televised leaders' debates in election campaigns, lead people to post comments on the unfolding events while watching and publicly exchange views and opinions online (Anstead and O'Loughlin 2011; Jungherr 2015). Suddenly people are not only watching media events (Dayan and Katz 1992) on the television screen but also keeping an eye out for the reactions of their friends and other people watching the same event on multiple other screens, such as their laptop or smartphone. Actively expressing opinions on unfolding events and receiving the opinions of others can change the way people assess the performance of politicians or form impressions of unfolding events. It might also impact the likelihood of participatory behavior later on. This has become a prominent topic in research under the terms second or dual screening (Gil de Zúñiga, Garcia-Perdomo, and McGregor 2015; Vaccari, Chadwick, and O'Loughlin 2015; Shah et al. 2016; McGregor et al. 2017; Vaccari and Valeriani 2018).

Political talk online is not only an object of study. Digital traces of political talk also create the opportunity to examine political events and shifts in public attention to politics (Jungherr and Jürgens 2013; Jungherr 2015). Political events and political media coverage are important sources of political talk online (Jungherr 2014; Bode et al. 2015; Jungherr and Jürgens 2016). In their shared reactions to political events, users point to moments in time, relevant individuals, and content (Meraz and Papacharissi 2013). This collective meaning-making process leaves digital traces that allow for subsequent analysis. We can thus interpret political talk as a process of collective filtering. References to actors, events, and content in posts and comments online provide in aggregate a map of what the participants in public exchanges on political events deemed important or relevant (Jungherr and Jürgens 2014a, 2014b). Data on the topics, actors, events, or content mentioned widely on public social media streams thus provide journalists and politicians with information on public reactions to political events in real time (Anstead and O'Loughlin 2015) and offer considerable analytical potential for researchers interested in the objects and dynamics of public attention (Jungherr, Schoen, et al. 2017; Zhang et al. 2019).

In the interpretation of these patterns, caution is advised. Digital traces documenting the focus and dynamics of political talk online do not offer an unbiased reflection of the events inspiring political talk. Instead, digital traces only document the actions of users of services that produce this data (Salganik 2018). This means that we only get insights into the behavior and interests of users of the respective service providing us with data. This means that any bias in the composition of active users will translate into biases in our analyses. Furthermore, not everything users pay attention to or feel is important will manifest in their interactions on digital media (Jungherr and Jürgens 2013). Public interactions document a selection of interests users feel comfortable sharing, expect to find public resonance, or that they have been pointed to by the platform itself, for example in the form of ads or sponsored content. Digital traces thus offer a biased reflection of reality mediated by the interests and motivations of users, and the usage conventions and underlying code of online platforms providing the data (Jungherr 2015; Jungherr, Schoen, and Jürgens 2016). Any interpretation of the resulting data not taking into account these mediating influences is bound to fail (Jungherr, Jürgens, and Schoen 2012; Jungherr, Schoen, et al. 2017; Jungherr 2019).

4.4 Effects on Society

Polarization

One very important claim with regard to the political impact of digital media is their perceived role in strengthening political polarization, the idea being that increasing choice in media offerings allows users to consume information supporting their previously held beliefs, thereby contributing to greater political polarization in societies. This argument is very popular but suffers from various empirical challenges. As with "echo chambers" and "filter bubbles," the intuitiveness of the argument does not fit with the available evidence once one looks at it more closely.

The claim that digital media contributes to increased political polarization among the general population has been raised most forcefully in the case of the United States (Sunstein 2001; Pariser 2011). Yet the available evidence does not seem to support this claim in its generality. Although it has been a staple of editorials for at least 20 years that public attitudes in the United States have become more polarized, there is little systematic evidence of this. Instead, various studies have repeatedly and over time found little indication that attitudes among the general US public have become more polarized across three of four polarization dimensions identified by DiMaggio, Evans, and Bryson (1996). Opinions among the general US public are not more widely dispersed across attitude distributions on topics (Evans 2003), opinions have not become increasingly clustered at extreme poles of attitude distributions (Fiorina, Abrams, and Pope 2010; Fiorina 2017), and attitudes across topics have not become increasingly linked to form coherent ideological systems (Converse 1964; Baldassarri and Gelman 2008). Only for the fourth dimension, the increased association of attitudes and salient personal characteristics or group identities, does there appear to be some supporting evidence, at least for political partisanship (DiMaggio et al. 1996). Overall, most available evidence seems to point to little, if any, political polarization in the attitudes of the general US public (DiMaggio et al. 1996; Fiorina et al. 2010; Prior 2013; Fiorina 2017). For political elites and partisans, the picture changes. Here, there is strong evidence of attitude polarization over time (Evans 2003; Baldassarri and Gelman 2008; Stoker and Jennings 2008; Levendusky 2009; McCarty, Poole, and Rosenthal 2016; Fiorina 2017).

Furthermore, there is little evidence for the claim that internet use necessarily leads to the exclusive consumption of political information in support of one's held opinion. As we discussed in the previous chapters, people who used the internet and digital media for news were likely to be exposed online to heterogeneous information to at least the same if not a greater degree as on other channels or in personal conversations (Gentzkow and Shapiro 2011). In addition, studies looking at polarization over time identify demographic groups for whom polarization appears most likely who are also least likely to use the internet (Boxell, Gentzkow, and Shapiro 2017). Thus even if we expect political polarization, digital media does not appear to be a driver of it.

The case of linking digital media to polarization might be stronger once we move away from the general population and focus on political partisans. Various studies point to attitudes of Democrats and Republicans becoming more polarized over time (Fiorina et al. 2010; Fiorina 2017). In this, politically charged topics, sometimes called wedge issues, play an important role. Specific attitudes on selected topics thus appear to become linked to group identities. It has been well established that either through a process of socialization or in-group signaling, political partisans' attitudes tend to converge on selected issues (Achen and Bartels 2016). Prominent wedge issues across which Democrat and Republican partisans tend to diverge are abortion, gun control, and health care (Hillygus and Shields 2008). Holding a specific attitude on these issues serves to identify people as members of a political group. The same mechanism has been raised recently with regard to the use of partisan news or even the consumption and sharing of potential disinformation or fake news. Belief in and sharing of demonstrably false information, rumors, and the use of highly partisan news outlets is thus not necessarily about information transmission but might instead serve the public performance of partisan identities (Huddy, Mason, and Aarøe 2015; Flynn, Nyhan, and Reifler 2017; Kahan 2017a, 2017b).

Another potential link between the expression of polarized opinions and digital media might lie in the characteristics of the communication environment online. As discussed in the section on political talk, communication environments characterized by incivility can lead people to fall back to previously held attitudes, which in political contexts can lead to the expression of polarized opinions (Anderson et al. 2014; A. A. Anderson et al. 2018).

The link between the supposed polarization of attitudes among the general public and digital media might prove to be elusive. Yet the role of digital media as a communication space to express partisan identities through the use and sharing of partisan news or disinformation might be a more promising topic. Moreover, the prevalence of political talk online increases the importance of understanding whether specific characteristics of the political communication environment online might lead users to revert to or voice polarized opinions online.

Digital Divides

Another important issue is the question of whether there are systematic differences between people who have access to the internet or digital tools and those who don't. Going beyond mere access, it is also important to understand if there are systematic differences between people able to use digital technology to their advantage and those who predominantly use it recreationally. Research into the "digital divide" was very prominent in the late 1990s and early 2000s. Recently it has declined somewhat in prominence but it is bound to remain relevant, especially with the steadily increasing use of algorithmic decision-making in political and governmental processes.

At its core, research into the digital divide is concerned with the consequences of having access to digital technology (DiMaggio et al. 2001; Norris 2001; Warschauer 2003; van Dijk 2005). Digital technology allows those with access richer participatory opportunities in social and political life. This can include furthering careers, enabling richer social lives, providing pathways to better education, and opening up more avenues of political participation. Conversely, those with no access run the risk of being left behind (Robinson et al. 2015). This divide is especially problematic as the determinants of having access to digital technology are material and mental resources. Digital technology thus allows those in society who are already well-to-do to advance further, while those who are already disadvantaged are at risk of being left behind. Digital technologies thus have the potential to reinforce already existing rifts in society. Consequences of the digital divide between those with access and those without are expected to become ever more crucial as digital technology becomes so deeply ingrained in social, political, and economic life that it does not merely work as an enabler of participation but becomes a prerequisite.

While the first wave of digital divide research focused on physical access to digital technology – such as computers and the internet – a second wave of studies focused increasingly on usage patterns (DiMaggio et al. 2004; Hargittai and Hsieh 2013; Pearce and Rice 2013) and the availability of skills necessary to maneuver and contribute to digital media (Hargittai 2002, 2010; Hargittai and Hsieh 2012; Hargittai and Shaw 2013). Since the early 2000s, the provision of public access to computers and the internet has been seen by many as a largely resolved issue. But researchers have pointed out that access alone does not solve the challenge of deviating opportunities to realize participatory potentials of digital technology. Instead, studies across various countries have shown that disadvantaged groups, who only a few years earlier were shown to be underrepresented with regard to access to digital technology, now had access to computers and the internet but were using this technology markedly differently from users comparatively richer in economic or educational resources. While users rich in material and mental resources were using digital technology for capital-enhancing purposes – such as information, news, education, and career purposes – users with fewer material and educational resources did so to a much smaller degree. For these users, social communication and recreational uses were more prominent than capital-enhancing uses (van Deursen and van Dijk 2014). This "second-level digital divide" (Hargittai 2002) perpetuates and potentially increases a divide in participatory opportunities for people with high or low material and mental resources. While studies vary in the exact terms used and operationalizations chosen, these findings appear to be robust over time and countries (Scheerder, van Deursen, and van Dijk 2017). Just providing access to digital technology does not solve the underlying problem. Instead, fixing digital inequalities also means addressing differentials in usage motives and usage skills.

Overcoming the problem of differential participatory gains from digital technology in society might be even more complicated than providing relatively disadvantaged groups with access to digital technology or with the proper training to use this technology to their benefit. Van Dijk (2012, 197–205) identifies access to digital technology as a process with four stages. The first of van Dijk's stages is motivation to gain access in the first place. The second stage is realizing this motivation by gaining physical and material access. The third stage is gaining the digital skills necessary to operate digital technology. Here, van Dijk differentiates between media-related skills – such as skills in operating digital technology and formal skills in navigating file structures or web browsing – and content-related skills – such as finding and evaluating information, communicating between users, skills in creating content on digital technology, and strategic skills in using digital technology in pursuing personal or professional goals (van Deursen and van Dijk 2014). The final stage is actual usage purposes – such as the use of digital technology for information and news, to further education and careers, for social communication and entertainment, and shopping and commerce (van Dijk 2012, 203). Across all stages, van Dijk and collaborators identify consistent inequalities between users rich in material and mental resources and comparatively poorer users (van Dijk and van Deursen 2014). This illustrates the challenges in ameliorating differential gains from digital technology across resource-rich and resource-poor groups in society.

Although the debate about digital divides has somewhat abated in public, evidence points to this being a persistent problem going well beyond physical access and skill provision. Changing the motivations of users is probably a much harder task than addressing either access or skills. Moreover, current technological development is bound to introduce new areas where divisions in access can come to matter with regard to participatory opportunities. For example, with the rise of data-driven campaigning, concerns have been raised with regard to the political representation of groups not represented in the databases used by politicians and campaigns in defining their target universes (Barocas 2012; Hersh 2015). Similar arguments can be made with regard to the use of public comments on digital media for assessing public opinion or reactions to policy initiatives given the well-known biases in the composition of users actively commenting on politics online. Perhaps even more disturbingly, data-driven decision-making in public policy or governmental action has been shown to risk reinforcing existing social inequalities as documented in data instead of ameliorating them (Eubanks 2018). These are only two examples of political and social practices increasingly relying on the use of digital technology that are part of a larger trend in society, politics, and business. Given these trends, systematic differential gains through digital technology along the lines of existing resource inequalities are a highly relevant concern, making research into determinants of digital divides in differing levels of access to digital technology highly relevant even when the opportunities for physical or material access can be accepted as a given (Barocas and Selbst 2016).

4.5 Misreading the Effects of Digital Media

Admittedly, our discussion of the effects of digital media on individuals and society has remained somewhat aloof. One could easily walk away from this chapter thinking of these concerns as just another case of academics discussing the finer points of angels dancing on needle points. This would be a mistake. In fact, it is crucially important for anyone trying to understand the role of digital media in contemporary politics to be very clear about which effects to expect from digital media and which claims to disregard. Getting this wrong risks not only investing in the wrong tools and campaign practices, it also risks weakening trust in democracy in general. An illustrative story of misreading the boundedness of the effects of digital media is the public scandal surrounding the role of the British consultancy Cambridge Analytica in the 2016 presidential campaign of Donald Trump.

The Setup

In March 2018, the journalist Carole Cadwalladr broke a sensational story that would lead to considerable controversy around Facebook and its perceived abuse of its users' privacy. The story culminated in a reported initial stock price loss approaching 80 billion dollars for Facebook (La Monica 2018) and two days of congressional hearings with Facebook CEO Mark Zuckerberg testifying before the US Senate and the House of Representatives. Cadwalladr reported the story of Christopher Wylie, a former employee of the British consultancy firm Cambridge Analytica (Cadwalladr 2018a). The company counted among its clients Donald Trump's 2016 presidential campaign (Cadwalladr and Graham-Harrison 2018), Ted Cruz's unsuccessful bid in the 2016 Republican primaries (Mohan 2015), and groups supporting Brexit in the UK European Union membership referendum (Cadwalladr 2017, 2018b). The consultants claimed to be able to design personalized campaign messages to exploit psychological pressure points of specific Facebook users. Cambridge Analytica promised clients that by playing to users' specific hopes and fears, their ads would be highly successful in getting supporters of their candidates to turn up to vote and those of their opponents to stay home (Cadwalladr 2018a; Cadwalladr and Graham-Harrison 2018; Rosenberg, Confessore, and Cadwalladr 2018).

At the core of Cambridge Analytica's service lay two promises: first, they promised to be able to correctly identify the personality of Facebook users through their likes; second, they promised that tailoring ads to recognizable personality traits would be specifically effective in getting voters to turn out for their clients or to stay at home if they opposed them. Both promises seem highly dubious at best in light of our previous discussion of the effects of digital media and the use of digital traces to infer traits of users. And yet, Cadwalladr's story and the fear of psychological manipulation through Facebook created a backlash that can still be felt at the time of this writing more than one year after the original story broke. For our purposes, this is an interesting case as the backlash against Facebook was based largely on unexamined and – in light of prior research – implausible expectations with regard to the effects of information transmitted through digital media.

In 2014, on behalf of Cambridge Analytica, a researcher based at the University of Cambridge had built the app *thisismydigitallife* and deployed it on Facebook (Weaver 2018). The primary purpose of the app was the administration of a short questionnaire to users assessing their psychological characteristics according to the widely used big five personality model. For Cambridge Analytica, the uses of the app differed. For them, it was a data collection effort that allowed them to connect the responses from users to queries about their psychological characteristics to other data available on their Facebook profiles. According to the terms of services in place at the time that were provided to the developers by Facebook, the app would have been able to collect demographic information available on users' profiles, news feeds, timelines, posts, private messages to other users, their responses, and their lists of Facebook contacts. Subsequently, the app would also have been able to collect all information publicly available on the profiles of contacts of users who had installed the app (Hern and Cadwalladr 2018). As of now, it is unclear how many Facebook users were touched by the app and what data it actually collected. While Facebook identified in total 270,000 users (Grewal 2018) who had installed the app, the subsequent data collection appears to have touched as many as 85 million users (Schroepfer 2018).

The Sales Pitch

According to the initial coverage of the scandal, Cambridge Analytica linked the survey answers of app users to their Facebook likes. The consultants claimed that this would allow them to infer personality types of Facebook users who did not take the survey on the app simply based on their Facebook likes. They then aimed to show users ads specifically designed to appeal to their personality type (Cadwalladr 2018a; Cadwalladr and Graham-Harrison 2018; Rosenberg et al. 2018). Since then, questions have been raised with regard to the effectiveness of this model and even with regard to whether the Trump campaign actually deployed it in scale (Butcher 2017; Stahl 2017; Hersh 2018; Hindman 2018a); still, much of the international coverage took this account and the effectiveness of psychometric targeting as a given. In the colorful words of Christopher Wylie, this constituted a "psychological warfare tool" (Cadwalladr 2018a) with which Cambridge Analytica "exploited Facebook to harvest millions of profiles. And built models to . . . target their [users'] inner demons" (Cadwalladr and Graham-Harrison 2018).

Yet despite its prominence in the coverage, the claim of the actual effects of psychometric targeting remains curiously unchallenged in the reporting. Instead, most of the coverage accepts Wylie's claims of its effectiveness at face value. This echoes earlier, much more enthusiastic coverage of Cambridge Analytica that appeared to be far more interested in the sales pitch of its executive Alexander Nix than in actual evidence.

In a 2016 article titled "25 Geniuses Who Are Creating the Future of Business," the magazine *Wired* listed Cambridge Analytica's then CEO Alexander Nix while describing the firm's sales proposition:

> Nix's company, Cambridge Analytica, can provide psychological profiling to help advertisers tailor their messages to specific personality types.... Using Cambridge's data, marketers combine a key trait with generic demographic information and then craft a message that's more likely to appeal to that type. So for someone who's neurotic, the message would play to fears about a subject. Agreeable people, on the other hand, gravitate toward information about how a given product or idea will benefit society.
>
> (Wired Staff 2016)

Again, this proposition rests firmly on the supposed ability to target people with specific psychological profiles and to tailor specific messages designed to appeal to them accordingly. This proposition thus promises significantly more than traditional micro-targeting models and practices using demographic characteristics, consumer data, and documented interests to identify recipients for communicative interventions. Nix claims to have a deeper knowledge about voters and to be able to communicate more effectively with them based on these insights. This would transform not just political communication but all of marketing and turn advertisers from "Mad Men to Math Men" (Butcher 2017).

In the breaking coverage of the Cambridge Analytica scandal of early 2018, the company's sales proposition was taken as a given. In fact, it was given more column inches, television hours, and eyeballs than Nix and associates could have hoped for in their wildest dreams. Both the original Observer and New York Times coverage simply repeated the claims of Nix and his former employee Christopher Wylie with regard to the effectiveness of psychometric targeting (Cadwalladr 2018a; Cadwalladr and Graham-Harrison 2018; Rosenberg et al. 2018). All investigative attention was focused on exposing how Facebook allowed a third-party developer to unethically share Facebook user data with Cambridge Analytica. In all likelihood, this element of the story alone would not have moved the needle much with regard to public attention. After all, Facebook's cavalier approach to its users' data privacy has been much discussed in the past without much discernible impact on its user numbers or its stock price. Thus all actors concerned – journalists exposing the story, informants hawking the story, and Cambridge Analytica owning the business model – share a common interest in psychometric targeting being a decisive tool in communication. Without it, the story deflates from a major sensation into just one episode among many where user data on a social media platform was misapprehended. A story, to be sure, but hardly as juicy as one on psychological manipulation and electoral fraud.

In fact, critical coverage of the scandal raised serious doubts about the veracity of the claims of Cambridge Analytica, its past performance with former clients, and the general fitness of psychometric targeting in politics. In fact, reporting by Kroll (2018) shows that both the Cruz and Trump campaigns appear to have been surprised by Cambridge Analytica's inability to satisfactorily fulfill such basic tasks as getting a campaign website up and running or to handle TV ad buys. Accordingly, both campaigns claim to have sidelined the company quickly. Nix himself is reported to have said that "marketing materials aren't given under oath" (Kroll 2018). Moreover, coverage and commentary focusing on the efficiency of psychometric targeting in politics cumulatively raise severe doubts as to its efficiency (Karpf 2017; Kavanagh 2018; Kroll 2018; Martínez 2018b; Resnick 2018; Simon 2018; Trump 2018) or even its actual deployment during the Trump campaign (Butcher 2017; Stahl 2017; Hindman 2018a). Yet these perspectives found recognition only at the fringes of the episode's coverage. The majority of the coverage with the greatest reach simply accepted the claims of Nix and associates, however implausible, and ran with the sensationalist take on how Facebook had allowed millions of its users to be psychologically manipulated against their will. But how plausible is this claim?

The Elusive Promises and Dangers of Psychometric Targeting

Assessing the potential impact of psychometric targeting through Cambridge Analytica rests on two questions: Is it possible to reliably identify a person's psychological characteristics through Facebook likes? And do psychological traits correspond reliably with political attitudes or behavior?

The big five scale ranks people on their accordance with five important personality traits: openness, conscientiousness, extraversion, agreeableness, and neuroticism (OCEAN for short) (Digman 1990). Various researchers have shown the possibility of using Facebook data to infer users' psychological characteristics on the big five personality scale (Azucar, Marengo, and Settanni 2018). While interesting in principle, this correspondence is limited, which renders any inference of personality characteristics based on Facebook likes error-prone. This raises the question of how precisely Cambridge Analytica was able to categorize people correctly according to their big five characteristics even if they had comprehensive access to current Facebook data of a significant part of the American electorate.

Furthermore, it is also far from clear that big five personality traits reliably correspond with politically relevant attitudes or behavior across contexts (Cawvey et al. 2017). So, even if Cambridge Analytica had been able to correctly identify the personality traits of a significant share of the US electorate, it is unclear that they would have been able to use this knowledge to influence people more effectively to turn up to or abstain from the vote than through the use of standardized campaign ads.

In addition, Cambridge Analytica has a well-documented history of overstating their capabilities and misrepresenting their methods. For example, Andy Kroll reports that in 2015 the Ted Cruz campaign sidelined Cambridge Analytica after the firm was unable to deliver on its promises (Kroll 2018). In another example, Brad Parscale, the Trump campaign's digital director, stated publicly that the use of Cambridge Analytica's models was widely exaggerated (Stahl 2017). In 2017, the New York Times ran a story reporting the skepticism among campaign professionals in the United States regarding the validity of Cambridge Analytica's professed methods and the veracity of the company overall (Confessore and Hakim 2017).

In combination, this raises serious doubts with regard to the viability of the psychometric targeting as a "psychological warfare tool" (Cadwalladr 2018a) (Hersh 2018). The truth might be a good deal more mundane. Based on an e-mail exchange with the developer of the original app, Matthew Hindman provided an alternative account of how Cambridge Analytica might have used Facebook's data. Instead of using Facebook likes to identify personality traits and to target ads accordingly, Cambridge Analytica might have simply proceeded based on the idea that people who are alike in some ways – such as sharing the same Facebook likes – might also be alike in others – such as supporting a specific candidate (Hindman 2018a). This would prove to be useful for a campaign in targeting its ad buys; similar approaches are routinely used in online marketing. Yet this approach is far from "reading voters' minds" (Rosenberg et al. 2018) with the help of all-knowing data wizards or the playing on Facebook users' psychology and "inner demons" (Cadwalladr 2018a) to manipulate them to act against their better impulses.

Of course, this is not to say that Donald Trump's campaign did not profit from its Facebook use. A variety of evidence gives the impression that the Trump campaign used Facebook very effectively to position ads (Frier 2018). It even took up Facebook on its offer to all campaigns to embed members of Facebook's ad team for better service delivery (Kreiss and McGregor 2018).

So, Trump used Facebook to reach people and Cambridge Analytica seems to have aided in that through potentially unethically obtained data. Whether or not this effort was decisive for Trump to win can only be guessed at. What seems pretty certain, though, is that the sensational hook in the Cambridge Analytica story, the psychometric targeting and manipulation of voters, was – if it happened at all – of little effect.

Where's the Harm?

This was not the first time that academics, journalists, and pundits misjudged the uses and effects of digital technology. Arguably, the campaigns of Howard Dean (Stromer-Galley and Baker 2006; Kreiss 2011), Barack Obama (Kreiss 2012a), and Donald Trump (Baldwin-Philippi 2017) were also successful in convincing the public that their uses of digital media substantially contributed to their candidates' successes without providing conclusive empirical evidence. But the largest downsides of believing these claims were a more optimistic assessment of the democratic potential of digital technology and a slightly more positive image of these campaigns than what might have been warranted through a more critical reading. This time the dangers of mistaking performance for fact go far beyond that.

The Cambridge Analytica scandal brought forward a colorful cast of "Bond villains" (Booth and Adam 2018), "math men" (Butcher 2017), and whistle blowers (Cadwalladr 2018a) who marched through Western media publicly celebrating their brilliance while at the same time raising doubts about the soundness of democratic elections. A widely perceived threat to democracy through psychometric targeting based on Facebook data is thus serving the interests of Cambridge Analytica, its employees current and former, and journalists alike while at the same time risking undermining public trust in elections and the quality of the democratic process in Western societies.

Getting the kind and strengths of the effects of digital media on politics wrong risks damaging public trust in democracy and electoral due process. The Cambridge Analytica episode illustrates this clearly. If the effects of digital media are limited and short-lived, as most of the literature seems to suggest, any fears of psychometric targeting allowing rogue actors to manipulate people into behaving against their own interests are overblown. If, in light of this and no convincing evidence to the contrary, we still repeat the narrative of how digital media allow shady figures to use our digital traces to manipulate us against our will, we risk increasing distrust in society and spread doubts about the soundness of electoral procedures. In this case our ill-founded warnings of digital media's imagined effects become the enemy of democracy, not digital media.

4.6 Coming to Terms with Limited and Contingent Effects of Digital Media

Getting it right in what to expect from the effects of digital media clearly matters. The collective findings discussed here should give pause to overly optimistic expectations with regard to digital technology transforming politics. Digital technology is used by resource-rich people for political information and participation. In this, we can expect digital media to facilitate information acquisition and participation. Yet an expected extension of the population of politically interested individuals through an activation of people not already motivated to engage in politics seems unlikely. Overall, there still appears to be a digital divide in the uses of digital technology, with resource-rich individuals being able to further their goals and standing while resource-poor individuals appear to use digital technology less productively and therefore benefit less. With regard to political influence and representation, this raises the question of whether digital technology further increases inequalities in society instead of ameliorating them.

Still, we should be careful not to underestimate the role of digital media in contemporary politics based on these findings. As shown in the previous chapters, digital technology is a pervasive element in politics. This is evident, for example, in changing practices of political actors and the changing economy of political information production. These changes are very real and obviously impact how electoral campaigns are run and the dynamics of public discourse. Yet we should be careful not to overestimate the associated effects on participating individuals. For example, even if people are exposed to disinformation, it is far from clear that this has persuasive effects. Instead, disinformation can serve in reinforcing existing attitudes or as signals demonstrating group membership. Although maybe not as impressive as persuasive effects, these are politically meaningful consequences of digital technology and play an important role in the development and expression of political partisanship.

Assessing the role of digital technology in politics thus means a constant balancing act between the two risks of overestimating directly measurable effects on individuals and society and underestimating the more pervasive but harder to measure changes in practices and structures governing political life. This challenge will reappear in Chapter 5, in which we will focus on the role of digital technology for the coordination of politics and collective action.

5

Digital Media and Collective Action

Ever since the protest cycle of 2010 and 2011, which included events such as the Arab Spring in North Africa and the Middle East, Occupy Wall Street in the United States, and anti-austerity movements in Spain and Greece, the question of whether digital media are transformative tools that facilitate collective action has been a major theme in the public imagination (Freelon, McIlwain, and Clark 2016). Although the potential of computer-mediated communication for social and political activism has been one of the central topics in the digital politics literature almost from the very beginning (see Margolis and Resnick 2000), with early milestones in the Zapatista movement in 1994 or the Seattle protests against the World Trade Organization (WTO) in 1999 (Kahn and Kellner 2004; Van Laer and Van Aelst 2010), it was in the 2010s, after the popularization of social media, that the public started to think of the internet as another tool in the political repertoire of social movements and not as just a novelty item.

Anderson et al. (2018) have documented that as many as 67 percent of Americans believe that social networking sites are important for "creating sustained movements for social change" and for accomplishing political goals. It thus seems as if we are collectively willing to believe that digital communication technologies played a significant role in the challenges to the authoritarian political regimes that we witnessed in Libya, Egypt, and Tunisia and that the social media-fueled demonstrations of Zuccotti Park, Puerta del Sol, and Syntagma Square are a blueprint for a new way in which democracies can articulate demands from below (Castells 2012). However, even if it has become commonplace to say that digital media did matter in all those events, we are still left with the question "how exactly did they matter?" (Aday et al. 2012, 4).

To better understand the mechanisms through which digital tools affect the way we organize ourselves to attain collective political goals, we will study in this chapter how digital media – and social media in particular – shape the decisions of the actors involved in mass protests and demonstrations: activists, participants, and governments. In doing so we will see how activists use digital tools to activate grievances and to manage the operational aspects of protests, how governments can counteract challenges on the internet, and how different affordances of digital media affect the motivation of potential participants to join the protest. We believe that the strategic interaction that unravels between these different political actors is part of the reason why a deceptively simple question such as whether digital media make it easier for individuals to organize collective action is unlikely to be answered with an unambiguous "yes" or "no."

Although this chapter is structured along the various roles that digital tools play for different political actors, there is a deeper discussion to keep in mind. Protests and demonstrations voice the concerns and grievances of those who feel underserved by the formal political process. Regardless of whether they are spontaneous or planned, successful or ineffective, protests and demonstrations embody in the streets what was not or could not be achieved through more standard methods of institutional representation. What do digital media mean for the overall strategy of activists? Are digital tools just another gadget in the toolbox of social and political movements or do they change the way in which citizens can present and articulate their demands (Gurri 2018)? One possibility is that, as we discussed in Chapter 3, digital media offer more bang for the buck – activists, through digital technologies, can reach more people at lower cost and more efficiently than they would otherwise. Another more enticing possibility is that digital tools render the old calculus of participation in collective action (see Section 5.1) obsolete. As Earl and Kimport (2011) point out we have to contemplate the possibility that digital media, rather than just "supersizing" traditional forms of organization and collaboration, could be transforming the constraints, incentives, and information that shape individual participation in politics. This debate on whether the changes that we are witnessing represent a matter of degree or a fundamental qualitative change in the dynamics of collective action underlies the discussion in this chapter.

A note about scope is important here. Collective action problems in the political domain are not limited to protests and demonstrations. As we will see in the next section, we could include under this banner events as diverse prima facie as petitions, distributed denial-of-service (DDoS) attacks, donations, boycotts, or even trolling. The fact that we restrict our attention here to expressions of discontent in the streets should not be taken as an indication that the only way to measure the impact of online coordination is by using an offline benchmark (Earl 2014). It is true that collective action problems around protests and demonstrations have been the object of special scrutiny in the literature, but our motivation to focus on them is not only their historical and academic relevance. Because of their offline component, protests raise the cost of participation relative to other modes of dissent that are native to digital spaces, making them a more reliable signal of the strength of social and political movements in the eyes of governments (Fearon 2011; Little, Tucker, and LaGatta 2015) and thus potentially more effective. The offline aspect of protests and demonstrations also makes them a better test ground to compare how activists and participants nowadays, equipped with digital tools, struggle with the classical collective action problems that have been common in the organization of mass movements, while still illustrating general lessons that can be applied more widely to other modes of political participation that share some of the same structural characteristics.

5.1 Two Types of Collective Dilemmas

Before jumping into the specifics, let's take a step back and think about what political protests have in common with other modes of mass political participation like the ones already mentioned, such as donations, petitions, or boycotts. If we look at them from a distance, we will be able to start appreciating the contours of the different ways in which technological innovations in digital communications can have an effect on events that seem unrelated.

The most obvious similarity is that, even if on the surface they require participants to undertake different types of actions (joining a protest, signing a request, giving money to a cause, abstaining from buying certain products), they are all examples of situations in which their success depends on a group of people jointly doing the *same thing*. In other words, they exemplify situations in which accomplishing a goal requires the willful and purposeful participation of a group of people.

This type of problem merits our attention because harmonizing "private desires" with "political actions" is not always an insignificant task (Laver 1997). Precisely for this reason, it is a class of problems that is linked to very fundamental questions about the relation between citizens and the government. As Hardin succinctly puts it, the government's authority "depends on coordination at the level of government and on lack of coordination at the level of any potential popular opposition" (Hardin 1995, 30). Our goal in this chapter is to elaborate on this general observation in the context of the transformations induced by digital media. To accomplish that, we will first draw a distinction between two different concepts that will point to different roles for information when it comes to building collective action. We will refer to them, borrowing from the jargon of the applied game theory literature (see, for instance, Chong 1991) as problems of *coordination* and problems of *cooperation*.

Consider the tactical challenges of organizing protests. Imagine for a moment that we are dissatisfied with a law that has just been passed, or that we want to express our frustration with the way things are going in our country. We know that there are others who want to take their discontent to the streets – we read it in the newspapers, we talk to our acquaintances, we just see it around us. It goes without saying that the more people join the protest, the more successful we will be in conveying our disapproval. One person protesting in the street is unlikely to draw more than derision from bystanders, but a few million may very well make the government reconsider and change course. But where and when to go? And what will we be doing there? Our demonstration needs many of us to show up at the same time, in the same place, and be willing to do the same thing. All we need is someone who can "choreograph" (Gerbaudo 2012) our efforts and ensure that everybody receives the necessary details about the plans for the protest. It does not sound like an unsurmountable problem based on what we discussed in Chapter 3 but it still needs to be addressed.

Think now about organizing the same protest under an authoritarian regime. We still want to express our unhappiness with the government but now we have to be cognizant of the very real possibility that we will face violent repression. As before, we will be better off if the protest succeeds: The protest may not topple the dictator, but perhaps it can pressure the regime into making some concessions. In our previous thought experiment we took for granted that people would participate, but now we need to reason more carefully about this problem. On the one hand, staying home if everybody else participates will make very little difference to the success of the protest – one fewer person will not have a noticeable effect on our collective capacity to bring political change. On the other hand, showing up can result in physical harm if the regime decides to unleash the military against protesters. One only needs to remember the Tlatelolco massacre of 1968 in Mexico, the Tiananmen Square protests of 1989 in China, or the repression of the protests around the 2009 election in Iran. It is not far-fetched to imagine that, faced with that decision, someone will prefer not to demonstrate hoping that everyone else does. If enough people make the same assessment, the protest will fail even if everybody would have benefited from its success.[1]

---

[1] Some recent empirical literature validates this argument. Cantoni et al. (2019) find direct evidence through surveys that people behave strategically and consider the success of the protest to assess whether to participate or not.

The two scenarios that we just described oversimplify the individual problem, and we will nuance them in the following pages, but they point to different roles for information and, in consequence, for communication technologies in the context of collective action (see Little 2016; Ananyev, Zudenkova, and Petrova 2017; Barbera and Jackson 2018). In the first case, the problem was one of sharing information to ensure the *coordination* of the actions of a group of people. We were dealing with a scenario in which we only needed to broadcast information across all the potential participants to obtain a favorable outcome. If that is the challenge that we are facing, collective action could immediately benefit from a decrease in the marginal cost of communication that makes transmitting information cheaper and faster. We have already seen this theme in previous chapters: It is where digital media shine.

The second scenario was different. The challenge there was to get around the individual incentives to free-ride and refrain from *cooperating* with the collective task. Providing people with information about the event, in the same way we did before, would not help. The problem was not that individuals did not know what to do, but rather that they would rather not do it. Digital tools are useful in this case only to the extent that they provide a way for groups to adjust how individuals perceive the net value of their participation or feel compelled to participate transcending self-centered strategic calculations.

The overarching point is that it seems natural to think that the affordances of digital media that tackle problems of the first kind will be different from those that affect the organization of protests in the second case and that, as a consequence, the value of the new toolkit for activists and participants will depend on the more general context in which the protest takes place. In the next section we will elaborate on this idea, and discuss how each of these two types of problems manifest in the case of protests and the way in which digital media help activists address them.

5.2 The Organization of Protests

Protests as a Coordination Problem

The Madrid bombings of 2004 occurred three days before a contentious parliamentary election. Controversy over the government's portrayal of the events emerged in the very first hours after the attack. A large-scale attack against civilians by the domestic terrorist organization ETA would have vindicated the government's policy of not entering into peace talks and probably garnered the incumbent additional support at the polls. If, however,

Al-Qaeda was behind the bombings, voters could have instead blamed the government for the very unpopular decision the previous year to participate in the invasion of Iraq. For two days, with election day closing in, the government spokesperson insisted that ETA was the main suspect. Then, on the eve of election day, a campaign originated on the internet and spread quickly through text messages. The messages called for a silent gathering in front of the headquarters of the Partido Popular to protest what was perceived as an electorally motivated narrative of the attacks. The texts famously ended with the request to "share it" (*"Pásalo"*) – to keep spreading the word among one's contacts. Reports indicate that network traffic across carriers increased between 20 and 40 percent relative to an average Sunday in March and around 4,000 people showed up at the protests (Delclós 2004).

It is immaterial to us whether these demonstrations were the ultimate cause of the ensuing defeat of the incumbent (see Lago and Montero 2006; Montalvo 2011). The events of the night of March 13 illustrate the role of communication technologies in the quick organization of mass mobilization. In only a few hours, activists managed to stage a protest that reached thousands of people. Using a technology as rudimentary as the SMS (short message service), activists raised awareness about the event and communicated the details about where and when to go by relying on the crowd to spread the message without any further instructions beyond telling others. It goes without saying how much harder it would have been to catalyze the outrage of the participants and cast it into a political action without an asynchronous texting system that demanded virtually no effort from recipients to keep distributing the messages. This notion of reach built on mobile technologies that require low-cost actions to amplify a message through a peer-to-peer network is precisely what is behind the debate about how digital technologies can help ease *coordination* problems.

Successful as they were in spreading the word in Madrid, SMS can exclusively distribute read-only short texts among recipients' lists of contacts, which means they can only navigate the network of phone users locally, step by step, from contact to contact, and only if the recipient takes a deliberate action of forwarding it. From that point of view, modern social networking sites (e.g., Facebook, VKontakte, Sina Weibo, Twitter), messaging and video-conferencing applications (e.g., Signal, Slack, WhatsApp, Skype), and collaboration tools (e.g., Google Docs, Wiki sites), to mention a few examples in an increasingly rich landscape, and the widespread adoption of smartphones have dramatically boosted both the reach and the usefulness of digital tools. Now activists and participants alike can stream video, share pictures, post messages for others to read, or team up to work on documents in real time and with an audience that is bounded only by their internet connection. Now, as Zucker-man (2007) colorfully expresses it, it is possible to disseminate a wider range of messages, from "cute cat pictures" to tactical information in reaction to a police charge during a mass protest, at any time, from any place, and with virtually no delay.

Broadcasting to a large audience scales up the potential for coordination. Survey evidence from participants in protests, in both democracies and autoc-racies – where information is not readily available outside closely monitored traditional media – shows that people often learn about the organization of events through digital media. For instance, Tufekci and Wilson (2012) esti-mate that 23 percent of the participants in the protests in Tahrir Square in Egypt in 2011 first heard about the demonstration through social media, a number that grows to 49 percent for the case of the Indignados movement in Spain (Anduiza, Cristancho, and Sabucedo 2014) and to a whopping 84 percent in the Euromaidan protests in Ukraine in 2013 (Onuch 2014). The variation in numbers reflects the diversity of contexts across three examples with different levels of internet penetration and at different points in time, but they capture the overall significance of horizontal communication networks in the diffusion of information.

The contribution of digital media may be better understood if we put it in historical context. Being a member of the opposition under an authoritarian regime is always a costly process. The challenge is phenomenal when it comes to communicating or spreading information to others who are not connected to the network of members of a social movement organization. Acquiring a printing press, circulating pamphlets, or putting up posters may carry enor-mous personal risks of being arrested, imprisoned, or even tortured. Of course, activists and participants alike in authoritarian countries are still exposed to retaliation and repression, but digital tools expand how supporters can collab-orate in the diffusion of antiregime information without even being physically present in the country. From this point of view, "there is a strong common-sense case that these new media mattered in the Arab uprisings" (Aday et al. 2012, 3).

The value of coordination can also be appreciated in modes of political participation such as political consumerism that, unlike protests, do not require such a costly offline component. We sometimes bring our political preferences to the marketplace and ground our decision of whether or not to purchase a good or service on our support or disagreement with the political stand of a given brand hoping to perhaps effect a change in its actions through its balance sheet. The effectiveness of a consumerist action is then tied to the number of people who join us and either buy or boycott a certain product or company, which then makes social media a natural tool to scale the organization, management, and staging of consumerism as a tactic (Wolf 2013). In fact, we have seen high-profile consumerist actions in recent years that originated on the internet. Think for instance about the boycotts against BP after the Gulf of Mexico spill of 2010 (Wolf 2013), against the ride-sharing application Uber after it was perceived to be profiting from the protests around the travel ban issued by the Trump administration in 2017 (Fraustino and Kennedy 2018), or the pressure on the brands advertising on the *Ingraham Angle* after the host ridiculed one of the Stoneman Douglas High School shooting survivors on Twitter (Victor 2018). A similar logic applies to the DDoS attacks that target a website with a flooding amount of requests to render it unusable (Sauter 2014), which became the staple tactic of Anonymous, perhaps most famous because of its attack against the Church of Scientology in 2008, or those against corporations like PayPal, MasterCard, Visa, or Amazon in retaliation for their collaboration with the US government after the release of US diplomatic cables on WikiLeaks (Beyer 2014; Coleman 2014; Sauter 2014).

Offline protests, however, introduce a layer of complexity to the problem of managing a crowd that does not appear in the case of purely online actions. Unlike instructing people "where and when to go," which is a challenge bounded only by the reach of the communication tools, telling them "what to do" carries all the complications that come with dealing with the clumsiness of the physical world. Participants need to receive instructions at the beginning of the protest but these instructions often need to be amended over the course of the event to react to changing circumstances. It is in this context that Gerbaudo (2012) argues that digital tools offer activists new methods to manage crowds that allow for the development of the "equivalent of military Command, Control and Communication" (Gerbaudo 2012, 128) that provides a coordination mechanism and a "minute-by-minute coverage of the events" (Gerbaudo 2012, 128), including the possibility of giving people "specific directions or suggestions on what to do" (Gerbaudo 2012, 128) at every moment. Such a tool is particularly useful to counteract public security forces by giving activists a bird's eye view of the events in the street that can be used to react to the strategic movements of police units (O'Rourke 2011; Earl et al. 2013). In other words, social media tools like Twitter serve as a noiseless bullhorn with which to steer the multitude once it is congregated in a physical, public space.

By allowing horizontal conversations in real time, digital tools also assist in the management of the logistical complexity of mass protests (Lotan et al. 2011; Anduiza et al. 2014; Jungherr and Jürgens 2014b), in a way that is not different from the role that social networks have played in reaction to emergencies (Hughes and Palen 2009). For instance, Jost et al. (2018) document the Facebook page helpgettomaidan, which organized carpools to travel to Maidan Square in Kiev during the demonstrations in Ukraine in 2013, and Tufekci (2017, 53) describes how the @TahrirSupplies Twitter handle was used in Egypt in 2011 and how "within a day, ... four young people were coordinating almost all supplies for ten field hospitals. To keep in touch with doctors on the ground, they also used Skype and other messaging apps. To keep track of supplies, they used publicly viewable Google documents and spreadsheets embedded on the website they hastily put up."

In sum, digital tools help activists guide the collective behavior of crowds at different stages, convening, shepherding, or soliciting collaboration from the participants as needed. These deceptively simple functions increase the reach but also the effectiveness of the event itself by making the audience capable of reacting to contingencies. But reach is not enough. Indeed, "the most infuriated and risk-acceptant citizen will not be able to participate in an anti-government demonstration if he or she does not know a demonstration event is actually taking place" (Breuer, Landman, and Farquhar 2014, 769). But what is true for the most risk-acceptant citizen may not hold for others who may need a nudge beyond telling them that an event is about to take place. We turn to this question now.

Recruitment and Mobilization

Zine El Abidine Ben Ali assumed the presidency of Tunisia in 1987 and, although he started his rule with a brief spell of timid political reforms, quickly established a de facto one-party regime that helped him stay in power for almost a quarter of a century. The tide turned when, in 2011, a small-scale street vendor, Mouhamed Bouazizi, set himself on fire after being harassed by the police for not having funds with which to bribe them. Protests erupted and spread throughout the country, escalating into a process that forced Ben Ali to flee the country three weeks later (Castells 2012). The events that unfolded in Egypt less than a month later resemble what happened in Tunisia although with a different timeline. Khaled Said, a 28-year-old from Alexandria, was picked up by the police and beaten to death in the street on June 6, 2010. A Facebook memorial page ("We are all Khaled Said") created by Wael Ghonim, a Google executive in Dubai, became a focal point for expressions of outrage over the incident and helped start a period of protests that began on January 25, 2011 and resulted in the resignation of Hosni Mubarak, the latest in a chain of civilian-clothed military rulers that had presided over the country since 1952 (Castells 2012; Herrera 2014).

In both Egypt and Tunisia the wave of protests resulted in the end of the dictator, but not necessarily in the end of the dictatorship. The echoes of these major disruptions reached Libya, Yemen, Syria, and Bahrain, although with different outcomes (Castells 2012), and had only relatively minor consequences in Morocco, Kuwait, Algeria, and Jordan. What needs explaining in all these cases is that in the span of a few months and after many years of successful authoritarian rule, we witnessed a political process that had seemed unfeasible until then. Digital media figure preeminently in narratives of the events (see, for instance, Gustin 2011; Preston 2011). However, it seems fruitless to try to explain what unfolded in 2010 and 2011 exclusively through the way in which digital tools assisted in the coordination of protests.

According to the *civic voluntarism model* (Verba, Schlozman, and Brady 1995), a common framework in political science, people participate in politics when they have a latent motivation that is aligned with the goals of what they are being asked to do, when they have the resources to participate, and, last but not least, when they are recruited to take part. If we take this view, digital tools help activists turn predisposed spectators with enough resources into participants, while engaging unpersuaded audiences that still have not formed a positive attitude towards the protests. Thus, activists are able to use a digital repertoire to, for instance, raise the visibility of a certain topic (Penney and Dadas 2014) with the goal of building "moral shocks" among the audience (Jasper 1998). In doing so, activists strategically manipulate the frame that is used by potential participants to understand the context in which the protest takes place (Snow et al. 1986; Benford 1993), guiding the audience into a particular diagnosis and interpretation of the problem and towards a potential solution that identifies the responsible for the situation that afflicts them (Snow and Benford 1988). Digital media thus help create the "attitudinal support" (Lee, Chen, and Chan 2017) that is necessary for a politicized collective identity (Simon and Klandermans 2001). In this way, in addition to allowing activists to reach out and ask others to participate (Enjolras, Steen-Johnsen, and Wollebæk 2012), digital media offer them the possibility to structure the political debate (Howard and Hussain 2011), exposing ordinary people to messages from the opposition and raising awareness of existing injustices and grievances (Breuer et al. 2014; Lee et al. 2017). As Gurri (2018) suggests, digital media as a result weaken the authority of the political elites by constantly putting their version of events into question.

For instance, the "We are all Khaled Said" Facebook page that we mentioned above is often credited as a central hub in the organization of the mass demonstrations that eventually toppled Mubarak in Egypt (Castells 2012;

Gerbaudo 2012; Herrera 2014; Alaimo 2015; Carty 2015). The site served as a rallying point in the mobilization efforts around the mass protests of January 25, 2011 in Cairo (Gerbaudo 2012) and involved participants who were typically not engaged with politics before, like the unemployed or the disaffected urban youth (Lim 2012). Similarly, Howard et al. (2011, 3) have argued that in Tunisia in 2011, "conversations about liberty, democracy, and revolution on blogs and on Twitter often immediately preceded mass protests." Moreover, Onuch (2015) documents, in a series of interviews with activists from the Euromaidan protests in Ukraine in 2013, how they transitioned from a "blind reliance" on Twitter and Facebook as a way to broadcast organizational content to induce cooperation and switched to an emphasis on mobilization strategies through the creation of discussion pages on which potential participants could be activated. This last observation thus points to the possibility that different channels and platforms are more suited to facilitate different tactics (Theocharis et al. 2014) depending on whether activists want to mobilize, facilitate the conversation with traditional media and social movement organizations or, as we saw in the previous pages, set the protest in motion.

This argument that social media facilitates mobilization is consistent with a number of studies at the individual level that show that use of platforms such as Facebook, Twitter, and blogs was a significant predictor of the likelihood of participating in protests (Tufekci and Wilson 2012; Boulianne 2015; Skoric et al. 2015), with perhaps some exceptions in authoritarian countries (Hassanpour 2014). For instance, Anduiza et al. (2014) find that participants in the Indignados protests in Madrid were younger and less likely to have formal memberships in traditional social and political organizations, which can be interpreted as evidence of being mobilized through the internet and outside the more traditional mobilization channels.

The civic voluntarism model not only recognizes the importance of the predisposition of potential participants and their recruitment by activists, it is also sensitive to the effect of the socioeconomic characteristics of individuals such as income level, educational achievement or even political and social skills in explaining who participates in politics. It is almost a truism that one's individual-level resources affect one's ability to engage in politics and, accordingly, the model recognizes that being available to participate and being capable of participating are conceptually different. In doing so, the model adds a new layer that is useful to explain who is mobilized. For instance, Aday et al. (2012) noticed that Twitter may have been more useful as a source of information for foreigners than for national activists, who shared and discussed more on Facebook (Gerbaudo 2012; Tufekci 2017), partly due to the different affordances of the two platforms that we discussed above and partly due to the marked class bias in the usage of Twitter in Egypt (Gerbaudo 2012). This type of observation is important because it brings to the table the question of who can be reached through different channels and speaks to the limits of mobilization on the internet. While social media caught the attention of analysts and academics alike, several scholars (for instance, Arafa and Armstrong 2016, McGarty et al. 2014 or Herrera 2014) have emphasized the impact of traditional media such as the Qatar-based Al-Jazeera TV network to "create and open an Arab public sphere by making live debate, talk shows, and news programs featuring interviews with exiled Arab opposition leaders and debates on touchy subjects a norm in Arab satellite TV" (Arafa and Armstrong 2016, 86) owing to its much wider reach than that of the internet (Miladi 2011).

This note of caution regarding the potential for the misattribution of effects of digital media on protests relative to other factors illustrates a more general lesson. As Boulianne (2015) points out, most of the results that are available for studying the effect of digital media on mobilization are driven by observational studies with very little capacity to control for unmeasured factors that simultaneously affect participation and internet use. In other words, given that access to the internet is entangled with socioeconomic characteristics that affect the probability of participating in politics (namely, resources like income or education), it is very difficult to identify the unique and independent contribution of the internet to engagement in politics. The exact same argument at the individual level can be exported to the effect of digital media on protests at the aggregate level. Focusing on cases in which protesters using digital tools were able to succeed in their political goals might lead us to exaggerate the role of technology in protests. It is unclear, based on the available evidence, whether digital media were as decisive as proponents and participants claim. In-depth studies on the origins and dynamics of particular movements and protests, like the Arab Spring, give us a rich view of mechanisms in play and a narrative of the process, but they are not sufficient to clarify whether digital tools played a causal role in mobilization. What we want to do is assess, from an empirical perspective, what would have happened had these protests not used digital media (i.e., would they have succeeded regardless?) or, more importantly, what happens in all the other situations in which people have access to the digital toolkit but a protest never occurs. In other words, the observational evidence that we have at the individual and the collective level, while suggestive, is still far from conclusive.

Nevertheless, throughout this section we have seen that, as a tool for horizontal and decentralized communication, digital media are useful in the organization of protests in two different ways. First, they serve as a coordination tool. In this case, it is the mere act of broadcasting the information about the protests that fosters the ability of social movement organizations to break out of the constraints to mobilization that prevail in the offline world. Second, they serve as a mobilization and recruitment tool. Digital media make it easier for activists to challenge the narrative of the government and therefore help *persuade* people to join the protest. Of course, neither of these two developments have gone unnoticed by those on the other side of protests: the government.

5.3 Counteracting Protests

The Strategic Problem for Governments

The image we painted in the previous section is one in which digital technologies make it easier for political and social entrepreneurs to assemble protests and demonstrations, which in turn should result in an increase in political contestation around the world. Based on what we discussed, it seems that even if we were skeptical about the way in which reducing the cost of communication would produce an increase in the number of protests, it would be hard to deny that digital media at best improve and at worst do not hinder the ability of activists to challenge the government. However, we should not be too quick to draw that conclusion.

Governments do not passively watch events unfold. Confronted with opposition in the streets, governments can take actions to minimize the damage. Dictatorships are a particularly interesting case. Dictators are less constrained in their reaction to protests than democratic leaders, but they are also more vulnerable to challenges from the street. For a democratic government, a demonstration signals unpopularity and may transform into poor electoral performance when election day comes. For a dictator, on the other hand, having people in the streets can indicate weakness and trigger a challenge to his authority (like a coup) that, more often than not, results in the death of the dictator (Escribà-Folch 2013).[2] The potentially fatal outcome that awaits dictators does not necessarily mean that the only option available to them is to swiftly repress any sign of discontent in the streets. However, small protests can escalate into larger, more dangerous ones, and thus it makes sense for governments to take steps to prevent, if possible, the expression of discontent in the public space.

---

[2] Dictators are virtually always men (Goemans, Gleditsch, and Chiozza 2009).

The coup attempt in Turkey in 2016 is a good example of how digital tools are not naturally biased in favor of political challengers and can instead serve the goals of incumbents. Rebel units from the Air Force attempted to depose Recep Tayyip Erdoğan on July 15. Following a time-proven tactic (Luttwak 1968), they attempted to take over the party headquarters and the main government buildings, and also tried to block the communication between Erdoğan and his supporters by occupying radio and television stations. Erdoğan was out of Ankara when the assault started. This circumstance was very favorable to the coup leaders; isolated outside the geographical center of power, he was supposed to be incapable of halting the events that were unfolding in the capital. However, a factor that would have been fatal not long ago was easily circumvented in 2016. Using a videotelephony tool (Facetime), Erdoğan was able to broadcast a message to CNN denouncing the military plotters. His image on TV helped him reassert his authority and provided the focal point that his supporters needed and pushed an uncertain state of affairs in his favor.

It is hard to ignore the irony of Erdoğan's government being saved by the tools that he had blamed for the organization of civil resistance in Gezi Park in 2013 (Healy 2016). More importantly, the example of the coup of 2016 shows how technology opens new possibilities for governments. It is possible to argue that due to their privileged access to the infrastructure that sustains digital communications, incumbents are in a particularly powerful position from which to counteract challenges.

If digital tools truly facilitate the mobilization of the opposition, autocrats can, for instance, hit the kill switch on the internet. Howard and Hussain (2011) document more than 220 network outages between 1995 and 2011 across authoritarian regimes, and the advocacy group Access Now shows that the number of internet shutdowns went from 75 in 2016 to 188 in 2018, mainly in Asia and Africa (Access Now 2019). Shutdowns are often explained by those who trigger them as for the purposes of public safety or the protection of the public from the spread of disinformation (Access Now 2019). However, it is not a stretch to think that the real goal often is different. As we saw in the previous section, blacking out the country reduces the ability of those in the streets to coordinate their actions and also curtails the spread of counter-narratives about the government (Zhuo, Wellman, and Yu 2011). Undoubtedly, these strategies are available to democracies and autocracies alike (for instance, della Porta and Reiter 1998; Noakes and Gillham 2007). Democracies can also deprive citizens of access to the internet during, for instance, periods of unrest to prevent the spread of riots (Somaiya 2011). United by a goal of securing public order, democratic governments and autocrats alike can then try to take forceful steps to return protesters to an offline age.

Yet autocracies offer a case with more delineated contours to study how governments can counteract challengers because their reaction can be much blunter. Dictators can go beyond trying to deter protests and take more aggressive steps. Assisted by informational darkness, they can unleash repression against the opposition if the latter cannot rely on the shielding gaze of international audiences (Gohdes 2015). However, restricting internet access has drawbacks. For one, activists can use alternative, if less effective, methods to broadcast information through mesh networks to communicate while in the streets (Bland 2014; Toor 2014). Furthermore, shutting down the internet raises the concern of the international community as it can reasonably infer an escalation in domestic repression (Howard and Hussain 2011; Gohdes 2015). Finally, Hassanpour (2014) argues that the strategy can backfire and actually bring even more people into the streets.

But the most important reason not to use network shutdown as a blanket strategy is that it only serves as a short-term patch when the protest is already in place. If a government needs to shut down the internet, it is probably too late. It is then not surprising that governments, and autocracies in particular,[3] have resorted to more sophisticated and targeted methods of engagement with digital media (Sanovich, Stukal, and Tucker 2018).

Controlling the Internet

Autocrats can engage in more refined methods of information management to help them *prevent* as opposed to *react* to protests. By its very nature, computer-mediated communication can make interactions (who talks to whom about what) more visible to central authorities. Governments can plug themselves into the communication network and use instruments that go beyond a simple on–off switch to shut down all traffic. With a networked population in place, they can more subtly interfere with the distribution of information online (Roberts 2018).

The method that we most commonly associate with autocracies is censorship. For instance, it is common to point out that Google purges from its Chinese site "search results of any Web sites disapproved of by the Chinese government, including Web sites promoting Falun Gong, a government-banned spiritual movement; sites promoting free speech in China; or any mention of the 1989 Tiananmen Square massacre" (White 2018). Restricting the distribution of content that can spark the creation of a shared anti-government frame among

---

[3] See Meserve and Pemstein (2018) for a discussion of similar strategies in democracies.

the public is certainly effective. But one needs to be careful in how censorship is used. Full censorship is hardly an optimal idea (Cairns and Plantan 2016). It is very costly to implement at scale and, more importantly, it can backfire. Curtailing the dissemination of some obviously subversive messages can open the door to more elaborated, more difficult-to-detect expressions of dissent or even to increased attention to the censored material. For instance, both Nabi (2014) and Hobbs and Roberts (2018) discuss several instances in which censorship in Pakistan, Turkey, and China produced a "Streisand Effect" in which, once it is known that the government is trying to hide some information, the public pays more attention to it, such as when the Turkish government blocked access to SoundCloud to stop the distribution of recordings that implicated the Prime Minister in a corruption case only to produce a surge in searches about the scandal on Twitter. Similarly, Hobbs and Roberts (2018) argue that knowing censorship is a possibility can induce users to acquire technical skills that can be useful to evade it and that they would otherwise not bother to learn, potentially making it harder for the government to catch up.

As a result, autocrats have an incentive to take a more fine-grained approach. For instance, Qiang (2011) and Hassid (2012) document that, in the case of China, messages criticizing officials are permitted while the encouragement of protests against the regime is prohibited. They confirm that criticism of the government in online forums and in social media is commonplace and even encouraged as a release valve for the opposition, as it also serves central authorities to, for instance, monitor the behavior and performance of officials from lower levels of government. At the same time, the same tools and the same topics are used to block chatter about anti-regime demonstrations that are deemed more dangerous to political stability. This kind of reasoning draws a very thin line between criticisms that are *harmful* to the government and those that are *innocuous* or even *helpful*. The distinction is sometimes difficult to navigate for users, and Roberts (2015) discusses whether the broad guidelines of what constitutes an inappropriate message can lead to self-censorship if the user is uncertain about whether a message will be suppressed or not.

Rather than blocking content, governments can take a more sophisticated approach and actively engage in the platform and use it to surveil and harass the opposition (Kovic et al. 2018). Governments can initiate campaigns themselves or through networks of supporters to uncover and intimidate opposition activists and participants in protests through the cooperation of distributed crowds, sometimes using bot farms that target dissenters to silence opposing voices. For instance, Burns and Eltham (2009) discuss how the Islamic Revolutionary Guard Corps in Iran used Twitter to target Iranian pro-democracy activists during the protests of 2009. Similarly, the Syrian Electronic Army manifested its support for the regime at the beginning of the Syrian civil war by using Facebook to recruit supporters to help in their targeting of accounts of government critics (Gunitsky 2015), which can in some cases take the form of the release of the personal information of activists, including their address or contact information (Tufekci 2017).

Finally, governments can engage in "regime activism" (Greitens 2013) through disinformation campaigns that manipulate the perception of the level of regime support. Regime activism can take a variety of forms. For instance, coordinated astroturfing campaigns can try to boost the official narrative of the government while at the same time misrepresenting the level of public support for the regime. Governments can also drown the voices of the opposition with irrelevant information to disrupt any attempt to use social media for coordination or initiate disinformation campaigns to counteract the narrative of dissenters.

We find numerous instances of these strategies in the literature. King, Pan, and Roberts (2017) estimate that the Chinese government fabricates 448 million social media comments a year to distract the public and strategically alter the subject of the public conversation online. By doing so, the government can engage in disinformation by saturating the debate, changing the topic when issues that are problematic for the regime become salient, or by "general pro-regime cheerleading so that the protesters' narrative appears to be only one of several possible readings of current events" (Munger et al. 2018, 2). Similar strategies were adopted, for instance, in Bahrain, where the government is said to have attempted to flood different social media sites with pro-regime messages in order to avoid the formation of a unified narrative by the opposition (King et al. 2017), and in Russia during the protests of 2011 and 2012 (Spaiser et al. 2017).

The previous discussion leaves us with a situation in which the effect of communication technologies on the ability of the opposition to present an effective challenge to governments is necessarily ambiguous. On the one hand, the opposition benefits from a communication tool that simplifies the process of broadcasting information to large groups of people. They can recruit, mobilize, and coordinate protests more effectively because digital tools give them unfettered access to the public. They can push messages to their audiences to shape the political debate and to call their attention to events and interpretations. On the other hand, the government can simply imitate those strategies with more resources, better access to the communication infrastructure, and a centralized (faster, more efficient) decision-making process. With governments adapting and catching up to the innovations adopted by activists and protesters, the inherent and unconditional advantage that analysts saw in digital media for challengers seems, if anything, short-lived.

5.4 The Social Side of Individual Decisions

The Cooperation Problem

In the first half of this chapter we discussed how digital media can help alleviate the coordination problems that pervade protests. However, when we think about mobilization, we think of it as a nudge to participate, as the "being asked" from the civic voluntarism model and responding to this call is a decision that, at the very least, involves an evaluation of the potential costs that may come with joining a protest (being physically harmed, repressed by the government, harassed, monitored, and a long list of personal and social effects). In other words knowing that the goal is a noble cause or that by the mere acting of participating we are contributing to its success may not be sufficient for any of us to take it to the streets.

A threat of physical harm is the norm for protest participants in authoritarian regimes. Breuer et al. (2014) fielded a survey among participants in the protests in Tunisia in 2011 and showed that 81.9 percent of respondents felt that by participating they were exposing themselves to "injury, arrest, or other forms of repression." Unless we dismiss their answers as self-serving attempts to boost the moral significance of their contribution, we need to address why people take decisions so at odds with their own personal interest. One could argue that there is no puzzle that needs to be explained. Not all participation in collective action involves the same level of personal cost that is associated with, for instance, the Civil Rights Movement (Sitkoff 1981), and certainly most conventional modes of political participation in modern societies do not involve more than minimal inconveniences. Joining a peaceful protest, signing a petition, going to vote, or donating money all involve sacrifices that can be measured in money, time, or even emotional weariness, but they are, for all intents and purposes, minuscule relative to the examples we have been discussing. Yet, small as they are, they can be sufficient to deter some people from participating.

The argument we are making here is not simply about the resources that are needed to overcome the costs of participation at the organizational and individual level (McCarthy and Zald 1977; Verba et al. 1995). Instead, what we argued in the previous pages is that, while resources do play a role, it is helpful to see them embedded in a larger strategic decision problem. Framing the individual decision to participate or not in a collective action (to *cooperate* in the sense we have used it here) from the point of the individual's perception of their own marginal contribution relative to their own personal costs gives us a way to reason about the effect of information and, consequently, about the way in which communication technologies shape what individuals finally do.

What needs to be addressed, as Mancur Olson states in *The Logic of Collective Action*, is that "unless the number of individuals in a group is small, or unless there is coercion or some other special device to make individuals act in their common interest, *rational, self-interested individuals will not act to achieve their common or group interests*" (Olson 1965, 2, emphasis in the original). In the remainder of the chapter we will deal with this apparent paradox and the different ways in which participation can be shaped so that individuals can get past their temptation to free-ride and the concern that their individual contribution will not have a meaningful impact (Willer 2009). Specifically, we will discuss the ways in which computer-mediated communication can affect an individual's motivation to join a protest.[4] In the following pages we will focus on mechanisms that start from the observation that individuals do not make decisions in isolation from each other and that something about that social component and the immediacy that is common in digital media shapes how individuals and organizations connect with each other, offering a way out of the collective action paradox.

Identity and Social Capital

Onuch (2015), based on her interviews of Euromaidan participants, discusses how some activists felt that Facebook was a risky choice for mobilization. While it is true that Facebook engaged people and gave them more options to participate, it also became clear that some people would feel they belonged to the Euromaidan collective without ever leaving their homes – without taking part in the actual protests. This observation poses an intriguing challenge. Digital tools can effectively help build a sense of identification with a movement, which may be so strong that some people may perceive participation online as a substitute for participation in the streets. What this observation brings front and center is that it is possible that what drives people to participate in protests or in other collective actions is connected to the fact that they *identify* with those who are participating.

The literature on social movements recognized early on the importance of social identity, shared interests, and social norms as tools to build and foster

---

[4] To be sure, our goal is not to argue whether the Olsonian model of collective action is an accurate description of reality. Instead, we see it as a powerful framework to think about the way in which social strategic interactions affect individual decisions in the context of participation in collective action. For a more careful discussion, we suggest Medina (2013), who offers a synthesis of different formal approaches to the collective action problem. The interested reader can also consult Rooij, Green, and Gerber (2009) or Chaudhuri (2011) for a review of the evidence about the tendency of individuals to cooperate above what is predicted in classical treatments of the collective action problem.

participation and collaboration in movements (see Polletta and Jasper 2001; Carty 2015; Jost et al. 2018). Identity, and specifically building a shared identity through a movement, has been argued as one of the most fundamental modes of bridging the grievances of the participants. Participants in collective action share a politicized collective identity (Tindall 2004; Klandermans et al. 2014), and it stands to reason that participants who identify with a collective are more likely to take part in events and actions by the collective than those who do not (Reicher 1984; Klandermans et al. 2014; Wilhoit and Kisselburgh 2015). As a result, the burden for the literature on digital media has been to show the extent to which the lack of synchronicity and colocation interfere in the capacity to create a shared link or identity among participants (Kavada 2015).

The early literature on digital media tended to downplay the importance of collective identity in online contexts (see Priante et al. 2018). The anonymity and pseudo-anonymity that characterize online interactions were pointed to as one of the reasons why social media could not help with the consolidation of a common identity (Gamie 2013). The bursts of protest activity and the lack of a long temporal horizon that is implied in the case of collective actions without organizations (see Chapter 6) means they run the risk of relying on short-term identifications that are cross-pressured in competing events (Rohlinger and Bunnage 2017). More recently, however, the literature has shown that online tools can help develop social and community ties (Priante et al. 2018). For instance, Gerbaudo (2012) has argued for the relevance of the "We are the 99%" Tumblr in building an identity for the participants of the Occupy movement and goes so far as to suggest that Occupy Wall Street's inability to build initial momentum was due to the fact that organizers adopted messaging strategies that focused on coordination instead of mobilization and did not try to create an emotional connection – contrary to the success of the Khaled Said memorial Facebook page in Egypt. However, as we have seen, if the identification is too strong, users will not feel compelled to take any additional steps, especially if it involves an offline component (Schumann and Klein 2015).

A "sense of belonging" is also a key component to the concept of social capital, which is the underlying theme of the discussion of whether digital media can facilitate the creation of social trust. Associational activity, as illustrated by Putnam's evocative title *Bowling Alone: The Collapse and Revival of American Community* (Putnam 2000), is expected to build trust, reciprocity, and cooperation among members. These relations are forged in any group or organization and can be seen as an alternative method to gain cooperation for collective action (Putnam 1993; Uslander 2002; Hooghe

2007). As a result, social capital researchers have focused on the relation between socializing and prosocial attitudes and behavior (Putnam 1993, 2000; Sampson, Raudenbush, and Earls 1997) and on the effects of internet use on these variables. Results point to a positive (Ellison, Steinfield, and Lampe 2007; Gil de Zúñiga, Jung, and Valenzuela 2012) if weak (Valenzuela, Park, and Kee 2009; Hooghe and Oser 2015) relationship between online activity and trust or socializing. Yet this relationship has not been causally established and it is very plausible that it is driven by the fact that people with high social capital are also the ones more likely to use the internet and digital technologies.

The same can be said about a group of studies that look at the characteristics of social connections between people. In this body of literature, social capital can be interpreted as the "resources that can be accessed or mobilized through ties in the network" (Lin 2008, 51) and shifts the attention from individual attitudes and behaviors to the effect of the structural position of people in a network of relations. Overall, while empirical studies across time and contexts tend to show an association between use of the internet and social networking platforms and various operationalizations of different types of social capital (Ellison et al. 2007; Brandtzæg 2012; Sajuria et al. 2015; Quinn 2016) the relationships that are identified are, as we saw previously, more safely interpreted as correlations and not as causal.

Social Effects and Networks

Not all sources of information have the same effect on us. Suggestions, recommendations, and advice weigh differently in our minds depending on whether they were shared by a friend or a stranger (see, for instance, Bond et al. 2012; Messing and Westwood 2014). It thus seems natural to expect that, when it comes to being mobilized for a demonstration or a protest, it matters who asks us to join (Huckfeldt and Sprague 1995; Passy 2003) and, conversely, that our own effectiveness and reach as we try to mobilize others depends on our relation with them (McAdam 1986; Opp and Gern 1993). Indeed, social connections play a role in overcoming the challenges of mobilization and recruitment through two different channels. On the one hand, our own response to a call for action will be mediated by the identity of those with whom we interact. On the other hand, how successful we are in spreading a call for action (and, consequently, the reach of recruitment and mobilization efforts) will depend on the structure of the network in which we are embedded. The two mechanisms are neither fully independent nor the only ones in play, as we will see, but they enrich the benchmark model of collective action by adding a background of social relations to the way individuals make decisions.

The intuition that there is a connection between the strength of the relations we have and how information spreads in our network was captured early on by Granovetter (1973) in his distinction between *strong* versus *weak* ties. The concepts emphasize the difference between people with whom we have a close connection (our friends) and those with whom we only interact occasionally (our acquaintances). Strong ties, as McAdam and Paulsen (1993) argue using the case of the Freedom Summer, have the higher level of influence that is needed to impact people's willingness to join social movements. The early literature on computer-mediated communication was rightly concerned about the possibility that digital media would be skewed in favor of the creation of weak ties between participants (Donath and boyd 2004), which would limit the possibility of mobilization using, for instance, social media (Gladwell 2010). The criticism was that while social media could spread the word about a protest, it was a tool that was limited in its ability to push people to take actions that required a level of commitment beyond, say, liking or sharing a post on Facebook or Twitter. If only strong ties are able to create interactions that lead to interpersonal trust, the argument goes, the impact of digital tools is necessarily limited. It is in this context that the concept of *slacktivism* or *clicktivism* (see Halupka 2014) was born, as a term that encapsulates how digital media favor the creation of a mass of passive participants who only "like" and "retweet" content but do not contribute to the actual results of collective action (Morozov 2011).

Nevertheless, weak ties do have value. As Granovetter (1973) shows, weak ties are superior to strong ones for the diffusion of information. His argument is based on the idea that connections across strong ties show more redundancies than those that happen through weak ties: The friends of my friends are oftentimes my friends, but the same type of relation does not hold for the case of acquaintances. As a result, acquaintances *bridge* the gap between disparate groups of friends, making it possible for information to move quickly through a network. Weak ties thus make it possible for distant people to hear about events such as protests (Kavanaugh et al. 2005) even if they are not connected to the activist elite. Using this argument, Steinert-Threlkeld (2017, 379), for instance, argues that the organization of protests is "not driven by the people who had tried for years to organize them" but instead owes much to those who, through their casual conversations about their participation, helped spread the word. Along the same lines, González-Bailón and Wang (2016) show how a minority of users bridged structural holes in the communication network of the Indignados movement, which facilitated the flow of information from cluster to cluster. These results, and similar ones (Bastos, Raimundo, and Travitzki 2013; Bastos and Mercea 2016), give non-central users a critical role in the diffusion of protest information, sometimes by merely sharing protest hashtags.

Looking at things from this perspective, even if it were true that digital media facilitate the creation of weak ties, we should not be too quick to dismiss the positive impact of slacktivism. As Barberá et al. (2015, 6) put it, "[p]eripheral users are less active on a per capita basis, but their power lies in their numbers: their aggregate contribution to the spread of protest messages is comparable in magnitude to that of core participants." As a consequence, we have a reason to rethink small acts of participation as part of a broader repertoire of new types of organizing (Karpf 2010b) instead of shrugging them off as substitutes for other modes of participation (Vaccari et al. 2015). In other words, it is more fruitful to see these actions through the lens of how they can contribute to the overall goal of the collective task as opposed to treating them as low-cost, low-effectiveness equivalents to offline activities.

However, it is important to keep in mind that the diffusion of information and the diffusion of behavior may be driven by different mechanisms. Ensuring the adoption of a behavior, like joining a protest, sometimes requires reinforcement (Centola and Macy 2007; Centola 2010). As we saw in the first half of this chapter, it is not sufficient to know that an event is taking place; it may require more than one person prompting us in order for us to get involved. For instance, González-Bailón et al. (2011) show that recruitment to the Indignados movement had high levels of redundancy and that the success is better accounted for by the fact that individuals were exposed to information from different sources. The mechanism is, of course, not unique to digital media (McAdam 1986; Opp and Gern 1993) and is consistent with the idea of "complex diffusion" (Centola and Macy 2007; Centola 2010).

There is, then, an argument to be made about how strong ties may be better for social coordination while weak ties are superior for information sharing (Chwe 2013). This specialization of functions maps well onto different tools in the digital environment, and Valenzuela, Arriagada, and Scherman (2012) have studied how different platforms induce different types of networks, which in turn may create different types of ties. In their argument, Facebook is more suitable for the creation of strong ties while Twitter, by its very nature, seems a better environment for the creation of weak links. In consequence, one could expect that the type of connections forged on Facebook may facilitate participation in costly, time-consuming actions like demonstrations.

At the same time, then, Twitter could be more useful for spreading information on the coordination of events, framing, or messaging. In this way, digital tools expand the repertoire of activists with tools that can be tuned to different needs, and they can jump from one to another depending on their goal throughout the organization process.

Getting Information about Others

A distinct affordance of digital tools is that they give us a way of observing not only what others intend to do – what they *say* they will do – but also what their actual behavior turns out to be. We see pictures of people attending protests in real time in our social media feed, we see the number of people who have donated so far to a given cause on a crowdfunding site, and we even see our friends flaunting online badges to let us know they have voted. With this information at hand, facilitated by how digital tools allow us to peek well beyond our immediate physical environment, we can reevaluate the impact of our contribution to a collective action. We evaluate our contribution differently being the first person who signs a petition or who donates the first dollar in a fundraiser compared to being the person whose contribution makes the cause meet its goal (Hale, Margetts, and Yasseri 2013; Hale et al. 2018), and similarly we look at the value of our participation differently if we can gauge the potential success of a demonstration through pictures on Twitter or Instagram (Breuer et al. 2014).

The number of people who have voted, participated, signed, or donated affects our own propensity to do the same. We could then argue that each of us is endowed with a different *participation threshold* (Granovetter 1978; Macy 1991), which measures how many people need to have donated before we do so ourselves, or how many need to join a protest before we do the same. From this perspective, we could then consider that some people, the *activists*, are happy to join early on, when there are still very few indications that the action will be successful. They would, in this view, have low participation thresholds. Others, however, have higher thresholds and need to see more people joining in order to join themselves. The core idea is that our decision to collaborate is guided by our evaluation of the social support for a given action.

The argument shows the value of social information (Margetts et al. 2015) as a way of facilitating cooperation in collective action. Digital media enable *observability*, which can reduce the need for selective incentives, as in the standard Olsonian model, which is another way of saying that collective action becomes more a process of contagion rather than one of designing an incentive scheme (González-Bailón and Wang 2016). An interesting consequence of this concept is that if participation in a protest is driven by individuals deciding when to join the "revolutionary bandwagon" (Kuran 1995), protests in particular become the result of small individual acts by potential protesters that do not depend on a strategy of recruitment. "Small, intrinsically insignificant event[s]" (Kuran 1995, 1533) can then start an unpredictable reaction as more people are encouraged to join depending only how many others have joined already.

5.5 Digital Media as a Strategic Tool

Protests are the most visible part of a complex organization process. Setting a protest in motion oftentimes requires more than an activist casually announcing it on the internet. From the moment the idea is conceived to the moment people return home after voicing their discontent, different organizational challenges need to be addressed. In this chapter, we have framed these challenges as informational problems in which communication tools and technologies play distinct roles and explored how the affordances of digital media change the strategies of activists, governments, and participants. Through an increased reach, digital media facilitate the marshaling of demonstrations by broadcasting information that helps participants assemble and react to changes in the environment of protest. In addition, although perhaps more questionable in the magnitude of its impact, digital tools embed activists and the public into a communication network in which political discussion takes place, fueling the activation of grievances and transforming onlookers into participants.

These *direct* effects are complemented by *indirect* effects that indicate that digital media not only change what the broadcasters can do, they also overhaul how the information is presented to the recipients. Digital tools place participants into a common infrastructure that can shape the formation of identity ties that further boost individual involvement in the event. Moreover, the very digital nature of the new platforms makes it possible to uncover information about who else is participating, which is useful in the decision to join. If we look back at the situations in which information, in and of itself, was not sufficient to ensure cooperation with a protest, we would then see how these social dimensions are crucial to give final, gentle nudges to potential participants who otherwise would be reluctant to leave their homes. In other words, the digital nature of new media, the way data and measurement are embedded in them, and even how information traverses the network of connections between participants bring about a social dimension of information that further contributes to the potential success of protests.

But this digital layer also poses a natural paradox. As a tool for organizers, we could argue that demonstrations have become more efficient. Many more new actors can arise amid the clamor of voices and trigger political actions that can spread defiantly through the public. In a sense, the organization of counter-politics is democratized. However, digital media facilitate this process by projecting all social interactions onto a single choke point – the technological infrastructure – over which governments have the upper hand. In fact, this might offer governments the most successful way ever to shut down collective action. Governments can use brute force methods, such as shutting down the internet, or they can limit conversation by either suffocating or flooding conversation with counternarratives and disinformation. Indeed, because communications and participation become *data*, they can access personal information and direct repression toward the opposition. The ease with which adversarial political entrepreneurs can join the political debate not only paves the way towards a more open society but also exposes it to hostile attacks.

6

Changing Organizations

Organizations are a fixture in democratic politics. Parties, business groups, advocacy groups, unions, and lobbies represent groups of people who share a common interest and who join forces to exert influence in the political process (Abrahamsson 1993). Pluralists see organizations as a natural component of liberal politics and they welcome them in a political arena that they perceive should provide opportunities for decentralized and balanced competition among organized interests (Dahl 1956). Others are less positive in their assessment and are concerned with the fact that inequality lies at the very heart of organizations. First of all, they tend to represent those who already have a disproportionate presence in politics to begin with. Second, organizations, more often than not, engender internal differentials of power between the leaders and the rank-and-file members (Michels 1915). These two layers of external and internal inequality thus shift representation from ordinary citizens to political elites, thus inspiring distrust in organizations as vehicles for political participation on both the political left and right (Abrahamsson 1993).

Regardless of how we evaluate them, organizations do exist and people collectively voice their interests and preferences in political systems through them. Yet organizations come with a decision dilemma for participants. Take, for example, labor unions. By bundling under a common voice the interests that are common to all members, unions strengthen the bargaining power of workers at the negotiation table with their employers (see Card 1996; Wallerstein 1999) and can push a labor-friendly agenda by supporting sympathetic parties and candidates (see Taylor 1993; Kitschelt 1999). Thus unions balance the scales between labor and capital by closing the gap of power in the political arena (Korpi 1983). But doing so represents a trade-off for each individual member (see Klandermans 1984). Presenting a common, unified position

158

means that the individual heterogeneity of preferences of its members needs to be smoothed out across the organization. Disagreements about strategy and goals are bound to arise as the ultimate position of any political organization has to reflect a collective goal that may not be in the specific interest of any of its members in particular. In addition, participating in a union demands a level of commitment and support (paying dues, participating in strikes, attending meetings, or joining other activities) that also carries opportunity costs, since participating in the union can exhaust the availability of members to collaborate with other organizations that represent them in other dimensions of their social and political life. Given this divergence between manifest costs and uncertain results that often requires activists to offer their support even when they do not fully endorse the leadership (May 1973; Kitschelt 1989) it is no wonder that disputes over tactics can fracture organizations internally (Downey 1986; Saunders 2008).

For an increasing number of observers, digital media seem to offer a promising alternative. By lowering the costs for likeminded people to find each other and coordinate around a shared cause, digital media might render traditional organizations obsolete. In their view, digital information is seen as contributing to a new "post-bureaucratic" age of political organizing:

> This process involves chiefly private political institutions and organizations such as
> civic associations, as well as interest groups, rather than formal governmental
> institutions rooted in law or the Constitution. To the extent that the central functions
> of these private institutions involve the collection, management, or distribution
> of information under circumstances where information has been costly and
> asymmetrically distributed, the contemporary information revolution has the
> capacity to alter organizational structures. The result is a diminished role on many
> fronts for traditional organizations in politics. ... The accelerated pluralism of the
> 1990s and 2000s increasingly involves situations in which the structure of group
> politics is organized around not interests or issues, but rather events and the
> intensive flow of information surrounding them.
>
> (Bimber 2003, 21f.)

A clear example are the books *Here Comes Everybody* (2008) and *Cognitive Surplus* (2010) by Clay Shirky. The books popularized the idea that digital technologies enable spontaneous organizing without having to depend on formal organizations. One of Shirky's prominent examples is illustrative of this kind of thinking. He tells us the story of Ivanna, who lost a phone in a cab, and how it ended up in the hands of someone who declined to return it. He then tells us how a quickly assembled website that became popular on the news aggregator Digg helped not only in locating the thief, but also in her identification and eventual arrest (Shirky 2008, 1–6). The moral is clear. A person alone, relying only on digital tools that are available to anyone at low or no cost, was able to mobilize a distributed contingent of helpers, whom she did not know before, to assist her with a single, well-defined, low-burden task once it is shared among many. Critics have pointed out that Shirky's argument is largely built on examples that may not adequately represent the types of problems that characterize the challenges and functions of organizations operating in the social and political domain (Earl and Kimport 2011). Yet the "organizing without organizations" (the subtitle of Shirky [2008]) view has gained a lot of traction in the face of the large-scale mobilizations in internet-enabled protests that we encountered in Chapter 5.

At its heart, this optimistic view suggests that digital communication technologies (online forums, social media networks, or group messaging applications) afford new ways of organizing that make formal organizations, and social movement organizations in particular, no longer critical. A networked infrastructure (Benkler 2006; Castells 2012; Bennett and Segerberg 2013) facilitated by low-cost communication (Lupia and Sin 2003; Earl and Kimport 2011) is there to help us escape Olson's dilemma of collective action. Participants now have the ability "to explore new ways of gathering together and getting things done" (Shirky 2008, 22) without going through the process of joining and committing to a collective structure, making it more obvious that "the fundamental solution to the challenges of collective action is not organization, but organizing" (Bimber, Flanagin, and Stohl 2012, 4–5).

If this argument resonates well, it is because it is consistent with early appreciations of digital technology that seek to disrupt the established power structures of the "weary giants of flesh and steel" (Barlow 1996). By creating networked relationships between formerly isolated individuals who share interests and preferences, digital technology creates new spaces liberated from hierarchical structures (Rheingold 1993; Hauben and Hauben 1997; Castells 2001). Beginning with the *Whole Earth Network*, countercultural expectations of digital technology offering a better alternative to established forms of organizing social and political interests have been central to thinking about the social effects of the internet (Turner 2006). These early high hopes about a fundamental political and social transformation driven by digital changes makes it hard to determine whether "organizing without organizations" is actually an empirical statement about how digital media *have* changed politics or rather a normative stance about how digital media *should* change politics. This makes it all the more important to look closely at the available evidence.

Digital tools are central to the coordination of political voice. Individuals are enabled to fulfill tasks that in the past demanded the support of coordinating structures. But does this necessarily spell the end of formal political and social organizations? Maybe the best way of addressing this question is by taking a wider look and thinking about the needs that organizations address in politics. This will show an often neglected role of digital media in politics, namely their incorporation by established political organizations in the pursuit of their goals and the representation of their constituents. This will put into focus how the operation of organizations has changed once they have found themselves embedded in an environment that offers the possibility of *organizationless organizing* (Davidow and Malone 1992) and make us reconsider as to whether rather than politics *without* organizations, we are seeing a transition towards politics with *different* organizations (Karpf 2012b, 3).

6.1 New Ways of Organizing in Politics

Organizing without Organizations

In an article about personalized political action and mobilization, Bennett (2012) reminds us whom Time magazine chose as their "Person of the Year" in 2006. The cover prominently showed a computer with a panel that reflected back the image of the reader. The person of the year was "You." Time's technology writer Lev Grossman (2006) explained the choice as a recognition of "the small contributions of millions of people" to a new idea of the internet as a collaborative endeavor. He also emphasized that "[i]t's a story about community and collaboration on a scale never seen before … It's about the many wresting power from the few and helping one another for nothing and how that will not only change the world, but also change the way the world changes." With the protest cycle of 2010 and 2011 (see Chapter 5) in hindsight, it was difficult not to read Time's cover as an early sign of the growing significance of the internet as a tool that favored an individualized role in politics at the expense of the power of established organizations (Bennett 2012). The internet afforded motivated individuals the possibility to choose the breadth and depth of their participation in politics (Earl and Kimport 2011; Bennett and Segerberg 2013). Using the reflected image of the reader, Time was hinting at the idea that to get things done, maybe organizations were not important after all.

The key mechanism behind this transformation has been the dramatic reduction of the cost of reaching out to others (Earl and Kimport 2011). A "team of one" (Earl and Kimport 2011) is sufficient to set up a discussion page on Facebook to advocate for a given issue, coin a hashtag on Twitter to give visibility to an event, initiate a new campaign on change.org to petition for economic or political reforms, or start a funding drive at gofundme.org to collect money to support an activity. One person alone can generate content and publish it; one person alone can set up what is needed to collect resources to support a cause; one person can roll out a call to mobilize others. The concept of a single-person operation may sound extreme, but tools in a service-oriented technological environment reduce the cost and simplify the management of the logistical complications that come with contacting and mobilizing people outside the immediate environment of activists, especially now that activists can use resources that do not require them to have a previous background in politics nor a technical education (Schussman and Earl 2004).

Participation, not only organization, can also be individualized. Participants can be reached outside the context of interpersonal mobilizing networks (Wahlström and Wennerhag 2014). For instance, Earl and colleagues document that individuals increasingly learn about political consumerism actions through social media, "draw[ing] on a sense of efficacy and responsibility and employ[ing] digital media to learn about civic affairs in order to strike out entrepreneurially and to make political choices part of their everyday buying" (Earl, Copeland, and Bimber 2017, 149–150).

Smaller teams are also conducive to specialization and diversification. Earl and Kimport (2011) show how "teams of one" sometimes view their activity as unique and differentiated from what everybody else is doing. This can be read either as indicative of a lack of awareness of the environment in which these new activists operate or, if we put it in a more positive light, as a sign of the ongoing personalization and individualization on the supply side of activism, with entrepreneurs targeting similar but, in their view, differentiated aims or tactics (Earl and Kimport 2011).

However, the main virtue of digital communication tools within this framework is the democratization of reach. Bennett and Segerberg (2013) put particular emphasis on the fact that activities can be "organized by the crowd largely without central or 'lead' organizational actors" (Bennett and Segerberg 2013, 46). The new methods of mobilization "draw on a new model of power that draws its power from its quick but overwhelming force" (Earl 2014, 41). These methods seem to be particularly effective for short-lived campaigns that address a single event and a single action. This is especially the case for protests that we can now view as ephemeral coalitions triggered on demand (Bennett and Segerberg 2013). These "flash organizations" (Valentine et al. 2017), "smart mobs" (Rheingold 2007), but also "cyber mobs" (Citron 2009) reflect a lower cost in recruiting, mobilizing, and managing participants as well as an additional flexibility and adaptability that is now available to activists. In addition, the online transition simplifies the planning of offline activities. As Agarwal et al. (2014, 648) put it, "[c]rowd-enabled networks are one result of a distinctive 'logic of connective action' in which large scale individual engagement is both highly personalized and technology enabled, creating diverse paths for individuals to participate in and activate their own social networks."

Consider, for instance, the hacktivist group Anonymous (Beyer 2014; Coleman 2014). The group, described as a crowd mobilized upon request, had "no internal structure, no clear boundaries between groups, and no leadership or identifiable hierarchy" (Beyer 2014, 29). In each of their actions, sometimes with virtually no planning, Anonymous were able to deploy a distributed action in which each participant took an undifferentiated low-cost task (Sauter 2014). Deciding on "what to do and when" and spreading the message through a network of potential participants could occur almost immediately with the help of Internet Relay Chats and, more importantly, without affecting its potential success, as shown by the precipitous events around the deployment of some of their distributed denial-of-service (DDoS) attacks (Coleman 2014).

The small cost of participation with on-demand activation also means that digital media can induce a shift toward "weaker patterns of allegiance" with a different conception of membership (Margetts et al. 2015, 50). Participants are no longer expected to commit the time or the energy that comes with being an active member of a political organization. They are free to engage in causes with more flexibility than before, joining actions and collaborating with others when it is convenient for them and fitting their interest in active political participation around their daily schedules (Earl and Kimport 2011). They can also carefully choose and plan the depth and breadth of their participation, tuning in and out of collaboration according to their level of interest: They can contribute money, donate time, sign a petition, or simply send a "like" on Facebook as a public demonstration of support for a given cause (Margetts et al. 2015).

Consequently, political activity does not have to be the main goal for people to engage in it. The reduced cost of both organizing and joining an online activity facilitates the building of mobilization on the back of other activities. Participation can arise as a by-product of users' involvement in activities or structures that do not have political activism as their primary goal, like online communities structured around media sharing or fan culture (Earl and Kimport 2009; Beyer 2014; Jenkins 2015). While it is not clear why some of these non-political activities or structures take a turn toward political activism while others do not (Beyer 2014), the fact that some do illustrates how digital media offer new, less burdensome paths for political engagement and mobilization. For this reason, new modes of organizing and participation are "fluid" (Faraj, Jarvenpaa, and Majchrzak 2011) and allow for "fleeting memberships that emphasize dynamic boundaries and membership" (Faraj et al. 2011, 1235).

The customization of participation on both the supply (organizers) and the demand (participants) sides does not immediately imply that organizations are entirely displaced from their core position in organizing. Organizations can take the place of entrepreneurs and activate networked structures themselves (Bennett 2012). However, in view of these arguments, it is fair to, at the very least, revisit the reasons that have been used to claim a core role for organizations. As Earl (2014) shows, the argument that needs to be made is about whether the dynamics of political participation through episodic events precipitated by small groups of activists are sufficient or not. In turn, this becomes a discussion about which goals can be achieved by on-demand crowds without sustained participation by activists and which other goals still require coordination by political organizations. Nevertheless, it puts additional pressure on legacy organizations to make their case in front of potential members and donors about why their seemingly old-school activities and tactics are still necessary to affect results in the long run.

Decentralization and Hierarchy

The idea that digitally organized participation, because of its bit-sized, individualized, and on-demand nature, is at odds with the formal hierarchies and structures of decision-making that are common in traditional organizations has been a common theme not only in the academic literature (Bennett 2012; Castells 2012), but also in the narrative of organizations and activists themselves (Gerbaudo 2018a). As Casaleggio and Grillo, founders of Movimento 5 Stelle (M5S), bluntly stated, "[t]he concept of 'leader' is blasphemy" (quoted in Natale and Ballatore [2014, 114]). There is indeed a long and illustrious genealogy to this anti-organizational view that provides us with arguments for resisting organizations grounded on ethical and practical reasons – ethical, since organizations might pose an obstacle to individual freedom and spontaneity, which thus runs the risk of alienating supporters; and practical, since they may favor irrational decisions that are not conducive to efficient gains for members (see Abrahamsson [1993, chapter 2] for a summary of the literature). A lot is riding on this rejection of organizations and therefore much is expected from, if not outright removing them, at least displacing them from their central position in political and social life.

The implicit claim is that digital tools lead to forms of organizing that offer alternatives to Michels's famous quip that "[w]ho says organization, says oligarchy" (Michels 1915, 401). In the view of Michels (1915) or Ostrogorski (1902), the sheer dynamics of any collective enterprise push towards the development of either a formal leadership or at least some structure with the ability to steer the direction of the organization using whatever institutional tools exist within their reach. Importantly, the argument is not exclusively based on the elite's desire to accumulate power and to establish their authority within the organization. Hierarchy and inequality arise as a mechanical result of the inner logic of organizations (Michels 1915). Because large groups cannot meet, delegation becomes necessary, and with delegation there is a need for professional bureaucracies that then become central nodes that regulate the inner life, creating an autonomous logic of behavior independent of the preferences of members (Michels 1915, 25f.). Because the management of an organization requires increasing levels of technical expertise, a bureaucracy is needed to manage a complex structure and to interact with the environment of the organization (Michels 1915, 31f.). Because longer tenures are necessary to understand and operate these more complex, bureaucratic structures, leaders tend to turn professionals and encroach in their positions (Michels 1915, 34f.).

Many people hope that digital media will offer an alternative to this seemingly inescapable trend. Instead of being closed, hierarchical, and plagued by relations of subordination, digitally enabled organizations are conceptualized as open, decentralized, and egalitarian. Crowd-enabled organizing removes the need for a formal bureaucracy and, if leadership manifests at all in these environments, it takes "charismatic," "organic," or "networked" forms, usually reached by consensus (Agarwal et al. 2014). In this way, "connective action" theorists expect that personal communication technologies favor "self-motivated sharing of already internalized or personalized ideas, plans, images, and resources with networks of others" (Bennett and Segerberg 2013, 36).

The optimistic view of networked models of collaboration has been fueled by the success of peer-production projects like Wikipedia or Linux that have captured the imagination of analysts (Raymond 1999; Benkler 2011). These projects are seen as the outcome of flat, distributed structures that managed to create a high-quality product without specific direction or top-down bureaucratic control (Konieczny 2009; Shaw and Hill 2014). There are, of course, differences across contributors, but they are seen as the reflection of differences in "time, labor, and attention to existing endeavors" (Coleman 2014, 75) or the capacity to get things done (Gerbaudo 2012). Variations in the influence of individuals across the organization are then the result of some individuals being more widely connected or trusted by their peers (Lee and Chan 2015), which, if anything, may result in a meritocratic "do-ocracy" (Coleman 2014) in which the power of individuals is directly associated with their contribution to the common enterprise.

In their analysis of Twitter usage during the 2011 Egyptian revolution, Wilson and Dunn (2011) noticed a concentration of online participation in a small number of "power accounts," a pattern that was replicated also in the communications of the Indignados (González-Bailón et al. 2011) and Occupy Wall Street (González-Bailón and Wang 2016) and that the authors see as evidence of the existence of "centralized and hierarchical" networks in these movements (González-Bailón, Borge-Holthoefer, and Moreno 2013). It is noteworthy that this central position is not occupied by traditional organizations, which counts as evidence of a transformation in the management of protest mobilization and coordination (González-Bailón et al. 2013). It is suggested that what has changed is not only the identity of those with more central positions in a protest or movement (from organizations to individuals), but the very nature of their responsibilities. It has been argued, for instance, that the new leaders merely "catalyze, fuel, and sustain" actions (Boler et al. 2014, 439) but do not centralize authority. Instead they hold performative roles (Bakardjieva, Felt, and Dumitrica 2018) that help consolidate its "collective identity and symbolic presence" (Bakardjieva et al. 2018, 912).

However, we do have evidence that more traditional forms of internal inequality have arisen in some of the digitally enabled protests. In a study of the social media teams of the Indignados movement, Gerbaudo (2016) shows that the more veteran activists gained access to the main social media accounts of the protest and limited access for others over fears about infiltration and to maintain a consistent message. Similarly, Poell et al. (2015) discuss how Wael Ghonim and Abdel Rahman Mansour, as the administrators of the Facebook page "We are all Khaled Said" (see Chapter 5), effectively shaped the protests in Egypt, even if they did not seek to play a predominant role in the movement and even actively avoided doing so. Gerbaudo (2012), in fact, characterizes this new type of leadership style as "soft leadership" in which certain participants play a key role by producing a "choreography of assembly."

Of course, the fact that there are no formally recognized leaders should not push us to think that all types of leadership are absent, or that the absence of formal leadership implies equality in participation and voice. At the same time, as Leach (2005) points out, inequality of influence or visibility of some actors is not sufficient to conclude that an organization is "oligarchic." This line is crossed, however, whenever "formal or informal power is wielded by someone who has not been given that right by the group or when a person with legitimate power either exceeds the scope of that power or exercises it in a manner that has not been sanctioned by the group" (Leach 2005, 326). To put it a different way, following Freeman's (1972) discussion of "the tyranny of structurelessness," the relevant question that needs to be addressed is not so much about the existence of a hierarchy but about whether, by refusing to institute a formal process for decision-making, informal leaders of these new organizations escape accountability.

Informality in the decision-making process, which translates into the lack of a system of rules about how leaders are selected and what they can and cannot do, oftentimes means that leaders are those who are perceived as the focal point of public attention, which oftentimes corresponds to spokespeople as they are recognized by the media (Gitlin 1980). This can be the result of them actively seeking that position or the outcome of an organic process in which, for whatever characteristics they possess, they emerge as the center of attention (Tufekci 2013, 2017). While these spokespeople are usually under intense scrutiny by the movement (Tufekci 2013) and while sometimes networked structures set up methods of internal control to check the behavior of their representatives (see Bülow 2018), their accountability remains a challenge. Freeman (1972, 158) offers a short diagnosis: "[B]ecause the movement didn't put them ... the movement cannot remove them," which greatly limits their ability to control informal leaders even if they are explicitly disapproved of by other members (Gerbaudo 2014).

Informality also has consequences for the overall effectiveness of the movement. The lack of explicit rules for deliberation and decision-making can bring resolution of conflicts to an impasse in the interactions with others. Achieving goals oftentimes requires making compromises and participants may differ in their willingness to sacrifice their original goals, which is another way of saying that groups within the movement differ in their evaluation of tactical gains if they involve making concessions (see Schorske 1955). Unanimity, which is equivalent to giving each participant veto power, instead of resolving conflicts, offers motivated participants the possibility to criticize any decision "openly, publicly and around the clock" (Tufekci 2017, 79), delaying a resolution, "derailing the movement and creating unnecessary polemics" (Gerbaudo 2018a, 102). Thus, they risk creating confrontational internal climates that could increase members' turnover and also cause the organization to be perceived as unreliable by the public and negotiation partners, a pattern that has been documented in political parties originating from grassroots organizations (Kitschelt 1993).

Last but not least, informal methods of membership expose organizations to the risk of being co-opted by outsiders, as Rohlinger and Bunnage (2017) show in a qualitative study of the Florida Tea Party movement and its increasing cannibalization by the Republican Party, and as it is reflected in the decisions of new digital parties like Podemos or the MS5 to recentralize (see section Rethinking Membership) in order not to have their local structures hijacked (Gerbaudo 2018a).

There is no such a thing as an optimal organizational structure that is appropriate to all cases and situations. Some organizations of their own accord adopt informal methods of decision-making and tolerate the possibility that organic and charismatic leaders may surface because a flat structure is consistent with their stated goals (Clemens 1993). This does not mean that by doing so they avoid the problems that led to the development of formal rules and procedures for deliberation and selection of leaders in brick-and-mortar organizations. Digitally enabled organizations are no different, at least not with regard to the challenges of aggregating the input of the members and participants in collective decisions. Maybe they are different because they target actions for which decisions do not need to be made; maybe their ephemeral nature ensures that they can remain "structureless" (Freeman 1972); but if that is indeed the case, what sets these new structures apart is not the fact that communications happen on digital platforms.

Many Paths to Organizing, Many Modes of Organizations

Claiming that digitally enabled forms of organizing have come to replace traditional forms of hierarchical organization misrepresents current developments (Earl 2014). In confronting social change, either/or thinking comes naturally but risks missing gradual change. Something similar happens in the discussion about changes in political organizations enabled by or reacting to digital tools when we think about the coordination of collective action. The idea of a digital transformation is a powerful element of the story, but adaption in traditional organizations is just as important (Earl 2014). This might take the form of organizational hybrids in which established structures, practices, and goals coexist with the realization of affordances brought by new technology and a pluralism of different types of political organizations (Bimber 2003; Earl and Kimport 2011; Bimber et al. 2012; Margetts et al. 2015). This perspective foregrounds a question about the conditions under which traditional organizations are able to outperform digitally networked structures and how digitally enabled forms of organizing can be incorporated in established organizations (Earl 2014).

A recent example illustrating the options of alternative modes of organizing are the choices of the #MeToo and Time's Up movements. Although they grew in popularity around the same time, #MeToo had a previous history as a classical organization that supported survivors of sexual violence. However, in October 2017 the hashtag #MeToo became viral on Twitter after the actress Alyssa Milano used it in an attempt to make visible the prevalence of sexual assault and harassment. From that moment on, the hashtag #MeToo has been a coordination and broadcasting tool for a decentralized issue public with celebrities as visible leaders and spokespeople. While pursuing similar goals and speaking to the same issue, Time's Up took the organizational route with more clearly defined goals and an aspiration for continuity (Langone 2017). After an early phase during which the group started out with a group of high-profile celebrity supporters, in 2018 Time's Up appointed a CEO to manage full-time staff, giving permanence and professional management to such initiatives as a legal defense fund (Lockett 2017). This example goes to show that contemporary movements that follow similar goals and even speak to similar publics have options with regard to organizational choices between traditional hierarchical structures with professional staff and decentralized, digitally enabled activism.

Traditionally, the power of traditional political organizations has been measured by their ability to bring people onto the streets and to translate attention, concerns, and interests into policy initiatives. While political action online can quickly rise to impressive heights, such activities seldom translate into persistent action in the brick and mortar world of policy-making (Earl 2014). Here, traditional political organizations have remained crucial contributors to the *supply side* of protests, by consistently creating opportunities, mobilizing the resources necessary for protests to take place, and funneling momentary attention into a long-term agenda that allows the pursuit of political goals in a longer timeframe (Earl and Kimport 2011). In this sense, organizations provide continuity and permanence (Earl 2014). By enduring beyond specific campaigns and outlasting every individual member, organizations expand the time horizon over which calculations can be made. In this way, organizations facilitate intertemporal decision-making, which offers members and activists an array of options to better balance present costs and future benefits in a way that is impossible for ephemeral coalitions. In other words, organizations deal in commitments and sacrifices that their members are willing to make in exchange for removing the problems of coordination and time consistency that may arise in their involvement in the political arena (Karpf 2012b). In addition, a longer lifespan opens up the possibility of accumulating popularity, experience, legitimacy, and reputation (Karpf 2012b), which are helpful in capturing resources and facilitating the support of high-risk activism (McAdam 1986). These observations lead us to a natural point of contention: Are the benefits of continuity and risk absorption still relevant if the digital age favors episodic events that do not require continuity (Earl 2014), and are there types of risks that participants are still willing to take without the intermediation of stable support networks?

Just as not every traditional organization will be replaced by groups of networked activism, not every digitally enabled network of activists will turn into an actual organization or follow the goals of politics as usual. For one, digitally enabled groups of networked activists might fail to turn into stable organizations because either they do not have the resources (McCarthy and Zald 1977) or the opportunities (McAdam 1982; Tarrow 2011), or they are not able to build a collective identity (Gamson 1992) around which to articulate the demands of would-be participants. Or they may simply reject formal structures on principle. As we have seen, by doing so they could be affecting their internal and external effectiveness, but their response could very well be that "the choice of organizational models is not governed solely by instrumental considerations" (Clemens 1993, 770).

Going beyond the existential question of the role of traditional organizations in contemporary politics, a more nuanced endeavor asks how digital tools and digital media have changed political organizations. Have organizations become *different* from what they used to be (Karpf 2012b)? Or do the tools that facilitate the coordination and mobilization of activists also affect how members engage within traditional organizations and with the organization's leadership? Organizations continuously adapt to their environment. The way they are internally structured, how decisions are made, how members participate, how leaders are selected and held accountable, how they recruit, and even how they communicate and present themselves to the exterior world have all been touched by the tools available to organizations in pursuit of their goals and purposes. We turn to this transformation next.

6.2 How Do Organizations Adapt?

Rethinking Membership

Even if leaders are the ones we would recognize if we saw them on the street (because of their preferential place in demonstrations, their signature underneath every official statement that is circulated in internal bulletins, or their captioned pictures in the media), it is the mass of undifferentiated card-carrying members marching behind them that measure the strength of an organization and are the only reason for them to exist.

Given the discussion in the previous pages, it is not unexpected that members can fine-tune the mode and amount of participation or that digital tools affect the relation between cadres and the rank and file. But if that is the case, what we are seeing is a transformation of the meaning of *being a member* (Bimber et al. 2012). Here we explore this idea. We draw mainly from the literature on political parties, if only because the apparent decline in membership around the world since the late 1980s (Whiteley 2011; Van Biezen, Mair, and Poguntke 2012) has turned the membership problem into a particularly pressing one with potential implications for democratic politics. However, the themes that arise are more general and apply broadly across political organizations of different types.

A common reaction to the pressures of declining membership has been to "blur the distinction" (Margetts 2001) between members and their wider environment – in the case of parties, the supporters and the electorate (Duverger 1954) – by creating different types of membership structures (Bimber et al. 2012; Scarrow 2014; Gauja 2015) that reduce the burden of joining the organization, personalize the experience for those who sign up, and facilitate the connection between the organization and its supporters (Scarrow 2014). This has been implemented through a menu of membership modes that vary in their level of intensity. Alongside traditional full members, political parties in particular have included other lighter types of membership, such as becoming a "friend" or a "supporter" (Scarrow 2014). Those oftentimes grant people the possibility to participate in the life of the party in exchange for being available for contact (Gauja 2015). Supporters can then fine-tune not only the level of involvement but also the type of contribution that they want to make. They can simply pay dues or contribute money, or they can become involved passively or actively in internal discussions, receiving regular updates through mailings or social media, or contributing feedback on policies and issues (Gibson et al. 2012). Through these spaces for communication and discussion, the grass roots can voice their discontent or raise criticisms, which helps leadership take the pulse of the concerns of the rank and file (Gibson et al. 2012) as well as incorporate new ideas or language from a larger community than before (Hatakka 2016).

Some parties, especially those born with a digital orientation like Podemos in Spain, M5S in Italy, or the different local versions of the original Pirate Party of Sweden, have taken the lead in the reevaluation of who is a member and how a member participates in collective decision-making (Bennett, Segerberg, and Knüpfer 2018; Gerbaudo 2018a). With variations across them, a common pattern has been a deliberate rejection of traditional notions of membership. Podemos, for instance, created a unique affiliation category with full participation rights that does not require any membership fee, probation period, or endorsement (Gomez and Ramiro 2019). Signing up and becoming a full member with the same rights as those in leadership positions could require as little as filling out an internet application (Pérez-Nievas, Rama-Caamaño, and Fernández-Esquer 2018). A similar pattern is found in other issue organizations (Bimber et al. 2012) like MoveOn, an advocacy organization (Karpf 2012b). Members participate through petitions and similar low-cost tactics and any email recipient in their database is automatically considered a member, which in turn means that MoveOn has an unconstrained incentive to constantly expand their membership (Karpf 2012b).

In most instances, new members can participate in the internal decisions on an equal footing with everybody else through a variety of internal tools that allow the party elites to continuously poll the opinion from the rank-and-file. This extends not only to issues of internal organization of the party but also, and more importantly, to legislation and the behavior of their elected representatives (Gerbaudo 2018a). In the collection of tools that parties use, we find a good a summary of different methods that have been tested to make democracy more open, inclusive, and meaningful (see Chapter 8). We find, for instance, tools that support the application of the concept of liquid democracy (such as LiquidFeedback, used by the Pirate Parties), tools to support discussion and deliberation for consensus building (Loomio or Plaza Podemos), Wiki-like systems for crowdsourced lawmaking (as in some areas within Rousseau, the "operating system" of M5S), or custom implementations of secure internet voting (like nVotes) (Hartleb 2013; Deseriis 2017; Gerbaudo 2018a; Kioup-kiolis and Pérez 2018), all living side by side with more common services like Facebook or Meetup (Casero-Ripollés, Feenstra, and Tormey 2016). These tools support the explicit goal of moving away from traditional forms of delegation or representation (Natale and Ballatore 2014), which for instance allows M5S to state that "every autonomous decision [of an elected member] can be interpreted as a betrayal of [their] mandate" (Manucci and Amsler 2018, 113–114).

An assessment of these digital transformations paints a sober landscape that does not always match the vivid narrative of leaders and supporters. While the reduction in the cost of joining has helped expand the rolls of the parties, the profile of the members is still substantially different (in education, employment status, or interest in public affairs) from that of the overall population of voters (Gomez and Ramiro 2019), which reflects underlying biases in political participation. Even with membership costs reduced to a minimum, new tools and new methods of participation maintain a divide in political parties by creating "opportunities for members to modulate the depth and width of their participation, increasing it or decreasing it according to their interest" (Lusoli and Ward 2004). A more common criticism, however, is that the party elites subtly exploit their position to control which issues are to be considered and the framing of the different alternatives (Gerbaudo 2018a) as well as the internal promotion of the initiatives (Simon et al. 2017), which often anticipate a disconnect between inputs from below and how decisions are taken.

More generally, Scarrow (2014) notes how, in spite the fact that there is enormous variation across parties, these initiatives tend to centralize power, shifting weight from regional and local chapters to their national organization – centralization that, in the case of new grassroots parties, may also be fostered by the need to compete in an electoral arena with more hierarchical parties and offer a more coherent election campaign (Bennett et al. 2018). While sometimes an unintended byproduct, this move toward a centralized structure can be the result of a more deliberate strategy by the leadership to consolidate their position (Pérez-Nievas et al. 2018), which is consistent with the observation that intra-party democracy helps party leaders unchain themselves from intermediary elites (Mair 2002). Parties then face the dilemma of "[h]ow to share authority between the membership and the executive party leadership in a stable manner" (Bennett et al. 2018, 1671), which in some cases leads to the demobilization and disillusionment of supporters (Kitschelt 1993; Casero-Ripollés et al. 2016). To put it bluntly, the use of digital tools and the move toward more participatory opportunities for the rank and file does not necessarily mean an erosion of power for the party leadership.

Against this backdrop it is thus easier to appreciate the two trajectories that Gibson et al. (2012) identify for political organizations depending on the depth and scope of the integration of digital tools. The first one is an increasingly decentralized, grassroots-led, internally transparent organization (Bimber et al. 2012) that requires very small setup costs (including being able to dispense with a central office) (Karpf 2012b), and that follows the lines of "the cyber party" proposed by Margetts (2001). This model has been associated with "insurgent social media-fueled grassroots" parties (Chadwick and Stromer-Galley 2016) like Syriza or Podemos that were born in the aftermath of the financial crisis of 2007–2008. The second model is an "increasingly centralized and 'techno-elite'-dominated organization that would erode members' collective power to hold their leaders accountable" (Gibson et al. 2012, 32) and that uses new modes of involvement to favor the creation of a "more passive and floating support base" (Gibson et al. 2012, 32) whose opinions are assessed every now and then but who cannot enforce accountability for the party leadership (Pérez-Nievas et al. 2018).

Rethinking Finance

A changing environment with a new conception of membership also implies a transformation of the ways in which organizations can capture resources from their environment, which, it goes without saying, affects their survival. While not much research exists about what resource-collection strategies are specific to new organizational forms, we can still locate organizations in a continuous space that ranges between two poles defined by security and regularity (Pfeffer and Salancik 2003). These two concepts map to funding either through regular membership fees that create a steady flow of income or through campaign-based donations that are, by nature, more irregular. The mix between the two strategies that organizations use affects their scope and overall strategy (Pfeffer and Salancik 2003) through the decision about how to structure themselves and the type of operations that can be supported (Stone, Hager, and Griffin 2001; Chavesc, Stephens, and Galaskiewicz 2004; Hodge and Piccolo 2005).

Small donations through crowdfunding are not a new development (Davies 2014) but the subject has attracted considerable attention (Agrawal, Catalini, and Goldfarb 2014), although the literature specific to "crowdfunded projects that provide services to communities" is underdeveloped (Davies 2014). Small, sporadic donations collected through digital services fit well within the narrative of a personalization of politics that we have encountered before. They provide more discretion and accountability to stakeholders, but at the same time they require additional administrative overhead. In addition, as with any other funding campaign, they are subject to strong temporal and social effects (Roberts 2015) due to the fact that they require a large number of small contributions and are impacted by their visibility to the general public.

Online fundraising has contributed significantly to the emergence of new activist organizations. The success of incident- and issue-based mobilization and fundraising has given rise to a set of new political organizations (Karpf 2012b). While these organizations have only shallow ties to traditional groups or interest-based collective action organizations, overall they share an internationalist, technologist leftist outlook. These organizations, like change.org, offer people the opportunity to mobilize through, for instance, publicity-friendly e-petitions. While they have drawn criticism from traditional political organizations, they nonetheless illustrate the power of post-bureaucratic pluralism for collective action organizations.

The importance of small donations for new organizations has also been particularly visible in the last few years in the case of the funding of political campaigns in the United States, with the growing importance of small donations via the internet. Campaigns driven by small, less-than-affluent donors making spontaneous contributes are behind a shift towards a pattern reliant on a wider base of supporters. In the early 2000s, the presidential campaigns of John McCain (Van Natta Jr. 2000) and Howard Dean (Hindman 2005) were highly successful in collecting donations online. This allowed candidates not backed by the political establishment or the mainstream of their parties to legitimately enter presidential bids. Following their early funding success, there soon emerged a consultancy industry focusing on the development of software and fundraising techniques optimized for the US case, the pinnacle of which turned out to be the two campaigns by Barack Obama in 2008 and 2012 (Johnson 2016). Obama's campaigns were highly optimized machines for generating the highest possible amount in donations from their supporters (Kreiss 2012b, 2016). The constant raising of money through email or other online approaches became so popular with US-based campaigns that critics started to speak of a culture of treating political supporters as ATMs instead of active political participants (Karpf 2015).

While this might constitute a shift in the quality of political participation invited by campaign organizations, the opportunity to repeatedly raise funds from a list of supporters, often in reaction to political events, changes the power dynamics within political organizations. While in the past the party machine drew considerable power from controlling lists of donors or members and thereby having a monopoly on contacting them, today email lists can be built quickly by challengers from the political wings of parties. Thus, fringe candidates that in the past would have had to vie for the support of the party machine can now throw their hat into the ring and fund their bid with decentralized financial support through their list. An optimistic view of this trend is that it makes politics much more flexible and open to new voices, all the while breaking open established power structures of traditional elites. A pessimistic view would counter that this development undermines some of the binding and balancing function of party bureaucracies and could potentially lead to a hollowing out of party structures. In this view, online fundraising could lead to the rise to prominence of ever more radical fringe candidates who would be able to attract ardent supporters and corresponding funds but who would also contribute to the polarization of political partisans.

Rethinking Networks

Political organizations are not isolated agents. Instead, they are embedded in complicated assemblages of other organizations, movements, and civil society actors forming temporal alliances in pursuit of shared goals (Magleby,

Monson, and Patterson 2007; Nielsen 2012a). The growing importance of digital media and services has also impacted these relationships and introduced new actors, especially in the context of political campaigns.

During the presidential cycles of 2004, 2008, and 2012, there emerged a view among American campaigners of the centrality of technological innovation for the success of campaigns. Central to this perception were the successes of the Obama campaigns and the consistently emphasized role of technology for the campaign (Kreiss 2012a; Madrigal 2012). This has put the roles of technology companies, technology consultants, and software platforms very much at the center of public debate on the nature of contemporary political campaigns. Already in 2005 Philip N. Howard warned of the increasing power of technology consultants in campaigns (Howard 2005). During the two Obama campaigns, this critical take on the role and perceived power of technology consultants in a campaign took a backseat, with academics and pundits focusing on the perceived participatory and empowering potential of campaign technology for outsiders and underprivileged groups. Some critical voices were heard with regard to extensive data collection by campaigns and political consultancies (Kreiss 2012c), but clearly these issues were not at the forefront of public and academic debate about the role of technology in campaigns.

Following Obama and amid the contentious fight between Hillary Clinton and Bernie Sanders for the official nomination for president by the Democratic Party in 2016, debate about the power of databases, models, and the political staff running them emerged. The two nominees fought over who should be rightfully allowed to access the vast information and know-how amassed by the Obama campaign (Lederman 2016). Ever since Howard Dean's primary campaign, the Democratic Party had been at the center of a strongly interlinked network of campaign vendors, consultancies, and technological service providers founded by former campaign staffers (Kreiss and Jasinski 2016). While interesting in itself, this outsourcing of core competencies previously handled directly by the party raises important questions with regard to shifts in organizational power and sustainability of skills across election cycles (Kreiss 2016).

While it is important to reflect on the changes brought about by the growing technological opportunities, we also have to start to more critically examine the role of privately run data vendors, technology firms, and commercial online platforms in politics. This means examining their activities as lobbyists before regulatory bodies. While governments in the United States and Europe have increased their attention on the tech sector (Foroohad 2017; Lynch 2017), they are still overmatched in interest group representation and spending by the companies they are trying to regulate (Solon and Siddiqui 2017). The resulting consequences are still far from clear. This is all the more important as online platforms have been shown to be significant service providers for campaigns, especially in the United States (Kreiss and McGregor 2018). What does this close interconnection between private companies and political campaigns mean for political campaigning and representation? And how does the heavy dependency of political actors on the services of these companies translate into access and influence on regulation once they are in office? The rules on these interrelations are currently being written. They should, therefore, also be in the focus of social scientists.

6.3 New Ways of Organizing, New Ways of Running Organizations

When examining collective action organizations, we see different phenomena happening at the same time. We see the emergence of new forms of digitally enabled activism, and movements quickly rising and disappearing in reaction to specific events. We also see traditional organizations trying to adapt to a new environment by rethinking membership models, financing, and networks of allies. There is not one simple story or one pattern of how digital media impacts political organizations. Instead, there are multiple trajectories occurring simultaneously that demand a nuanced examination of the practices of "new" and "old" organizations.

The phenomena discussed here and in Chapter 5 show that new tools and technologies can muster large crowds and direct their efforts to a particular goal without the laborious and often ineffective efforts that were required not long ago. But there is a deeper question beyond the simple fact that digital tools help activists. *If* digital technologies indeed open the door to the *commoditization* of organizing, then we have to contemplate the possibility that they also undermine the foundations of traditional modes of organization. The same channels that can be used to communicate information about protests and events can be used to discuss, collaborate, or deliberate. If hierarchy were the answer to the inability of crowds to reach effective decisions due to the difficulty of scaling up decision-making, digital technologies would not only reduce the role for structured and formal organizations, they would also *inherently* offer more democratic and horizontal solutions. If true, this would shake up the foundations of the way politics is run.

However, the prognosis of politics turning into an arena without formal organizations seems more normatively motivated than empirically founded. It is easy to lose sight of the reasons that led traditional organizations to adopt formal structures. By making it easier to resolve internal conflicts, formal organizational arrangements prolong the lifespan of organizations, facilitate the capture of resources from the environment, and make interactions with the external network of political agents more effective. While it is true that we have seen the development of new forms of organizing – ranging from formal hierarchies to digitally enabled networked activism – that reflect a plurality of goals and needs, we should not forget that new organizations, even if they have arisen in an environment with new methods and tools that confer on them more flexibility than was available to their traditional counterparts, are organizations nonetheless.

On the other side of the coin, digital tools have made traditional organizations look more like internet-enabled groups. Traditional organizations have reacted to the public's demands for responsiveness by adopting strategies of participation that include more fluid and less formal modes of membership. Through digital technologies, organizations also have available new methods to capture resources and enter into new types of relations with other actors in their environment. In doing so, traditional political organizations have borrowed tactics and structures from the playbook of organizations native to the internet. So, rather than conceptualizing them in a strict dichotomy between online and offline forms of organizing, it seems more fruitful to think of them as placed along a continuum between more online- and more offline-based forms of organizing.

7

Data in Politics

Digital media and technology have created vast new datasets documenting behavior and traits of people. New analytical tools and increasing computational resources facilitate data access and analysis at low cost and with limited effort. The combination of the two has resulted in an increase in the use of data in various areas of politics and administration, building on the logic of state and organizational power, which requires, above all, making things countable. As with earlier cultural and technological developments – such as writing, the printing press, and archives (Goody 1977; Beniger 1989; Scott 1998) – digital media and technology have been used by governments to increase their ability to make more elements social life countable and, by implication, actionable. This trend follows consistent hopes in management, administration, and science that an increase in the available measurement of social life can enable managers, politicians, and scientists to identify underlying mechanisms and to intervene in order to achieve more efficient or normatively desired processes or outcomes (Porter 1996; Fourcade and Healy 2017; Mau 2019). After all, the goals of quantification have never been merely descriptive but are "part of a strategy of intervention" (Porter 1996, 42). The current hopes and fears for a societal transfiguration through digital data arise in this context.

Fears materialize in the expectation that every conceivable piece of data that *can* be collected, no matter how trivial it may seem at face value, *will* be collected. Disparate data, integrated into enormous and highly heterogeneous datasets, can be mined by actors for a wide range of purposes: lawful or unlawful, ethical or unethical, to tune a political message to the taste of some part of the electorate, to determine the performance of a candidate during a live-broadcast debate, to learn about the appeal of a recently implemented policy, to try to forecast an election, to determine if a given convict deserves parole, or to monitor a protest in real time through social media.

179

These examples show an underlying conflict. While increasing opportunities to measure and influence the behavior of people might in some cases allow for better provision of services, it does so at a cost of making subjects more "visible" (Scott 1998) to an authority. Without proper accountability, monitoring can slide into surveillance while at the same time providing rogue actors with opportunities for interference and manipulation. Campaigns can target unlikely voters and mobilize them to participate; at the same time, campaigns might use the same methods to demobilize supporters of the other side. Using data-driven procedures, the police might be able to tailor their resources to better fight crime; at the same time, data-driven policing might perpetuate discrimination by targeting subpopulations with high rates of criminality in the past.

Data-driven practices will thus look positive or negative depending on which of their dimensions we emphasize. To understand the trade-off better, we need to delve into the process of data collection. Currently, there is little public awareness of what data is collected through what means and to what ends. It remains opaque how or to what degree data is used as the basis of services or governmental action. This has to change if we want to asses meaningfully the inherent trade-off between increased opportunities for socially beneficial measurement and interventions and socially detrimental surveillance and vulnerability to potentially malicious actors.

We also face a deeper challenge: How do we do know what these data-driven processes do and what their actual effects are? Current debate tends to rely on the claims made by companies selling data-driven solutions, journalistic accounts of innovations in business and politics, and public intellectuals sharing their opinions on these perceived developments. To put it mildly, this does not make for optimal evidence. In any discussion of the role of data-driven processes in politics, we have to remain skeptical and assess critically the evidence that is available to us. Importantly, we have to distinguish between evidence of data-driven techniques being used by political actors and evidence of the effects of these techniques. As we will show, the first type of evidence is often shaky, while the second type of evidence is currently all but missing.

In this chapter we will discuss the impact of digital media and technology on the measurement of politics. We will discuss the nature of digital data, pointing to areas where it is qualitatively different from earlier measurement revolutions. We will then focus on areas in politics where data-driven procedures have had a strong impact. This will allow us to illustrate the conflicts identified previously: How do we navigate the expected efficiency benefits introduced by the collection and analysis of digital data and the dangers of ubiquitous surveillance and control? And how do we know what these techniques contribute and where we fall for claims originating in marketing departments? For a start, let us take a brief look at the history of making societies more efficient through data.

7.1 Making Social Life Countable

The idea that counting elements of social life allows for its optimization and management runs deep through modernity up to the present (Porter 1996; Scott 1998). By counting entities – be they inputs, outputs, or actions – one might gain greater knowledge about society, identify and implement best practices, and ultimately control the future.

In the eighteenth and nineteenth centuries, we find these hopes expressed in the shared attempt by states to systematically collect data on their citizens and economies (Woolf 1989; Osterhammel 2009, 57–62; Igo 2018). These historical roots can be found even in the very term "statistics," which was originally coined in German from New Latin and translates as the "science dealing with the facts of a state" (Woolf 1984, 82). Statistics was thus originally seen as a science dedicated to making government operations more efficient, especially for the goals of taxation and conscription (Behrisch 2016). In the twentieth century the idea of making social life more controllable through counting entities – metrics – found forceful expression in the Taylorist approach to "scientific management" (Taylor 1911) and its manifold aftershocks, such as Robert McNamara's attempts at quantifying progress during the Vietnam War (Halberstam 1972), metrics-based management (Wooldridge 2011), and its public sector expression in "new public management" (Pollitt and Bouckaert 2017). The impulse is of course not exclusive to those who attempt to manage states as if they were privately owned companies. Economic planners in socialist economies were also enamored with the potential of collecting and processing data to make central decision-making about what and where to produce more efficient (Medina 2011; Peters 2016). In this, both the right and the left followed an intellectual tradition that connects to the intellectual program of Norbert Wiener's *Cybernetics* and the hope for more governable social systems (Wiener 1950, 1961).

From the beginning, there was always a tension in expectations of whether digital technology would increase social control by governments and big business or strengthen the power and opportunities for expression and coordination of citizens (Turner 2006; Medina 2011; Peters 2016). Increasing the ability to measure or represent processes or events can also be used to decentralize decision-making by providing real-time information to distributed organizational units who, on the basis of this information, can form decisions independently and act accordingly. This is particularly true in the development of fully decentralized organizations based on algorithmic governance (DuPont 2017; Filippi and Wright 2018). But we can also see a reflection of this power in other areas, such as expanding the abilities of nongovernmental organizations (NGOs) (Livingston 2016), the reformation of warfare through more independent units (Arquilla and Ronfeldt 2000; McChrystal et al. 2015), or the abilities of insurgents in areas of contested statehood or challengers in established states (Arquilla and Ronfeldt 2001).

Underlying the attempt at measurement and control is the idea of regularity. If what is true today will also be true tomorrow, successfully identifying the relationship between the right combination of a set of inputs and a desired output today will allow one to reproduce this relationship at will tomorrow. This implicit belief in the constancy of historical patterns under future conditions logically leads to attempts at forecasting conditions, outcomes, and behaviors. Based on these predictions, scenarios are developed and individuals are assigned scores reflecting the estimated likelihood of their sharing specific traits, attitudes, or future behaviors. Data-driven prediction has gained a lot of attention in light of the massive increases in available data and computing power provided by digital technology (Brynjolfsson and McAfee 2016; Agrawal, Gans, and Goldfarb 2018). While these approaches seem to work fine for often repeated low-impact decisions, such as buying decisions for consumer goods online or the use of specific search terms to look for holiday destinations or used cars, the record of these approaches in even slightly more complex prediction tasks has been spotty at best (Lazer et al. 2014).

By measuring the relationship between inputs and outputs, we can hope to increase the efficiency by which outputs are produced or outcomes achieved. These elements can then be counted, put in relation to one another, and tracked over time. This allows for the optimization of processes, the evaluation of actors, the prediction of outcomes or behaviors, and the provision of actionable information to organizational units. In a very direct way, this is part of the optimization of production processes in industries (Grove 1983). Hatry (1978) captures these hopes evocatively: "Unless you are keeping score, it is difficult to know whether you are winning or losing. This applies to ball games, card games, and no less to government productivity for specific services and activities." But transporting efficiency-oriented metrics into other areas without clearly identifiable inputs and outputs, such as the provision of many public services, like education and health care, or the public sector in general is intrinsically problematic (Smith and Street 2005; Poister, Aristigueta, and Hall 2015; Muller 2018).

We find these developments also in politics. Take election campaigning. Campaign organizations increase the efficiency of their voter outreach by automatically testing if digitally deployed ads or mailings lead to the wished-for outcomes or if variations do so more effectively. They monitor the activities of campaigners, volunteers, and even elected politicians in campaigns and rank them according to their efforts or intervene if they fall behind. They assign potential voters scores on their likely partisan leaning, their persuadability, and their likelihood to turn out to vote. They also use digital technology to empower field offices and volunteers on the ground in providing them with lists of people to contact and talking points to stick to during their intervention (Kreiss 2012b, 2016; Nickerson and Rogers 2014; Stromer-Galley 2019). Data-driven practices are thus deeply ingrained in electoral politics.

Data-driven practices also allow for the scoring of individuals according to a set of traits, behaviors, or predicted outcomes. These scores then serve as the basis for standardized interventions, shaping the option space in which scored individuals find themselves (Citron and Pasquale 2014). This has long been true for credit ratings determining the conditions under which people can borrow money (Citron and Pasquale 2014). But scoring individuals has become prominent in other domains as well, such as their perceived likelihood to break the law (Brayne 2017; Ferguson 2017), the chances of convicted criminals to reoffend (Dressel and Farid 2018), the provision of social services (Eubanks 2018), the likelihood to vote for a given party (Nickerson and Rogers 2014), or in the context of the Chinese social credit system the likelihood of individuals engaging in antisocial deviant behavior (Liang et al. 2018; Ahmed 2019). Rolling out interventions at scale promises increased efficiency in service provision and less waste by focusing on individuals for whom interventions are likely to bring the expected effects. Yet rolling out interventions automatically and at scale also involves high risks of unintended consequences (Ferguson 2017; Eubanks 2018).

While these potentials and practices have been widely documented, there have also been instructive critiques of data-driven practices. For one, there are long-standing fundamental critiques doubting the possibility of measuring the relevant aspects of social processes comprehensively so as to allow for a meaningful reflection of social life (Merleau-Ponty 1945; Oakeshott 1947; Hayek 1948; Polanyi 1958). Going beyond the question of whether what matters can be measured, other authors have examined how what is measured starts to matter regardless of its correspondence with the social process in focus. Here, authors have discussed how once measures are established that ostensibly capture social processes, people start reacting to the reflection of the social world arising from this abstract representation. Over time, the representation of the world emerging from its reflection in data and measurements comes to matter more than other, less quantified representations. We should thus remain aware that the representation of the social world in data is mediated by the process of translating social phenomena into data points. Potentially important elements that prove reluctant to this translation might even be missing altogether. In a world emphasizing measurement and quantification, over time only those elements of the social world that can be expressed in data matter (Fourcade and Healy 2017). Consequently, these come to matter disproportionately. Instead of representing reality, data and measures can be seen to be reconstructing reality subject to their inherent foci and blind spots (Espeland and Sauder 2007). This forces us to identify the biases in the selection of elements of the social world that come to be represented in data. It also guides our attention to the practices of people working with data and measures and their interpretative approaches in contextualizing these abstract reflections of reality.

Any attempt at using data-driven procedures thus demands critical reflection: Do we know enough about the underlying process to be able to reduce it to a simple set of quantifiable inputs and outputs? Are we reasonably sure that our chosen metrics represent inputs and outputs accurately? Can we quantify the remaining errors or biases between data-driven representation and the actual process at hand? How do we develop processes of quality control to ensure the correspondence of said links in the future? These questions are just as relevant for traditional forms of measuring social life as for new measurement approaches enabled through digital data and computational power.

7.2 Promises of Digital Data

Digital technology and the opportunities of data processing in modern computing environments have increased significantly the data available to companies, governments, and organizations. This has led to the collection of vast datasets on people's behavior and traits by governments, companies, third-party data vendors, or directly by organizations themselves (Salganik 2018). The term "big data" has been widely used to capture the supposed potential of these data sources to increase the opportunities of governments to control and incentivize their citizens and the development of new business models and services for companies and organizations to interact with people in order to achieve their goals (De Mauro, Greco, and Grimaldi 2015).

The main promise of digital data is that, contrary to other data collection tasks, it is oftentimes readily available. Behavior on digital tools maps to events that can be recorded, not only as part of an analytical goal (e.g., how much time do users spend on the platforms, why do they unsubscribe from services, what features of the site are more attractive to prospective customers) but also as part of the operation of digital tools (think of wearable devices, captchas, online games). Individuals thus leave digital traces that can be used to document and, more importantly, analyze their interactions with digital services (Howison, Wiggins, and Crowston 2011), their history of web navigation (Mayer and Mitchell 2012), or their online purchases (Chen et al. 2012). But analysts also have access to footage from CCTVs (Valera and Velastin 2005), records of people's movements, interactions, or environmental conditions provided by sensors embedded in digital devices (Pentland 2008; Ferguson 2016), or even conversations captured by digital assistants. It is not only digitally born services that collect data in the process of their operation. The digitalization of administrative data collected as part of the regular operations of services, including the government (e.g., electronic health records, tax and property records, crime reports), can be used as sources for analysis. This information can then be combined to get a better picture of what people do as opposed to what they say, opening the scope from what happens in a single site to more general behaviors whenever a person is online. These data sources are seen by some as being superior to self-reports as they document actual behavior and are thus ostensibly not subject to people lying or forgetting what they did, a common theme in the survey methodology literature (Tourangeau, Rips, and Rasinski 2000).

In politics, a wide variety of datasets have found prominent uses. Centrally, voter files collected and provided by governments help campaigns find prospective voters (Hersh 2015). Companies provide data vendors with data on commercial transactions by consumers, who then link them with publicly available datasets and sell them to organizations and consultancies (Ramirez et al. 2014). Parties and NGOs collect data on any person who comes into contact with them, uses their services, or voices interest or support in their platforms or candidates (Karpf 2016a; Kreiss 2016). These various datasets are routinely enriched by merging them with other sets containing additional data points on the individuals concerned. The merging of big datasets allows the development of predictive models using signals in the dataset to predict outcomes of interest (Nickerson and Rogers 2014).

These practices by private actors are most pronounced in the United States, as data protection laws offer considerable leeway for companies and organizations to collect, sell, enrich, and store data on individuals. More restrictive data protection laws restrict these opportunities in many other countries. This divide is made starker as different regulatory regimes appear to be driven by deep cultural divides in the origin of data protection regulation. For example, privacy laws, which determine what data can be stored, for how long, and for what purpose, stem from different legal traditions in the United States and in Europe (Jones 2016). This has given rise to comparatively lenient data privacy laws in the United States and strong data protection in Europe, such as the right to be forgotten and the General Data Protection Regulation (GDPR) (Hert and Papakonstantinou 2016). But even in rather restrictive data protection regimes, such as Germany, political actors invest heavily in realizing the opportunities provided to them by digital data (Kruschinski and Haller 2017). Consequently, while the United States is at the forefront of data-driven policy-making (Zarsky 2011; Ferguson 2017; Eubanks 2018), other governments like China (K.-F. Lee 2018) or those in the European Union (Engin and Treleaven 2019) are establishing vast data collections on their citizens and experimenting with data-driven policy-making, surveillance, and enforcement programs. While the specifics might vary given variations in data protection regulation, the use of data-driven approaches is an international phenomenon.

Another import promise of these new data sources is that they collect data continuously and nonresponsively – they are always on (Salganik 2018, 21ff.). By observing people continuously over long periods of time, these data collections allow researchers to gain a deeper understanding of social processes and human behavior. Traditionally, social scientists had to run data collections documenting behavior or traits at a given time, such as in cross-sectional surveys. If researchers were lucky and secured the necessary funding, they were able to combine a series of surveys into a panel survey by repeatedly surveying a selected group of individuals. Using this approach works well for identifying correlations between traits and behavior at the time of the survey, but is less well suited to identify small changes over time. By having the behavior of large numbers of people tracked over long periods of time, new data sources offer a fine-grained view of individual behavior over time in which even small or temporally bounded shifts become visible and can be connected to external stimuli.

These data collections are also unobtrusive (Salganik 2018, 23f.). More often than not, data is collected automatically without subjects necessarily being aware or caring that their behavior is being watched and recorded. This increases the reliability of the data, as subjects do not adjust their behavior in response to being watched. This reduces well-known confounders in active data collection such as social desirability bias, where respondents adjust their answers in surveys in order to conform with what they perceive to be socially acceptable (Tourangeau et al. 2000).

The collection and merging of these diverse datasets allows for the development of statistical models that predict future behavior by individuals given specific traits, behaviors, or contextual conditions. Other than in theory-driven statistical modeling, in principle, these models do not rely on the researcher explicitly telling the model which signals should be predictive of which outcome (Breiman 2001; Maass et al. 2018). Instead, the vast amounts of data collected allow for automated model building. Statistical learning promises the identification of hidden relationships between observable signals and outcomes of interest (Agrawal et al. 2018). Such relationships could include the increased propensity of an individual to donate money to a campaign when a donation mailer contains an appeal by the candidate's spouse. This could also lead an individual to be perceived as a heightened reoffender risk if she shares traits and behaviors with other reoffenders. Once such a link is identified, the appearance of a specific signal by an individual can automatically trigger a specific treatment. This could be the specific targeting of said person with campaign mailers in which the candidate's spouse acts as speaker. Or this could be an algorithmically determined sentencing suggestion for a judge hearing a parolee's case. Vast amounts of data thus allow the development of statistical models of observable signals linked to outcomes of interest. Once observed, these signals can then trigger algorithmically determined interventions in an effort to get the person in question to behave in a way intended by the government, company, or political organization.

7.3 Challenges of Digital Data

While the promises of these new digital data sources are widely propagated, their limitations are often neglected. The very nature of digital communications enhances the visibility of subsets of a population active on digital platforms to administrators and analysts. Every information or interaction circulating through communication devices can be mapped to a data point that can be stored, processed, aggregated, and analyzed. But this does not translate into perfect visibility. Who and what gets counted is limited by the nature of the platform and the process of measurement itself. This goes for each measurement approach, device, and encoding, bringing with it a mediation process that encodes an interpretation of reality, a measurement, into data points (Hand 2004). On a more pragmatic level, measurement, as a technical process, involves decisions and challenges that affect the data we collect and that

may transform how we think about reality. Borrowing from the survey literature (see Biemer 2010), one could separate errors associated with coverage
(who can be studied because she has a nonzero probability of being observed),
specification (the mismatch between what needs to be measured and what can
be measured), and measurement (the effect of the act of measuring itself).

How much these errors matter depends on the nature of the specific data
source and the purposes for doing the measuring. The project manager
working for Facebook will worry about different errors in trying to understand
the platform's users than will the researcher trying to understand reality by
using data collected on Facebook. While the challenges in working with digital
trace data are manifold, they are experienced in different ways by different
users of the data.

The first obvious problem is that digital data is essentially data about a slice
of reality – things that happen on the digital platform. This means not everyone
is likely to be represented in these new datasets (Hargittai 2015). Inferences
drawn based on these data sources are likely to miss voices and interests of
people not represented in the respective datasets. A trivial example is internet
surveys: They cannot reach everyone. The only voices that can be heard are
those who can receive a survey and those represented online. For instance, in
the United States, where in 2010 95 percent of adults younger than 33 used the
internet, only 30 percent of those older than 74 used it (Zickuhr 2010). Without
further correction, there is a systematic bias in which voices are registered and
analyzed. Whether this becomes a problem depends on what the analytical
goal is. Trying to understand the opinions of the users of the digital service
providing us with data is different from inferring what nonusers or even the
general population thinks based on our data. In the latter case, we need
corrections to jump from the data we collected in order to make a statement
about cases that were beyond the coverage of our data. This discussion
becomes even more relevant in the use of digital trace data collected on social
networking platforms in the study of public opinion. Here, the demographic
biases in the composition of active users of these platforms and the general
population is even more blatant than in internet use overall. Using the same
report as before, we see a solid age gap between users and nonusers of social
media: 83 percent vs. 16 percent for social networking sites (SNS), 80 percent
vs. 20 percent for watching online videos, and 43 percent vs. 15 percent for
reading blogs (Zickuhr 2010). This issue is made more problematic still, as
usage patterns of different social media services are not homogeneous across
groups. Consequently, the user bases of different platforms show very different
mixes of gender, racial, ethnic, and socioeconomic status, and even ideological
background (Rainie et al. 2012; Duggan et al. 2015).

Even if some people can be reached, this does not mean that their information will be available. Consider again internet surveys. Not all the users of our product will want to take consumer surveys. This becomes a problem once people who express their opinion in a survey systematically differ from those who do not. This self-selection bias is a pervasive and notorious problem that affects all areas of digital research. Who takes surveys about their experience in a hotel? Who talks about airlines on Twitter? Who participates in opinion surveys in digital newspapers? The answer will hardly be a representative cross-section of the population of interest. This has most clearly been shown for political talk in social media. In one of the first studies addressing this question, Mustafaraj et al. (2011) showed that topical content on social media is frequently the product of small but very vocal groups, with large majorities of users remaining mostly silent. Other studies have shown that politically vocal social media users tend to have firmer and more extreme opinions (Rainie et al. 2012; Barberá and Rivero 2015) while tending to self-identify as opinion leaders (Park 2013). Users with more moderate opinions are less likely to express them, while others who might even be highly interested in politics do not use social media to voice political opinions (Gustafsson 2012). Additionally, the composition of users voicing political opinions drifts depending on issues and events (Mitchell and Hitlin 2013).

The degree to which these biases matter depends on the contexts and purposes of their use. On the one hand, Hersh (2015) showed that voter files provided by the US government offered campaigns data of a quality that they could not reproduce using extensive additional data sources available to them. Here, administrative records produced a ground truth superior to biased data sources collected by data vendors or online. On the other hand, the experiences of the Vote Leave campaign for the 2016 United Kingdom European Union membership referendum (Brexit) vote showed that running ads on Facebook provided campaigners access to people invisible in other records, thereby providing the campaign an edge over competitors (Shipman 2016, 407–424). This shows that under conditions of data scarcity even biased data collected online can provide campaigns with a powerful edge.

Going beyond who is covered by these new data sources, we also find issues with what gets covered. The widely touted advantage of digital data is that, contrary to surveys, they supposedly provide an unescapable gaze capturing much more than can be identified by a survey. The discussion about bias thus might not apply to the same degree as long as we are only interested in what happens within the platform of interest. In these cases, we do not have to explicitly ask for cooperation by subjects. Everything they do on or through the digital service of interest is covered and available in the data. Think about

Facebook. To identify their usage behavior, we do not need users to take surveys; everything they do or say on Facebook can be measured, from the moment they log in to the moment they log out. Additionally, through partnerships with other sites and platforms, Facebook can even gain information about what users have done before and after they interact with the platform. Moreover, by being able to identify users by name or contact details, Facebook can merge data on the behavior of these users on their platform with data available on them from other sources. Facebook thus gets information on its users that they did not explicitly disclose or share on Facebook.

However, while behavioral data is interesting, often social scientists want to go beyond merely mapping behavioral patterns. Instead their goal is the identification of latent drivers of behavior, such as traits, attitudes, or motives, and their relationship with outcomes of interest. Here, it is far from clear if and how we can use behavior documented in digital trace data to infer underlying traits, attitudes, or motives. Many studies do use digital trace data to do just this, for example to infer political ideology and partisanship (Conover, Goncalves, et al. 2011; Colleoni, Rozza, and Arvidsson 2014; Barberá 2015; Bond and Messing 2015; Rivero 2019). Yet it is far from clear how to infer traits, attitudes, or motives based simply on behavioral data (Jungherr, Schoen, et al. 2017; Jungherr 2019). This attempt creates challenges about the linking of what users do and what this can tell us about the latent divers of this behavior. An example is Jungherr, Schoen, et al. (2017), who showed that studies trying to measure political support for parties through Twitter data were instead likely to measure the level of public attention parties received. While political attention is an important and ill-documented phenomenon, it is not the same as political support. Without robust attempts at indicator validation, it is hard to be sure one is actually measuring the one and not the other. How to do so reliably currently remains an open question.

This challenge is made even more difficult as individuals can behave strategically and unobserved changes in the design of a platform may induce changes in behavior. Most online platforms have opted to algorithmically incentivize users in order to get them to behave in a specific way, be it to spend more time on the platform, click on ads, post more content, or buy more products. These algorithmic interventions remain invisible to observers without access to the workings and inputs of platform-specific algorithms. There is thus a high risk of mistakenly perceiving specific user behavior as being driven by outside factors or observable events when in fact it was driven by algorithmic interventions of the platform itself (Salganik 2018, 35ff.). As a result, shifts in platform design or algorithms incentivizing users to act a certain way on a platform can break statistical links between signals and outcomes of interest

(Lazer et al. 2014). This adds to the general question of whether relationships identified in the past still hold in the present or the future (Lucas 1976).

An often neglected question in the use of data-driven approaches in politics is the one of data ownership, accessibility, and privacy. In fact, we are far from a universally data-rich society. Instead, we find a crass divide between a few data-haves and a large group of data-have-nots, and a consistent trade-off between the privacy rights of the observed and the hoped-for payoffs of data-driven practices. The resulting conflicts lie at the heart of the future of data-driven politics.

Data is not free. Instead, data is collected and owned by companies that use it in furthering their business models. At times this can entail providing access to predefined slices of this data to the outside, such as the public or researchers. Yet it would be naive to think that providing data access to the outside lies at the heart of these companies' purpose. Instead, it is more likely that they provide access to data as long as it serves their growth or supports their public image. For example, Twitter's early steep growth in users and available applications was deeply linked to the opportunities for developers to build tools and services on Twitter's platform. This was enabled by Twitter providing anyone broad access to user data through its API. Once growth slowed and Twitter was forced to look more actively for a viable business model, the service started to restrict access to its data in order to control ad display to users and sell access to data to interested parties instead of providing it for free. Or take Facebook. After the scandal around illicit uses of Facebook data by the English consultancy Cambridge Analytica in 2018, Facebook restricted access to data on its platform through its API. The company framed this as an effort to put user privacy first, but the move was just as likely driven by public relations considerations given Facebook's rather callous approach to user privacy in the past. In both cases, companies that own massive amounts of data decided from one day to the next to heavily restrict access to said data to the outside. Any insight to be gained from this data thus lies with these companies. It is exclusively their decision which questions to address with this data and which to ignore. While this data on social and political reality thus is produced collectively by user behavior and interactions, its gains and insights are held privately by the companies providing services and devices. This is a problematic balance especially when it comes to auditing the platforms provided by these companies and independently assessing their impact on society. Just ask yourself how likely these platforms are to support studies that might show their detrimental political or societal footprints.

All of this goes to show that instead of being error-free, these new data sources might come with new biases that we just have not yet identified or consciously have chosen to ignore. The important takeaway is that there are trade-offs we have to face when using these new data sources. The data comes with different challenges than data traditionally used by social scientists. These challenges have to be addressed. While new data is readily available, it comes with problems in access, coverage, and being fit-for-purpose (Keller et al. 2016), compromising its validity. In addition to these technical problems, we also find new legal and ethical issues that researchers have to answer.

7.4 Extending Transparency

The steady flow of digital data documenting activities, processes, decisions, and events allows ever more actors a broad and deep view of ever more areas of social and political life. This leads to a significant increase in transparency. As with any data-driven practice, transparency turns out to be a mixed blessing. Inherent to the idea of data-driven transparency are normatively wished-for opportunities for civil society actors to shine a light on illicit goings on and make visible what remained hidden in the past. On the other hand, digitally enabled transparency can also mean the publication of information that legitimately held a claim on remaining secret. The unblinking eye of digitally enabled transparency thus does not necessarily lead to a strengthening of a healthy monitorial civil society.

On the positive side, digital data provided by ubiquitous sensors, such as satellites or mobile telephones, has extended the opportunities in the work of nongovernmental organizations (NGOs) and activists in documenting illicit activities by governments and human rights violations (Livingston 2016). The same data and sensors also allow NGOs, activists, and first responders to coordinate rescue or relief efforts (Gao, Barbier, and Goolsby 2011; Imran et al. 2013). Similarly, satellite data can help researchers to measure remotely wealth and income, for example by analyzing light emission patterns, thereby providing crucial information on areas for which only few reliable statistics exist (Weidmann and Schutte 2017). While these are generally positive cases of increased transparency and measurability driven by digital data, negative cases are just as prominent. For example, collective use of the popular fitness app Strava by US military personnel inadvertently revealed locations of US overseas military bases. By recording their daily jogging routes and uploading them to the service, soldiers revealed the location of their bases (Hern 2018). This illustrates the unexpected and sometimes detrimental effects of continuous data collection through sensors. This is only bound to grow through the pervasive use of ill-understood and only weakly secured sensors in internet-of-things applications (Schneier 2018). Similarly, digital data not only enables activists but also makes them visible to government agencies, allowing autocratic regimes to learn about individual activists and their networks and pursue targeted crackdowns (Morozov 2011; Benner et al. 2018). Potential gains in efficiency are seen as being offset by an associated loss in privacy on behalf of the individual (Beniger 1989; Igo 2018; Zuboff 2019).

Transparency is also a central element in the relation between citizens and governments (see Chapter 8). Digital technologies are at the heart of various leaks of confidential information by various actors in various fields. Famously, large amounts of confidential digital data have been leaked from inside the US military and secret service community by insiders like Chelsea Manning or Edward Snowden (The Editorial Board 2014; Shear 2017). Prominent leaks have also happened in the realm of finance, such as the Panama papers (The Editorial Board 2016). The aggregation of large amounts of data in easily accessible databases makes the unsanctioned collection and extraction of confidential information possible in the first place. In a second step, digital distribution of information through platforms like WikiLeaks makes possible the publication of data dumps that otherwise might be filtered or held back by more traditional newsroom practices (Khatchadourian 2010). Ironically, in this process the transparency thus enforced on organizations from which data is taken is not mirrored by transparency on leaking actors or organizations, which remain largely opaque with regard to their identity, motives, or backing (Khatchadourian 2017).

Hacks and leaks, even when associated with transparency and accountability of governments, are also double-edged swords. Someone, somewhere will always feel dissatisfied with any level of information sharing established by governments. With sufficient technical expertise, adversarial agents can take it into their own hands to publish information that governments have not released. WikiLeaks and the release of secret diplomatic cables from the United States triggered a public debate about the ethical limits of unauthorized disclosures of information. The discussion addressed the question of the optimal level of secrecy that citizens should grant governments and the tension that naturally exists between legitimation-via-transparency and reassurance-via-secrecy (Pasquale 2011). With increased transparency, not only could the legitimacy of decisions increase, but a high level of transparency also reassures citizens that governments are not covering up actions deemed illegitimate by the public. On the other hand, increased transparency could reduce the effectiveness of officials (Stasavage 2004), who sometimes need to make compromises that would not be easily accepted by the public. Similarly, transparency can be used to feed a narrative of waste and corruption (O'Neill 2002) to manipulate the frame with which governments are evaluated.

Normatively, we might think about transparency as an unconditionally positive attribute and of secrecy as an unconditionally negative one. While popular, this reading ignores the inherent trade-off between society's legitimate need for transparency and actors' and organizations' just as legitimate need for secrecy to get their job done. A balance between the two has to be established that takes into account the nature and uses of digital data, allowing for large data dumps and immediate far-reaching distribution. In this, it is important to move beyond any visionary cyber-rhetoric of a post-privacy world without any secrets determined by the perceived nature of digital data. Instead of rhetorical grandstanding, this new balance has to be built on the basis of practicality and the nature of social organizations.

So again, the effect of digital data on politics is not clear-cut. Digital data can be used effectively to force an increase in transparency and shine a light on illicit activities by governments, big business, or elites. Yet it can also be used effectively against civil society itself in constituting a pervasive surveillance tool and by eroding trust in confidentiality necessary to social and political life. The beneficial potential of increased transparency through digital data thus has to be seen in the context of its detrimental or malicious use.

7.5 Manipulating Digital Metrics

Once people start paying attention to digital metrics as sources of intelligence, incentives to manipulate them increase. One prominent example is the attempt to gauge public opinion based on publicly available social media metrics, such as mention counts on Twitter of politicians or topics, retweet counts of tweets by politicians, or the number of clicks on news articles. Metrics like these are becoming ever more important for politicians, journalists, and consultants to infer public opinion or interest in stories, or to publicly cite evidence of the apparent popularity of their stances (Anstead and O'Loughlin 2012). For strategic actors like campaign consultants or communication professionals working for companies or NGOs, this provides an interesting opportunity. By actively pushing the mentions of their candidates or campaign topics, they can hope to influence media coverage and create the impression of large public support. Increasing public reliance on digital metrics thus also means increased incentives for interfering with them.

Digital data is easy to collect, store, and analyze. It is also easy to manipulate. After all, how can we be sure that a technologically mediated expression online actually represents a legitimate human voice? While it is surprisingly cheap to create thousands of posts on social media protesting against a policy, it is much more expensive to hire thousands of demonstrators to protest the same policy on the streets. Manipulating public opinion becomes easy once it is about simply counting virtual instead of actual hands. This is equally true for the manipulation of digital data points feeding models and algorithmic decision-making systems in other areas of social or political life. The growing reliance on digital data thus makes an increasing set of areas vulnerable to malicious interference or manipulation. The more decisions depend on mediated reflections of reality, the more manipulating that image becomes attractive (Holiday 2012; Singer and Brooking 2018). Echoing Campbell (1979) and Goodhart (1975), David Karpf notes:

> Any metric of digital influence that becomes financially valuable, or is used to determine newsworthiness, will become increasingly unreliable over time.... The perverse result here is that digital listening works best when no one is aware it is going on.... If governments chose to make public policy decisions on the basis of online sentiment analysis, organized interests would start figuring out how to game those government systems.... [T]he more public value we place on a given digital metric, the muddier the metric is likely to become.
>
> (Karpf 2016a, 41)

In discussing the potential for manipulation, we have to differentiate between the difficulty of actually manipulating a data source underlying a given data-driven decision-making process, the intended outcomes of the manipulation, and the incentives of those wittingly or unwittingly contributing to the process. In theory it might be possible to hack administrative databases and manipulate information stored there, but this is probably more likely to occur in a Hollywood movie than in real life. In contrast, it is trivially easy to manipulate metrics trying to identify popularity or attention online. By themselves, these manipulations might not mean much. But as ever more media organizations use social media metrics to identify hot topics or personalities, this is a cheap way to capture media attention and create or shift coverage on given topics. It is no surprise to find most public examples in the manipulation of data-driven processes in the area of trend and public opinion manipulation.

Manipulation of public opinion measures online can take different forms, from comparatively direct and easy to complicated and elaborate. On the direct and easy side, we have attempts at buying followers, likes, or retweets on Facebook or Twitter in the hope of signaling relative importance or public interest. On the more complicated and elaborate side of the spectrum of manipulation are coordinated efforts to push actors, topics, or specific pieces of information into public attention (Metaxas and Mustafaraj 2012; Tucker et al. 2017). For example, Metaxas and Mustafaraj have conducted extensive research, particularly in relation to electoral campaigns. They have explored the use of link-bombing techniques by bloggers to boost negative results in search engines (Metaxas and Mustafaraj 2009), and similar uses of Twitter (Mustafaraj and Metaxas 2010). Their findings suggest that these activities are relatively common: "In times of political elections, the stakes are high, and advocates may try to support their cause by active manipulation of social media" (Metaxas and Mustafaraj 2012). This research spearheaded later developments such as "Truthy" (Ratkiewicz, Conover, Gonçalves, et al. 2011; Ratkiewicz, Conover, Meiss, et al. 2011), a system to detect astroturfing campaigns at early stages.

While there are serious doubts about whether social media metrics are able to reflect public opinion accurately even before accounting for manipulation (Gayo-Avello 2013; Murphy et al. 2014; Schober et al. 2016; Jungherr, Schoen, et al. 2017), these doubts have done nothing to lower the public enthusiasm for these metrics. Of course, focusing on the accuracy of social media-based public opinion measures might actually miss the point of why they are so popular with journalists and politicians alike. After all, the purpose of traditional opinion polls for practitioners is not necessarily about their accurate representation of political support, that is, their "instrumental use" (Herbst 1993). Instead, they are often used in order to represent the overwhelming levels of public support or the unstoppable momentum of a candidate or party. These "symbolic uses" (Herbst 1993) are powerful and largely independent from their factual representation of public opinion. For these strategic uses, the biases in social media representations of public opinion do not matter much as long as the message fits. This might explain the persistence of social media-based public opinion mining among practitioners and journalists and also account for its longevity even in the face of potential manipulation.

Similar tactics have been used in the dissemination of disinformation. This has led to extensive research trying to establish the credibility of posts in digital media (Castillo, Mendoza, and Poblete 2011; Gupta, Zhao, and Han 2012; Kang, O'Donovan, and Höllerer 2012; Abbasi and Liu 2013; Y. A. Kim and Ahmad 2013; Sikdar et al. 2013; Metaxas, Finn, and Mustafaraj 2015; Mocanu et al. 2015). These manipulation attempts are often conducted through coordinated automated or semi-automated accounts, so-called bot nets (Bessi and Ferrara 2016) or troll farms (Zelenkauskaite and Niezgoda 2017; Badawy, Ferrara, and Lerman 2018). This has led to extensive research into the detection and analysis of corresponding accounts and campaigns (Chu et al. 2010; Boshmaf et al. 2011; Wang et al. 2012) and dissemination patterns of misleading information and purposefully introduced and disseminated disinformation (Castillo et al. 2011; Qazvinian et al. 2011; Metaxas et al. 2015; Mocanu et al. 2015).

The goals of these interventions are multiple. For one, the goal could be to shift public perception of a selected candidate's electoral chances of success or to goad media organizations into covering candidates, events, topics, or arguments through manipulating the intensity of online reactions they generate (Holiday 2012). Or these interventions could be about creating distrust in information environments and media coverage in general (Farrell and Schneier 2018). On a more tactical level, these targeted interventions can also attempt to disrupt information flows between activists and civil society who are attempting to coordinate actions (King, Pan, and Roberts 2017; Spaiser et al. 2017). Getting a clear bearing on these goals is important as this determines the effectiveness of chosen countermeasures (Flynn, Nyhan, and Reifler 2017; Kovic et al. 2018).

Similarly, it is important to correctly identify the incentives of actors in reacting to these manipulation attempts. For example, no amount of fact-checking or media literacy will stop media organizations from picking up and in turn amplifying disinformation and manipulated content if they are driven by economic reasons to do so. Similarly, if the sharing of misleading information by users would not represent their actual belief in the factualness of said content but instead would serve the expression of their partisan beliefs or group affiliation, the impact of fact-checking and media literacy programs will remain limited (Nyhan, Reifler, and Ubel 2013; Kahan et al. 2017; Marwick 2018).

Using digital metrics effectively thus means being clear about one's purpose and their vulnerability for manipulation. As long as the use of digital metrics is "symbolic" instead of "instrumental" (Herbst 1993), one probably does not have to think too closely about their accurateness or susceptibility to strategic manipulation. In these cases, the more important question is whether the output of digital metrics corresponds with one's goals. If instead the purpose of the use of digital media is "instrumental," one has to be much more careful about the correspondence of these metrics with the measurement targets. In general, metrics that reliably document actual behavior of interest in controlled environments, such as an online platform provided by one's own organization, are likely to be more reliable than public activity on third-party platforms.

These different aspects of the use of data-driven approaches in politics become more clearly apparent once we focus on a specific case. While there are many potential areas that we could use as examples, we will focus on the use of data-driven approaches in election campaigns. This is one of the best documented and publicly visible political arenas for the use of data-driven approaches and practices.

7.6 Data-Driven Campaigning

One of the areas in politics most publicly shaped by data-driven practices is campaigning. This area therefore offers a very promising example of the impact and challenges of data-driven practices in politics. While data-driven campaigning has been most visible in the United States, campaign organizations worldwide use data-driven practices to decide which voters to contact, how to raise funds, where to run ads, or how to allocate resources. This has given rise to both hopes and fears. The ability to mobilize people and allocate resources efficiently has been seen as an opportunity for outsiders to build successful organizations independent of major party organizations, thereby opening up political discourse – with beneficial or detrimental consequences, depending on the challenger (Jungherr, Schroeder, and Stier 2019). Others have emphasized the perceived risks emerging from political parties or candidates being too skillful in manipulating the public through their use of digital media (Howard 2005). Data-driven campaigning holds trade-offs between promising political organizations more effective means of reaching, mobilizing, and persuading people and a general fear that once political organizations become too skillful in the use of these tools, they turn into master manipulators of the public. As so often, neither the hopes nor the fears seem to materialize fully.

The two presidential campaigns of Barack Obama in 2008 and 2012 put data-driven campaigning on the map. His campaign organization used data-driven methods extensively to target and coordinate voter outreach, for fundraising from supporters, test messages and campaign materials, and to allocate resources. Daniel Kreiss has called this pervasive culture of data-driven decision-making "computational management" (Kreiss 2012b, 2016). The Obama campaign built on the experiences of many other campaigns (Stromer-Galley 2019), the most important of which was probably Howard Dean's 2004 campaign for the Democratic primaries. This campaign had proven beyond a doubt the powers of digital tools for fundraising and the coordination of volunteers (Trippi 2004). At least as important was a shift in campaigning practices in the United States toward evidence-based practices whose persuasive power had been tested in experiments (Issenberg 2012c; Green and Gerber 2015). While the Obama campaigns thus invented neither the use of digital tools in campaigning nor the use of experiments in establishing what works, they were highly successful in combining both innovations and establishing an organization structure and practices that were able to fully capitalize on their potential (Kreiss 2012b).

Specific to the Obama campaign organization was the commitment to develop the technology and analytical approaches used within the campaign organization itself. Following this model, campaign organizations resemble technology firms like Facebook, Google, or Twitter, companies that develop both technology and data-driven services in-house (Kreiss 2016). This approach is highly resource- and skill-dependent. An alternative to this can be found one campaign cycle later. Instead of building technological or analytical solutions in-house, the campaign of Donald Trump had the ad divisions of companies like Facebook, Google, or Twitter compete for ad buys (Kreiss and McGregor 2018). Thus the Trump campaign did not try to replicate the technological or analytical capabilities of these platforms, but instead rented their services. They used digital technology and data-driven products as commodities to be bought or rented at will (Vaccari 2010).

Creating Data Infrastructures

By now, a large number of companies offer campaigns custom-made software and contact lists, either as an offshoot of a larger online ad business, as in the cases of targeted advertising opportunities on Google or Facebook, or in the provision of dedicated services and solutions customized for politics, such as NGP VAN or the GOP Data Center. Online platforms promise campaigns the ability to reach out to people otherwise invisible to political parties, such as those not registered to vote or disinterested in politics (Simon 2019).

Probably the most famous examples of the use of services and databases dedicated for campaign work are the Obama campaigns in 2008 and 2012. The Obama campaign built on previous efforts by the Democratic Party to establish a common high-quality voter database and a common set of tools supporting Democratic candidates on the local and national level (Blaemire 2012; Pearlman 2012; Sullivan 2012). This included tools supporting outreach by phone, email, or door-to-door canvassing as well as donation runs. For these purposes the party had settled on the services of what is now NGP VAN, a company providing services exclusively to Democratic campaigns and allied interest groups, and encouraged local party organizations and campaigns to run their campaigns with these tools. The resulting economics of scale allowed for the development of a highly sophisticated campaigning toolbox available to campaigns on the national as well as the local level. At the heart of the service lies a voter list that contains contact information for every voter in the United States with additional meta-data collected through various different sources, such as additional data provided by official voter files, consumer data, or behavioral data from social media services. The continuous use of this data in campaigns on the local, state, and national level ensures a continuous evaluation of data quality (Kreiss 2012b; Stromer-Galley 2019). Pooling collective resources with one vendor and continuously using these services allowed Democrats to break the usual four-year product cycle of presidential campaigning and enabled them to switch to software as a service model of continuous updates (Kreiss 2016). Yet, given the vagaries of political funding, the interests of donors, and the attention of the party elites, it is an open question whether this provides them with an edge over Republicans in 2020 (Lapowsky 2019).

Accounts of Barack Obama's two presidential runs often focus on the use of databases and data-driven practices by the campaigns. An indication of this is headlines like "Obama Does it Better" followed by the teaser "When it comes to targeting and persuading voters, the Democrats have a bigger advantage over the GOP than either party has ever had in the modern campaign era" (Issenberg 2012b), or "How Obama's Team Used Big Data to Rally Voters" (Issenberg 2012a). One reason for this is the campaigns' very conscious featuring of data-driven tactics in their self-description to the press, which led campaign process stories to focus heavily on this aspect (Madrigal 2012). Yet, while there is definitely a public relations aspect to the prominent role that databases and data-driven campaigning appear to have had for the Obama campaign (Kreiss 2012a), they were in fact a key element in the strategic decision-making, organization, and running of the campaigns (Kreiss 2012b). Early on, the 2008 Obama campaign made the conscious strategic choice to try to extend the realized electorate by mobilizing hard-to-reach populations with low propensity to turn up to vote but with high affinity to Obama or to Democrats (Plouffe 2009). This meant the campaign had to employ mobilizing tactics with strong impact to overcome the disinclination of targets to turn out to vote. This led them to emphasize personal interventions through volunteers either at the doorstep or through telephone calls (Nielsen 2012a). Both campaigning tactics are empirically associated with a good ratio between investment and realized votes (Green and Gerber 2015). While these tactics might have a larger impact than other mobilizing approaches, they are also significantly more time and resource intensive (Nielsen 2012a). This made it crucial for the campaign to organize outreach efforts efficiently. Dedicated software allowing local campaign organizers to access voter information and local volunteers to access talking points helped in this.

The Obama approach is highly resource intensive and depends on electoral and privacy regulation allowing for the purchase and merging of extensive individual-level datasets. The marginal return on investment depends on the strategic choices of a campaign. If, as in the case of the Obama campaign, one tactically relies on comparatively expensive contact modes, such as door-to-door canvassing, increased precision in targeting allows you to spend scarce resources better. If, alternatively, a wasted contact does not cost you much, heavy investments in targeting solutions are likely to be of little relevance. Moreover, the United States is an exceptionally permissive campaign environment providing campaigns with high-quality voter contact information through the government and allowing the buying and merging of individual-level datasets (Hersh 2015). Political actors in an electoral context where this is not possible to such a degree will have to evaluate if their respective legal environment allows them to develop an adequate database to realize the hoped-for increases in targeting precision over other traditional targeting approaches, such as geographic targeting.

Furthermore, the heavy reliance on providers of databases and digital campaign tools creates a new set of intermediaries on whose services parties, campaigns, and candidates have to depend in reaching voters. This transfers a significant amount of knowledge of practices of how to reach people away from party organizations to commercial vendors. While the economies of scale connected with the decision to outsource these functions matter, this also creates new dependencies and raises significant ethical concerns with regard to the legitimacy of commercial actors being as heavily and opaquely involved in the democratic process as they currently are. The growing awareness of these new dependencies can be seen in the public debate about data breaches at political data vendors (Cameron and Conger 2017), acrimonious discussion between competing campaigns and central party organizations about who actually owns databases with voter information and who has access to which tools and vendors when (Haberman and Corasaniti 2015; Newell 2016), and the role of targeted political advertisements on online platforms such as Facebook (Glaser 2017; Martínez 2018a). This debate is still in its infancy and lacks a sophisticated basis with regard to a pragmatic assessment of the marginal effects of the use of these techniques as well as a balanced assessment of the role and power of these new intermediaries.

A potential answer lies in political parties and campaigns becoming data collectors themselves. For example, the German conservative Christian Democratic Union (CDU), during the campaign for the general election in 2017, had their canvassers ask a series of questions of contacts and mark the quality of contact through a mobile app connected to a central database. The goal was to develop an extensive map of political support over a series of campaign cycles and also to get some real-time input during the campaign (Clemens 2018). While it is an open question whether this approach yields reliable data and can be maintained consistently over campaign cycles, it is one attempt by a party campaigning in a much less forgiving regulatory environment than the United States.

Another interesting example comes from the Vote Leave campaign during the 2016 Brexit vote. The Vote Leave campaign issued a public football competition. Anyone able to guess the results of all 51 matches in the Euro 2016 tournament was set to win 50 million pounds. To be eligible, participants had to enter their prediction on a website, leave their contact information, and assess the likelihood that they were going to vote for Britain to stay in the EU. While the exact participation numbers have not been released, this potentially allowed the Vote Leave campaign to quickly build an extensive database containing contact information of hundreds of thousands of potential voters, including email addresses and mobile phone numbers, and referendum preferences. Without any statistical wizardry, the campaign was then able to send out an email and SMS blast on the eve of the vote mobilizing likely supporters to turn up during the referendum. Moreover, given the astronomically low chance of successfully guessing the results of all the games in the competition, the Vote Leave campaign could do so without any undue resource expenditures (Cummings 2017).

While clearly different, these approaches share a central idea. Parties and campaigns use digital technology and digital media to establish contact lists of potential voters that are either held by themselves, a close subsidiary, or allies. This data then forms the basis of different methods varying in sophistication to differentiate between promising and less promising targets of direct outreach. In this approach, parties, campaigns, or their close allies remain in possession of data and models and thereby develop and maintain significant power and knowledge over the democratic core practice of reaching voters.

Data-Driven Targeting

The data-driven targeting of prospective and likely voters has featured especially strongly in public debate. Here, breathless accounts of the perceived transformative power of this procedure dominate public discourse. In reality, the role of data-driven procedures is important in politics but far from decisive. Fundamentally, targeting for a campaign is all about deciding whom to contact. Campaigns have limited resources in time and money and therefore have to decide where to focus their efforts. Targeting can consist of focusing voter outreach on a given geographical area that, given its voting history or income distribution, appears promising to a campaign. It can consist of focusing on the readership of specific politically aligned newspapers or viewers of television stations. Or targeting can consist of identifying specific individuals based on known characteristics or past behavior and contacting them (Issenberg 2012c; Lundry 2012; Castleman 2016).

On a very basic level, the goal of micro-targeting is to predict for every individual on the voter list the likelihood of voting for a given party and for turning out to vote, and the likelihood of a campaign intervention shifting their behavior in the direction wished for (Nickerson and Rogers 2014). This approach has been pioneered in the United States and its efficiency is largely driven by two factors: one, the majority electoral system in the United States limits electoral competition predominantly to two parties, making the prediction task of whom people will vote for easier; second, administrative records in the United States offer campaigns dependable information about voting behavior of individuals, namely for which elections they turned up and voted and often also party registration (Hersh 2015). This provides statisticians with very promising data to start with. Administrative records then get merged with other publicly or commercially available datasets from commercial data vendors, historical data collected by parties, or that matched with records of social media platforms. This increases the available information on each potential voter. Based on voters for whom parties know their political affiliation and their history of turning up to vote, statisticians build models of which elements of the other available information predict this behavior. Based on these models, people for whom there is only little information about party affiliation and turnout likelihood are ranked and potentially contacted by the campaign (Nickerson and Rogers 2014; Hersh 2015).

While public imagination tends to equate these outcomes of probabilistic models with deterministic knowledge of campaigns about voting behavior, a closer look shows that things are far from as certain as consultants and pundits like to suggest. For one, public debate often focuses on the size and variety of the data available on US citizens. Here, the use of datasets documenting commercial transactions or social media use in targeting feature strongly. But various studies show that the precision of targeting largely depends on the availability of voter files, data that is collected by the state and provided to campaigns (Ansolabehere and Hersh 2014; Igielnik et al. 2018). In fact, it has been shown that traits or behaviors of people that are not provided in voter files but inferred from publicly available data sources (such as consumer data or social media activity) is of far lower quality and adds little to the precision of voter targeting (Hersh 2015). This holds even more strongly for so-called psychometric targeting, such as the approach supposedly used by the campaign consultancy Cambridge Analytica in support of Donald Trump's presidential bid in 2016 (Confessore and Hakim 2017; Karpf 2017; Hersh 2018).

The rise of data-driven targeting has been heavily criticized. It has been argued that campaigning practices focusing very specifically only on parts of the electorate deemed as being susceptible to influence might lead to a focusing of political attention on only this small subset of the electorate. Other groups might end up being disenfranchised as data-driven models tell politicians that they might not be swayable in the wished-for direction (Hersh 2015). Others have focused on the negative consequences of politicians being able to pinpoint their message to only those people who are supposed to hear it. This would give rise to targeted extremist messages or communication on wedge issues, thereby increasing partisanship in society while reducing accountability of campaigns (Howard 2005; Bennett and Manheim 2006; Barocas 2012).

After the publicized successes of the Obama campaigns, data-driven campaigning practices have become pervasive in US campaigns (Stromer-Galley 2019). They have also expanded to the work of NGOs and activists (Karpf 2016a). Still, it is far from certain how well data-driven practices can be used outside of highly resource- and personnel-rich campaign organizations or even beyond the context of Obama's campaign organization (Baldwin-Philippi 2015, 2017).

Similarly, it is unclear which of these practices travel internationally. Various studies from France (Pons 2018), Germany (Wuttke, Jungherr, and Schoen 2019), and the United Kingdom (Foos and Rooij 2017; Foos and John 2018) show that political parties across Western democracies see promise in experimentally determining the effects of communicative interventions. While this points to evidence-based campaigning approaches being able to translate to contexts outside of the United States, this is far from clear with regard to large data-driven micro-targeting efforts. Electoral campaigns in the United States are conducted under unique political, regulatory, and organizational conditions that are crucial for the instrumental use of data-driven campaigning (Vaccari 2013). For one, political campaigning in the United States is a multi-billion-dollar industry (Johnson 2016). This offers campaigns a rich environment of specialized vendors skilled in developing data-driven services (Kreiss and Jasinski 2016). Furthermore, the operating budgets of presidential campaigns allow these organizations to develop technological solutions themselves and hire dedicated staffers (Kreiss and McGregor 2018). These conditions do not translate to other countries. There, campaign budgets are usually too small to even cater for the emergence of a healthy local campaign vendor environment, never mind the running of technology or analytics departments within the campaign organization itself. Moreover, privacy and campaign financing laws in the United States are much more lenient than in other countries. This makes fundraising an important feature in resource gathering for campaigns. In this, even small improvements delivered by data-driven fundraising practices translate into high absolute payoffs. With fundraising being of more limited importance in other electoral systems, this driver of innovation has much less appeal (Jungherr 2016b). In addition, US data protection laws allow the collection, merging, and selling of large and varied datasets on electorates (Rubinstein 2014). This serves as the foundation of fine-grained data-driven micro-targeting in the United States. Other countries have much stricter data protection laws. Accordingly, data-driven targeting produces much coarser results. This again limits the appeal for political organizations to invest heavily in this option as its payoff can be expected to be limited at best (Jungherr 2016a; Anstead 2017; Kruschinski and Haller 2017). Given these limitations, it might thus be too early to speak of a new age of pervasive data-driven campaigning.

Looking closely, it might even turn out that the potential of data-driven targeting of just the right individuals for interventions might be overblown, especially since, as we have shown in Chapter 4, changing people's minds especially about closely held beliefs, such as whom to vote for, is much harder than public debate seems to assume. While we know a lot about the supposed use of these techniques, there is very little evidence of the marginal effect of data-driven campaigning on votes gained and funds raised when compared with less data-intensive targeting approaches.

Data-Driven Outreach

While most of the debate on data-driven campaigning focuses on the often elusive magic of micro-targeting, the actual impact of data in campaigns might lie in the provision of actionable information to organizational branches on the ground and a documentation of their activity available for evaluation at the campaign headquarters. Through software and mobile devices, it has become much easier to coordinate a large number of volunteers and for these volunteers to efficiently contribute to the campaign (Hendler 2012; Nielsen 2012a; Jungherr 2016a).

While centrally maintained databases containing voter contact information form the backbone of modern campaign software, they also offer local field offices access to actionable information. Field office coordinators have access to contact information of voters in their district and they see the scores of potential voters provided by the central campaign office. This allows them access to condensed information on potential voters in their district that are expected to react favorably to interventions. The software then allows local coordinators to group likely voters with promising scores in walk or call lists so that volunteers can proceed to contact them. Volunteers who go from door to door are thus supported through a geographically clustered list of promising contacts that they can access on apps on their smartphones. The outcome of the contact is subsequently protocoled on the platform, which allows for local and central quality control of the outreach effort's progress.

On the face of it, these features of data-driven campaigning might seem less thrilling than those provided by data-driven targeting, but they are crucial for the successful running of a dispersed and relatively resource-poor organization like a campaign. For example, while publicly the direct voter outreach by the Obama campaigns has been heralded as a massive groundswell of public support, a true form of organizing without organization, and a form of grassroots support (Margetts et al. 2015), it is probably best thought of as a hybrid form of organization. Or, in the words of one campaign organizer: "The bottom up stuff needs to be enforced from the top down" (Scola 2009). In this enforcement the use of digital tools was highly important in the Obama campaigns as it allowed the campaign leadership to centrally define targets, coordinate the work of local teams, and evaluate the impact of its measures.

Furthermore, campaigns can also use behavioral data of people who are interacting with them on their platforms and link it with information available on social media services, like Facebook. For example, in 2012 the Obama campaign pulled the Facebook contacts of users who installed the official campaign app and mapped those contact lists onto lists of potential voters. They then prompted their supporters with promising targets among their Facebook friends to contact them and make sure they voted (Scherer 2012). Thus, the campaign linked different data sources in order to increase their outreach effort.

Campaigns can also use behavioral data of their supporters in order to optimize their interactions with them. Online marketing has developed into a vibrant field for A/B testing (Kohavi and Longbotham 2017). In its most simple version, visitors to a website or subscribers to a newsletter are randomly divided into two groups. One group is shown the standard version of a website or an email (version A) while the second group sees the website or email with a slight variation (version B). This could be a change in the positioning or design of a donation button, or the phrasing in which the campaign asks for donations. Following this, analysts compare the two groups with regard to their compliance with an outcome of interest, such as remaining on the website longer, clicking the donate button, or maximizing their donation amount. Depending on the size of the lists and the abilities of organizations to establish meaningful content variations, this simple adaption of the experimental method (Rosenbaum 2017) of comparing outcomes in two groups given slightly different stimuli can be extended at will and to all areas where campaigns have rich behavioral data on their supporters. As recounted by Kreiss (2012b), the Obama campaigns believed strongly in the use of A/B testing and grounded decisions on design and resource allocation heavily on results from their internal experiments (Saatchi 2012). This resulted in a management style that Kreiss termed "computational management." Currently, the debate on A/B testing focuses on the optimization of ads on social media platforms. Yet the associated opaqueness makes it difficult to assess the relative importance of these activities and their true impact on campaign success.

Impact of Data-Driven Campaigning

While consultants never got tired of emphasizing the applicability of the lessons of Obama's campaign for races across the United States and internationally (Vaccari 2010), a closer look at the campaigns and their uses of technology illustrates the large organizational challenges of actually running a data-driven, technologically savvy campaign (Kreiss 2016). Given these considerable preconditions, it was no surprise to find down-ticket campaigns in the United States relying on much more mundane uses of digital technology than the high-precision and high-impact uses by the Obama campaign (Nielsen 2011; Baldwin-Philippi 2015). Similar patterns hold for the use of digital tools by international campaigns (Jungherr 2016b). Given the decidedly low-tech approach taken by the subsequently successful presidential bid of Donald Trump (Tankersley 2016; Baldwin-Philippi 2017), we should also be wary of expecting each subsequent US presidential campaign to continuously build on the technological success of its predecessors. On the contrary, given the strategic nature of campaigning and the competitive advantage lying in doing the opposite of what is expected or seemingly common knowledge, we might expect periods of successful campaigns relying heavily on technology to be followed by phases in which successful campaigns consciously neglect technology in favor of other campaigning tools or rhetorical gestures and vice versa. As with any strategic competition, success usually does not follow established rulebooks but instead upturns what is then perceived as common knowledge. As Lawrence Freedman has shown for strategic thinking about the future of conflict, the most confident prognoses about the future of campaigning and the role of technology might tell much more about contemporary concerns and convictions than about the future (Freedman 2017).

Instead of actually using data-driven practices, campaigns might instead be simply mirroring the Obama campaigns' narratives as being highly innovative data-driven operations. After the 2012 Obama campaign, the use of data-driven campaigning became a common element in the self-presentations of international campaigns. To take but two examples, the 2016 Vote Leave campaign emphasized the importance of data and the sophistication of their efforts (Cummings 2017). Even in Germany, a country with famously strict data privacy laws and a population highly sensitive to issues of data protection, during the federal election 2017 the German conservatives emphasized their use of data in order to drive their door-to-door campaign in public presentations of the campaign (Jungherr 2016a). While data undoubtedly played a role in these campaigns, given differences in institutional, legal, and resource contexts the uses and effects of data-driven approaches varied strongly between these campaigns and the template provided by the Obama campaign (Jungherr 2016b). Still, irrespective of these differences and the actual impact of data-driven approaches on the success of these campaigns, campaigners shared the conviction that talking about data-driven campaigning in public would positively contribute to the image of their campaigns. In this, employing and talking about data-driven approaches served a rhetorical function for international campaigns in campaign cycles from 2012 onwards.

The Future of Data-Driven Campaigning

In early 2016, it looked to researchers as if the question of the dominant model of data-driven campaigning was settled. The US Democrats had developed a vibrant network of technology developers and consultancy firms in close contact with the party, associated campaigns, and allied interest groups. This ensured quick, innovative iterative cycles allowing for the development and testing of technological solutions in Democratic campaigns and those of their allies. The use of digital technology appeared to be deeply ingrained in Democratic organizational structures and work routines. This was the model of ensuring efficient uses of data-driven campaigning tactics (Kreiss 2016). And then Donald Trump happened.

Early reports focusing on the tactics used by Donald Trump's 2016 bid for the US presidency tended to note condescendingly the apparent lack of data-driven campaigning efforts, throwing doubt on the seriousness of his bid and the professionalism of his staff (Lapowsky 2016; Marshall 2016). Shortly before the election, this was countered by the campaign in providing one of the United States' leading tech-in-politics journalists, who was instrumental in creating the buzz around Obama's micro-targeting efforts in the first place, insights into their clandestine data-driven campaign techniques (Green and

Issenberg 2016). Yet that report probably spoke more about the desire of Trump's campaign consultants to appear less as atavistic stooges and more as data-savvy wizards, than offering an accurate version of the campaign's use of data-driven campaigning and its effects (Karpf 2016b). Currently, the best available evidence indicates that the Trump campaign, instead of collecting data itself or running analyses on data available through the Republican Party, simply outsourced both these tasks. Instead of investing heavily in directed voter outreach through volunteers, the Trump campaign focused on running targeted ads on online platforms, such as Google, Facebook, and Twitter. To decide where and how to spend their ad dollars, it seems the Trump campaign had the platforms propose solutions and bid for ad buys. In this, the Trump campaign relied on the efforts of the platforms themselves to find and propose the most efficient way to spend money with them (Kreiss and McGregor 2018; Martínez 2018a). While this is cost efficient and follows the practice of outsourcing ad buys in business, the practice has obvious challenges in the mid- to long term. For one, following this tactic, a campaign completely relies on black-box models by third parties. Potentially even more problematic, parties and campaigns following this approach neglect to develop in-house capacities of reaching voters and supporters while at the same time transferring existing knowledge and resources to an intermediary who over time becomes increasingly knowledgeable about this former core competency. This makes political actors ever more dependent on these intermediaries. These in turn grow more powerful and potentially might even develop into competitors. This dependency might render political actors largely helpless once vendors transfer their services to other actors, such as challengers of the political status quo. This development thereby contributes to a further hollowing out of established political parties (Mair 2013).

That being said, the Trump example shows that there is not one superior model of reaching voters through data-driven campaigning. Instead, there are different modes available whose success at any point in time might depend on the electoral system, level of technological sophistication in a campaign organization, and available resources. For example, a mixture of a restrictive regulatory context and limited campaign resources forces German parties to predominantly rely on targeting models provided by third parties. In practice, these models remain black-boxes to campaigns using them with no access to the underlying data, contact information, or inner workings of the models identifying promising contacts. Moreover, strategically it makes sense to search for alternatives to the "dominant campaign tactics" of the day and instead choose approaches ignored by the rest of the field.

7.7 Making Politics Countable

The discussion of data-driven campaigning has provided an instructive overview of how data-driven practices can shape politics. We have seen the challenge for established political actors to develop data infrastructures at great cost in order to profit from data-driven practices. We have also seen that the practice most heralded in public, data-driven targeting, might not actually be the form of data use that is most transformative to the practice of campaigning. Instead, a less chic but more mundane use of data in the coordination of supporters and the provision of actionable information to local organizational units might be more important for the running of contemporary campaigns. We have also seen that the impact of these practices and their contribution to the success of campaigns are hard to quantify and to evaluate. Finally, the story of data-driven campaigning also shows that there is no irreversible trend favoring one model of perpetual data-driven campaigning.

In this, data-driven campaigning provides a promising template of how to assess the use of data in politics. First, we have to establish the necessary preconditions for data-driven practices to work. What data points are of interest, what kind of infrastructure is necessary to establish at what cost for the practices to develop impact, and what kind of new mediating actors emerge in political fields by their skill in data collection, provision, and analysis? Second, we have to look closely at actual uses of data-driven practices in politics. What traditional functions do they fulfill for political actors, and what new functions do they create? Maybe most importantly, we should not be deceived by headline-grabbing tales about the use of data in politics, but instead look closely at how they are actually used. The true transformation of political practice might happen in the mundane, not in the exceptional (Nielsen 2011). Third, we have to search for metrics that allow the quantification of the success of data-driven practices for political actors and organizations. Without establishing these success metrics, it will be hard to differentiate data-driven practices from the next hot flavor of the month. Finally, we should not succumb to lazy thinking and prognosticate an irreversible trend toward a transformation of politics through data just because we see its increasing use in a variety of areas. The case of data-driven campaigning has shown us that there is no clear trend in innovation. While everyone is focusing on data, the next big thing might happen somewhere else completely. After all, in any competition one is unlikely to gain an edge in doing exactly what everybody else is doing.

On a larger scale, the chapter has shown that data-driven practices have evolved into the basis of decisions in ever more political areas. This increases the incentives for companies, political actors, and governments to measure customers, publics, and citizens. This leads to a twin problem of the conceptual standardization of social life in countable metrics and its constant monitoring. After all, the more of social life that can be translated into metrics and measured over time, the better the decisions, products, or services provided by companies, political actors, and governments will be. But this is built on a rather naive conception of a sustainable alignment between the interests of the measurer and the measured. Over time, this will lead to strong incentives for the measured to evade measurement, game it, or downright reject it.

We appear to have reached a point where there has emerged a cleavage between what is technologically feasible and what is socially legitimate, ethically desired, or legally allowed. This calls for a broad public debate on shared goals and acceptable trade-offs between data-driven increases in the common good and decreases in freedom from observation. Yet this debate is currently only held among small interested circles without broad salience or the involvement of the public. Even the most fundamental basis of this debate, a transparent account of which data-driven processes and algorithms are at work in politics and societies, is lacking. This is unfortunate, as this opaqueness creates room for wild speculation driven by the imaginations of proponents and opponents of data-driven politics.

In this chapter, we have reviewed prominent data sources, practices, and principles underlying data-driven politics. These practices promise new insights into public opinion, better policy-making and enforcement, more efficient campaigning, and increased transparency of government actions and elite behavior. Yet upon closer examination it is clear that these promises come with associated limitations or dangers. At the heart of these drawbacks is the question of the legitimate use of data documenting far-reaching areas of social and political life. What level of expected efficiency gains allow for the associated increase in surveillance and corporate and government control? Debating this fundamental trade-off underlying the use of data-driven practices must accompany any meaningful discussion of the use and regulation of the associated technology, business models, and practices.

8

Digital Media and Democracy

Two episodes from 2011 and 2016 bookend public expectations regarding the role of digital media in politics. In the wake of the protests and demonstrations in North Africa and the Middle East that we discussed in Chapter 5, the dominant public narrative portrayed social media as the keystone that enabled the opposition to coordinate a challenge to otherwise seemingly unwavering autocracies. Only social media offered disgruntled citizens the possibility of taking their discontent to the streets. Decentralized networks on top of real-time communication systems enabled activists to level the playing field against authoritarian regimes that previously had taken full advantage of their control over the official media and showed an unfettered capacity to repress any sign of dissent. It does not matter whether we see digital media as a causal factor; no account of the events in Egypt would be complete without a reference to the #jan25 hashtag on Twitter or the "We are all Khaled Said" site on Facebook (see Chapter 5).

The second decisive event is the election of Donald Trump to the presidency of the United States. One prominent reading of Trump's electoral success emphasizes the malicious uses of digital media to manipulate the American public. Through a series of orchestrated cyberattacks, a foreign power, Russia, was able to take advantage of new communication tools to actively trying to influence the electoral results (Jamieson 2018). The element that had the most visibility for the general public was the high-profile disinformation campaign that sought to disparage the Democratic candidate, Hillary Clinton (Mueller 2019). This vast and yet inexpensive operation exposed American audiences to false information and polarizing content on Twitter, Facebook, and Instagram (Singer and Brooking 2018) and helped Russia "sow discord in the U.S. political system" (Mueller 2019, 4). The actual effects of Russian activities are yet to be quantified and so their impact in the election of Donald Trump should be taken with a grain salt (see Chapter 3). However, the events shifted the public perception of digital media from being inherently beneficial to democracy to being a danger to a healthy public sphere (Carr 2015; Persily 2017).

These two events did not create their corresponding narratives. The views they embody about how digital media impact politics have run in parallel, one next to the other, since the 1990s, their prominence waxing and waning according to their seasonal resonance with current events and the political fortunes of their sponsors. While the two accounts have evolved to adapt to new technologies, events, or actors, they seem to revolve around a stable, common core of ideas.

One side sees the internet as an archetypal tool for citizen empowerment (Benkler 2006). Digital communication technologies enable deliberation and participation at a scale that escapes the limits of the world of "flesh and steel" (Barlow 1996). Horizontal, flat, decentralized networks are the base upon which individuals can build new forms of collective action and decision-making, allowing citizens to rethink and reshape the foundations of political life:

> There is no scientific law that prevents 100 people who find each other on the internet from coming together for a month, or 1,000 such people from coming together for a year. And as that increases to 10,000 and 100,000 and beyond, for longer and longer durations, we may begin to see cloud towns, then cloud cities, and ultimately cloud countries materialize out of thin air.
>
> (Srinivasan 2013)

Freed from the shackles of the physical context, the internet creates a space in which the concepts and limitations of the offline world no longer apply (Barlow 1996). Local politics, the politics of proximal communities, can in that way be meshed with global governance, connecting us with others who share our concerns, who are affected by similar problems, regardless of where they are (Barber 2013). As a result, it is natural that some authors see the internet as "the most democratizing innovation we've ever seen, more so than the printing press" (Trippi 2004, 235), one that is "founded on the primacy of individual liberty and a commitment to pluralism, diversity, and community" (Kapor 1993), all of which are principles that we want to associate with modern liberal democracies.

The contrasting narrative focuses on how digital media induce an augmentation of the same vices that characterize mass communication in the offline world (Carr 2015), bolstered by tools that quantify, regulate, and control citizens at a new scale (see Chapter 7). Over the last few years, we have been peppered with a spate of essays that take a fatalistic viewpoint of digital media and that argue that digital communication technologies are at odds with a healthy body politic. An attention economy that prizes "emotionalism over reason" (Carr 2015) creates a natural link between new media and populism (Gerbaudo 2018b) and constitutes fertile ground for the spread of disinformation and the creation of informational silos that deepen political polarization (Vaidhyanathan 2018). Similarly, an unstoppable process of datafication of every aspect of our domestic and social lives, driven by a push toward a personalization economy, narrows the private sphere of individuals and becomes indistinguishable from a state of surveillance (Marx 2016). Thus, there is something harrowing about digital tools that, rather than being conducive to a more open society founded upon "pluralism, diversity, and community," may instead be better aligned with new modes of authoritarianism (Beauchamp 2019; Deibert 2019).

These narratives are neither new nor specific to digital media (Strömberg 2015). They might not even be truly contradictory. As Tucker et al. (2017) discuss, digital technologies are a platform on which "political interests battle for influence, and not all these interests are liberal or democratic" (Tucker et al. 2017, 48). Samidh Chakrabarti, Facebook's Civic Engagement Product Manager, articulated a similar view in his assessment of the events of 2016 from the perspective of a platform: "At its best, it [digital media] allows us to express ourselves and take action. At its worst, it allows people to spread misinformation and corrode democracy. This is a new frontier and we don't pretend to have all the answers" (Chakrabarti 2018). For that reason, if the two assessments of the impact of digital tools are different, it is because they focus on affordances that favor different political actors. On the one hand, optimists emphasize the potential that digital tools unlock for addressing the challenges of collective action and organization, shifting the power away from the elites, as we saw in Chapters 5 and 6. Pessimists, on the other hand, fear that the same toolkit can be used to regulate the reach of voices, boosting or muffling opinions coming from the edges of the political system (Tucker et al. 2017).

Distilling an overarching interpretation of the effect of digital media in politics faces the challenge of adjudicating which political players – challengers or incumbents, insiders or outsiders – stand to benefit the most from a given toolkit. But it also forces us to adopt a yardstick to measure whether digital media are moving us and our political systems in the right or the wrong direction. It is incontrovertible, for instance, that exposing individuals to false information – regardless of whether it has small or large impact – is socially undesirable. To make similar statements about other dimensions and assess whether they help us build more effective democracies, we first need to spell out how they affect the mechanics of current institutions and practices. As Dahlberg (2011) helpfully pointed out, disagreement over whether digital tools strengthen democracies is rooted in broader ideological arguments over what is an ideal democratic system and what features of digital media to focus on. Some emphasize the value of the internet as a tool to gather political information; others, how it can improve deliberation and collective decision-making, or the way in which digital media facilitate the coordination of contestation in the public arena (Buchstein 1997; Dahlberg 2011). Each of these possibilities is associated with different interpretations of how modern democracies work –perhaps more importantly, how they *should* work – and, in consequence, carry different evaluations of the impact of digital media and their capacity to bring us closer to their particular version of an ideal political system.

The unruly variety of normative goals implicit in the evaluation of modern digital technologies is by no means exclusive to this particular field (Cunningham 2002; Dunn 2005; Shapiro 2005; Held 2006). What makes digital media unique is the fact that the object of study is still maturing. It involves an ever expanding set of agents, tools, and affordances (Karpf 2012a). Since 2000 we have witnessed a transition from bulky desktops to smartphones and from Usenet to Facebook. Along the way we have seen a transition towards an economy in which the market capitalization of Facebook, Apple, or Alphabet surpasses that of classical behemoths like General Electric, Exxon Mobile, or Walmart; a dramatic expansion of the number of internet users; and a transformation of the structure and rules governing internet service providers. The internet that inspired the "Declaration of Independence of Cyberspace" (Barlow 1996) is not the same one that sustained the ecosystem of tools that were at the center of the discussion about the Arab Spring. With such an elusive target, it is hardly surprising that it is frequently not clear which aspect of digital technology or which concept of democracy is at stake in the debate, and that makes it exceedingly difficult to extract clear lessons from the literature.

In light of how the discussion includes many moving pieces, it seems fruitful to constrain ourselves to be able to reason more clearly. In the following pages we do just that. We will commit to a barebones view of democracy that will lead us to evaluate the role of digital media through the prism of whether they improve the way in which citizens (voters) can control the political elites (politicians). This approach will help us move past an argument that sees representative democracy as an unfortunate workaround to the limitations of the offline world. The value of doing so is that regardless of whether we see the definition that will drive the discussion as a satisfying interpretation of what democracy *should be*, it offers a valuable viewpoint to evaluate the effect of digital media on the mechanics of *existing* political systems. Only after doing that, and having a firm grasp on the role and effects of digital media in current democracies, can we then circle back and rethink representation, if we are so inclined, to ponder whether digital media can offer us a way to make democratic discussion and decision-making more meaningful.

8.1 Democracy as Delegation

Modern democratic systems are structured around the notion of delegation. Underneath the unwieldy variation of institutional systems around the world, the fundamental trait that is common to all of them is that citizens elect politicians and that politicians, not citizens, write and implement legislation and policies. Simplifying things to some degree, we can describe democratic systems through the cadence of their electoral cycles (Przeworski 2018). At regular intervals, qualifying citizens are called to cast a vote. Those who are selected according to some known electoral rules convene and pass and execute laws for a predetermined period of time. Then, a new election takes place and voters are given an opportunity to either retain their representatives or give a chance to the opposition.

Such a system unburdens citizens from the immense majority of legislative and executive decisions, which are delegated to specialized and, more often than not, professional bodies. As a result, participation in politics does not consume more than a minimal amount of the citizens' time except for those who choose to become politicians and run for office. But we are then forced to face an obvious question: What makes politicians take decisions that are consistent with what citizens want? In this question rests the debate about the viability of democratic systems, and tackling it will occupy us for the next two sections. We will discuss, in very broad strokes, how elections induce politicians to behave as representatives of voters. Our goal is not to persuade the reader that this is the most realistic way of conceiving how democracies work, but rather to use this framework to better understand the role of political information in democratic systems. Armed with this analytical toolkit, it will then be easier to revisit the discussion about the effects of digital media with a clearer picture of the context in which it operates.

Controlling Politicians

As we said, our hope is that elections in modern democracies are mechanisms to incentivize politicians to keep in line with the preferences of the electorate (Przeworski, Stokes, and Manin 1999). Elections achieve this in two ways. On the one hand, voters can hold politicians accountable by voting out of office those who do not perform well, which motivates incumbents to avoid electoral retribution and exert effort in producing outcomes that satisfy a majority of voters. On the other hand, voters can select candidates that best reflect their own political preferences, voting for the candidate who is best aligned with them on any issues that voters consider relevant.

Accountability is a retrospective mechanism (Fiorina 1981)[1] that allows voters to "throw the rascals out." It hinges on an expectation that voters are able to correctly blame or reward politicians for whatever happened on their watch (Barro 1973; Ferejohn 1986). The second mechanism is instead a prospective one: On election day, voters need to select good politicians (Fearon 1999). What makes a candidate "good" is in the eye of the beholder. It can be someone who shares our views on social or economic issues, or we may want our candidate to have attributes that we consider valuable, such as decisiveness or empathy. Whatever it is, the goal is to select someone whose preferences align with those of voters because, if those preferences are one and the same, we can then relieve voters from having to closely monitor the behavior of politicians in office (Pitkin 1967).

These two notions of control correspond with two types of information that voters can use to evaluate politicians. To keep incumbents accountable, voters need to know what politicians *do*; to select from among all candidates the one that will best represent them, voters need information on what politicians *want*. In either case, voters depend on the media to acquire and process that information on their behalf. It is precisely from this point of view that the media are a "fourth estate" (McQuail 2010, 168f.) that is key in sustaining a well-functioning democracy. An informed public, a public able to keep the bad apples out of office, is thus a public protected against abuse or simple incompetence.

The connection between a more informed public and higher performance of politicians has been established in a number of empirical studies (Ahrend 2002; Brunetti and Weder 2003; Snyder and Strömberg 2010). Not only does voters' access to media improve the policies provided for them (Besley and Burgess 2002; Strömberg 2004), we also have evidence that politicians are more likely to exploit their position and to deviate from the preferences of the general public when the news media are not paying attention (Durante and Zhuravskaya 2018; Kaplan, Spenkuch, and Yuan 2018). Additional empirical research also points out that the link between what voters know and what

---

[1] See Ashworth (2012) for a more nuanced discussion.

politicians do is driven by the regulative contexts in which news media are situated and the way in which they are financed (Curran et al. 2009; Aalberg, Aelst, and Curran 2010; Iyengar et al. 2010; Soroka et al. 2013). By changing these settings, digital media might positively or negatively impact the provision of information necessary for voters to successfully control politicians. Accordingly, the role of digital media needs to be evaluated with regard to how voters consume information that is relevant to select and punish politicians and how voters' behavior may be affected by it.

Information and Democracy

One prominent view in the political science literature offers very dim prospects for the existence of an informed electorate that can be capable of evaluating politicians in the sense we have defined here. In this framework, partisan loyalties rather than a thoughtful weighing of the information available to voters are the basis for electoral decision-making. Affective and social attachments with political parties, often formed before we even start to participate in politics, do the heavy lifting in the formation of political attitudes (Campbell et al. 1960; Carpini and Keeter 1996), a possibility that offers little hope for the development of a consistent set of independent political beliefs with which to make decisions on election day (Converse 1964). In short, the decisions of the public may, without being irrational, stay disconnected from the foundations of individual behavior needed to keep politicians accountable and responsive. It is not surprising, then, that we can spot results in the literature that support the idea that voters are ready to punish or reward incumbents for events that do not bear any relation to the actions of the government, like shark attacks (Achen and Bartels 2016) or the outcome of college football games (Healy, Malhotra, and Mo 2010).[2]

Pessimistic as this view may seem, it still carries a certain dose of "realism" (Achen and Bartels 2016) that stands in opposition to the expectations of a "folk theory of democracy [that] celebrates the wisdom of popular judgments by informed and engaged citizens" (Achen and Bartels 2016, 53) in which voters do not spare any effort to sharpen a political worldview with which to make sense of political events and to understand the ideological inclinations of candidates. According to this approach, voters are capable of identifying their own interests, mapping them into an articulated political position, and selecting the party that is closer to their own political viewpoint (Downs

---

[2] For a reassessment of this literature, see Fowler and Hall (2018) and Fowler and Montagnes (2015).

1957), which consequently assumes a level of sophistication and motivation on the side of citizens that is very much absent in the previous model.

Our goal here is not to decide on the merits of either perspective but rather to outline the contours of two common but opposing views about how voters make decisions on election day. Between these two extremes there is, of course, a range of grays. What these intermediate positions have in common is that the voters can perform a competent job of keeping politicians motivated without regular citizens being asked to spend the time and effort that is implicit in the caricature version of the rational choice model and without at the same time imagining them to be so detracted from politics that they make their electoral decisions based entirely on partisan grounds.

True, voters typically score low in assessments of political knowledge in surveys (Page and Shapiro 1992) and have a superficial understanding of political information (Gomez and Wilson 2001). However, limited sophistication at the individual level does not immediately spell trouble for elections as a measure of effective democratic control of political elites. While it is necessary to accept that politics is not a major interest for average citizens (Hibbing and Theiss-Morse 2002), it seems reasonable to expect that they would develop strategies to assist them in their political behavior. This idea has been a major theme in the literature. Accountability, for instance, can be simplified so that the burdensome task of deciding whether a politician did a good job in office can be reduced to evaluating some simple metrics that summarize the prevalent economic conditions during the tenure of the incumbent (Kramer 1971). Voters then do not need to follow closely what the incumbent does, but rather inspect whether they are themselves better off than since the last election (Fiorina 1981).

In this regard, we can think about voters as agents that are trying to behave optimally while at the same time minimize their cognitive burden (Simon 1957; Fiske and Taylor 2017). Through rules of thumb and heuristics, they can then assess the consequences of actions or attributes of politicians (Nadeau and Niemi 1995; Lupia and McCubbins 1998; Lau and Redlawsk 2001; Dancey and Sheagley 2013) and, similarly, they can make use of summaries like political affiliations of candidates to help them decide how to interpret the messages coming from the political elites. Most important for us is the fact that, in this view, voters do not fully absorb or dismiss all the information they encounter. Instead, they are adept at evaluating it according to whether it is consistent with cues they have previously received, through its compatibility with previously held ideas, or by making an assessment based on the source of the information (Jost, Hennes, and Lavine 2013). For us, this means that voters are not unaware that the media may be biased (Gentzkow and Shapiro 2006) and that sources are politically motivated (Bullock 2011), but they can use those biases to help them pick and choose how to make sense of the world (see Chapter 4).

This brief discussion, admittedly unfair to a voluminous and sophisticated body of literature, informs the rest of the chapter. Two ideas developed here are of particular importance to what follows. First, looking at democracy as the institutional setting through which voters can control politicians allows us to identify the players on whom we should focus our attention (voters, politicians, and the media) and the type of information that is central to a well-functioning democracy. Second, a realistic view of the way political information is processed by voters should give us some comfort that voters do not take every message they receive at face value. While the "hypodermic needle model," a theory that mass media audiences are ready to accept all information presented to them in their information environment, has experienced a surprising renaissance of late, it has little empirical support (see a classical treatment by Lazarsfeld, Berelson, and Gaudet [1944]). By filtering new information through preexisting attitudes and beliefs or by comparing it against cues from the elites, various mechanisms cause the effects of information to be more indirect and subtle than is often suggested in the public debate (see Chapter 4). With this toolkit at hand, we can now move into a more grounded exploration of different dilemmas in which digital media are effecting a change in the relation between politicians and voters.

8.2 Digital Media, Accountability, and Representation

Monitoring Politicians

One of the key themes that animates this book is the digitalization of the institutions whose purpose is to monitor politics and politicians (Schudson 2008; Keane 2013). We have witnessed a transformation of the landscape of providers of political information that has affected the resources available to old players (such as traditional news media) but that, at the same time, has incorporated participants with new expertise and orientation. The dilemma that is yet to be resolved is which of the two effects dominates.

As we saw in Chapter 2, one of the critical changes associated with digital media has been the reshaping of the business model of news media. This is especially true for countries relying predominantly on commercial news. News organizations are experimenting widely with new financing models (Nielsen 2012b) but it remains an open question whether alternative schemes – like public funding, crowdsourcing, or sponsorship by individuals or foundations – can successfully provide pluralistic, continuous, and competent coverage of politics on national, state, and local levels or invest in high-risk, high-reward investigative journalism that is necessary for meaningful political accountability at different institutional levels.

At the same time, digital tools empower alternative players to go beyond the opportunities afforded by conventional news media. A new environment that favors the proliferation of media with a higher diversity of views and functions (Schudson 1999; Keane 2013) provides fertile ground for specialization and, consequently, for improved control of the elites. With more and more varied eyes (e.g., citizen-journalists or fact-checking organizations), there are more opportunities to trigger "burglar alarms" (Zaller 2003). New players can bring in new resources, interests, and perspectives that can cover areas traditionally ignored by the media, often with more topic expertise (Powers 2016). It remains unclear, however, if the values of impartiality and objectivity to which newsrooms aspire can be reproduced outside of professional news organizations (see Pressman 2018), especially for those coming from a background of political advocacy. It is also debatable whether topics of general interest that are not tied to particularistic goals, like the economy or national news, can be competently addressed by these new organizations (Powers 2016).

Unmediated Connections

The sociologist Ralph Schroeder has described the increasing linkage between political elites, information producers, and consumers that is furnished by digital media through the concept of "tethering" (Schroeder 2018, 161), which emphasizes the mutual visibility between citizens and politicians. Through a more direct and unmediated connection, each of them can then fine-tune their decisions to a particularized and even personalized measurement of the other side.

A body of literature suggests that politicians follow the preferences of the public during their term in office. Politicians who move outside of the "zone of acquiescence" of voters are likely to face the consequences on electoral day (Erikson, MacKuen, and Stimson 2002), which translates into an empirical observation that the status of aggregate public opinion should have an effect on the policy environment (Wlezien 1995). As we saw in Chapter 7, political elites and journalists use digital media to measure public opinion (Anstead and O'Loughlin 2015; McGregor 2019), slicing and dicing the reaction of the potential electorate to any speech, announcement, or scandal. What topics are at the center of attention online? To what topics or slogans do my supporters react most strongly? Digital media offer political elites a mediated and skewed reflection of reality (Jungherr, Schoen, and Jürgens 2016) but accessibility oftentimes trumps validity. While there is a fruitful debate to be had in academia on whether social media allow one to infer public opinion (Jungherr, Schoen, et al. 2017), practitioners will be tempted to incorporate metrics based on digital media regardless.

Digital media, and particularly social media, make it easier for citizens to individually and directly scrutinize what politicians do and say, avoiding the potentially biased perspective of gatekeepers. While it is true that online presence is oftentimes performative (Jungherr 2016c), citizens are still afforded a way of reaching politicians (or, more realistically, their staff) to have their concerns heard. In this way, politicians can use the same tools to signify their individuality, especially in political systems that have traditionally relied on parties as the main interface between voters and their representatives (Ceron 2017), airing disagreements with official positions if necessary and turning previously hidden intra-party conflicts into more public affairs (Grant, Moon, and Busby Grant 2010; Ceron 2017).

Reshaping Representation

A lower cost of reach (see Chapter 3) translates into smaller barriers of entry for new participants in the public debate. More voices are heard and, without gatekeepers to modulate their presence, they can attempt to push their message across to gather support beyond their traditional networks and increase their relevance. But the same mechanism can be exploited by those on the fringes who are not reluctant to build their political space through provocation, personal attacks, or outright abuse.

As we have seen in Chapters 5 and 6, digital media reduce the costs of political coordination and organizations significantly. The impact of this has been seen most clearly in collective action and in the work of social movements, but it also affects the functioning of other institutions like political parties. Digital media enable new and formerly underrepresented groups to coordinate and run effective campaigns by allowing them to identify and establish lists of supporters, get the word out cheaply and effectively, and circumvent former gatekeepers of the political process, such as party elites or traditional news organizations. We have seen these processes at work in the emergence of new political parties in multi-party systems, such as Alternative für Deutschland (AfD) in Germany, Podemos in Spain, or Movimento 5 Stelle (M5S) in Italy; the emergence of political outsiders who manage to take over established parties, such as Donald Trump or Jeremy Corbyn; or the emergence of highly successful ad hoc organizations in referendum campaigns, such as Vote Leave during the British Brexit referendum.

At the same time, this can lead to a strengthening of political fringes that political gatekeepers, such as party elites or media organizations, had previously excluded from political competition (Jungherr, Schroeder, and Stier 2019). It also means that there are more groups and positions available to the public that contentiously compete for attention and votes, which may lead to new forms of political discourse and could contribute to the deterioration of shared political norms, which are highly important for the workings of representative democracy (Levitsky and Ziblatt 2018). Since incivility online, especially that directed toward politicians (Theocharis et al. 2016), predominantly targets women and minorities (Jane 2014; Marwick and Caplan 2018), it can further retract the presence of already underrepresented groups in the public debate.

The Fragility of Information Spaces

The narratives of disinformation and polarization have taken a central role in recent discussions about politics (see Chapters 2 and 3). Without gatekeepers that control the flow of information and behave as central and trusted authorities (see Chapter 3), the spread of information is easier, faster, and freer. While this may be good news for the purposes of solving collective action problems (see Chapter 5), it also has a darker side. Adversarial attacks spreading disinformation or attempting to exploit wedge issues to polarize public opinion are now easier to conduct, too. Yet how decisive is their impact on voters?

The reach of disinformation originating on digital media is not as broad as the public debate sometimes seems to suggest (Alcott and Gentzkow 2017; Guess, Nyhan, and Reifler 2018b; Nelson and Taneja 2018; Guess, Nagler, and Tucker 2019). People who tend to receive or share disinformation predominantly appear to have already made up their minds about what to believe and whom to trust or, maybe even more importantly, whom to distrust in politics (Guess et al. 2018b; Guess et al. 2019). In other words, political partisans are those predominantly exposed to disinformation (Alcott and Gentzkow 2017). Previously held beliefs and available information about politics will limit the effects of disinformation on this audience. Less politically involved people who end up receiving disinformation might ending up not thinking too hard about it or dropping it quickly from their mind (Bronstein et al. 2019; Pennycook and Rand 2019). In other words, consistent with what we discussed in the previous sections about the effect of political information, belief in disinformation is likely limited to people predisposed toward the goal independent of the persuasive effects of the content itself (Flynn, Nyhan, and Reifler 2017).

Yet this does not mean that we should rule out that a steady diet of disinformation can indeed produce strong effects on individuals. Events like #pizzagate in Washington, DC or the terror attack in Christchurch, New Zealand can be traced back to online disinformation (Aisch, Huang, and Kang 2016; Lorenz 2019) and serve as reminders of the destructive power of exposure to politically motivated disinformation. Even so, the causal direction is still unclear as we are far from being able to tell whether radicalization is a cause or a result of the consumption of untrustworthy and misleading information.

Disengaged Citizens?

Any democracy is unquestionably in a better place if voters are engaged in the process and believe that their voices are heard and that institutions are not rigged against them. This opens up a different perspective on the potential effects of disinformation online. While public debate focuses predominantly on manipulation of audience members, it is possible that effects are indirect. The goal of disinformation might not lie in persuading people whom to vote for but instead in casting doubt on the viability of public discourse and the functioning of democratic institutions (Arquilla and Ronfeldt 2001; Farrell and Schneier 2018). Rather than correcting isolated misconceptions, ubiquitous fact-checking might thus contribute to a pervasive feeling that political information cannot be trusted. In this direction, findings indicate that fact-checks increase distrust not only in dubious information but also in news coverage in general (Clayton et al. 2019).

Given the growing importance of digital platforms for information distribution and public discourse in representative democracies, trust in them now plays a role akin to that of trust in traditional news media. Digital platforms are hosts to an ever increasing share of public discourse, their parent companies have been made de facto arbiters of free speech, and even electronic voting appears to some to be an attractive alternative to paper-based ballots. Their growing importance is not matched, however, by public transparency in the inner workings of these digital platforms in the service of democracy. Instead, the way these platforms operate remains essentially a black box for users and regulators (Pasquale 2015). There is widespread distrust in the algorithmic shaping of political discourse on platforms like Facebook, Google, or Twitter, with widespread speculation about whether they might be able to hand candidates or parties an election (Zittrain 2014). Not only that, legislation making online platforms liable for disinformation or personal attacks has led to highly controversial editorial decisions blocking legitimate accounts following opaque procedures (Sarovic 2019)

*****

The information that voters have available to them is crucial in the task of ensuring that politicians are adequate representatives of their interests. Politicians, meanwhile, benefit from being able to poll their constituents to avoid surprises on election day. Thus, both sides, principals and their agents, welcome transformations that reduce frictions in the distribution of information about one another. In this way, digital media insert themselves into the democratic process by changing who can communicate with whom and how, and in doing so, who can participate in the political process. As a result, we have witnessed the surge of new participants in the political arena representing voices that were previously unable to get sufficient reach. But digital tools do not discriminate among the voices they carry and have opened the gates to participants galloping from the borderlands of the political discourse. We have observed not only a rise in incivil behavior online, but also more opportunities for those on the fringes to contact and, potentially, persuade disaffected citizens. It is thus of little surprise that one of the challenges we deal with nowadays is related to distrust, not only in institutions, but also in the platforms that sustain digital media.

However, these transformations do not mean that digital media are dismantling the foundations of democracy. Political actors interact in the same way they did before in order to satisfy the same needs they had in an offline world. New participants may have elbowed their way into the political arena and the distribution of resources among political actors may have shifted with them, but the crucial relation in democracies, the one between voters and politicians, still operates under similar parameters as before. Voters' behavior neither passively reflects the latest piece of information they have seen, nor is it unaware of the biases and motivations of the elites from which they take cues or that inform their reasoning process. From this point of view, we should rest somewhat more at ease with regard to the widespread fears of digital media "breaking democracy." By that, we do not mean to convey a message of unconditional resilience of democratic regimes, but rather to raise a cautionary note about where to find the causes of the current political challenges.

Our view in the preceding discussion has been driven by setting our eyes on elections above everything else. In that regard, we need to be ready to accept that, if the effects of digital technologies do not seem large, it is maybe due to the fact that we are looking at things through a peephole that misses the main transformations that digital media bring into the political space. By limiting ourselves to a narrow understanding of democracy, perhaps we have missed the fundamental transformative potential of digital tools in politics. To understand that, we need to switch to alternative definitions of how democracies should operate in order to better view other modes of engaging people through new models of participation.

8.3 Deepening Democracy

It does not take much to feel disillusioned if one thinks about the potential for political transformation that is associated with digital media and then contrasts it with our discussion about democratic governance in the previous pages. With new communication tools at hand, the traditional logic of representative democracy seems if not insufficient, at least unsatisfactory. Much less clear is what the road ahead should look like. The ideal form of a digitally fueled democracy is still very much open to debate (see Susskind 2018). And yet, as often happens, even the most innovative of the proposals that attempt to forge a new road ahead fit well within a long tradition of projects of democratic transformation. Examining those roots, we can discern two distinct, although not necessarily divergent, goals.

One approach emphasizes that participation can go much further and deeper than the way in which we conceived it in the previous pages. Democracy in the form of regular elections, used to fill a small number of offices by means of a very rough tool such as a ballot, unnecessarily removes people from the political sphere. It is hoped that digital media will give citizens many more channels to make their opinion count. This could either mean an expansion of the offices that are elected by the public or an adoption of direct democracy to vote on issues directly. Either way, digital tools provide the necessary infrastructure to involve the public in more decisions.

Another approach takes the view that voting cannot be equated to an actual voice in politics. Voting restricts political expression and turns opinions into an arithmetic of approval versus disapproval that hides the arguments and, as a result, makes it impossible to build consensus. Digital tools, in this case, are the platform that enables more active involvement in the decision-making process through a rational exchange of ideas that, one hopes, converges on a satisfactory solution for all parts.

The participatory and deliberative approaches are not fully separate, either in theory or in practice. In fact, the vast majority of the designs that implement them tends to include elements of both. As should be clear, the goal of these transformative outlooks is not simply to replace offline participation methods with their technological cousins, for example replacing town halls with online town halls or voting with electronic voting. Instead, they aspire to take advantage of the possibilities of new technologies to improve participation and representation, engage diverse participants to provide new insights (Mergel 2015), and improve the legitimacy of democratic structures and institutions (Simon et al. 2017). This goes beyond gradually improving current democratic practices and attempts to build stronger forms of democracy with a more active citizenship (see, for instance, Barber 2003). In this endeavor, digital tools, one would hope, make it possible to "enhanc[e] civic participation and democratic decision making" (Halpern and Gibbs 2013. 1160). Thus, a sizable chunk of the discussion on digital democracy devotes its attention to engineering solutions to problems of democratic politics that we originally tried to solve through delegation of power. In this, they see representative democracy as a second-best solution limited by the technologies of the day and express the hope that digital technology can lead us to a more direct and vibrant form of politics.

The Deliberative Turn

Representative democracy, at least in the way we have described it here, aggregates preferences through elections. Deliberative theorists try to move past this approach to offer an alternative that gives citizens a more meaningful way to engage in collective decision-making. Where electoral democracy focuses on votes to choose representatives, the deliberative method primes instead the public exchange of arguments with the goal of finding a solution that is agreeable to all participants (Habermas 1992). An open discussion in the public sphere, precisely because it involves an active contribution by participants, achieves a level of legitimacy, acceptance, and quality (Gimmler 2001; Friess and Eilders 2015) that is not attainable in representative methods.

Uncovering the truth together, listening to others as opposed to imposing the will of the majority (Buchstein 1997), helps participants understand not only who supports a proposal but the reasons behind that support (Meijer, Curtin, and Hillebrandt 2012). To this process-oriented throughput legitimacy theorists add the expectation that deliberation can indeed produce better outcomes as new participants bring in new expertise that was unavailable in representative democracies, where all citizens could do was express approval or rejection. Not only that, each individual participant benefits directly from deliberation because joining rational and open discussions strengthen attributes that we associate with a virtuous citizenry. Accordingly, empirical studies on the effects of deliberation try to uncover how deliberation increases political knowledge (Luskin, Fishkin, and Jowell 2002; Iyengar, Luskin, and Fishkin 2003), feelings of political efficacy, engagement, or trust (Min 2007). As one probably would expect, mixed results are the norm (Morrell 2005), partially due to the inherent difficulty of designing and measuring both causes and effects in this context.

Perhaps ironically, no consensus has been reached on what the deliberative method should look like or how to delimit the set of deliberative practices beyond a rejection of preference aggregation and voting. To be fair, while no unified definition exists on what deliberation is, there is wide agreement on how deliberative discussion is different from its non-deliberative counterpart. This variety of perspectives should not be seen as a fatal flaw and, if anything, speaks to the wealth of contributions to the field, sparked by the variety of proposals for democratic reform in which deliberation plays different roles (see Etzioni 1993; Barber 2003), which has prompted Dryzek (2002) to talk about a deliberative turn in political thought.

Whatever deliberation may be, the challenge we need to address is whether meaningful exchanges can happen online. In other words, does deliberation offline translate well to an online environment? Adapting deliberation to the internet would certainly help expand who can participate in politics, which is one of the most commonly voiced criticisms about deliberation – namely that even if we were to accept that it is useful for small groups, it is not viable for large modern democratic systems (Coleman and Gotze 2001; Goodin 2003; Goodin and Niemeyer 2003) without design changes (e.g., Fishkin and Luskin 2005). As a result, the comparison between offline and online, and whether – scale issues aside – computer-mediated communication technologies are conducive to rational discussions (see Neuman, Bimber, and Hindman [2011] for an overview), has been a major empirical program in the literature. Positive results point to the possibility of achieving meaningful deliberation in online contexts (Iyengar et al. 2003; Min 2007; Neblo, Esterling, and Lazer 2018), although they are probably drowned out by the narrative about the prevalence of incivility, polarization, and harassment in digital contexts (Anderson et al. 2014; Coe, Kenski, and Rains 2014; Mutz 2015).

This issue goes beyond the malaise that the public has come to associate with social networking platforms. Some authors have identified a series of patterns that spell trouble for deliberation, including evidence that individuals agree with whatever opinion is expressed by the majority (Myers and Lamm 1976), the entrenchment of positions or even increased polarization of opinions as the conversation progresses instead of convergence (Mendelberg and

Oleske 2000; Mendelberg 2002), and even growing resentment among those who are challenged during a discussion, which can in turn make them retreat from further participation (Gervais 2015). This same literature shows that advocates of political deliberation have to face the problems of opinion polarization (Esterling, Fung, and Lee 2015; Grönlund, Herne, and Setälä 2015) and the extent to which small group discussions may induce anger, aversion, or the growth of incivility (Gervais 2015).

An assessment of whether online deliberation is feasible also has to account for the riotous variety of formats and designs in which deliberative conversation could take place (Janssen and Kies 2005). Taking a fairly wide-ranging view of deliberation to include all sorts of spaces that allow for online conversation, the literature has studied discussion dynamics in Usenet newsgroups (Wilhelm 1998), on dedicated participation platforms (Borge Bravo and Sáez 2016; Aragón et al. 2017; Neblo et al. 2018), in the comments section of newspapers (Ruiz et al. 2011; Rowe 2015) on content-sharing platforms, and, of course, in social media (Stroud et al. 2014). This literature shares an interest in the degree to which the design choices of these platforms can help shape discussions to converge with deliberative ideals (Wright and Street 2007).

What all these studies have in common is that they force us to explicitly deal with ubiquitous attributes that make computer-mediated communication special. Some of them, like asynchronicity (interactions in online conversations can be delayed), are if anything a convenient feature and the problems that come with them may be read as a matter of unfulfilled potentials. The possibility of stepping back and revisiting assumptions or finding new information has been associated with greater reflexibility in debates (Janssen and Kies 2005; Stromer-Galley and Wichowski 2011). Asynchronicity also enables broad participation in debates (Coleman, Hall, and Howell 2002), as users can read contributions at their own pace. While it is true that the lack of contextual cues that are common in face-to-face interactions could make consensus harder to reach in online discussions (Baek, Wojcieszak, and Delli Carpini 2012), or that users may find it easy to withdraw from participation and to "lurk" (Preece, Nonnecke, and Andrews 2004; Kim and Sundar 2014), these are best seen as hurdles that can be addressed with the proper design.

Other features of online conversations are more problematic. Perhaps the most prominent of these controversial affordances is anonymity (Moore 2018). Anonymity is commonly associated with a disposition towards a candid and honest expression of opinions that participants would otherwise be discouraged from sharing if they perceive them to be socially undesirable (Tourangeau and Yan 2007). At the same time, anonymity appears to be clearly associated with uncivil conduct and hate speech (Halpern and Gibbs 2013), as illustrated by the public attention garnered by sites like 8chan or Gab, or some political threads on Reddit, as the most visible spaces of abuse (Marwick and Lewis 2017). Targets are commonly marginalized groups, which reflects the fact that attackers lack accountability (Beyer 2014), even if the social norms of civility may be sustained, for example, by appropriate interventions to limit interactions with toxic users (Fredheim, Moore, and Naughton 2015).

Redefining Participation

Delegation as the basis for democratic decision-making feels unsatisfactory in two distinct ways. On the one hand, we, the voters, are given a chance to express our opinion only every few years and using a tool that gives us no more expressiveness than a thumbs up or down. Additionally, we are constrained to a limited set of choices (i.e., parties or candidates) that, as a consequence, need to offer broad platforms that force us to decide on proposals that do not match exactly our own preferences. The deliberative approach, described previously, is interested in changing the way political decisions are made, bypassing both issues altogether. There is, however, a case to be made about taking collective decisions according to whether a majority approves or disapproves of a given proposal (Przeworski 2018). In that case, what needs to be addressed is not so much whether voting and majoritarianism work but rather what additional decisions, within the frame of current electoral democracies, can be reverted back to citizens. For this, the internet and digital technologies have been welcomed as disruptive forces for their capacity to overcome the logistical difficulties of organizing the electoral process in an offline world, which is in itself a natural offshoot of the core tenet that digital technologies generally reduce the costs of communication, which could then mean that "[e]lections and public participation in politics could become as mundane as replying to an email" (Wright and De Filippi 2015, 39). In this context, the concern we have is not so much with making decisions through voting but rather what decisions qualify as relevant and clear enough to be used in referendums (Lupia and Matsusaka 2004).

The expansion of the scope of participation can also be understood in a different way, as a complement to the current mechanisms of representative democracy. Citizens can be involved earlier in the decision process, not only deciding between alternatives that are presented on election day but instead joining others in the elaboration of proposals, bringing voters into the legislative process earlier (Lathrop and Ruma 2010). Digital tools offer not only a possibility for "voting on more things" but rather a much larger set of opportunities for the insertion of citizens in everyday politics. It is worth noting that a less structured form of participation in the elaboration of proposals makes the distinction between participatory and deliberative approaches increasingly artificial, as illustrated by the fact that the tools and platforms used to harness "collective intelligence" often combine elements of both (see Simon et al. 2017).

Citizens can be called on to create petitions to draw the attention of legislators to specific issues, review and comment on existing legislative proposals, collaboratively draft new ones, or decide on execution through participation in participatory budget initiatives. Examples of each kind abound across the world and several organizations have attempted to catalogue them (Patel et al. 2013; Simon et al. 2017; The GovLab 2018). Some of the most well-known initiatives allow citizens and representatives to collaborate with each other to gather comments on bills (like "Parlement et Citoyens" in France), offer stakeholders the opportunity to participate in discussions about policy (as in "vTaiwan" used by the Taiwanese government), or open the door to suggestions about the allocation of funding across competing projects (for instance, "Decide Madrid" in Spain). Perhaps unsurprisingly, there is substantial overlap between the tools adopted to gather input from members in political parties (see Chapter 6) and those used by government agencies and institutions.

The argument that led us to involve citizens in the legislative process can be applied to other spheres of government, and the collaboration between governments and citizens can be expanded to include other tasks that are typically the domain of public employees (Simon et al. 2017). Most notably, citizens can use digital platforms to assist local governments to improve their performance by "doing what they do best: noticing issues that arise in a neighborhood" (Schrock 2018, 54). From mapping potholes that need to be repaired and identifying broken streetlights (with applications like SeeClickFix or Fix My Street) to involving individuals in presenting ideas to improve municipal services (such as "Better Reykjavik"), the overarching idea is that communication technologies allow governments to identify relevant stakeholders in the population and poll their knowledge, skills, and resources. In some cases, it may simply mean having eyes in every street to spot issues with the urban infrastructure, but it can be scaled to the identification of individuals with useful expertise that are usually removed from the network of advisors that is available to the government (Noveck 2015). In a way, the government is increasingly transformed into a platform that aggregates decisions and provides basic infrastructure (Johnson and Robinson 2014), which is "a convener and an enabler – ultimately, it is a vehicle for coordinating the collective action of citizens" (O'Reilly 2009).

Yu and Robinson (2012) have pointed out that open data is neither sufficient nor necessary for open government, but the two concepts go hand in hand. For successful collaboration between governments and citizens, it is helpful to "lift the veil of secrecy" from government (Attard et al. 2015), and consequently national and regional institutions have been building portals that centralize information produced by the government, such as data.gov in the United States or data.gov.uk in the United Kingdom (Attard et al. 2015). In doing so, governments navigate a strategic dilemma between releasing information and increasing the participation from citizens." Governments benefit from presenting themselves as transparent and open. At the same time, precisely because openness exposes them to potential criticism from the public (see Chapter 7), pushback to keep portions of their actions away from public scrutiny is expected. Thus, it is reasonable for governments to carefully select both the content and the format of what is released so that it is least harmful to their interests (Lourenço 2015). Within this context, we can then make more sense of the observation that governments tend to focus their efforts on tools that increase participation in discussions rather than on building applications that scrutinize public actions (Simon et al. 2017) which raises the risk that these initiatives turn into largely rhetorical enterprises for governments to score points with the public through gestures of transparency while keeping under the rug more contested areas.

Participation and Inequality

Underlying any notion of democracy there is a common concern: How do we ensure a link between what citizens want and what governments do? When we discussed the concept of representative democracy, the connection was established through electoral incentives that motivate politicians to pursue the interests of *voters*. The emphasis on voters is important: Elections push politicians to cater to those who may keep them accountable at the polls, which is a way of saying that they will be reactive to those who show up and ignore those who stay out of politics. Alternative approaches to collective decision-making do not fare better in this regard. More profound and consequential participation demands additional attention, time, and effort from citizens and it is not obvious that, in doing so, transformations that seek to deepen democratic practices may not just drive some people away from politics. The literature on digital democracy has grappled with this challenge, although, as Hansson, Belkacem, and Ekenberg (2015) report, many research articles in the field tend to ignore the fact that groups like "the public" or "the citizens" hide heterogeneous groups with different interests or with unequal means to participate. We discussed in Chapter 4 how varying levels of access to the internet induce a layer of inequality in the voices that are heard, a divide that is amplified even further through the decision by political organizations and politicians on what is to be measured, as we saw in Chapter 7. This problem is compounded even further here. As we outlined in Chapter 5, political participation is mediated by socioeconomic characteristics of individuals, and moving towards more costly methods of citizen involvement runs the risk of pushing aside individuals with low political interest, low economic resources, or simply those who are not within reach of mobilizing organizations (Verba, Schlozman, and Brady 1995). What this means is that particular attention needs to be paid to ensure that methods of participation do not reproduce the distortions in turnout by class that have already been documented in the United States (Campbell et al. 1960; Wolfinger and Rosenstone 1980; Verba et al. 1995) and Europe (Gallego 2007; Armingeon and Schädel 2015). Indeed, evidence from internet voting is suggestive that even if the cost of participation drops, the effect on turnout may be small (Germann and Serdült 2017; Goodman and Stokes 2018) and that those who do show up reflect biases favoring those who are younger, have higher education levels, higher income, or are more tech savvy (Serdült et al. 2013; Goodman et al. 2018) Thus, although the internet was originally praised for its homogenizing value, which would "give new voice to people who've felt voiceless" (Gillmor 2004. xxix), there is a danger that it instead provides more opportunities to those who are already overrepresented in politics (Margolis and Resnick 2000; Hindman 2009).

On the flip side, it is understandable that representative democracy could lead to disenchantment with the political process. People may feel disconnected from the political process, that their votes do not count, or maybe, not too incorrectly, that other political actors may have more influence in the political domain. Declining participation rates are thus to be expected and it may even be surprising that people participate in politics at all. It is not hard to put ourselves in the shoes of a citizen thinking that "if my participation is only required every few years in the form of a yes-or-no ballot, why would I bother to behave as if it was fundamental?" We find traces of this argument in much of the literature. Underneath it, there is the expectation that changing the institutional conditions in which citizens operate will produce more engaged and informed citizens. After all, how could one fairly evaluate a new way of organizing politics by presenting evidence established under the parameters of a system that precludes full and engaged participation? We could seek support for this view in findings that suggest that participating in deliberation appears to follow different reasons than other modes of political participation and that those who are willing to participate in deliberation might indeed be less likely to participate in politics as usual (Neblo et al. 2010). The question, however, is one that goes beyond the feasible empirical record. At the end of the day, the problem becomes one of disentangling whether people's motivation to engage in politics is mediated by institutional constraints and whether, by raising the stakes of participation, we can also achieve deeper involvement of citizens in politics.

8.4 Digital Solutions and Non-digital Problems

While there currently seems to be wide agreement about the negative impact of digital media in politics, it seems at least questionable that all the malaise of contemporary democracies can be traced back to them. It cannot be disputed that we are seeing the rise of unquestionably concerning phenomena, but a look at the empirical record on how voters behave does not support an assumption, implicit in the public debate, that voters are powerless in the face of whatever information they encounter in their communication environments or that digital media have fundamentally transformed how they manage their political participation. We should not, of course, blindly disregard disinformation, polarization, abuse, or radicalization as threats to political conversation. They pose risks for a healthy public debate in that they can silence minority voices, strengthen animosities among the public, feed distrust, or push individuals towards militant extremism. It is not our goal to minimize these problems. Our view here is driven by an admittedly narrower question about how digital media impact the way in which democracies – conceived as institutional arrangements in which voters control politicians – work. From this point of view, the challenge is to square the current consensus in the public debate with what we know about the strategies that voters use in order to effectively participate in politics. Looking at the existing evidence on how voters process information, the transformation in the landscape of media organizations, and the new ways in which political actors can communicate and interact with each other, what has emerged in this chapter is a variety of effects, most of which are indirect and remain somewhat hidden from view. Based on them, while it is hard to make a sweeping assessment, the main message that transpires from our discussion is that informational threats to democracy are more nuanced than pessimists would have us believe.

There is a counterpart to this argument. Kreiss (2015, 2), observing the tension that pervades the literature on digital democracy, asks: "How do we reconcile academic skepticism about e-democracy in many quarters with practitioner enthusiasm about the power of digital and social media to restore the health of contemporary democracy?" It is easy to feel optimistic about the many ways in which new tools could help us rebuild democracies and get rid of the vestiges that we inherited from a time in which delegation was the only way to manage large-scale polities. In this chapter, we discussed two alternative but closely related approaches that embody the hopes of a digitally fueled transformation of current democratic practices. They both have deep roots in the literature in political science and, through these origins, they are connected to discussions that predate the digital revolution. By placing these two theoretical approaches in context, we can more clearly see that some of the challenges these alternatives face are not technological in nature, but are instead entrenched in how and why individuals participate in politics to begin with. With that, our argument here has not been that these initiatives cannot improve how democracies work (they surely can), but rather that we need to evaluate their optimistic promises with more critical eyes, attentive to what we have learned about how citizens engage in politics.

We can think of the institutional design of current democracies as an attempt to reduce the cost of political participation in order to minimize inequalities in representation while at the same time maintaining a link between public opinion and policy outputs. Alternative designs that hope to improve this link need to be cognizant that democratic institutions are, and more likely will be, resting on voters that do not correspond to the rational ideal (Achen and Bartels 2016), and it is thus only reasonable to expect that all the challenges that affected deliberative or participatory methods offline, especially with regard to differentials in participation, will not be solved simply by moving them to a new technological infrastructure. At the same time, with all our flaws, we, the voters, are equipped with instruments that help us parse a complex informational environment using minimal resources that are yet sufficient to keep politicians accountable and representative. The digital context may be new, but the challenges that we have discussed throughout the book resemble those that are built into any system of self-government. Looking at things from this perspective, it is tempting to conclude that, in the relation between digital media and politics, optimists have come to expect too much from voters and pessimists too little.

9

Digital Media in Politics

We have started with two questions in mind: What are the ways in which digital media have influenced and changed politics? And how can we best go about identifying them? In other words, what are digital media doing to politics and how do we know?

In answering the first question, there is the consistent danger of missing small but significant changes. As a consequence, the discussion tends to focus on imagined hopes and nightmares. While these regularly fail to materialize, they still draw the oxygen from any pragmatic and empirically grounded discussion of the real-world effects of digital media. Their persistence in public discourse also leads to misguided regulation attempts and focuses the attention of decision-makers on movie-plot threats (Schneier 2005) and an imagined internet full of terrors.

It certainly feels like the imagined effects of digital media are much more at the fore of regulators' minds than the need for establishing empirically grounded evidence. Recently, for example, we witnessed attempts to regulate so-called fake news without knowing the scope of its reach, its effects, or even agreeing on a definition of what constitutes "fake news." Other regulatory initiatives touch on free speech, with internet companies becoming de facto arbiters of users' legal rights, the size and scope of internet companies, and the right to privacy of individuals. The far-reaching consequences of these regulatory efforts mean that we have to be much clearer about what we know about digital media's effects and how we know.

Getting information on the effects of digital media is inherently difficult. Everybody who is involved in political uses of digital technology and who might offer insights about its effects has incentives to consciously or subconsciously mislead us. Accounts of tent-pole campaigns promise insights into how campaigns were using digital technology to gain votes. Investigative reports promise insights into the nefarious dealings of companies selling us services and selling our attention to the highest bidder. These accounts do not sell if the use of technology is not new or expected to have little impact. Anybody working in political tech has strong incentives to exaggerate the role and impact of digital technology as well. They tell stories about a steady stream of revolutionary uses of technology with supposedly pervasive effects whether or not these perceived innovations are actually new, pervasive, or have strong effects. This does not mean there is an attempt to actively mislead the public. Instead, structural incentives lead to the emergence of accounts that actively look for revolutionary innovation or scandalous misuses, all against the background of assumed massive effects of the technology in use. The everyday mundane uses of digital technology and their often at best limited effects remain under-covered.

We are thus faced with a non-trivial challenge in determining the role of digital media in politics. Actual effects are probably subtle and hidden in small but significant changes in the practices of people and organizations. Yet our imagination is continuously drawn toward extreme visions of hope or doom, while practitioners and chroniclers have compelling incentives for consciously or subconsciously misleading us by pushing narratives of revolutionary change.

The days of digital exceptionalism are over in politics. Digital media have become a crucial element in the perception, performance, and practice of politics all over the world, and assessing the actual impact of the use of digital media increasingly matters. For this, we have to take a more structured approach to the topic in the social sciences that is more aware of subtle but significant and small but persistent changes. Getting this assessment wrong risks damaging public trust in the functioning of democracy and might inspire futile or harmful regulation of digital media.

In this chapter, we will give our answers to two questions: What role do digital media play in shaping democracy by providing political actors with new tools to fulfill their needs in pursuit of political goals? And how can we go about finding out? This means identifying the structural reasons of why we keep getting things wrong and providing an outlook on how to get things right. For a balanced and nuanced assessment of the role of digital media in politics, we need to start by identifying actors, their incentives, their opportunities and limitations in the option space available to them, and the bounded impact of digital media depending on specific constellations and contexts. We will close by offering an outlook on the research potential provided by this perspective.

9.1 What Have We Learned?

Looking back on the ground we have covered, there is a central takeaway that has appeared over and over: digital media matter in politics. They matter since they provide political actors with new tools and new affordances in the pursuit of their political goals. While their uses are pervasive, the changes they introduce are limited and bounded by larger political contexts. They deeply impact the practice of politics and sometimes allow political actors to shift the balance of power in their favor. Yet mostly these changes do not lead to a transformation of politics on a fundamental level. While important, gaining an advantage over political competitors is often simply one element contributing to an actor's political success overall. In addition, more often than not these advantages are fleeting as political competitors tend to adapt their practices following defeats.

For us the key to understanding the impact of digital media in politics is to focus on the strategic needs of a variety of political actors. Doing so offers a view of digital media's contribution to the everyday pursuit of politics. We saw digital media's contribution to the actions and practices of political actors. Their strategic interactions with allies and competitors are shaped by the communicative tools at their disposal. Digital media have provided them with new tools helping them to fulfill their needs emerging from the pursuit of politics. While digital media have changed the way they address these needs, they existed and were addressed differently well before the advent of digital media. Political actors:

- still try to get their message injected into media and popular discourse;
- still try to reach people either directly or indirectly;
- still try to change minds and to mobilize people; and
- still face challenges in the coordination of supporters and getting them to cooperate in the first place.

Furthermore:

- political organizations remain important in translating attention and engagement in sustainable political action and change; and
- political actors still try to orient themselves in the world through quantification and metrics.

Thus, on a fundamental level the nature of political competition does not change. Those engaged in it in an age of digital media need to achieve similar goals as those engaged in it in the age of mass media or those engaged in it in the age of newspapers. What has decidedly changed, though, are the way these challenges are met. Digital media are deeply ingrained in the everyday practice of politics:

- they shape the way political actors try to become part of the flow of political information;

- they shape the approaches political actors take in their attempt to reach people either directly or indirectly through new partners;
- their technology, usage practices, and conditions shape the type and strength of effects information develops on recipients;
- they contribute to the success of collective action by allowing people to coordinate more cheaply and quickly, while at the same time do not necessarily change the underlying willingness of people to cooperate;
- they even shape the form political organizations take by providing them with new models of membership, monetization, and building networks; and
- they shape the image political actors have of reality by providing them with new, deceptively easy and cheap quantified metrics and data.

These changes stop short of a fundamental transformation of politics or political power. The areas touched by them are only part of the calculus of political power, which depends on many other inputs, many of them independent of communication. Moreover, as we are dealing with strategic actors who are in direct competition for political influence, any gain one side develops will over time be met with adaptation from the competition. Any gains will be offset a few cycles later by the competition adapting, either by copying a new dominant tactic or by countering it through a flanking move offsetting the previous advantage.

Digital media provide new tools to political actors in their pursuit of politics. This retooling of politics shapes their practices and for a limited time can provide them with an edge over the competition. In this sense digital media shape democracy by allowing political actors to follow their needs in pursuit of political goals in new ways that change their practices and the shape political competition takes. These changes are likely to be most pervasive in the mundane world of everyday politics (Nielsen 2011): a pundit's tweet intended to shape news coverage, a politician's choice of Instagram filters to reach first-time voters, an email blast ostensibly coming from the candidate's spouse asking recipients for money, the protestor sending out SMS to get people to rally at a location to avoid confrontation with the police, new ways to take part in political organizations, or the consultant with a keen eye on Twitter trends to fine-tune her candidate's message. These are all mundane ways in which digital media shape the opportunities, perceptions, and actions of political actors without transforming political power fundamentally. Yet they matter deeply as they change the way people practice and encounter politics.

While pervasive, these changes are at risk of being overlooked and under-appreciated. Our attention naturally wanders toward the exceptional and the surprising. We should keep these impulses in check if we want to understand the role of digital media in politics. Luckily, most of the time politics is boring. The everyday grind of politics is only for the enthusiasts and the not-easily-bored. These are the realms where the impact of digital media can be seen most clearly. We therefore have to be brave enough to face the mundane and the boring to get to the heart of digital media's impact on politics.

As we have shown, digital media have led to the emergence of new practices and structures shaping information distribution and political coordination. Digital media have also led to the emergence of new actors in politics, such as groups forming directly in reaction to inciting events or the growing influence of companies providing the backbone of digital media infrastructure as political actors, such as Facebook, Google, or Twitter. We have also seen attempts at regulating this new environment politically. All of these are real and potentially deep changes in politics that as of now we do not fully understand. This is at least partly due to structural factors that contribute to why these changes might be overlooked.

9.2 Why Do We Keep Getting This Wrong?

If our perspective focusing on how digital media allow political actors to pursue political goals is indeed helpful in describing and understanding the impact of digital media on politics, why is it not more prominent? Why does the debate seem to continuously oscillate between extreme takes, either those diagnosing a fundamental transformation of politics or relativistic accounts confidently denying there has been any change at all? In other words: Why are we getting this wrong? We believe the reasons for the persistence of the false dichotomy between radical transformation and no change at all lie in the economy of attention in scientific and public discourse and the limitations in prominent research approaches.

Go Big or Go Home

The attention economy favors speakers who are ready to go big or go home. There is an apparently infinite space available for accounts that declare the fundamental transformation of politics by digital media. After revolutions fail to materialize, these prophetic takes are replaced by ones declaring just as confidently that there is no change at all in politics. And as reliably as spring follows winter, these accounts will be replaced in time by hot takes seeing political revolution in every protest and campaign using the new tool *du jour*. Accounts discussing limited changes dependent on contextual conditions lack an intuitive hook and attract fewer readers. This makes them less likely to become prominent in public discourse.

The structure of academic discourse also contributes to this state. Political scientists, on the one hand, tend to be interested in questions addressing political institutions or large-scale social events, like elections. As we have seen over the course of the book, this perspective invites a view of digital media as introducing minimal changes to these phenomena. Communication scientists, on the other hand, focus much more on selected cases or practices in which the use of digital media figures prominently. Communication scientists also find themselves in a field in which the strongest institutions and organizations – the news media – have indeed been transformed radically by digital media. This invites a view of deeply transformative effects of digital media on politics and society.

Both perspectives have merit but each underestimates the contribution of the other. Political science focuses on the structures and outcomes of a complicated multi-level process of collective collaboration and coordination in which the effects of digital media are bound to be small if we only focus on the outcome. Communication focuses on the building blocks of said process: the fate of selected actors in engaging with digital media, changing practices of actors and publics, and episodes that illustrate these changes most clearly. This perspective automatically leads to a sense of a deep transformation introduced by digital media. But as long as the two fields do not widen their gaze, we risk getting the actual role of digital media wrong. Political science has to become more open to the limited but very real changes in the practice of politics among actors and publics, while communication science has to become more aware of the context in which the episodes and practices it focuses on are embedded. This might mean having to come to terms with the limited and bounded role of communication in politics, but it would also lessen the incentive to panic in the face of phenomena indicating a deterioration in political communication spaces.

Tricksters Tell Tall Tales

Another issue arises from the accounts of practitioners we choose to trust. There has emerged a veritable subgenre in the coverage of political campaigns focusing on campaign technology. Very important to this subgenre is that every new campaign cycle brings a fresh technological innovation, changing campaigning fundamentally. Usually this new key technology is shown to be exploited successfully by only one campaign, with another falling hopelessly behind.

In 2008, this was Obama's use of digital media, enabling what was portrayed as a groundswell of volunteer support. In 2012, this was Obama's use of data to identify likely voters and reach out to them in a meaningful way. In 2016, it was the supposedly uncanny ability of the consultancy Cambridge Analytica to infer psychological traits of potential voters from their Facebook posts and to mobilize them by exposing them to content targeted toward their specific psychological traits.

The factualness of these accounts does not matter. To varying degrees each of these narratives has been contested after the fact with regard to the actual use of the tools in question, the emphasis the campaign put on them, or the contribution of these tools and services to the subsequent electoral successes of the respective campaigns. What matters is that they are compelling stories allowing the attribution of electoral success to the use of a specific new tool or campaigning practice. They thus create a public narrative of ongoing technological innovation in campaigning. Not only does this narrative make for good reading, it also allows people to sell new tools or services, so it comes as no surprise to find consultants pushing the narrative of the transformative power of digital media on politics. Usually these accounts are linked to an offer to harness this transformative potential at a surprisingly reasonable fee. What is more surprising is that academics seem more than happy to repeat these narratives in their work as fact or as a blueprint of how things should be done.

Academics have to become much better at critically investigating the claims of self-interested actors with regard to the supposed effects of digital media on politics and the supposed use of specific tools and practices in campaigns. The most recent example is the role of Cambridge Analytica in the 2016 election of Donald Trump. Among published opinion and interested publics there is little doubt that Cambridge Analytica used Facebook data to infer key psychological traits of American voters and showed them ads optimized for their specific psychological traits. This is widely thought to have helped Donald Trump win the election. Never mind that reports indicate that Cambridge Analytica was sidelined early in the campaign as the company was seen as unreliable by the Trump campaign. Never mind that the quality of psychological profiling based on Facebook data is dubious at best. Never mind that in politics the likely effects of psychologically optimized ads are small. A combination of Trump's surprising win needing an extraordinary explanation, a successful sales pitch by Cambridge Analytica, a suspenseful journalistic process story, and stunningly unsuccessful crisis management by Facebook have all contributed to establishing the social fact of Trump's electoral success being the product of successful psychometric targeting through Facebook data.

Academics have to become better at challenging these accounts in public discourse and not repeat them uncritically in their work. If we want to understand the actual impact of digital media on politics, we have to do a better job of establishing empirical facts instead of perpetuating social facts. This means developing a more critical approach to the claims of consultants and politicians about the uses and effects of digital media in their campaigns and the fawning campaign-technology coverage.

Success Is More Interesting Than Failure

Another problem in identifying the role of digital media in politics lies in the selection of cases that academics focus on. Cases in which digital media played a large role in the political success of political actors, groups, or organizations are, of course, highly attractive. They receive a lot of public and scholarly attention and are well observed. In turn, they become blueprints for the successful use of a given technology, tool, or practice. But is this justified? Can an Indian member of parliament learn from the use of Twitter by Donald Trump? Can a French union learn from the tactics used by the #Occupy movement?

By focusing on successful cases while largely ignoring unsuccessful ones, we cannot identify how digital media drove these successes. If we are interested in examining what contributes to the successful use of digital media in politics, we must not only examine successful cases. Instead, we have to examine cases in which digital media were used unsuccessfully but that otherwise resemble the cases of successful use. Only in doing so will we able to identify not only the actual contributions of digital media to the success of political endeavors but also the contextual dependencies necessary for this contribution to emerge (see e.g. Medina 2011; Peters 2016). Currently, failed approaches to the use of digital media in politics are not nearly as prominently studied as successes and are usually presented as unsuccessful deviations from a blueprint due to a lack of understanding by the protagonists. The much more interesting cases of where adherence to a blueprint led to failure are too often ignored.

Closely related is the question of how far findings for each selected case can be expected to travel. Current practice favors the detailed presentation of selected cases documenting an interesting phenomenon. This could be an imaginative form of protest or an innovative use of a new digital tool in a campaign. The respective case is then discussed in detail. Yet instead of providing an account of the specific contextual dependencies of the case or a pragmatic assessment of its representativeness for politics as a whole, far too often these interesting but highly contingent cases are taken as a sign for the future of campaigning or protest in general. Conversely, the much more mundane uses of digital media by political actors and organizations at the center of politics are too often ignored as they are not in themselves interesting. This leads the field to develop a skewed view of the political world, with a lot of information about fringe groups and fringe practices and a gaping hole in the evidence with regard to the everyday practices of central actors and organizations.

For the field to evolve, we have to develop a more comprehensive view. The uses of digital media in different political contexts, by different political actors, with different degrees of success have to be charted while systematically accounting for the specific characteristics of each case. Only then will a coherent picture of the role of digital media in politics emerge.

The Missing Long View

There is also the problem that most discussions of successful uses of digital media in politics focus on isolated cases over a limited amount of time. This is an important limitation. Politics is the complex continuous interplay of actors, groups, and organizations over a long period of time. Here, political organizations play an important role in bundling often disparate interests of issue publics over time to translate interests and grievances into policy, by developing and transmitting important procedural knowledge and trust with opposing actors, or by providing a political brand consistent over time. At any one time independent actors or groups might emerge and perform a given task better than an established organization. Yet often these successes will remain limited to a specific area of politics and remain limited in time.

For example, in 2011 #Occupy protesters might have been more successful than unions in focusing public attention on the issue of economic inequality. An account of the Occupy movement focusing on the events of 2011 might identify this digitally enabled issue movement as the future of protest movements. But taking a longer time frame into account would show that the movement had difficulties in forming coherent political demands going beyond catchy slogans that in turn might have been translated into policy and also disintegrated over time. In the short view, #Occupy might have indeed looked like a powerful new form of political movement, highly successful in capturing the public agenda and forming a powerful alliance across different groups. Yet, in the long view, the fragility of this alliance and movement type becomes much more apparent, as does its inability to translate interests or grievances into policy.

Similarly, by focusing on campaign innovations over one or two campaign cycles, it is easy to mistake a fad for a trend or a contextually successful tactic for a new strategic blueprint. Only by taking the long view and seeing how actors react to this new trend or blueprint and strategically position themselves in alignment or opposition can we understand the phenomenon. For example, after the Obama campaigns of 2008 and 2012, data-driven campaigning was supposed to be the new transformative element of international campaigns. Yet, as we have seen, Trump's campaign broke that new paradigm already in 2016 by outsourcing analytics to commercial vendors. Following Trump's campaign, regulators and online platforms themselves reacted to this by clamping down hard on the kind of data use they allowed to political organizations. This puts the deterministically transformative role of data-driven practices in campaigns in question. Yet we only see this taking the long view.

By privileging the short view, we are overestimating the actual political success of our selected cases and prematurely underestimating the current political influence of existing organizations. Unfortunately, this does not remain an academic problem. By publicly emphasizing the short-term success of digitally enabled movements while turning a blind eye to their long-term fragility, we run the risk of devaluing established political organizations. As most of these are dependent on external financing, there exists a real danger that the current enthusiasm for new forms of "organizing without organizations" could lead to the defunding of traditional political organizations whose continued value only emerges if observers take the long view.

9.3 Getting It Right: Putting Digital Media into Context

With this book, we have tried to avoid these traps. We have done so by consistently featuring work by authors who reflected deeply on the role of digital media in politics and who did not go for easy answers if their subject demanded complicated ones. Looking at this literature, we can identify a set of approaches and research tactics that might allow us to get things more consistently right.

Focus on Actors

One way to get a clearer view of the impact of digital media on politics is to focus on how different political actors go about pursuing their goals. By focusing on political outcomes or large-scale phenomena, we tend to miss the small but significant changes in the way politics is practiced and experienced by people. Focusing on actors and their practices brings these changes to the fore.

By examining the way political actors use digital media to achieve specific goals, we get a ground-level view of how digital media impact the practice and experience of politics directly. We see, for example, if digital media allow actors to become more efficient in achieving their goals, to pursue new tactics, or to be countered by opponents. Moving too far from this level means getting only a diluted impression of the impact of digital media on politics. The farther you move from political actors toward political outcomes, the weaker the imprint of digital media becomes in competition with many other contributing factors.

For example, digital media have shaped the way political campaigns are run. But this does not mean that a campaign challenging the status quo will necessarily win just because it happens to use digital media skillfully. Just focusing on the election outcome as an indicator of the political impact of digital media would mean missing the very real effect they might have had for the challenger to be able to run a campaign operation in the first place or to reach people with limited budgets. The campaign might not have been successful in shifting the balance of political power, but digital media helped to articulate a challenge to the political status quo that would otherwise have remained unvoiced. This has been made possible by digital media providing actors with new tools that allow them to act more efficiently or to extend their opportunity space. This is how digital media are shaping politics.

We have to look closely at the actual uses of digital media in politics. In this, we have to differentiate between actual usage practices and the way actors describe them to us. In short, it is not just about providing evidence about the use of digital media, but also about providing evidence of their effects and contributions to outcomes. We also need to be critical of the actors and sources providing us with information: Who is claiming what effects of digital media on politics? What are their incentives to do so? Does their claim help them to better sell a story, a service, or their expertise? In other words, do they have a vested interest in their claims of how digital media change politics becoming social facts? What is the evidence they present? Is it just evidence of someone using some service some of the time? Or do they provide actual evidence of effects? A vast number of claims of the supposed effects of digital media on politics are based on isolated anecdotes documenting that someone appears to have been using a digital tool while having success politically. Yet more often than not these accounts fall short of empirically demonstrating, or even conceptualizing, a systematic link between the use of digital tools and subsequent political success. This is not good enough.

In practice, this means we will have to look closely at the actual uses of digital media by political actors. This will often mean spending time with political actors and organizations in order to understand their goals, resources, and tactics to achieve them. This will get you into the weeds of political organizing, coordinating, and communicating. Do not shy away from this. Mundane practices that on the face of it look boring shape everyday politics. Understanding how they shift through the use of digital media will give you a deeper understanding of how digital media are actually changing politics and perhaps over time contributing to large-scale outcomes. Additionally, only by knowing about the regularities of the mundane can we confidently recognize the exceptional when it occurs.

Develop Mechanisms Linking Digital Media and Politics

We also need to be much more explicit about the ways we believe digital media impact political outcomes. If we want to move beyond showing that digital media change the practices of political actors in their pursuit of political goals or their experience of politics, we need to propose mechanisms by which these changes link to changes in political outcomes of interest.

For example, how does the opportunity to choose information freely supposedly impact political polarization in societies? Proponents of the echo chamber hypothesis would argue that deeply ingrained within each individual there is a psychological preference for information supporting her beliefs. If given the choice, people will thus gravitate to information and sources supporting their political beliefs. This is deemed problematic since if people are allowed to only consume information supporting their beliefs they are seen as likely to lose sight of opposing arguments and the legitimacy of political opponents. In traditional media environments this tendency was kept in check by people only having limited choice of information and sources. In contrast, the informational abundance of digital media would allow people to move ever farther apart in their political opinions and thus contribute to political polarization.

As discussed in Chapter 3, this expectation is highly contested. What is of interest to us right now is the mechanism presented in this account. By presenting the hypothesis "digital media increase political polarization" by way of a detailed mechanism, we make explicit which hypotheses of human behavior ground these expectations and identify a series of steps that can be empirically tested. The echo chamber is a good example of a rich research program emerging from a detailed mechanistic account of the underlying hypotheses.

Mechanisms have proven to be rich tools in the social sciences (Hedström and Swedberg 1998; Elster 2015; Glennan 2017). They also provide us with a powerful way to interrogate claims regarding digital media's role in politics: How explicit are these claims in linking specific features or usage practices of digital media to political outcomes? Is it possible to reconstruct such mechanisms if they are left unspecified? Even if a claimed impact of digital media on politics might not be testable, steps proposed in the underlying mechanism should be. Their plausibility then allows us to judge the respective claim overall.

Going beyond checking the plausibility of claims regarding the role of digital media in politics, mechanisms also allow for an abstract account of the link between specific features of digital media and specific outcomes in politics. Explicitly linking political outcomes to the way specific features of digital media change specific practices and extend opportunities of political actors makes expectations testable and allows the linking of cases beyond their specific contexts. Given the temporal shifts in digital technology and usage patterns (Neuman, Bimber, and Hindman 2011; Karpf 2012a), enabling an abstract account of the links between digital media and political outcomes is especially important, as a case-by-case analysis risks getting lost in specific findings without a clear understanding of how findings travel to different contexts or stages of technological development.

Establish Context and Constraints

In looking at how digital media have been integrated into the practices of political actors, we also have to explicitly establish the contexts under which this happens. Political actors are embedded in specific contexts that influence their tactics, goals, and practices and determine their success or failure. They find themselves to be resource-deprived challengers, dominant incumbents, or arbiters of the political status quo. They are embedded in cultural, legal, and commercial environments that support or hinder their adaption of digital media. Ignoring these contexts in the analysis of digital media's effect on politics risks losing sight of contextual determinants of adoption choices and their successes or failures.

Politics does not happen in a vacuum. Political actors and publics are embedded in institutional and social structures that constrain their ability to adapt to digital media or to achieve their goals. Resource-strapped challengers will not be able to shift the balance of political power simply by using digital media. Actors working in a legal environment that limits fundraising efforts will have smaller incentives to invest heavily in the use and development of digital tools than actors working in legal environments that favor fundraising. By ignoring these constraints and others like them, we are likely to misestimate the political impact of digital media.

Analyses that focus on identifying relevant contexts will likely show that although digital media are regularly employed in the pursuit of politics, their transformative power remains harnessed by persisting constraints. Digital media might change aspects of the political economy of reaching out to people or coordinating them, but they do not necessarily change the underlying political power balances. Digital media definitely change the practice of politics, but not necessarily the nature of politics and of political power itself. While we might find it disappointing that constraints tend to limit the effects of digital media in politics when we hope for an invigoration of politics, we might find solace as the same factors also limit the impact of malicious effects of digital media on political communication environments, such as disinformation.

As a consequence, we have to be very explicit about the contexts in which the actors in our selected cases find themselves. This makes it possible to map their experiences not only to an abstract mechanism but also to contextual conditions, allowing us to establish common patterns across cases with comparable contexts. Here, it is also necessary to broaden our understanding of what constitutes a valuable case. As we have seen, everybody is talking about the successful uses of digital media in politics, but what about the cases where the best practice blueprint failed? Only by documenting the uses of digital media in politics much more broadly will we understand the hidden contextual conditions determining the usage patterns and effects of digital media. This means considering successes and failures. It also means considering the uses of digital media internationally and not just in Western democracies. Just as importantly, we should not fall for the shiny object syndrome. Just because a new service or tool has been used successfully by some does not mean it will become the future of politics. By all means be aware of new developments, but do not equate them automatically with the imminent transformation of politics as we know it.

Most of all, we have to stop treating digital media as an isolated element in contemporary politics. Instead, as we have shown, digital media have been integrated fully in the pursuit of basic tasks of political actors, such as distributing information, coordinating people, and getting votes. While in the past it might have been enough to speak of the contribution of digital media to these tasks, today we have to see digital media as an integral part of politics. This means that instead of discussing voter mobilization online as if it were an isolated feature in a campaign, we have to discuss contemporary voter mobilization with digital media as part of a campaign's overall voter mobilization across channels and tools. This allows us to see the relative contribution of digital media in the context of other tools and communication channels. This allows us to identify which specific, if any, uses or constraints political actors face when they are using digital media compared with their uses of other communication tools.

9.4 What Comes Next?

Currently, we are experiencing an understandable but limiting topical fixation on the role of digital media in the success of Donald Trump and the rise of right-wing populism: understandable, as these topics are very much at the forefront of current public debate, and limited, as this research is especially drawn to attributing to digital media a decisive role in these events while ignoring alternative and more plausible explanations. It is also limiting as the focus on a small set of cases of seemingly obvious relevance leads researchers to neglect the larger picture. If explaining the election of Donald Trump is of obvious appeal, then we do not have to think about what larger phenomenon this one case actually represents. This produces a lot of detailed case studies of aspects of digital media use in the context of the electoral successes of Donald Trump and right-wing populists, but larger, more general theory building is neglected. In other words, there might be a lot of sound and fury in current research activity but ultimately the field risks remaining unsure of what this activity actually signifies beyond the current moment in time. The novelty of this current moment is bound to pass. The question is what comes next.

One obvious answer points to the growing opportunities for theory-driven research. While the empirical research into political uses of digital media has made great strides, theory building and the development of concepts has somewhat lagged behind (Neuman 2016). While the practice, performance, and participation in politics has changed visibly, social scientists have only recently begun to adjust theories and concepts – an area of significant research potential in the near future. Identifying relevant phenomena, conceptualizing them, and making them measurable across contexts is hugely important and highly rewarding. Examples like "networked gatekeeping" (Meraz and Papacharissi 2013), the "END framework" (Settle 2018), the "news finds me perception" (Gil de Zúñiga, Weeks, and Ardèvol-Abreu 2017), the "hybrid media system" (Chadwick 2017), "discursive power" (Jungherr, Posegga, and An 2019a), "connective action" (Bennett and Segerberg 2013), or a framework of political participation accounting for the extension of action repertoires by digital media (Theocharis and van Deth 2018b) show that theory and concept building is deeply important in increasing our understanding of the role of digital media in politics by creating new categories and phenomena that can be considered and measured.

Another promising area is the growing attention paid to internal governance and external regulation of companies providing access to digital platforms and tools (Kreiss and McGregor 2019). The growing maturation and pervasive uses of digital media have put both firmly in the focus of public debate. Here, the rich tradition in the comparison of institutions and policy fields provides rich frameworks by which to address these phenomena.

The third area providing promising perspectives for future research is the development and application of new data sources and methods. Researchers interested in the use and effects of digital media have the opportunity to use digital trace data, data consciously or unconsciously produced as a byproduct of user interactions with digital services (Howison, Wiggins, and Crowston 2011; Jungherr 2015). This data provides researchers with a true documentation of user behavior, or at least the slices of the behavior expressed on the service providing the data (Jungherr 2019). This data is vast in size while at the same time offering very fine-grained accounts of user behavior. Data with these characteristics has until now not been available to social scientists. Its availability therefore promises a significant jump in the reach of the social sciences (Salganik 2018), with some expecting a measurement revolution (Watts 2011) or a transformation of the social sciences into a "hard" science through an increase in data, which might allow the formulation of law-like theories comparable to other sciences like physics (González-Bailón 2017).

Yet, while the research potential of these new data sources has been well charted, it has to be said that there is still a lot of room in its manifestation in the social sciences (Jungherr and Theocharis 2017; Jungherr 2019). The connection between meaningful theories in the social sciences and signals identified in these new datasets by advanced computational methods is still in its infancy but offers tremendous research potential. The current trend of online platforms shutting down or at least heavily restricting access to their data for researchers and the public might slow this effort down or stop it altogether (Freelon 2018). While it was comparatively easy to collect vast amounts of data using public APIs of popular online services like Facebook, Twitter, or YouTube, newly implemented restrictions make this harder. While some researchers and institutions might be able to engage in privileged partnerships with companies running online platforms in order to get access to data in research-grade quality, most researchers will have to develop dedicated data collection approaches. This increases the effort that goes into the collection of high-quality datasets documenting user behavior online or the larger informational environment. It also means that there is an increasing demand for interdisciplinary collaboration with computer or information scientists. At first light, this approach might appear as obviously inferior to engaging in negotiations for privileged access to data with companies running online platforms. In the long run, though, it might turn out to be the more robust approach. For one, it demands the explicit development and implementation of a research design, a step often forgotten in face of apparent riches of available data. More importantly, in privileged partnerships researchers depend on the persistent will of companies to provide access to data and their willingness for continued collaboration even in face of research findings potentially at odds with the bottom line of their business. Betting the future of a research field on this calculation might be putting a little too much trust in the kindness of strangers.

The study of political uses and effects of digital media as a field is far from settled. Other than in more established fields, it is thus more difficult to identify trends that can be reliably projected in the future. Technological innovation provides a moving target, making the next big trend hard to foresee. Moreover, researchers from many different backgrounds as diverse as computer science, communication, the humanities, political science, and sociology contribute to the study of digital media in politics. This makes it a field in which there is little methodological consensus on what counts as evidence or the role and nature of theory. The resulting pluralism and parallelism in theories, methods, and findings make this a much more chaotic research field than areas that are well settled within either of the connected scientific fields. All of this makes the future difficult to predict but at the same time a highly energizing and rewarding endeavor to work toward.

9.5 The Final Account

Digital media clearly matter in politics. We have charted many cases in which digital media have led to changes in the practices, performance, and reception of politics around the world. Maybe these changes are not as big as sometimes suggested, but they are real and they are pervasive. Yet these changes also depend on a lot of factors, such as political systems or the specific contexts in which actors find themselves. Accordingly, the available evidence does not point to a fundamental transformation of politics through digital technology. It is easy to be surprised by this, as in other areas digital media have had a deeply disruptive effect, be it journalism (Williams and Carpini 2011; Rusbridger 2018) or the economy (Parker, Alstyne, and Choudary 2016; Baldwin 2019).

In the face of the major recalibration of business models and social fields, the relative resistance to change in politics might seem surprising. But politics is different. The transformative power of digital technology in various fields lies in reducing transaction costs by eliminating inefficiencies created by information asymmetries enabled by digitalizing information. Yet politics is about much more than information flows. Politics is about bringing people together in alliances, forming bonds of trust, and sharing risks and resource expenditure. This makes politics a psychologically and sociologically rich phenomenon in which technology is only one factor and limits the applicability of lessons learned in other areas. Finally, politics remains a relatively data-poor arena. This limits the potential of data-driven procedures.

That being said, it might also be that our focus on what constitutes political change directly caused by digital media might turn out to be too narrow. It might very well be that digital media impact societies very deeply. These underlying social changes might then impact politics. Our discussion of changes to the public sphere driven by the disruption to the economics of news in Chapter 2 provides an example of one of these deep social changes. Over time this might lead to changes in political competition and accountability that might not be directly attributable to digital media but still follow from their transformation of politically important institutions. Other indirect effects on politics might be found in the deepening representation crisis driven by the erosion of public trust in elites (Gurri 2018; Mair 2013) or the weakening of public support for democratic institutions driven by society-wide job crises 2019(Baldwin 2019). Here, digital media might have an indirect effect on politics, one that could remain hidden in an analysis focused only on direct effects.

Correctly identifying the role of digital media in politics is more important than ever. Rumors and accusations fly regarding the perceived power of digital media supporting malicious actors intent on undermining democracies, spawning disinformation, and dividing countries by appealing to the worst inclinations of their citizens. At the same time, we see digital media playing an ever more crucial role in how people find information, socialize, and coordinate. Dividing fact from fiction on the political and social impact of digital media's widespread use matters.

As our account has shown, there are no obvious answers to these questions. Establishing the role of digital media comes with specific challenges. The speed of innovation in digital services and their spread in society are a persistent challenge for researchers, especially as the continuously evolving nature of digital media makes digital media of the past different from digital media of today and the future (Karpf 2012a). This is much more true for digital media than for technologically more stable media such as newspapers or television. This rate of change in technology and user base raises the question of which findings established for earlier stages of digital media still hold now or will hold in the future. This makes the usual cumulative process of research more difficult and fragile than in other areas.

Social scientists, journalists, practitioners, and publics face the same challenge of deciding how to use digital media to achieve their purposes without succumbing to their risks. This means establishing shared standards for theorizing and evidence creation. This is an impressive collective challenge. At the same time, it also makes it a thrilling and rewarding endeavor.

We have tried to provide some guidance by emphasizing actors' needs arising in their pursuit of politics and the impact of digital media on how these needs are filled. We hope this allows for a more focused debate with an eye on changes of different magnitudes and the contextual dependencies for their realization. Some of our assessments will age better than others. In case we gave you reason to disagree with us, we hope these will be interesting disagreements. We hope that the needs-oriented, actor-centric framework we provided will prove useful for others beyond the next wave of technological innovation. As with any discussion of a rapidly changing environment, we see our contribution not so much in specific assessments or prognoses – although we hope time will not contradict us too harshly. Instead, we hope that the interpretative framework we have offered will prove a useful tool to structure the continuous debate on the political impact of digital media. But most of all, we are excited to see what comes next! There is much to do.

So let's get back to work!

References

Aalberg, Toril, Peter van Aelst, and James Curran. 2010. "Media Systems and the Political Information Environment: A Cross-National Comparison." *The International Journal of Press/Politics* 15 (3): 255–271.

Abad-Santos, Alexander. 2013. "Politico Has No Time for Your Loser Attitude." *The Atlantic.* www.theatlantic.com/politics/archive/2013/10/politico-has-no-time-your-loser-attitude/354515/.

Abbasi, Mohammad-Ali, and Huan Liu. 2013. "Measuring User Credibility in Social Media." In *Social Computing, Behavioral-Cultural Modeling and Prediction,* edited by Ariel M. Greenberg, William G. Kennedy, and Nathan D. Bos, 441–448. Heidelberg: Springer.

Abrahamsson, Bengt. 1993. *The Logic of Organizations.* Newbury Park, CA: SAGE.

Access Now. 2019. *Keep It On.* www.accessnow.org/keepiton/.

Achen, Christopher H., and Larry M. Bartels. 2016. *Democracy for Realists: Why Elections Do Not Produce Responsive Government.* Princeton, NJ: Princeton University Press.

Acquire Media. 2017. "ComScore Ranks the Top 50 U.S. Digital Media Properties for June 2017." *comScore.* http://ir.comscore.com/news-releases/news-release-details/comscore-ranks-top-50-us-digital-media-properties-june-2017.

Aday, Sean, Henry Farrell, Marc Lynch, John Sides, and Deen Freelon. 2012. *Blogs and Bullets II: New Media and Conflict after the Arab Spring.* Washington, DC: United States Institute of Peace.

Agrawal, Ajay, Christian Catalini, and Avi Goldfarb. 2014. "Some Simple Economics of Crowdfunding." *Innovation Policy and the Economy* 14 (1): 63–97.

Agrawal, Ajay, Joshua Gans, and Avi Goldfarb. 2018. *Prediction Machines: The Simple Economics of Artificial Intelligence.* Boston, MA: Harvard Business Review Press.

Agarwal, Sheetal D., W. Lance Bennett, Courtney N. Johnson, and Shawn Walker. 2014. "A Model of Crowd Enabled Organization: Theory and Methods for Understanding the Role of Twitter in the Occupy Protests." *International Journal of Communication* 8: 646–672.

Ahmed, Shazeda. 2019. "The Messy Truth about Social Credit." *Logic: A Magazine About Technology* 7: 111–123. https://logicmag.io/07-the-messy-truth-about-social-credit/.

Ahrend, Rudiger. 2002. "Press Freedom, Human Capital and Corruption." DELTA Working Paper No. 2002-11. Paris: Ecole normale supérieure.

Aisch, Gregor, Jon Huang, and Cecilia Kang. 2016. "Dissecting the #Pizzagate Conspiracy Theories." *The New York Times*. www.nytimes.com/interactive/2016/12/10/business/media/pizzagate.html.

Alaimo, Kara. 2015. "How the Facebook Arabic Page 'We Are All Khaled Said' Helped Promote the Egyptian Revolution." *Social Media + Society* 1 (2): 1–10.

Albuquerque, Afonso de. 2005. "Another 'Fourth Branch': Press and Political Culture in Brazil." *Journalism* 6 (4): 486–504.

Albuquerque, Afonso de. 2016. "Voters against Public Opinion: The Press and Democracy in Brazil and South Africa." *International Journal of Communication* 10: 3042–3061.

Albuquerque, Afonso de. 2019. "Protecting Democracy or Conspiring against It? Media and Politics in Latin America: A Glimpse from Brazil." *Journalism* 20 (7): 906–923.

Alcott, Hunt, and Matthew Gentzkow. 2017. "Social Media and Fake News in the 2016 Election." *Journal of Economic Perspectives* 31 (2): 211–236.

Allen, Stuart, and Einar Thorsen, eds. 2009. *Citizen Journalism: Global Perspectives*. New York: Peter Lang.

Altheide, David L., and Robert P. Snow. 1979. *Media Logic*. Beverly Hills, CA: SAGE.

An, Jisun, Haewoon Kwak, Oliver Posegga, and Andreas Jungherr. 2019. "Political Discussions in Homogeneous and Cross-Cutting Communication Spaces: Interaction Patterns and Linguistic Strategies on Reddit." In *ICWSM 2019: Proceedings of the Thirteenth International AAAI Conference on Web and Social Media*, edited by Jürgen Pfeffer, Ceren Budak, Yu-Ru Lin, and Fred Morstatter, 68–79. Menlo Park, CA: Association for the Advancement of Artificial Intelligence (AAAI).

Ananny, Mike, and Leila Bighash. 2016. "Why Drop a Paywall? Mapping Industry Accounts of Online News Decommodification." *International Journal of Communication* 10: 3359–3380.

Ananyev, Maxim, Galina Zudenkova, and Maria Petrova. 2019. "Information and Communication Technologies, Protests, and Censorship." Working Paper. Available at SSRN: https://ssrn.com/abstract=2978549.

Anderson, Ashley A., Dominique Brossard, Dietram A. Scheufele, Michael A. Xenos, and Peter Ladwig. 2014. "The 'Nasty Effect': Online Incivility and Risk Perceptions of Emerging Technologies." *Journal of Computer-Mediated Communication* 19 (3): 373–387.

Anderson, Ashley A., Sara K. Yeo, Dominique Brossard, Dietram A. Scheufele, and Michael A. Xenos. 2018. "Toxic Talk: How Online Incivility Can Undermine Perceptions of Media." *International Journal of Public Opinion Research* 30 (1): 156–168.

Anderson, Monica, Skye Toor, Lee Rainie, and Aaron Smith. 2018. *Activism in the Social Media Age*. Washington, DC: Pew Research Center. www.pewinternet.org/2018/07/11/activism-in-the-social-media-age/.

Anduiza, Eva, Camilo Cristancho, and José M Sabucedo. 2014. "Mobilization through Online Social Networks: The Political Protest of the Indignados in Spain." *Information, Communication & Society* 17 (6): 750–764.

Anduiza, Eva, Michael J. Jensen, and Laia Jorba, eds. 2012. *Digital Media and Political Engagement Worldwide: A Comparative Study*. Cambridge, UK: Cambridge University Press.

Aneez, Zeenab, Sumandro Chattapadhyay, Vibodh Parthasarathi, and Rasmus Kleis Nielsen. 2016. *Indian Newspapers' Digital Transition: Dainik Jagran, Hindustan Times, and Malayala Manorama*. Oxford, UK: Reuters Institute for the Study of Journalism.

Angelos, James. 2016. "The New Europeans." *The New York Times Magazine*. www.nytimes.com/2016/04/10/magazine/the-new-europeans.html.

Ansolabehere, Stephen, and Eitan Hersh. 2014. "Voter Registration: The Process and Quality of Lists." In *The Measure of American Elections*, edited by Barry C. Burden, and Charles Stewart III, 61–90. Cambridge, UK: Cambridge University Press.

Anstead, Nick. 2017. "Data-Driven Campaigning in the 2015 United Kingdom General Election." *The International Journal of Press/Politics* 22 (3): 294–313.

Anstead, Nick, and Ben O'Loughlin. 2011. "The Emerging Viewertariat and BBC Question Time: Television Debate and Real-Time Commenting Online." *The International Journal of Press/Politics* 16 (4): 440–462.

Anstead, Nick, and Ben O'Loughlin. 2012. *Semantic Polling: The Ethics of Online Public Opinion*. London: The London School of Economics. http://eprints.lse.ac.uk/46944/.

Anstead, Nick, and Ben O'Loughlin. 2015. "Social Media Analysis and Public Opinion: The 2010 UK General Election." *Journal of Computer-Mediated Communication* 20 (2): 204–220.

Arafa, Mohamed, and Crystal Armstrong. 2016. "'Facebook to Mobilize, Twitter to Coordinate Protests, and YouTube to Tell the World': New Media, Cyberactivism, and the Arab Spring." *Journal of Global Initiatives: Policy, Pedagogy, Perspective* 10 (1): 73–102.

Aragón, Pablo, Andreas Kaltenbrunner, Antonio Calleja-López, Andrés Pereira, Arnau Monterde, Xabier E Barandiaran, and Vicenç Gómez. 2017. "Deliberative Platform Design: The Case Study of the Online Discussions in Decidim Barcelona." In *International Conference on Social Informatics*, edited by Giovanni Luca Ciampaglia, Afra Mashhadi, and Taha Yasseri, 277–287. Cham: Springer.

Aretz, Eckart. 2018. "Auf Den Knien Senden?" *Tagesschau.de*. https://web.archive.org/web/20180620172304/www.tagesschau.de/ausland/rundfunk-vergleich-101.html.

Armingeon, Klaus, and Lisa Schädel. 2015. "Social Inequality in Political Participation: The Dark Sides of Individualisation." *West European Politics* 38 (1): 1–27.

Armstrong, Jerome, and Markos Moulitsas Zúniga. 2006. *Crashing the Gate: Netroots, Grassroots, and the Rise of People-Powered Politics*. West River Junction, VT: Chelsea Green Publishing.

Arquilla, John, and David Ronfeldt. 2000. *Swarming and the Future of Conflict*. Santa Monica, CA: RAND Corporation.

Arquilla, John, and David Ronfeldt. 2001. *Networks and Netwars: The Future of Terror, Crime, and Militancy*. Santa Monica, CA: RAND Corporation.

Ashworth, Scott. 2012. "Electoral Accountability: Recent Theoretical and Empirical Work." *Annual Review of Political Science* 15: 183–201.

The Associated Press. 2017. "NBC Wins Ratings Week, Narrows Season's Gap with CBS." Business Insider (November 29). https://web.archive.org/web/20191201102543/ www.businessinsider.com/ap-nbc-wins-ratings-week-narrows-seasons-gap-with-cbs-2017-11?r=DE&IR=T.

Atkins, Ralph. 2018. "Swiss TV Licence Vote a Concern for All Public Broadcasters." *Financial Times.* www.ft.com/content/4bd801cc-1ad2-11e8-aaca-4574d7dabfb6.

Attard, Judie, Fabrizio Orlandi, Simon Scerri, and Sören Auer. 2015. "A systematic review of open government data initiatives." *Government Information Quarterly* 32 (4): 399–418.

Auletta, Ken. 2018. *Frenemies: The Epic Disruption of the Advertising Industry.* New York: Penguin Books.

Azari, Julia R. 2016. "How the News Media Helped to Nominate Trump." *Political Communication* 33 (4): 677–680.

Azucar, Danny, Davide Marengo, and Michele Settanni. 2018. "Predicting the Big 5 Personality Traits from Digital Footprints on Social Media: A Meta-Analysis." *Personality and Individual Differences* 124 (1): 150–159.

Badawy, Adam, Emilio Ferrara, and Kristina Lerman. 2018. "Analyzing the Digital Traces of Political Manipulation: The 2016 Russian Interference Twitter Campaign." In *ASONAM'18: Proceedings of the 2018 IEEE/ACM International Conference on Advances in Social Networks Analysis and Mining*, edited by Ulrik Brandes, Chandan Reddy, and Andrea Tagarelli, 258–265. Washington, DC: IEEE.

Baek, Young Min, Magdalena Wojcieszak, and Michael X Delli Carpini. 2012. "Online versus Face-to-Face Deliberation: Who? Why? What? With What Effects?" *New Media & Society* 14 (3): 363–383.

Bailard, Catie Snow. 2014. *Democracy's Double-Edged Sword: How Internet Use Changes Citizens' Views of Their Government.* Baltimore, MD: Johns Hopkins University Press.

Bakardjieva, Maria, Mylynn Felt, and Delia Dumitrica. 2018. "The Mediatization of Leadership: Grassroots Digital Facilitators as Organic Intellectuals, Sociometric Stars and Caretakers." *Information, Communication & Society* 21 (6): 899–914.

Bakos, Yannis, and Erik Brynjolfsson. 2000. "Bundling and Competition on the Internet." *Marketing Science* 19 (1): 63–82.

Bakshy, Eytan, Solomon Messing, and Lada A. Adamic. 2015. "Exposure to Ideologically Diverse News and Opinion on Facebook." *Science* 348 (6239): 1130–1132.

Baldassarri, Delia, and Andrew Gelman. 2008. "Partisans without Constraint: Political Polarization and Trends in American Public Opinion." *American Journal of Sociology* 114 (2): 408–446.

Baldwin, Richard. 2019. *The Globotics Upheaval: Globalization, Robotics, and the Future of Work.* New York: Oxford University Press.

Baldwin-Philippi, Jessica. 2015. *Using Technology, Building Democracy: Digital Campaigning and the Construction of Citizenship.* New York: Oxford University Press.

Baldwin-Philippi, Jessica. 2017. "The Myths of Data-Driven Campaigning." *Political Communication* 34 (4): 627–633.

Ball, James. 2017. *Post-Truth: How Bullshit Conquered the World.* London: Biteback Publishing.

Barbaro, Michael. 2015. "Pithy, Mean and Powerful: How Donald Trump Mastered Twitter for 2016." *The New York Times*. www.nytimes.com/2015/10/06/us/polit ics/donald-trump-twitter-use-campaign-2016.html.

Barber, Benjamin R. 2003. *Strong Democracy: Participatory Politics for a New Age (Twentieth Anniversary Edition)*. Berkeley: University of California Press.

Barber, Benjamin R. 2013. *If Mayors Ruled the World: Dysfunctional Nations, Rising Cities*. New Haven, CT: Yale University Press.

Barberá, Pablo. 2015. "Birds of the Same Feather Tweet Together: Bayesian Ideal Point Estimation Using Twitter Data." *Political Analysis* 23 (1): 76–91.

Barberá, Pablo, and Gonzalo Rivero. 2015. "Understanding the Political Representativeness of Twitter Users." *Social Science Computer Review* 33 (6): 712–729.

Barberá, Pablo, Ning Wang, Richard Bonneau, John T. Jost, Jonathan Nagler, Joshua A. Tucker, and Sandra González-Bailón. 2015. "The Critical Periphery in the Growth of Social Protests." *PLoS ONE* 10 (11): e0143611.

Barbera, Salvador, and Matthew O Jackson. 2018. "A Model of Protests, Revolution, and Information." Available at SSRN: https://ssrn.com/abstract=2732864.

Barlow, John Perry. 1996. "Declaration of the Independence of Cyberspace." *Electronic Frontier Foundation*. www.eff.org/cyberspace-independence.

Barnard, Lisa, and Daniel Kreiss. 2013. "A Research Agenda for Online Political Advertising: Surveying Campaign Practices, 2000–2012." *International Journal of Communication* 7: 2046–2066.

Barocas, Solon. 2012. "The Price of Precision: Voter Microtargeting and Its Potential Harms to the Democratic Process." In *PLEAD'12: Proceedings of the 1st Edition Workshop on Politics, Elections and Data*, edited by Ingmar Weber, Ana-Maria Popescu, and Marco Pennacchiotti, 31–36. New York: ACM.

Barocas, Solon, and Andrew D. Selbst. 2016. "Big Data's Disparate Impact." *California Law Review* 104: 671–732.

Barrett, Nicholas. 2016. "Brexit Has Locked Us Millennials Out of the Union We Voted for." *Financial Times*. www.ft.com/content/82a1a548-3b93-11e6-8716-a4a71e8140b0.

Barro, Robert. 1973. "The Control of Politicians: An Economic Model." *Public Choice* 14 (1): 19–42.

Bartels, Larry M. 2014. "Remembering to Forget: A Note on the Duration of Campaign Advertising Effects." *Political Communication* 31 (4): 532–544.

Bastos, Marco T., and Dan Mercea. 2016. "Serial Activists: Political Twitter beyond Influentials and the Twittertariat." *New Media & Society* 18 (10): 2359–2378.

Bastos, Marco T., and Dan Mercea. 2019. "The Brexit Botnet and User-Generated Hyperpartisan News." *Social Science Computer Review* 37 (1): 38–54.

Bastos, Marco T., Rafael Luis Galdini Raimundo, and Rodrigo Travitzki. 2013. "Gatekeeping Twitter: Message Diffusion in Political Hashtags." *Media, Culture & Society* 35 (2): 260–270.

Bear, Drake. 2016. "The 'Filter Bubble' Explains Why Trump Won and You Didn't See It Coming." *New York Magazine*. www.thecut.com/2016/11/how-facebook-and-the-filter-bubble-pushed-trump-to-victory.html.

Beauchamp, Zack. 2019. "Social Media Is Rotting Democracy from Within." *Vox*. www.vox.com/policy-and-politics/2019/1/22/18177076/social-media-facebook-far-right-authoritarian-populism.

Behrisch, Lars. 2016. "Statistics and Politics in the 18th Century." *Historical Social Research/Historische Sozialforschung* 41 (2): 238–257.

Bell, Emily, and Taylor Owen. 2017. *The Platform Press: How Silicon Valley Reengineered Journalism*. New York: The TOW Center for Digital Journalism.

Benford, Robert D. 1993. "Frame Disputes within the Nuclear Disarmament Movement." *Social Forces* 71 (3): 677–701.

Beniger, James. 1989. *The Control Revolution: Technological and Economic Origins of the Information Society*. Cambridge, MA: Harvard University Press.

Benkler, Yochai. 2006. *The Wealth of Networks: How Social Production Transforms Markets and Freedom*. New Haven, CT: Yale University Press.

Benkler, Yochai. 2011. *The Penguin and the Leviathan: How Cooperation Triumphs over Self-Interest*. New York: Crown Publishing Group.

Benkler, Yochai, Robert Faris, and Hal Roberts. 2018. *Network Propaganda: Manipulation, Disinformation, and Radicalization in American Politics*. New York: Oxford University Press.

Benner, Katie, Mark Mazzetti, Ben Hubbard, and Mike Isaac. 2018. "Saudis' Image Makers: A Troll Army and a Twitter Insider." *The New York Times*. www.nytimes.com/2018/10/20/us/politics/saudi-image-campaign-twitter.html.

Bennett, W. Lance. 1990. "Towards a Theory of Press–State Relations in the US." *Journal of Communication* 40 (2): 103–125.

Bennett, W. Lance. 2004. "Gatekeeping and Press–Government Relations: A Multigated Model of News Construction." In *Handbook of Political Communication Research*, edited by Lynda Lee Kaid, 283–313. Mahwah, NJ: Lawrence Erlbaum Associates.

Bennett, W. Lance. 2005a. "Beyond Pseudoevents: Election News as Reality TV." *American Behavioral Scientist* 49 (3): 364–378.

Bennett, W. Lance. 2005b. "News as Reality TV: Election Coverage and the Democratization of Truth." *Critical Studies in Media Communication* 22 (2): 171–177.

Bennett, W. Lance. 2012. "The Personalization of Politics." *The Annals of the American Academy of Political and Social Science* 644 (1): 20–39.

Bennett, W. Lance. 2016. *News: The Politics of Illusion*. 10th ed. Chicago, IL: The University of Chicago Press.

Bennett, W. Lance, and Alexandra Segerberg. 2013. *The Logic of Connective Action: Digital Media and the Personalization of Contentious Politics*. Cambridge, UK: Cambridge University Press.

Bennett, W. Lance, Alexandra Segerberg, and Curd B. Knüpfer. 2018. "The Democratic Interface: Technology, Political Organization, and Diverging Patterns of Electoral Representation." *Information, Communication & Society* 21 (11): 1655–1680.

Bennett, W. Lance, Alexandra Segerberg, and Yunkang Yang. 2018. "The Strength of Peripheral Networks: Negotiating Attention and Meaning in Complex Media Ecologies." *Journal of Communication* 68 (4): 659–684.

Bennett, W. Lance, and Barbara Pfetsch. 2018. "Rethinking Political Communication in a Time of Disrupted Public Spheres." *Journal of Communication* 68 (2): 243–253.

Bennett, W. Lance, and Jarol B. Manheim. 2006. "The One-Step Flow of Communication." *The Annals of the American Academy of Political and Social Science* 608 (1): 213–232.

Bennett, W. Lance, Regina G. Lawrence, and Steven Livingston. 2007. *When the Press Fails: Political Power and the News Media from Iraq to Katrina.* Chicago, IL: The University of Chicago Press.

Bennett, W. Lance, and Steven Livingston. 2018. "The Disinformation Order: Disruptive Communication and the Decline of Democratic Institutions." *European Journal of Communication* 33 (2): 122–139.

Bensinger, Ken, Miriam Elder, and Mark Schoofs. 2017. "These Reports Allege Trump Has Deep Ties to Russia." *BuzzFeed.* www.buzzfeed.com/kenbensinger/these-reports-allege-trump-has-deep-ties-to-russia?utm_term=.qan6BA50WA#.lqxx7orkQo.

Benson, Rodney. 2006. "News Media as a 'Journalistic Field': What Bourdieu Adds to New Institutionalism, and Vice Versa." *Political Communication* 23 (2): 187–202.

Benton, Joshua. 2015a. "Facebook's Instant Articles Are Live: Either a Shrewd Mobile Move by Publishers – or Feeding the Borg." *NiemanLab.* www.niemanlab.org/2015/05/facebooks-instant-articles-are-live-either-a-shrewd-mobile-move-by-publishers-or-feeding-the-borg/.

Benton, Joshua. 2015b. "Get Amp'd: Here's What Publishers Need to Know About Google's New Plan to Speed up Your Website." *NiemanLab.* www.niemanlab.org/2015/10/get-ampd-heres-what-publishers-need-to-know-about-googles-new-plan-to-speed-up-your-website/.

Berry, Jeffrey M., and Clyde Wilcox. 2018. *The Interest Group Society.* 6th ed. Oxon: Routledge.

Besley, Timothy, and Robin Burgess. 2002. "The Political Economy of Government Responsiveness: Theory and Evidence from India." *The Quarterly Journal of Economics* 117 (4): 1415–1451.

Bessi, Alessandro, and Emilio Ferrara. 2016. "Social Bots Distort the 2016 U.S. Presidential Election Online Discussion." *First Monday* 21 (11). http://firstmonday.org/article/view/7090/5653.

Beyer, Jessica L. 2014. "The Emergence of a Freedom of Information Movement: Anonymous, Wikileaks, the Pirate Party, and Iceland." *Journal of Computer-Mediated Communication* 19 (2): 141–154.

Biemer, Paul P. 2010. "Total Survey Error: Design, Implementation, and Evaluation." *Public Opinion Quarterly* 74 (5): 817–848.

Bimber, Bruce. 2001. "Information and Political Engagement in America: The Search for Effects of Information Technology at the Individual Level." *Political Research Quarterly* 54 (1): 53–67.

Bimber, Bruce. 2003. *Information and American Democracy: Technology in the Evolution of Political Power.* Cambridge, UK: Cambridge University Press.

Bimber, Bruce, Andrew J. Flanagin, and Cynthia Stohl. 2012. *Collective Action in Organizations: Interaction and Engagement in an Era of Technological Change.* Cambridge, UK: Cambridge University Press.

Bimber, Bruce, and Lauren Copeland. 2013. "Digital Media and Traditional Political Participation over Time in the U.S." *Information, Communication & Society* 10 (2): 125–137.

Bimber, Bruce, and Richard Davis. 2003. *Campaigning Online: The Internet in U.S. Elections.* Oxford: Oxford University Press.

Blaemire, Robert. 2012. "An Explosion of Innovation: The Voter-Data Revolution." In *Margin of Victory: How Technologists Help Politicians Win Elections*, edited by Nathaniel G. Pearlman, 107–120. Santa Monica, CA: ABC-CLIO.

Bland, Archie. 2014. "FireChat – the Messaging App That's Powering the Hong Kong Protests." *The Guardian*. www.theguardian.com/world/2014/sep/29/firechat-messaging-app-powering-hong-kong-protests.

Blumler, Jay G. 1970. "The Political Effects of Television." In *The Political Effects of Television*, edited by James G. Halloran, 68–104. London: Panther.

Boast, Robin. 2017. *The Machine in the Ghost: Digitality and Its Consequences.* London: Reaktion Books LTD.

Boczkowski, Pablo J., Eugenia Mitchelstein, and Mora Matassi. 2018. "'News Comes across When I'm in a Moment of Leisure': Understanding the Practices of Incidental News Consumption on Social Media." *New Media & Society* 20 (10): 3523–3539.

Bode, Leticia. 2012. "Facebooking It to the Polls: A Study in Online Social Networking and Political Behavior." *Journal of Information Technology & Politics* 9 (4): 352–369.

Bode, Leticia. 2016. "Political News in the News Feed: Learning Politics from Social Media." *Mass Communication and Society* 19 (1): 24–48.

Bode, Leticia, Alexander Hanna, Junghwan Yang, and Dhavan V. Shah. 2015. "Candidate Networks, Citizen Clusters, and Political Expression: Strategic Hashtag Use in the 2010 Midterms." *The ANNALS of the American Academy of Political and Social Science* 659 (1): 149–165.

Bode, Leticia, Emily K. Vraga, Porismita Borah, and Dhavan V. Shah. 2014. "A New Space for Political Behavior: Political Social Networking and Its Democratic Consequences." *Journal of Computer-Mediated Communication* 19 (33): 414–429.

Bode, Leticia, Emily K. Vraga, and Sonya Troller-Renfree. 2017. "Skipping Politics: Measuring Avoidance of Political Content in Social Media." *Research & Politics* 4 (2): 1–7.

Boler, Megan, Averie Macdonald, Christina Nitsou, and Anne Harris. 2014. "Connective Labor and Social Media." *Convergence: The International Journal of Research into New Media Technologies* 20 (4): 438–460.

Bond, David. 2017. "Incoming BBC Chairman Warns of Budgetary Constraints." *Financial Times*. www.ft.com/content/0e49c198-dcc0-11e6-9d7c-be108f1c1dce.

Bond, Robert M., Christopher J. Fariss, Jason J. Jones, Adam D. I. Kramer, Cameron Marlow, Jaime E. Settle, and James H. Fowler. 2012. "A 61-Million-Person Experiment in Social Influence and Political Mobilization." *Nature* 489 (7415): 295–298.

Bond, Robert, and Solomon Messing. 2015. "Quantifying Social Media's Political Space: Estimating Ideology from Publicly Revealed Preferences on Facebook." *American Political Science Review* 109 (1): 62–78.

Bond, Shannon. 2014. "Bezos-Owned Washington Post Offers Technology to Other Publishers." *Financial Times*. www.ft.com/content/0ee6686a-8707-11e4-982e-00144feabdc0.

Booth, William, and Karla Adam. 2018. "Cambridge Analytica's Alexander Nix: Bond Villain, Tech Genius or Hustler?" *The Washington Post*. www.washingtonpost

.com/world/europe/cambridge-analyticas-alexander-nix-bond-villain-tech-genius-or-hustler/2018/03/27/14c99112-2e34-11e8-8dc9-3b51e028b845_story.html.

Borge Bravo, Rosa, and Eduardo Santamarina Sáez. 2016. "From Protest to Political Parties: Online Deliberation in New Parties in Spain." *Medijske Studije/Media Studies Journal* 7 (14): 104–122.

Borgesius, Frederik J. Zuiderveen, Damian Trilling, Judith Möller, Balázs Bodó, Claes H. de Vreese, and Natali Helberger. 2016. "Should We Worry about Filter Bubbles?" *Internet Policy Review* 5 (1): 1–16.

Boshmaf, Yazan, Ildar Muslukhov, Konstantin Beznosov, and Matei Ripeanu. 2011. "The Socialbot Network: When Bots Socialize for Fame and Money." In *ACSAC'11: Proceedings of the 27th Annual Computer Security Applications Conference*, edited by Robert Hobbes Zakon, John McDermott, and Michael Locasto, 93–102. New York: ACM.

Boulianne, Shelley. 2009. "Does Internet Use Affect Engagement? A Meta-Analysis of Research." *Political Communication* 26 (2): 193–211.

Boulianne, Shelley. 2011. "Stimulating or Reinforcing Political Interest: Using Panel Data to Examine Reciprocal Effects between News Media and Political Interest." *Political Communication* 28 (2): 147–162.

Boulianne, Shelley. 2015. "Social Media Use and Participation: A Meta-Analysis of Current Research." *Information, Communication & Society* 18 (5): 524–538.

Boulianne, Shelley, and Yannis Theocharis. 2018. "Young People, Digital Media, and Engagement: A Meta-Analysis of Research." *Social Science Computer Review*.

Boxell, Levi, Matthew Gentzkow, and Jesse M. Shapiro. 2017. "Greater Internet Use Is Not Associated with Faster Growth in Political Polarization among US Demographic Groups." *PNAS: Proceedings of the National Academy of Sciences of the United States of America* 114 (40): 10612–10617. https://doi.org/10.1073/pnas.1706588114.

boyd, danah. 2011. "Social Network Sites as Networked Publics: Affordances, Dynamics, and Implications." In *A Networked Self: Identity, Community, and Culture on Social Network Sites*, edited by Zizi Papacharissi, 47–66. New York: Routledge.

boyd, danah. 2017. "Hacking the Attention Economy." *Medium: Points*. https://points.datasociety.net/hacking-the-attention-economy-9fa1daca7a37.

Boykoff, Jules. 2012. "US Media Coverage of the Cancún Climate Change Conference." *PS: Political Science & Politics* 45 (2): 251–258.

Brandtzæg, Petter Bae. 2012. "Social Networking Sites: Their Users and Social Implications – a Longitudinal Study." *Journal of Computer-Mediated Communication* 17 (4): 467–488.

Brayne, Sarah. 2017. "Big Data Surveillance: The Case of Policing." *American Sociological Review* 82 (5): 988–1008.

Breiman, Leo. 2001. "Statistical Modeling: The Two Cultures." *Statistical Science* 16 (3): 199–215.

Breitbart, Andrew. 2011. *Righteous Indignation: Excuse Me While I Save the World!* New York: Grand Central Publishing.

Breuer, Anita, Todd Landman, and Dorothea Farquhar. 2014. "Social Media and Protest Mobilization: Evidence from the Tunisian Revolution." *Democratization* 22 (4): 764–792.

Bronstein, Michael V., Gordon Pennycook, Adam Bear, David G. Rand, and Tyrone D. Cannon. 2019. "Belief in Fake News Is Associated with Delusionality, Dogmatism, Religious Fundamentalism, and Reduced Analytic Thinking." *Journal of Applied Research in Memory and Cognition* 8 (1): 108–117.

Brooks, Tim, and Earle Marsh. 2007. *The Complete Directory to Prime Time Network and Cable TV Shows 1946–Present*. 9th ed. New York: Ballantine Books.

Brundage, Miles, Shahar Avin, Jack Clark, Helen Toner, Peter Eckersley, Ben Garfinkel, Allan Dafoe, et al. 2018. *The Malicious Use of Artificial Intelligence: Forecasting, Prevention, and Mitigation*. Oxford: Future of Humanity Institute (FHI) et al. https://arxiv.org/abs/1802.07228.

Brunetti, Aymo, and Beatrice Weder. 2003. "A Free Press Is Bad News for Corruption." *Journal of Public Economics* 87 (7–8): 1801–1824.

Bruns, Axel. 2005. *Gatewatching: Collaborative Online News Production*. New York: Peter Lang Publishing.

Brynjolfsson, Erik, and Andrew McAfee. 2016. *The Second Machine Age: Work, Progress, and Prosperity in a Time of Brilliant Technologies*. New York: W. W. Norton & Company.

Buchstein, Hubertus. 1997. "Bytes That Bite: The Internet and Deliberative Democracy." *Constellations* 4 (2): 248–263.

Bullock, John G. 2011. "Elite Influence on Public Opinion in an Informed Electorate." *American Political Science Review* 105 (3): 496–515.

Bülow, Marisa von. 2018. "The Survival of Leaders and Organizations in the Digital Age: Lessons from the Chilean Student Movement." *Mobilization: An International Quarterly* 23 (1): 45–64.

Burns, Alex, and Ben Eltham. 2009. "Twitter Free Iran: An Evaluation of Twitter's Role in Public Diplomacy and Information Operations in Iran's 2009 Election Crisis." In *Record of the Communications Policy & Research Forum*, edited by Franco Papandrea and Mark Armstrong, 298–310. Sydney: Network Insight Institute.

Butcher, Mike. 2017. "Cambridge Analytica CEO Talks to Techcrunch About Trump, Hillary and the Future." *Techcrunch*. https://techcrunch.com/2017/11/06/cambridge-analytica-ceo-talks-to-techcrunch-about-trump-hilary-and-the-future/

Cadwalladr, Carole. 2017. "The Great British Brexit Robbery: How Our Democracy Was Hijacked." *The Guardian*. www.theguardian.com/technology/2017/may/07/the-great-british-brexit-robbery-hijacked-democracy.

Cadwalladr, Carole. 2018a. "'I Made Steve Bannon's Psychological Warfare Tool': Meet the Data War Whistleblower." *The Guardian*. www.theguardian.com/news/2018/mar/17/data-war-whistleblower-christopher-wylie-faceook-nix-bannon-trump.

Cadwalladr, Carole. 2018b. "The Brexit Whistleblower: 'Did Vote Leave Use Me? Was I Naive?'." *The Guardian*. www.theguardian.com/uk-news/2018/mar/24/brexit-whistleblower-shahmir-sanni-interview-vote-leave-cambridge-analytica.

Cadwalladr, Carole, and Emma Graham-Harrison. 2018. "Revealed: 50 Million Facebook Profiles Harvested for Cambridge Analytica in Major Data Breach." *The Guardian*. www.theguardian.com/news/2018/mar/17/cambridge-analytica-facebook-influence-us-election.

Cairns, Christopher, and Elizabeth Plantan. 2016. "Why Autocrats Sometimes Relax Online Censorship of Sensitive Issues: A Case Study of Microblog Discussion of Air Pollution in China." Working Paper.

Calin-Jageman, Robert J., and Geoff Cumming. 2019. "The New Statistics for Better Science: Ask How Much, How Uncertain, and What Else Is Known." *The American Statistician* 73 (sup1): 271–280.

Cameron, Dell, and Kate Conger. 2017. "GOP Data Firm Accidentally Leaks Personal Details of Nearly 200 Million American Voters." *Gizmodo*. https://gizmodo.com/gop-data-firm-accidentally-leaks-personal-details-of-ne-1796211612.

Campbell, Angus, Philip E. Converse, Warren E. Miller, and Donald E. Stokes. 1960. *The American Voter*. Chicago, IL: The University of Chicago Press.

Campbell, Donald T. 1979. "Assessing the Impact of Planned Social Change." *Evaluation and Program Planning* 2 (1): 67–90.

Cantoni, Davide, David Y. Yang, Noam Yuchtman, and Y. Jane Zhang. 2019. "Protests as Strategic Games: Experimental Evidence from Hong Kong's Antiauthoritarian Movement." *The Quarterly Journal of Economics* 134 (2): 1021–1077.

Card, David. 1996. "The Effect of Unions on the Structure of Wages: A Longitudinal Analysis." *Econometrica: Journal of the Econometric Society* 64 (4): 957–979.

Carpini, Michael X. Delli. 2000. "Gen.com: Youth, Civic Engagement, and the New Information Environment." *Political Communication* 17 (4): 341–349.

Carpini, Michael X .Delli, and Scott Keeter. 1996. *What Americans Know about Politics and Why It Matters*. New Haven, CT: Yale University Press.

Carr, Nicholas. 2008. *The Big Switch: Rewiring the World, from Edison to Google*. New York: W. W. Norton & Company.

Carr, Nicholas. 2015. "How Social Media Is Ruining Politics." *Politico*. www.politico.com/magazine/story/2015/09/2016-election-social-media-ruining-politics-213104.

Carty, Victoria. 2015. *Social Movements and New Technology*. Boulder, CO: Westview Press.

Casero-Ripollés, Andreu, Ramón A Feenstra, and Simon Tormey. 2016. "Old and New Media Logics in an Electoral Campaign: The Case of Podemos and the Two-Way Street Mediatization of Politics." *The International Journal of Press/Politics* 21 (3): 378–397.

Castells, Manuel. 2001. *The Internet Galaxy: Reflections on the Internet, Business and Society*. New York: Oxford University Press.

Castells, Manuel. 2009. *Communication Power*. New York: Oxford University Press.

Castells, Manuel. 2012. *Networks of Outrage and Hope: Social Movements in the Internet Age*. Cambridge, UK: Polity Press.

Castillo, Carlos, Marcelo Mendoza, and Barbara Poblete. 2011. "Information Credibility on Twitter." In *WWW'11: Proceedings of the 20th International Conference on World Wide Web*, edited by S. Sadagopan, Krithi Ramamritham. Arun Kumar, M. P. Ravindra, Elisa Bertino, and Ravi Kumar, 675–684. New York: ACM.

Castleman, Dan. 2016. "Essentials of Modeling and Microtargeting." In *Data and Democracy: How Political Data Science Is Shaping the 2016 Elections*, edited by Andrew Therriault, 1–6. Sebastopol, CA: O'Reilly Media.

Cawvey, Matthew, Matthew Hayes, Damarys Canache, and Jeffery J. Mondak. 2017. "Personality and Political Behavior." In *Oxford Research Encyclopedia of Politics*, edited by William R. Thompson, 1–20. New York: Oxford University Press. https://doi.org/10.1093/acrefore/9780190228637.013.221.

Centola, Damon. 2010. "The Spread of Behavior in an Online Social Network Experiment." *Science* 329 (5996): 1194–1197.

Centola, Damon, and Michael Macy. 2007. "Complex Contagions and the Weakness of Long Ties." *American Journal of Sociology* 113 (3): 702–734.

Ceron, Andrea. 2017. *Social Media and Political Accountability*. London: Palgrave Macmillan.

Chadwick, Andrew. 2006. *Internet Politics: States, Citizens, and New Communication Technologies*. Oxford: Oxford University Press.

Chadwick, Andrew. 2011a. "Britain's First Live Televised Party Leaders' Debate: From the News Cycle to the Political Information Cycle." *Parliamentary Affairs* 64 (1): 24–44.

Chadwick, Andrew. 2011b. "The Political Information Cycle in a Hybrid News System: The British Prime Minister and the 'Bullygate' Affair." *The International Journal of Press/Politics* 16 (1): 3–29.

Chadwick, Andrew. 2017. *The Hybrid Media System: Politics and Power*. 2nd ed. Oxford: Oxford University Press.

Chadwick, Andrew, Cristian Vaccari, and Ben O'Loughlin. 2018. "Do Tabloids Poison the Well of Social Media? Explaining Democratically Dysfunctional News Sharing." *New Media & Society* 20 (11): 4255–4274.

Chadwick, Andrew, and Jennifer Stromer-Galley. 2016. "Digital Media, Power, and Democracy in Parties and Election Campaigns: Party Decline or Party Renewal?" *The International Journal of Press/Politics* 21 (3): 283–293.

Chakrabarti, Samidh. 2018. "Hard Questions: What Effect Does Social Media Have on Democracy?" *Facebook Newsroom*. https://newsroom.fb.com/news/2018/01/effect-social-media-democracy.

Chan, Michael. 2018. "Reluctance to Talk about Politics in Face-to-Face and Facebook Settings: Examining the Impact of Fear of Isolation, Willingness to Self-Censor, and Peer Network Characteristics." *Mass Communication and Society* 21 (1): 1–23.

Chaudhuri, Ananish. 2011. "Sustaining Cooperation in Laboratory Public Goods Experiments: A Selective Survey of the Literature." *Experimental Economics* 14 (1): 47–83.

Chavesc, Mark, Laura Stephens, and Joseph Galaskiewicz. 2004. "Does Government Funding Suppress Nonprofits' Political Activity?" *American Sociological Review* 69 (2): 292–316.

Chen, Hsinchun, Roger H. L, Chiang, and Veda C. Storey. 2012. "Business Intelligence and Analytics: From Big Data to Big Impact." *MIS Quarterly* 36 (4): 1165–1188.

Chen, Hsuan-Ting. 2018. "Spiral of Silence on Social Media and the Moderating Role of Disagreement and Publicness in the Network: Analyzing Expressive and Withdrawal Behaviors." *New Media & Society* 20 (10): 3917–3936.

Chong, Dennis. 1991. *Collective Action and the Civil Rights Movement*. Chicago, IL: University of Chicago Press.

Chozick, Amy. 2015. "New Book, 'Clinton Cash,' Questions Foreign Donations to Foundation." *The New York Times*. www.nytimes.com/2015/04/20/us/politics/new-book-clinton-cash-questions-foreign-donations-to-foundation.html.

Chozick, Amy. 2016. "Hillary Clinton Calls Many Trump Backers 'Deplorables,' and G.O.P. Pounces." *The New York Times*. www.nytimes.com/2016/09/11/us/politics/hillary-clinton-basket-of-deplorables.html.

Christensen, Clayton M. 1997. *The Innovators Dilemma: When New Technologies Cause Great Firms to Fail*. Boston, MA: Harvard Business Review Press.

Christin, Angèle. 2018. "Counting Clicks: Quantification and Variation in Web Journalism in the United States and France." *American Journal of Sociology* 123 (5): 1382–1415.

Chu, Zi, Steven Gianvecchio, Haining Wang, and Sushil Jajodia. 2010. "Who Is Tweeting on Twitter: Human, Bot, or Cyborg?" In *ACSAC'10: Proceedings of the 26th Annual Computer Security Applications Conference*, 21–30. New York: ACM.

Chwe, Michael Suk-Young. 2013. *Rational Ritual: Culture, Coordination, and Common Knowledge*. Princeton, NJ: Princeton University Press.

Citron, Danielle Keats. 2009. "Cyber Civil Rights." *Boston University Law Review* 89: 61–125.

Citron, Danielle Keats, and Frank Pasquale. 2014. "The Scored Society: Due Process Fo Automated Predictions." *Washington Law Review* 89 (1): 1–33.

Clayton, Katherine, Spencer Blair, Jonathan A. Busam, Samuel Forstner, John Glance, Guy Green, Anna Kawata, et al. 2019. "Real Solutions for Fake News? Measuring the Effectiveness of General Warnings and Fact-Check Tags in Reducing Belief in False Stories on Social Media." *Political Behavior*, 1–23. https://doi.org/10.1007/s11109–019-09533-0.

Clemens, Conrad. 2018. "Motivating Voters Door-to-Door in Germany." *Campaigns & Elections*. www.campaignsandelections.com/europe/motivating-voters-door-to-door-in-germany.

Clemens, Elisabeth S. 1993. "Organizational Repertoires and Institutional Change: Women's Groups and the Transformation of US Politics, 1890–1920." *American Journal of Sociology* 98 (4): 755–798.

Coe, Kevin, Kate Kenski, and Stephen A. Rains. 2014. "Online and Uncivil? Patterns and Determinants of Incivility in Newspaper Website Comments." *Journal of Communication* 64 (4): 658–679.

Cohan, William D. 2011. "Huffing and Puffing." *Vanity Fair*. www.vanityfair.com/news/2011/02/ariana-huffington-201102.

Cohan, William D. 2016a. "How Arianna Huffington Lost Her Newsroom." *Vanity Fair*. www.vanityfair.com/news/2016/09/how-arianna-huffington-lost-her-newsroom.

Cohan, William D. 2016b. "The Inside Story of Why Arianna Huffington Left the Huffington Post." *Vanity Fair*. www.vanityfair.com/news/2016/09/why-arianna-huffington-left-the-huffington-post.

Coleman, Gabriella. 2014. *Hacker, Hoaxer, Whistleblower, Spy: The Story of Anonymous*. London: Verso.

Coleman, Stephen, and John Gotze. 2001. *Bowling Together: Online Public Engagement in Policy Deliberation*. London: Hansard Society.

Coleman, Stephen, Nicola Hall, and Milica Howell. 2002. *Hearing Voices: The Experience of Online Public Consultation and Discussion in UK Governance*. London: Hansard Society.

Colleoni, Elanor, Alessandro Rozza, and Adam Arvidsson. 2014. "Echo Chamber or Public Sphere? Predicting Political Orientation and Measuring Political Homophily in Twitter Using Big Data." *Journal of Communication* 64 (2): 317–332.

Confessore, Nicholas, Gabriel J. X. Dance, Richard Harris, and Mark Hansen. 2018. "The Follower Factory." *The New York Times*. www.nytimes.com/interactive/2018/01/27/technology/social-media-bots.html.

Confessore, Nicholas, and Daisuke Wakabayashi. 2017. "How Russia Harvested American Rage to Reshape U.S. Politics." *The New York Times*. www.nytimes .com/2017/10/09/technology/russia-election-facebook-ads-rage.html.

Confessore, Nicholas, and Danny Hakim. 2017. "Data Firm Says 'Secret Sauce' Aided Trump; Many Scoff." *The New York Times*. www.nytimes.com/2017/03/06/us/ politics/cambridge-analytica.html.

Conover, Michael D., Bruno Goncalves, Jacob Ratkiewicz, Alessandro Flammini, and Filippo Menczer. 2011. "Predicting the Political Alignment of Twitter Users." In *SocialCom 2011: The 3rd IEEE International Conference on Social Computing*. Washington, DC: IEEE.

Conover, Michael D., Jacob Ratkiewicz, Matthew Francisco, Bruno Goncalves, Alessandro Flammini, and Filippo Menczer. 2011. "Political Polarization on Twitter." In *ICWSM 2011: Proceedings of the 5th International AAAI Conference on Weblogs and Social Media*, edited by Nicolas Nicolov, James G. Shanahan, Lada Adamic, Ricardo Baeza-Yates, and Scott Counts, 89–96. Menlo Park, CA: Association for the Advancement of Artificial Intelligence (AAAI).

Conroy, Meredith, Jessica T. Feezell, and Mario Guerrero. 2012. "Facebook and Political Engagement: A Study of Online Political Group Membership and Offline Political Engagement." *Computers in Human Behavior* 28 (5): 1535–1546.

Converse, Philip. 1964. "The Nature of Belief Systems in Mass Publics." In *Ideology and Discontent*, edited by David E. Apter, 206–261. New York: Free Press.

Cook, Timothy E. 2005. *Governing with the News: The News Media as a Political Institution*. 2nd ed. Chicago, IL: The University of Chicago Press.

Copeland, Lauren, and Bruce Bimber. 2015. "Variation in the Relationship between Digital Media Use and Political Participation in U.S. Elections over Time, 1996–2012: Does Obama's Reelection Change the Picture?" *Journal of Information Technology & Politics* 12 (1): 74–87.

Cornia, Alessio, Annika Sehl, and Rasmus Kleis Nielsen. 2017. *Developing Digital News Projects in Private Sector Media*. Oxford: Reuters Institute for the Study of Journalism.

Couldry, Nick. 2012. *Media, Society, World: Social Theory and Digital Media Practice*. Cambridge, UK: Polity Press.

Cramer Walsh, Katherine. 2004. *Talking about Politics: Informal Groups and Social Identity in American Life*. Chicago, IL: University of Chicago Press.

Cummings, Dominic. 2017. "On the Referendum #22: Some Basic Numbers for the Vote Leave Campaign." *Dominic Cummings's Blog*. https://dominiccummings .files.wordpress.com/2017/01/20170130-referendum-22-numbers.pdf.

Cunningham, Frank. 2002. *Theories of Democracy: A Critical Introduction*. London: Routledge.

Curran, James, Shanto Iyengar, Anker Brink Lund, and Inka Salovaara-Moring. 2009. "Media System, Public Knowledge and Democracy: A Comparative Study." *European Journal of Communication* 24 (1): 5–26.

Dahl, Robert A. 1956. *A Preface to Democratic Theory*. Chicago, IL: The University of Chicago Press.

Dahl, Robert A. 1989. *Democracy and Its Critics*. New Haven, CT: Yale University Press.

Dahlberg, Lincoln. 2011. "Re-Constructing Digital Democracy: An Outline of Four 'Positions':" *New Media & Society* 13 (6): 855–872.

Dahlgren, Peter. 1995. *Television and the Public Sphere: Citizenship, Democracy and the Media*. London: SAGE.

Dahlgren, Peter. 2013. *The Political Web: Media, Participation and Alternative Democracy*. Basingstoke: Palgrave Macmillan.

Dancey, Logan, and Geoffrey Sheagley. 2013. "Heuristics Behaving Badly: Party Cues and Voter Knowledge." *American Journal of Political Science* 57 (2): 312–325.

D'Ancona, Matthew. 2017. *Post-Truth: The New War on Truth and How to Fight Back*. London: Ebury Press.

Darschin, Wolfgang, and Bernward Frank. 1997. "Tendenzen im Zuschauerverhalten." *Media Perspektiven* 4: 174–185.

Davenport, Thomas H., and Laurence Prusak. 1997. *Information Ecology: Mastering the Information and Knowledge Environment*. Oxford: Oxford University Press.

Davidow, William H., and Michael S. Malone. 1992. *The Virtual Corporation: Structuring and Revitalising the Corporation for the 21st Century*. New York: HarperBusiness.

Davies, Rodrigo. 2014. "Three Provocations for Civic Crowdfunding." *Information, Communication & Society* 18 (3): 342–355.

Davis, Clayton A., Onur Varol, Emilio Ferrara, Alessandro Flammini, and Filippo Menczer. 2016. "BotOrNot: A System to Evaluate Social Bots." In *WWW'16: Proceedings of the 25th International Conference on World Wide Web*, edited by Jacqueline Bourdeau, Jim A. Hendler, Roger Nkambou Nkambou, Ian Horrocks, and Ben Y. Zhao, 273–274. New York: ACM.

Davis, Evan. 2017. *Post-Truth: Why We Have Reached Peak Bullshit and What We Can Do about It*. London: Little, Brown.

Davis, Richard. 1999. *The Web of Politics: The Internet's Impact on the American Political System*. Oxford: Oxford University Press.

Davis, Richard. 2009. *Typing Politics: The Role of Blogs in American Politics*. New York: Oxford University Press.

Dayan, Daniel, and Elihu Katz. 1992. *Media Events: The Live Broadcasting of History*. Cambridge, MA: Harvard University Press.

Deibert, Ronald J. 2019. "The Road to Digital Unfreedom: Three Painful Truths about Social Media." *Journal of Democracy* 30 (1): 25–39.

Delclós, Tomàs. 2004. "Pásalo." *El País*. https://elpais.com/diario/2004/03/16/catalunya/1079402853_850215.html.

della Porta, Donatella, and Herbert Reiter, eds. 1998. *Policing Protest: The Control of Mass Demonstrations in Western Democracies*. Minneapolis: University of Minnesota Press.

De Mauro, Andrea, Marco Greco, and Michele Grimaldi. 2015. "What Is Big Data? A Consensual Definition and a Review of Key Research Topics." In *AIP Conference Proceedings*, edited by Georgios Giannakopoulos, Damianos P. Sakas, and Daphne Kyriaki-Manessi, 1644: 97–104. 1. AIP Publishing LLC.

Deseriis, Marco. 2017. "Direct Parliamentarianism: An Analysis of the Political Values Embedded in Rousseau, the 'Operating System' of the Five Star Movement." In *2017 Conference for E-Democracy and Open Government (Cedem)*, 15–25. Washington, DC: IEEE.

Diakopoulos, Nicholas, and Michael Koliska. 2017. "Algorithmic Transparency in the News Media." *Digital Journalism* 5 (7): 809–828.

Digman, John M. 1990. "Personality Structure: Emergence of the Five-Factor Model." *Annual Review of Psychology* 41: 417–440.

DiMaggio, Paul, Eszter Hargittai, Coral Celeste, and Steven Shafer. 2004. "Digital Inequality: From Unequal Access to Differentiated Use." In *Social Inequality*, edited by Kathryn Neckerman, 355–400. New York: Russell Sage Foundation.

DiMaggio, Paul, Eszter Hargittai, W. Russell Neuman, and John P. Robinson. 2001. "Social Implications of the Internet." *Annual Review of Sociology* 27: 307–336.

DiMaggio, Paul, John Evans, and Bethany Bryson. 1996. "Have Americans' Social Attitudes Become More Polarized?" *American Journal of Sociology* 102 (3): 690–755.

Dimitrova, Daniela V., Adam Shehata, Jesper Strömbäck, and Lars W. Nord. 2014. "The Effects of Digital Media on Political Knowledge and Participation in Election Campaigns: Evidence from Panel Data." *Communication Research* 41 (1): 95–118.

Doherty, Carroll, Jocelyn Kiley, and Bridget Johnson. 2017. *Public Trust in Government Remains Near Historic Lows as Partisan Attitudes Shift*. Washington, DC: Pew Research Center.

Donath, Judith, and danah boyd. 2004. "Public Displays of Connection." *Bt Technology Journal* 22 (4): 71–82.

Döpfner, Mathias. 2017. *Rede von BDZV-Präsident Dr. Mathias Döpfner bei der Mitgliederversammlung am 18. September in Stuttgart*. Stuttgart: BDZV: Bundesverband Deutscher Zeitungsverleger. www.bdzv.de/fileadmin/bdzv_hauptseite/ver anstaltungen/2017/zeitungskongress2017/assets/Rede_Dr._Döpfner_Medienpoli tik_Mitgliederversammlung.pdf.

Downey, Gary L. 1986. "Ideology and the Clamshell Identity: Organizational Dilemmas in the Anti-Nuclear Power Movement." *Social Problems* 33 (5): 357–373.

Downs, Anthony. 1957. *An Economic Theory of Democracy*. New York: Harper.

Dressel, Julia, and Hany Farid. 2018. "The Accuracy, Fairness, and Limits of Predicting Recidivism." *Science Advances* 4 (1): eaao5580.

Druckman, James N., and Arthur Lupia. 2016. "Preference Change in Competitive Political Environments." *Annual Review of Political Science* 19: 13–31.

Drudge, Matt. 2000. *Drudge Manifesto*. New York: NAL.

Dryzek, John S. 2002. *Deliberative Democracy and Beyond: Liberals, Critics, Contestations*. Oxford: Oxford University Press.

Dubois, Elizabeth, and Grant Blank. 2018. "The Echo Chamber Is Overstated: The Moderating Effect of Political Interest and Diverse Media." *Information, Communication & Society* 21 (5): 729–745.

Duggan, Maeve, and Aaron Smith. 2016. *The Political Environment on Social Media*. Washington, DC: Pew Research Center.

Duggan, Maeve, Nicole B. Ellison, Cliff Lampe, Amanda Lenhart, and Mary Madden. 2015. *Social Media Update 2014*. Washington, DC: Pew Research Center.

Dunaway, Johanna, Kathleen Searles, Mingxiao Sui, and Newly Paul. 2019. "The Move to Mobile: What's the Impact on Citizen News Attention?" In *New Directions in Media and Politics*, edited by Travis N. Ridout, 2nd ed., 143–158. New York: Routledge.

Dunn, John. 2005. *Democracy: A History.* New York: Atlantic Monthly Press.

DuPont, Quinn. 2017. "Experiments in Algorithmic Governance: A History and Ethnography of 'the Dao', a Failed Decentralized Autonomous Organization." In *Bitcoin and Beyond: Cryptocurrencies, Blockchains, and Global Governance,* edited by Malcolm Campbell-Verduyn, 157–177. London: Routledge.

Durante, Ruben, and Ekaterina Zhuravskaya. 2018. "Attack When the World Is Not Watching? US News and the Israeli-Palestinian Conflict." *Journal of Political Economy* 126 (3): 1085–1133.

Dutton, William H. 2009. "The Fifth Estate Emerging through the Network of Networks." *Prometheus: Critical Studies in Innovation* 27 (1): 1–15.

Duverger, Maurice. 1954. *Political Parties: Their Organization and Activity in the Modern State.* New York: Methuen.

Earl, Jennifer. 2014. "The Future of Social Movement Organizations." *American Behavioral Scientist* 59 (1): 35–52.

Earl, Jennifer, Heather McKee Hurwitz, Analicia Mejia Mesinas, Margaret Tolan, and Ashley Arlotti. 2013. "This Protest will be Tweeted." *Information, Communication & Society* 16 (4): 459–478.

Earl, Jennifer, and Katrina Kimport. 2009. "Movement Societies and Digital Protest: Fan Activism and Other Nonpolitical Protest Online." *Sociological Theory* 27 (3): 220–243.

Earl, Jennifer, and Katrina Kimport. 2011. *Digitally Enabled Social Change: Activism in the Internet Age.* Cambridge, MA: MIT Press.

Earl, Jennifer, Lauren Copeland, and Bruce Bimber. 2017. "Routing Around Organizations: Self-Directed Political Consumption." *Mobilization: An International Quarterly* 22 (2): 131–153.

Easton, David. 1965. *A Systems Analysis of Political Life.* New York: John Wiley & Sons.

Eddy, Melissa, and Mark Scott. 2017. "Delete Hate Speech or Pay up, Germany Tells Social Media Companies." *The New York Times.* www.nytimes.com/2017/06/30/business/germany-facebook-google-twitter.html.

The Editorial Board. 2014. "Edward Snowden, Whistle-Blower." *The New York Times.* www.nytimes.com/2014/01/02/opinion/edward-snowden-whistle-blower.html.

The Editorial Board. 2016. "Financial Secrecy in Panama and Beyond." *The New York Times.* www.nytimes.com/2016/04/08/opinion/financial-secrecy-in-panama-and-beyond.html.

Editorital Team. 2016. "EU Referendum: Results." BBC News. www.bbc.com/news/politics/eu_referendum/results.

Edmonds, Rick. 2017. "Politico Is Trying to Turn the Business Model for Magazines on Its Head." *Poynter.* www.poynter.org/news/politico-trying-turn-business-model-magazines-its-head.

Eilperin, Juliet. 2015. "Here's How the First President of the Social Media Age Has Chosen to Connect with Americans." *Washington Post.* www.washingtonpost.com/news/politics/wp/2015/05/26/heres-how-the-first-president-of-the-social-media-age-has-chosen-to-connect-with-americans/.

El-Bermawy, Mostafa M. 2016. "Your Filter Bubble Is Destroying Democracy." *Wired.* www.wired.com/2016/11/filter-bubble-destroying-democracy/.

Ellison, Nicole B., Charles Steinfield, and Cliff Lampe. 2007. "The Benefits of Facebook 'Friends:' Social Capital and College Students' Use of Online Social Network Sites." *Journal of Computer-Mediated Communication* 12 (4): 1143–1168.

Elster, Jon. 2015. *Explaining Social Behavior: More Nuts and Bolts for the Social Sciences*. Rev. ed. Cambridge, UK: Cambridge University Press.

Engin, Zeynep, and Philip Treleaven. 2019. "Algorithmic Government: Automating Public Services and Supporting Civil Servants in Using Data Science Technologies." *The Computer Journal* 62 (3): 448–460.

Enjolras, Bernard, Kari Steen-Johnsen, and Dag Wollebæk. 2012. "Social Media and Mobilization to offline demonstrations: transcending participatory divides?" *New Media & Society* 15 (6): 890–908.

Enos, Ryan D., and Eitan D. Hersh. 2015. "Party Activists as Campaign Advertisers: The Ground Campaign as a Principal-Agent Problem." *American Political Science Review* 109 (2): 252–278.

Entman, Robert M. 1989. *Democracy without Citizens: Media and the Decay of American Politics*. New York: Oxford University Press.

Entman, Robert M. 2004. *Projections of Power: Framing News, Public Opinion, and U.S. Foreign Policy*. Chicago, IL: The University of Chicago Press.

Entman, Robert M., and Nikki Usher. 2018. "Framing in a Fractured Democracy: Impacts of Digital Technology on Ideology, Power and Cascading Network Activation." *Journal of Communication* 68 (2): 298–308.

Erikson, Robert S., Michael B. MacKuen, and James A. Stimson. 2002. *The Macro Polity*. Cambridge, UK: Cambridge University Press.

Escribà-Folch, Abel. 2013. "Accountable for What? Regime Types, Performance, and the Fate of Outgoing Dictators, 1946–2004." *Democratization* 20 (1): 160–185.

Espeland, Wendy Nelson, and Michael Sauder. 2007. "Rankings and Reactivity: How Public Measures Recreate Social Worlds." *American Journal of Sociology* 113 (1): 1–40.

Esser, Frank. 2008. "Dimensions of Political News Cultures: Sound Bite and Image Bite News in France, Germany, Great Britain, and the United States." *The International Journal of Press/Politics* 13 (4): 401–428.

Esterling, Kevin M., Archon Fung, and Taeku Lee. 2015. "How Much Disagreement Is Good for Democratic Deliberation?" *Political Communication* 32 (4): 529–551.

Etzioni, Amitai. 1993. *The Spirit of Community: Rights, Responsibilities and the Communitarian Agenda*. New York: Crown Publishing Group.

Eubanks, Virginia. 2018. *Automating Inequality: How High-Tech Tools Profile, Police, and Punish the Poor*. New York: St. Martin's Press.

Eulau, Heinz, and Paul D. Karps. 1977. "The Puzzle of Representation: Specifying Components of Responsiveness." *Legislative Studies Quarterly* 2 (3): 233–254.

Evans, David S., Andrei Hagiu, and Richard Schmalensee. 2006. *Invisible Engines: How Software Platforms Drive Innovation and Transform Industries*. Cambridge, MA: MIT Press.

Evans, David S., and Richard Schmalensee. 2007. *Catalyst Code: The Strategies Behind the World's Most Dynamic Companies*. Boston, MA: Harvard Business School Press.

Evans, David S., and Richard Schmalensee. 2016. *Matchmakers: The New Economics of Multisided Platforms*. Boston, MA: Harvard Business School Publishing.

Evans, John H. 2003. "Have Americans' Attitudes Become More Polarized? An Update." *Social Science Quarterly* 84 (1): 71–90.

Evans, Jonathan St. B. T. 2008. "Dual-Processing Accounts of Reasoning, Judgment, and Social Cognition." *Annual Review of Psychology* 59: 255–278.

Faraj, Samer, Sirkka L. Jarvenpaa, and Ann Majchrzak. 2011. "Knowledge Collaboration in Online Communities." *Organization Science* 22 (5): 1224–1239.

Farrell, Henry, and Bruce Schneier. 2018. *Common-Knowledge Attacks on Democracy. Berkman Klein Center Research Publication No. 2018-7.* Cambridge, MA: Berkman Klein Center for Internet & Society.

Fearon, James D. 1999. "Electoral Accountability and the Control of Politicians: Selecting Good Types versus Sanctioning Poor Performance." In *Democracy, Accountability, and Representation,* edited by Adam Przeworski, Susan C. Stokes, and Bernard Manin, 55–97. Cambridge, UK: Cambridge University Press.

Fearon, James D. 2011. "Self-Enforcing Democracy." *The Quarterly Journal of Economics* 126 (4): 1661–1708.

Ferejohn, John. 1986. "Incumbent Performance and Electoral Control." *Public Choice* 50 (1/3): 5–25.

Ferguson, Andrew Guthrie. 2016. "The Internet of Things and the Fourth Amendment of Effects." *California Law Review* 104 (4): 805–880.

Ferguson, Andrew Guthrie. 2017. *The Rise of Big Data Policing: Surveillance, Race, and the Future of Law Enforcement.* New York: New York University Press.

Ferrara, Emilio, Onur Varol, Clayton A. Davis, Filippo Menczer, and Alessandro Flammini. 2016. "The Rise of Social Bots." *Communications of the ACM* 59 (7): 96–104.

Festinger, Leon. 1957. *A Theory of Cognitive Dissonance.* Redwood City, CA: Stanford University Press.

Filippi, Primavera De, and Aaron Wright. 2018. *Blockchain and the Law: The Rule of Code.* Cambridge, MA: Harvard University Press.

Filloux, Frédéric. 2011. "Politico: What Are the Secrets of Its Success?" *The Guardian.* www.theguardian.com/media/2011/sep/05/politico-secrets-success.

Fiorina, Morris P. 1981. *Retrospective Voting in American National Elections.* New Haven, CT: Yale University Press.

Fiorina, Morris P. 2017. *Unstable Majorities: Polarization, Party Sorting, and Political Stalemate.* Stanford, CA: Hoover Institution Press.

Fiorina, Morris P., Samuel J. Abrams, and Jeremy C. Pope. 2010. *Culture War? The Myth of a Polarized America.* 3rd ed. New York: Longman.

Fishkin, James S., and Robert C. Luskin. 2005. "Experimenting with a Democratic Ideal: Deliberative Polling and Public Opinion." *Acta Politica* 40 (3): 284–298.

Fiske, Susan T., and Shelley E. Taylor. 2017. *Social Cognition: From Brains to Culture.* 3rd ed. Los Angeles, CA: SAGE.

Flaxman, Seth, Sharad Goel, and Justin M. Rao. 2016. "Filter Bubbles, Echo Chambers, and Online News Consumption." *Public Opinion Quarterly* 80 (1): 298–320.

Fletcher, Richard, Alessio Cornia, Lucas Graves, and Rasmus Kleis Nielsen. 2018. *Measuring the Reach of "Fake News" and Online Disinformation in Europe.* Oxford: Reuters Institute for the Study of Journalism.

Fletcher, Richard, and Rasmus Kleis Nielsen. 2017a. "Are News Audiences Increasingly Fragmented? A Cross-National Comparative Analysis of Cross-Platform

News Audience Fragmentation and Duplication." *Journal of Communication* 67 (4): 476–498.

Fletcher, Richard, and Rasmus Kleis Nielsen. 2017b. "Are People Incidentally Exposed to News on Social Media? A Comparative Analysis." *New Media & Society* 20 (7): 2450–2468.

Fligstein, Neil, and Doug McAdam. 2012. *A Theory of Fields*. Oxford: Oxford University Press.

Flynn, D. J., Brendan Nyhan, and Jason Reifler. 2017. "The Nature and Origins of Misperceptions: Understanding False and Unsupported Beliefs About Politics." *Political Psychology* 38 (Supplement S1): 127–150.

Foos, Florian, and Eline A. de Rooij. 2017. "All in the Family: Partisan Disagreement and Electoral Mobilization in Intimate Networks – a Spillover Experiment." *American Journal of Political Science* 61 (2): 289–304.

Foos, Florian, and Peter John. 2018. "Parties Are No Civic Charities: Voter Contact and the Changing Partisan Composition of the Electorate." *Political Science Research and Methods* 6 (2): 283–298.

Foroohad, Rana. 2017. "Big Tech Can No Longer Be Allowed to Police Itself." *Financial Times*. www.ft.com/content/ce1d6a00-89a0-11e7-bf50-e1c239b45787.

Fourcade, Marion, and Kieran Healy. 2017. "Seeing Like a Market." *Socio-Economic Review* 15 (1): 9–29.

Fowler, Anthony, and Andrew B. Hall. 2018. "Do Shark Attacks Influence Presidential Elections? Reassessing a Prominent Finding on Voter Competence." *The Journal of Politics* 80 (4): 1423–1437.

Fowler, Anthony, and B. Pablo Montagnes. 2015. "College Football, Elections, and False-Positive Results in Observational Research." *Proceedings of the National Academy of Sciences* 112 (45): 13800–13804.

Frankel, Todd C., and Thomas Heath. 2017. "David Bradley Is Selling the Atlantic Magazine to Laurene Powell Jobs's Nonprofit." *The Washington Post*. www .washingtonpost.com/business/economy/david-bradley-is-selling-atlantic-media-to-laurene-powell-jobs-nonprofit/2017/07/28/be0517b0-739f-11e7-8839-ec48ec4 cae25_story.html.

Fraustino, Julia Daisy, and Amanda K. Kennedy. 2018. "Care in Crisis: An Applied Model of Care Considerations for Ethical Strategic Communication." *The Journal of Public Interest Communications* 2 (1): 18–40.

Fredheim, Rolf, Alfred Moore, and John Naughton. 2015. "Anonymity and Online Commenting: The Broken Windows Effect and the End of Drive-by Commenting." In *WebSci'15: Proceedings of the ACM Web Science Conference,* edited by David De Roure, Pete Burnap, and Susan Halford, 11. New York: ACM.

Freedman, Lawrence. 2017. *The Future of War: A History*. New York: Public Affairs.

Freelon, Deen. 2018. "Computational Research in the Post-Api Age." *Political Communication* 35 (4): 665–668.

Freelon, Deen, Charlton D. McIlwain, and Meredith D. Clark. 2016. *Beyond the Hashtags: #Ferguson, #Blacklivesmatter, and the Online Struggle for Offline Justice*. Washington, DC: Center for Media & Social Impact, American University.

Freeman, Jo. 1972. "The Tyranny of Structurelessness." *Berkeley Journal of Sociology* 17: 151–164.

Frenkel, Sheera. 2016. "This Is What Happens When Millions of People Suddenly Get the Internet." *BuzzFeed*. www.buzzfeed.com/sheerafrenkel/fake-news-spreads-trump-around-the-world.

Frier, Sarah. 2018. "Trump's Campaign Said It Was Better at Facebook. Facebook Agrees." *Bloomberg Politics*. www.bloomberg.com/news/articles/2018-04-03/trump-s-campaign-said-it-was-better-at-facebook-facebook-agrees.

Friess, Dennis, and Christiane Eilders. 2015. "A Systematic Review of Online Deliberation Research." *Policy & Internet* 7 (3): 319–339.

FT View. 2015. "Preserving the BBC for the Nation." *Financial Times*. www.ft.com/content/004ff4d0-a3fb-11e5-8218-6b8ff73aae15.

Fuchs, Christian. 2009. "Information and Communication Technologies and Society: A Contribution to the Critique of the Political Economy of the Internet." *European Journal of Communication* 24 (1): 69–87.

Fuchs, Christian. 2017. *Social Media: A Critical Introduction*. 2nd ed. London: SAGE.

Fuller, Matthew. 2005. *Media Ecologies: Materialist Energies in Art and Technoculture*. Cambridge, MA: The MIT Press.

Gallego, Aina. 2007. "Unequal Political Participation in Europe." *International Journal of Sociology* 37 (4): 10–25.

Gamie, Samaa. 2013. "The Cyber-Propelled Egyptian Revolution and the de/Construction of Ethos." In *Online Credibility and Digital Ethos: Evaluating Computer-Mediated Communication*, edited by Moe Folk and Shawn Apostel, 316–330. Hershey: IGI Global.

Gamson, William A. 1992. *Talking Politics*. Cambridge, UK: Cambridge University Press.

Gamson, William A., and Andre Modigliani. 1989. "Media Discourse and Public Opinion on Nuclear Power: A Constructionist Approach." *American Journal of Sociology* 95 (1): 1–37.

Gans, Herbert J. 1979. *Deciding What's News: A Study of CBS Evening News, NBC Nightly News, Newsweek, and Time*. New Brunswick, NJ: Random House.

Gao, Huiji, Geoffrey Barbier, and Rebecca Goolsby. 2011. "Harnessing the Crowd-sourcing Power of Social Media for Disaster Relief." *IEEE Intelligent Systems* 26 (3): 10–14.

Garber, Megan. 2012. "'New York Times' + Buzzfeed = Omg." *The Atlantic*. www.theatlantic.com/technology/archive/2012/06/new-york-times-buzzfeed-omg/258658/.

Garrett, R. Kelly. 2009a. "Echo Chambers Online? Politically Motivated Selective Exposure among Internet News Users." *Journal of Computer-Mediated Communication* 14 (2): 265–285.

Garrett, R. Kelly. 2009b. "Politically Motivated Reinforcement Seeking: Reframing the Selective Exposure Debate." *Journal of Communication* 59 (4): 676–699.

Gauja, Anika. 2015. "The Construction of Party Membership." *European Journal of Political Research* 54 (2): 232–248.

Gayo-Avello, Daniel. 2013. "A Meta-Analysis of State-of-the-Art Electoral Prediction from Twitter Data." *Social Science Computer Review* 31 (6): 649–679.

Gearhart, Sherice, and Weiwu Zhang. 2015. "'Was It Something I Said?' 'No, It Was Something You Posted!' A Study of the Spiral of Silence Theory in Social Media Contexts." *Cyberpsychology, Behavior, and Social Networking* 18 (4): 208–213.

Gearhart, Sherice, and Weiwu Zhang. 2018. "Same Spiral, Different Day? Testing the Spiral of Silence across Issue Types." *Communication Research* 45 (1): 34–54.

Geiß, Stefan, Melanie Magin, Birgit Stark, and Pascal Jürgens. 2018. "'Common Meeting Ground' in Gefahr? Selektionslogiken politischer Informationsquellen und ihr Einfluss auf die Fragmentierung individueller Themenhorizonte." *M&K: Medien & Kommunikationswissenschaft* 66 (4): 502–525.

Gentzkow, Matthew, and Jesse M. Shapiro. 2006. "Media Bias and Reputation." *Journal of Political Economy* 114 (2): 280–316.

Gentzkow, Matthew, and Jesse M. Shapiro. 2011. "Ideological Segregation Online and Offline." *The Quarterly Journal of Economics* 126 (4): 1799–1839.

Gerbaudo, Paolo. 2012. *Tweets and the Streets: Social Media and Contemporary Activism.* London: Pluto Press.

Gerbaudo, Paolo. 2014. "The Persistence of Collectivity in Digital Protest." *Information, Communication & Society* 17 (2): 264–268.

Gerbaudo, Paolo. 2016. "Social Media Teams as Digital Vanguards: The Question of Leadership in the Management of Key Facebook and Twitter Accounts of Occupy Wall Street, Indignados and UK Uncut." *Information, Communication & Society* 20 (2): 185–202.

Gerbaudo, Paolo. 2018a. *The Digital Party: Political Organisation and Online Democracy.* London: Pluto Press.

Gerbaudo, Paolo. 2018b. "Social Media and Populism: An Elective Affinity?" *Media, Culture & Society* 40 (5): 745–753.

Gerbner, George. 1998. "Cultivation Analysis: An Overview." *Mass Communication and Society* 1 (3–4): 175–194.

Germann, Micha, and Uwe Serdült. 2017. "Internet Voting and Turnout: Evidence from Switzerland." *Electoral Studies* 47: 1–12.

Gervais, Bryan T. 2015. "Incivility Online: Affective and Behavioral Reactions to Uncivil Political Posts in a Web-Based Experiment." *Journal of Information Technology & Politics* 12 (2): 167–185.

Gibson, Rachel K., Kevin Gillan, Fabienne Greffet, Benjamin J. Lee, and Stephen Ward. 2012. "Party Organizational Change and ICTs: The Growth of a Virtual Grassroots?" *New Media & Society* 15 (1): 31–51.

Gil de Zúñiga, Homero, Brian Weeks, and Alberto Ardèvol-Abreu. 2017. "Effects of the News-Finds-Me Perception in Communication: Social Media Use Implications for News Seeking and Learning About Politics." *Journal of Computer-Mediated Communication* 22 (3): 105–123.

Gil de Zúñiga, Homero, Logan Molyneux, and Pei Zheng. 2014. "Social Media, Political Expression, and Political Participation: Panel Analysis of Lagged and Concurrent Relationships." *Journal of Communication* 64 (4): 612–634.

Gil de Zúñiga, Homero, Nakwon Jung, and Sebastián Valenzuela. 2012. "Social Media Use for News and Individuals' Social Capital, Civic Engagement and Political Participation." *Journal of Computer-Mediated Communication* 17 (3): 319–336.

Gil de Zúñiga, Homero, and Sebastián Valenzuela. 2011. "The Mediating Path to a Stronger Citizenship: Online and Offline Networks, Weak Ties, and Civic Engagement." *Communication Research* 38 (3): 397–421.

Gil de Zúñiga, Homero, Victor Garcia-Perdomo, and Shannon C. McGregor. 2015. "What Is Second Screening? Exploring Motivations of Second Screen Use and Its

Effect on Online Political Participation." *Journal of Communication* 65 (5): 793–815.

Gillespie, Tarleton. 2010. "The Politics of 'Plattforms'." *New Media & Society* 12 (3): 347–364.

Gillmor, Dan. 2004. "We the Media: The Rise of Citizen Journalists." *National Civic Review* 93 (3): 58–63.

Gimmler, Antje. 2001. "Deliberative Democracy, the Public Sphere and the Internet." *Philosophy & Social Criticism* 27 (4): 21–39.

Gitlin, Todd. 1980. *The Whole World Is Watching: Mass Media in the Making and Unmaking of the Left*. Berkeley: University of California Press.

Glaberson, William. 1995. "The Media Business: Circulation Drops at Many Large Papers." *The New York Times*. www.nytimes.com/1995/10/31/business/the-media-business-circulation-drops-at-many-large-papers.html.

Gladwell, Malcolm. 2010. "Small Change : Why the Revolution Will Not Be Tweeted." *The New Yorker* 4: 42–49. www.newyorker.com/magazine/2010/10/04/small-change-malcolm-gladwell.

Glaser, April. 2017. "Political Ads on Facebook Now Need to Say Who Paid for Them." *Slate*. https://slate.com/technology/2017/12/political-ads-on-facebook-now-need-to-say-who-paid-for-them.html.

Glennan, Stuart. 2017. *The New Mechanical Philosophy*. Oxford: Oxford University Press.

Goel, Sharad, Ashton Anderson, Jake Hofman, and Duncan J. Watts. 2016. "The Structural Virality of Online Diffusion." *Management Science* 62 (1): 180–196.

Goemans, Henk E., Kristian Skrede Gleditsch, and Giacomo Chiozza. 2009. "Introducing Archigos: A Dataset of Political Leaders." *Journal of Peace Research* 46 (2): 269–283.

Gohdes, Anita R. 2015. "Pulling the Plug: Network Disruptions and Violence in Civil Conflict." *Journal of Peace Research* 52 (3): 352–367.

Gomez, Brad T., and J. Matthew Wilson. 2001. "Political Sophistication and Economic Voting in the American Electorate: A Theory of Heterogeneous Attribution." *American Journal of Political Science* 45 (4): 899–914.

Gomez, Raul, and Luis Ramiro. 2019. "The Limits of Organizational Innovation and Multi-Speed Membership." *Party Politics* 25 (4): 534–546..

González-Bailón, Sandra. 2017. *Decoding the Social World: Data Science and the Unintended Consequences of Communication*. Cambridge, MA: The MIT Press.

González-Bailón, Sandra, Javier Borge-Holthoefer, Alejandro Rivero, and Yamir Moreno. 2011. "The Dynamics of Protest Recruitment through an Online Network." *Scientific Reports* 1 (197): 1–7.

González-Bailón, Sandra, Javier Borge-Holthoefer, and Yamir Moreno. 2013. "Broadcasters and Hidden Influentials in Online Protest Diffusion." *American Behavioral Scientist* 57 (7): 943–965.

González-Bailón, Sandra, and Ning Wang. 2016. "Networked Discontent: The Anatomy of Protest Campaigns in Social Media." *Social Networks* 44 (1): 95–104.

Goodhart, Charles. 1975. "Problems of Monetary Management: The U.K. Experience." In *Papers in Monetary Economics*. Vol. 1. Sydney: Reserve Bank of Australia.

Goodin, Robert E. 2003. *Reflective Democracy*. Oxford: Oxford University Press.

Goodin, Robert E, and Simon J Niemeyer. 2003. "When Does Deliberation Begin? Internal Reflection Versus Public Discussion in Deliberative Democracy." *Political Studies* 51 (4): 627–649.

Goodman, Nicole, and Leah C Stokes. 2018. "Reducing the Cost of Voting: An Evaluation of Internet Voting's Effect on Turnout." *British Journal of Political Science*, 1–13. https://doi.org/10.1017/S0007123417000849.

Goodman, Nicole, Michael McGregor, Jérôme Couture, and Sandra Breux. 2018. "Another Digital Divide? Evidence That Elimination of Paper Voting Could Lead to Digital Disenfranchisement." *Policy & Internet* 10 (2): 164–184.

Goody, Jack. 1977. *The Domestification of the Savage Mind*. Cambridge, UK: Cambridge University Press.

The GovLab. 2018. *CrowdLaw Manifesto: A Statement of 12 Principles for Online, Participatory Lawmaking*. New York: CrowdLaw. http://manifesto.crowd.law.

Graham, David A. 2017a. "The Trouble with Publishing the Trump Dossier." *The Atlantic*. www.theatlantic.com/politics/archive/2017/01/why-did-buzzfeed-publish-the-trump-dossier/512771/.

Graham, David A. 2017b. "What CNN's Report on Trump and Russia Does and Doesn't Say." *The Atlantic*. www.theatlantic.com/politics/archive/2017/01/what-cnns-bombshell-report-does-and-doesnt-say/512747/.

Granovetter, Mark. 1973. "The Strength of Weak Ties." *American Journal of Sociology* 78 (6): 1360–1380.

Granovetter, Mark. 1978. "Threshold Models of Collective Behavior." *American Journal of Sociology* 83 (6): 1420–1443.

Grant, Will J., Brenda Moon, and Janie Busby Grant. 2010. "Digital Dialogue? Australian Politicians' Use of the Social Network Tool Twitter." *Australian Journal of Political Science* 45 (4): 579–604.

Graves, Lucas. 2016. *Deciding What's True: The Rise of Political Fact-Checking in American Journalism*. New York: Columbia University Press.

Green, Donald P., and Alan S. Gerber. 2015. *Get Out the Vote: How to Increase Voter Turnout*. 3rd ed. Washington, DC: Brookings Institution Press.

Green, Joshua. 2015. "This Man Is the Most Dangerous Political Operative in America." *Bloomberg Businessweek*. www.bloomberg.com/politics/graphics/2015-steve-bannon/.

Green, Joshua. 2017. *Devil's Bargain: Steve Bannon, Donald Trump, and the Storming of the Presidency*. New York: Penguin Press.

Green, Joshua, and Sasha Issenberg. 2016. "Inside the Trump Bunker, with Days to Go." *Bloomberg Businessweek*. www.bloomberg.com/news/articles/2016-10-27/inside-the-trump-bunker-with-12-days-to-go.

Greitens, Sheena Chestnut. 2013. "Authoritarianism Online: What Can We Learn from Internet Data in Nondemocracies?" *PS: Political Science & Politics* 46 (2): 262–270.

Grewal, Paul. 2018. "Suspending Cambridge Analytica and Scl Group from Facebook." *Facebook Newsroom*. https://newsroom.fb.com/news/2018/03/suspending-cambridge-analytica/.

Grimme, Christian, Dennis Assenmacher, and Lena Adam. 2018. "Changing Perspectives: Is It Sufficient to Detect Social Bots?" In *Social Computing and Social Media. User Experience and Behavior. SCSM 2018*, edited by Gabriele Meiselwitz, 445–461. Springer.

Grinberg, Nir, Kenneth Joseph, Lisa Friedland, Briony Swire-Thompson, and David Lazer. 2019. "Fake News on Twitter During the 2016 U.S. Presidential Election." *Science* 363 (6425): 374–378.

Grönlund, Kimmo, Kaisa Herne, and Maija Setälä. 2015. "Does Enclave Deliberation Polarize Opinions?" *Political Behavior* 37 (4): 995–1020.

Grossman, Lawrence K. 1995. *Electronic Republic: Reshaping American Democracy for the Information Age*. New York: Viking.

Grossman, Lev. 2006. "You – Yes, You – Are Time's Person of the Year." *Time*. http://content.time.com/time/magazine/article/0,9171,1570810,00.html.

Grove, Andrew S. 1983. *High Output Management*. New York: Vintage Books.

Grueskin, Bill, Ava Seave, and Lucas Graves. 2011. *The Story So Far: What We Know About the Business of Digital Journalism*. New York: Columbia University Press.

Guess, Andrew, Brendan Nyhan, Benjamin Lyons, and Jason Reifler. 2018a. *Avoiding the Echo Chamber about Echo Chambers: Why Selective Exposure to Like-Minded Political News Is Less Prevalent Than You Think*. Miami, FL: Knight Foundation.

Guess, Andrew, Brendan Nyhan, and Jason Reifler. 2018b. "Selective Exposure to Misinformation: Evidence from the Consumption of Fake News during the 2016 U.S. Presidential Campaign." Working Paper. www.dartmouth.edu/~nyhan/fake-news-2016.pdf.

Guess, Andrew, Jonathan Nagler, and Joshua A. Tucker. 2019. "Less Than You Think: Prevalence and Predictors of Fake News Dissemination on Facebook." *Science Advances* 5 (1): eaau4586.

Gunitsky, Seva. 2015. "Corrupting the Cyber-Commons: Social Media as a Tool of Autocratic Stability." *Perspectives on Politics* 13 (1): 42–54.

Guo, Zhongshi, and Patricia Moy. 1998. "Medium or Message? Predicting Dimensions of Political Sophistication." *International Journal of Public Opinion Research* 10 (1): 25–50.

Gupta, Manish, Peixiang Zhao, and Jiawei Han. 2012. "Evaluating Event Credibility on Twitter." In *SIAM'12: 2012 Siam International Conference on Data Mining*, edited by Joydeep Ghosh, Huan Liu, Ian Davidson, Carlotta Domeniconi, and Chandrika Kamath, 153–164. Philadelphia, PA: Society for Industrial; Applied Mathematics.

Gurri, Martin. 2018. *The Revolt of the Public and the Crisis of Authority in the New Millennium*. 2nd ed. San Francisco, CA: Stripe Press.

Gustafsson, Nils. 2012. "The Subtle Nature of Facebook Politics: Swedish Social Network Site Users and Political Participation." *New Media & Society* 14 (7): 1111–1127.

Gustin, Sam. 2011. "Social Media Sparked, Accelerated Egypt's Revolutionary Fire." *Wired*. www.wired.com/2011/02/egypts-revolutionary-fire/.

Haberman, Maggie, and Nick Corasaniti. 2015. "Democrats and Bernie Sanders Clash over Data Breach." *The New York Times*. www.nytimes.com/politics/first-draft/2015/12/18/sanders-campaign-disciplined-for-breaching-clinton-data/.

Habermas, Jürgen. 1992. "Further Reflections on the Public Sphere." In *Habermas and the Public Sphere*, edited by Craig Calhoun, 421–461. Cambridge, MA: The MIT Press.

Haenschen, Katherine. 2016. "Social Pressure on Social Media: Using Facebook Status Updates to Increase Voter Turnout." *Journal of Communication* 66 (4): 542–563.

Halberstam, David. 1972. *The Best and the Brightest*. New York: Random House.

Hale, Scott A., Helen Margetts, and Taha Yasseri. 2013. "Petition Growth and Success Rates on the UK No. 10 Downing Street Website." In *Proceedings of the 5th Annual Acm Web Science Conference*, edited by Hugh Davis, Harry Halpin, Alex Pentland, Mark Bernstein, Lada Adamic, Harith Alani, Alexandre Monnin, and Richard Rogers ,132–138. New York: ACM.

Hale, Scott A., Peter John, Helen Margetts, and Taha Yasseri. 2018. "How Digital Design Shapes Political Participation: A Natural Experiment with Social Information." *PLoS ONE* 13 (4): e0196068.

Hallin, Daniel C. 1992. "Sound Bite News: Television Coverage of Elections, 1968–1988." *Journal of Communication* 42 (2): 5–24.

Hallin, Daniel C., and Paolo Mancini. 2004. *Comparing Media Systems: Three Models of Media and Politics*. Cambridge, UK: Cambridge University Press.

Hallin, Daniel C., and Paolo Mancini. eds. 2012. *Comparing Media Systems Beyond the Western World*. Cambridge, UK: Cambridge University Press.

Halpern, Daniel, and Jennifer Gibbs. 2013. "Social Media as a Catalyst for Online Deliberation? Exploring the Affordances of Facebook and YouTube for Political Expression." *Computers in Human Behavior* 29 (3): 1159–1168.

Halupka, Max. 2014. "Clicktivism: A Systematic Heuristic." *Policy & Internet* 6 (2): 115–132.

Hamblin, James. 2014. "It's Everywhere, the Clickbait." *The Atlantic*. www.theatlantic.com/entertainment/archive/2014/11/clickbait-what-is/382545/.

Hamby, Peter. 2013. *Did Twitter Kill the Boys on the Bus? Searching for a Better Way to Cover a Campaign*. Boston, MA: Joan Shorenstein Center on the Press, Politics, Public Policy.

Hampton, Keith N., Inyoung Shin, and Weixu Lu. 2017. "Social Media and Political Discussion: When Online Presence Silences Offline Conversation." *Information, Communication & Society* 20 (7): 1090–1107.

Hand, David J. 2004. *Measurement Theory and Practice: The World through Quantification*. London: Wiley.

Hanfeld, Michael. 2018. "Am Scheideweg." *Frankfurter Allgemeine*. www.faz.net/aktuell/feuilleton/medien/ard-zdf-und-der-rundfunkbeitrag-15424656.html.

Hansson, Karin, Kheira Belkacem, and Love Ekenberg. 2015. "Open Government and Democracy: A Research Review." *Social Science Computer Review* 33 (5): 540–555.

Hardin, Russell. 1995. *One for All: The Logic of Group Confict*. Princeton, NJ: Princeton University Press.

Hargittai, Eszter. 2002. "Second-Level Digital Divide: Differences in People's Online Skills." *First Monday* 7 (4). http://firstmonday.org/article/view/942/864.

Hargittai, Eszter. 2010. "Digital Na(t)ives? Variation in Internet Skills and Uses among Members of the 'Net Generation'." *Sociological Inquiry* 80 (1): 92–113.

Hargittai, Eszter. 2015. "Is Bigger Always Better? Potential Biases of Big Data Derived from Social Network Sites." *The ANNALS of the American Academy of Political and Social Science* 659 (1): 63–76.

Hargittai, Eszter, and Aaron Shaw. 2013. "Digitally Savvy Citizenship: The Role of Internet Skills and Engagement in Young Adults' Political Participation Around the 2008 Presidential Election." *Journal of Broadcasting & Electronic Media* 57 (2): 115–134.

Hargittai, Eszter, and Yuli Patrick Hsieh. 2012. "Succinct Survey Measures of Web-Use Skills." *Social Science Computer Review* 30 (1): 95–107.

Hargittai, Eszter, and Yuli Patrick Hsieh. 2013. "Digital Inequality." In *The Oxford Handbook of Internet Studies*, edited by William H. Dutton, 129–150. New York: Oxford University Press.

Hartleb, Florian. 2013. "Anti-Elitist Cyber Parties?" *Journal of Public Affairs* 13 (4): 355–369.

Hasebrink, Uwe, and Hanna Domeyer. 2012. "Media Repertoires as Patterns of Behaviour and as Meaningful Practices: A Multimethod Approach to Media Use in Converging Media Environments." *Participations: Journal of Audience & Reception Studies* 9 (2): 757–779.

Hasebrink, Uwe, and Jutta Popp. 2006. "Media Repertoires as a Result of Selective Media Use: A Conceptual Approach to the Analysis of Patterns of Exposure." *Communications: The European Journal of Communication Research* 31 (3): 369–387.

Hassan, Abdalla F. 2015. *Media, Revolution and Politics in Egypt*. London: I. B. Tauris.

Hassanpour, Navid. 2014. "Media Disruption and Revolutionary Unrest: Evidence from Mubarak's Quasi-Experiment." *Political Communication* 31 (1): 1–24.

Hassid, Jonathan. 2012. "Safety Valve or Pressure Cooker? Blogs in Chinese Political Life." *Journal of Communication* 62 (2): 212–230.

Hatakka, Niko. 2016. "When Logics of Party Politics and Online Activism Collide: The Populist Finns Party's Identity under Negotiation." *New Media & Society* 19 (12): 2022–2038.

Hatry, Harry P. 1978. "The Status of Productivity Measurement in the Public Sector." *Public Administration Review* 38 (1): 28–33.

Hauben, Michael, and Ronda Hauben. 1997. *Netizens: On the History and Impact of Usenet and the Internet*. Los Alamitos, CA: IEEE Computer Society Press.

Hayek, Friedrich August von. 1948. *Individualism and Economic Order*. Champaign, IL: The University of Chicago Press.

Healy, Andrew J, Neil Malhotra, and Cecilia Hyunjung Mo. 2010. "Irrelevant Events Affect Voters' Evaluations of Government Performance." *Proceedings of the National Academy of Sciences* 107 (29): 12804–12809.

Healy, Kieran. 2016. "Turkey Coup: How Facetime and Social Media Helped Erdogan Foil the Plot." *Vox*. www.vox.com/2016/7/16/12206304/turkey-coup-facetime.

Hedström, Peter, and Richard Swedberg, eds. 1998. *Social Mechanisms: An Analytical Approach to Social Theory*. Cambridge, UK: Cambridge University Press.

Heidenheimer, Arnold J. 1986. "Politics, Policy and Policey as Concepts in English and Continental Languages: An Attempt to Explain Divergences." *The Review of Politics* 48 (1): 3–30.

Helbing, Dirk, Bruno S. Frey, Gerd Gigerenzer, Ernst Hafen, Michael Hagner, Yvonne Hofstetter, Jeroen van den Hoven, Roberto V. Zicari, and Andrej Zwitter. 2017. "Will Democracy Survive Big Data and Artificial Intelligence?" *Scientific American*. www.scientificamerican.com/article/will-democracy-survive-big-data-and-artificial-intelligence/.

Held, David. 2006. *Models of Democracy*. 3rd ed. Cambridge, UK: Polity.

Hendler, Josh. 2012. "Organizing Technology: The Marriage of Technology and the Field Campaign." In *Margin of Victory: How Technologists Help Politicians Win Elections*, edited by Nathaniel G. Pearlman, 121–132. Santa Monica, CA: ABC-CLIO.

Herbst, Susan. 1993. *Numbered Voices: How Opinion Polling Has Shaped American Politics*. Chicago, IL: The University of Chicago Press.

Hermida, Alfred. 2014. "The Fall and Rise of the News Bundle." *In NiemanLab: Predictions for Journalism 2015*. Cambridge, MA: Nieman Foundation at Harvard. www.niemanlab.org/2014/12/the-fall-and-rise-of-the-news-bundle/.

Hermida, Alfred, Fred Fletcher, Darryl Korell, and Donna Logan. 2012. "Share, Like, Recommend: Decoding the Social Media News Consumer." *Journalism Studies* 13 (5–6): 815–824.

Hern, Alex. 2018. "Fitness Tracking App Strava Gives Away Location of Secret Us Army Bases." *The Guardian*. www.theguardian.com/world/2018/jan/28/fitness-tracking-app-gives-away-location-of-secret-us-army-bases.

Hern, Alex, and Carole Cadwalladr. 2018. "Revealed: Aleksandr Kogan Collected Facebook Users' Direct Messages." *The Guardian*. www.theguardian.com/uk-news/2018/apr/13/revealed-aleksandr-kogan-collected-facebook-users-direct-messages.

Herrera, Linda. 2014. *Revolution in the Age of Social Media: The Egyptian Popular Insurrection and the Internet*. London: Verso.

Hersh, Eitan D. 2015. *Hacking the Electorate: How Campaigns Perceive Voters*. Cambridge, UK: Cambridge University Press.

Hersh, Eitan D. 2018. "Cambridge Analytica and the Future of Data Privacy: Written Testimony of Eitan Hersh." In *Hearing Before the United States Senate Committee on the Judiciary*. Washington, DC: United States Senate. www.judiciary.senate.gov/imo/media/doc/05-16-18%20Hersh%20Testimony1.pdf.

Hert, Paul de, and Vagelis Papakonstantinou. 2016. "The New General Data Protection Regulation: Still a Sound System for the Protection of Individuals?" *Computer Law & Security Review* 32 (2): 179–194.

Hess, Amanda. 2017. "How to Escape Your Political Bubble for a Clearer View." *The New York Times*. www.nytimes.com/2017/03/03/arts/the-battle-over-your-political-bubble.html.

Hibbing, John R, and Elizabeth Theiss-Morse. 2002. *Stealth Democracy: Americans' Beliefs About How Government Should Work*. New York: Cambridge University Press.

Hill, Seth J., James Lo, Lynn Vavreck, and John Zaller. 2013. "How Quickly We Forget: The Duration of Persuasion Effects from Mass Communication." *Political Communication* 30 (4): 521–547.

Hillygus, D. Sunshine, and Todd G. Shields. 2008. *The Persuadable Voter: Wedge Issues in Presidential Campaigns*. Princeton, NJ: Princeton University Press.

Hindman, Matthew. 2005. "The Real Lessons of Howard Dean: Reflections on the First Digital Campaign." *Perspectives on Politics* 3 (1): 121–128.

Hindman, Matthew. 2009. *The Myth of of Digital Democracy*. Princeton, NJ: Princeton University Press.

Hindman, Matthew. 2018a. "How Cambridge Analytica's Facebook Targeting Model Really Worked – According to the Person Who Built I." *The Conversation*. https://

theconversation.com/how-cambridge-analyticas-facebook-targeting-model-really-worked-according-to-the-person-who-built-it-94078.

Hindman, Matthew. 2018b. *The Internet Trap: How the Digital Economy Builds Monopolies and Undermines Democracy.* Princeton, NJ: Princeton University Press.

Hirschfeld Davis, Julie. 2015. "A Digital Team Is Helping Obama Find His Voice Online." *The New York Times.* www.nytimes.com/2015/11/09/us/politics/a-digital-team-is-helping-obama-find-his-voice-online.html.

Hobbs, William R., and Margaret E. Roberts. 2018. "How Sudden Censorship Can Increase Access to Information." *American Political Science Review* 112 (3): 621–636.

Hodge, Matthew M., and Ronald F. Piccolo. 2005. "Funding Source, Board Involvement Techniques, and Financial Vulnerability in Nonprofit Organizations: A Test of Resource Dependence." *Nonprofit Management and Leadership* 16 (2): 171–190.

Hoffman, Donna L., and Thomas P. Novak. 1996. "Marketing in Hypermedia Computer-Mediated Environments: Conceptual Foundations." *Journal of Marketing* 60 (3): 50–68.

Hoffmann, Christian Pieter, and Christoph Lutz. 2017. "Spiral of Silence 2.0: Political Self-Censorship among Young Facebook Users." In *#SMSociety17: Proceedings of the 8th International Conference on Social Media & Society*, 1–12. 10. New York: ACM.

Holbert, R. Lance. 2005. "Intramedia Mediation: The Cumulative and Complementary Effects of News Media Use." *Political Communication* 22 (4): 447–461.

Holiday, Ryan. 2012. *Trust Me, I'm Lying: Confessions of a Media Manipulator.* New York: Portfolio.

Holiday, Ryan. 2018. *Conspiracy: Peter Thiel, Hulk Hogan, Gawker, and the Anatomy of Intrigue.* New York: Portfolio/Penguin.

Holt, Kristoffer, Adam Shehata, Jesper Strömbäck, and Elisabet Ljungberg. 2013. "Age and the Effects of News Media Attention and Social Media Use on Political Interest and Participation: Do Social Media Function as Leveller?" *European Journal of Communication* 28 (1): 19–34.

Hooghe, Marc. 2007. "Social Capital and Diversity Generalized Trust, Social Cohesion and Regimes of Diversity." *Canadian Journal of Political Science* 40 (3): 709–732.

Hooghe, Marc, and Jennifer Oser. 2015. "Internet, Television and Social Capital: The Effect of 'Screen Time' on Social Capital." *Information, Communication & Society* 18 (10): 1175–1199.

Howard, Philip N. 2005. *New Media Campaigns and the Managed Citizen.* Cambridge, UK: Cambridge University Press.

Howard, Philip N., Duffy, A., Freelon, D., Hussain, M. M., Mari, W., and Maziad, M. 2011. *Opening closed regimes: what was the role of social media during the Arab Spring?* Available at SSRN 2595096.

Howard, Philip N., and Muzammil M Hussain. 2011. "The Role of Digital Media." *Journal of Democracy* 22 (3): 35–48.

Howard, Philip N., and Muzammil M Hussain. 2013. *Democracy's Fourth Wave? Digital Media and the Arab Spring.* New York: Oxford University Press.

Howison, James, Andrea Wiggins, and Kevin Crowston. 2011. "Validity Issues in the Use of Social Network Analysis with Digital Trace Data." *Journal of the Association for Information Systems* 12 (12): 767–797.

Huckfeldt, R. Robert, and John Sprague. 1995. *Citizens, Politics and Social Communication: Information and Influence in an Election Campaign.* Cambridge, UK: Cambridge University Press.

Huddy, Leonie, Lilliana Mason, and Lene Aarøe. 2015. "Expressive Partisanship: Campaign Involvement, Political Emotion, and Partisan Identity." *American Political Science Review* 109 (1): 1–17.

Hughes, Amanda Lee, and Leysia Palen. 2009. "Twitter Adoption and Use in Mass Convergence and Emergency Events." *International Journal of Emergency Management* 6 (3–4): 248–260.

Igielnik, Ruth, Scott Keeter, Courtney Kennedy, and Bradley Spahn. 2018. *Commercial Voter Files and the Study of U.S. Politics.* Washington, DC: Pew Research Center.

Igo, Sarah E. 2018. *The Known Citizen: A History of Privacy in Modern America.* Cambridge, MA: Harvard University Press.

Imran, Muhammad, Shady Elbassuoni, Carlos Castillo, Fernando Diaz, and Patrick Meier. 2013. "Extracting Information Nuggets from Disaster-Related Messages in Social Media." In *Proceedings of the 10th International Iscram Conference*, edited by T. Comes, F. Fiedrich, S. Fortier, J. Geldermann, and T. Müller, 1–10. Baden-Baden: ISCRAM

Ingram, Mathew. 2016. "Facebook Traffic to U.S. News Sites Has Fallen by Double Digits, Report Says." *Fortune.* http://fortune.com/2016/08/16/facebook-traffic-media/.

Isaac, Mike. 2014. "Amazon's Jeff Bezos Explains Why He Bought the Washington Post." *The New York Times.* https://bits.blogs.nytimes.com/2014/12/02/amazons-bezos-explains-why-he-bought-the-washington-post/.

Issenberg, Sasha. 2012a. "How Obama's Team Used Big Data to Rally Voters." *MIT Technology Review.* www.technologyreview.com/s/509026/how-obamas-team-used-big-data-to-rally-voters/.

Issenberg, Sasha. 2012b. "Obama Does It Better." *Slate.* www.slate.com/articles/news_and_politics/victory_lab/2012/10/obama_s_secret_weapon_democrats_have_a_massive_advantage_in_targeting_and.html.

Issenberg, Sasha. 2012c. *The Victory Lab: The Secret Science of Winning Campaigns.* New York: Crown Publishing Group.

Iyengar, Shanto, James Curran, Anker Brink Lund, Inka Salovaara-Moring, Kyu S. Hahn, and Sharon Coen. 2010. "Cross-National versus Individual-Level Differences in Political Information: A Media Systems Perspective." *Journal of Elections, Public Opinion and Parties* 20 (3): 291–309.

Iyengar, Shanto, Robert C. Luskin, and James S. Fishkin. 2003. "Facilitating Informed Public Opinion: Evidence from Face-to-Face and Online Deliberative Polls." Working Paper.

Jamieson, Kathleen Hall. 1992. *Dirty Politics: Deception, Distraction, and Democracy.* New York: Oxford University Press.

Jamieson, Kathleen Hall. 1996. *Packaging the Presidency: A History and Criticism of Presidential Campaign Advertising.* 3rd ed. New York: Oxford University Press.

Jamieson, Kathleen Hall. 2018. *Cyberwar: How Russian Hackers and Trolls Helped Elect a President*. New York: Oxford University Press.

Jane, Emma A. 2014. "'Your a Ugly, Whorish, Slut': Understanding E-Bile." *Feminist Media Studies* 14 (4): 531–546.

Jankowski, Nicholas W. 2002. "Creating Community with Media: History, Theories and Scientific Investigations." In *Handbook of New Media: Social Shaping and Consequences of Icts*, edited by Leah A. Lievrouw and Sonia Livingstone, 34–49. London: SAGE.

Janowitz, Morris. 1952. *The Community Press in an Urban Setting: The Social Elements of Urbanism*. Glencoe, IL: Free Press.

Janssen, Davy, and Raphaël Kies. 2005. "Online Forums and Deliberative Democracy." *Acta Politica* 40 (3): 317–335.

Jasper, James M. 1998. "The Emotions of Protest: Affective and Reactive Emotions in and Around Social Movements." *Sociological Forum* 13 (3): 397–424.

Jenkins, Henry. 2006. *Convergence Culture: When Old and New Media Collide*. New York: New York University Press.

Jenkins, Henry. 2015. "'Cultural Acupuncture': Fan Activism and the Harry Potter Alliance." In *Popular Media Cultures*, edited by Lincoln Geraghty, 206–229. Basingstoke: Palgrave Macmillan.

Jenkins, Henry, Sam Ford, and Joshua Green. 2013. *Spreadable Media: Creating Value and Meaning in a Networked Culture*. New York: New York University Press.

Jensen, Klaus Bruhn. 2010. *Media Convergence: The Three Degrees of Network, Mass, and Interpersonal Communication*. London: Routledge.

Jensen, Klaus Bruhn, and Rasmus Helles. 2017. "Speaking into the System: Social Media and Many-to-One Communication." *European Journal of Communication* 32 (1): 16–25.

Jerit, Jennifer, Jason Barabas, and Toby Bolsen. 2006. "Citizens, Knowledge, and the Information Environment." *American Journal of Political Science* 50 (2): 266–282.

Johnson, Dennis W. 2016. *Campaigning in the Twenty-First Century: Activism, Big Data, and Dark Money*. 2nd ed. New York: Routledge.

Johnson, Peter, and Pamela Robinson. 2014. "Civic Hackathons: Innovation, Procurement, or Civic Engagement?" *Review of Policy Research* 31 (4): 349–357.

Jones, Meg Leta. 2016. *Ctrl + Z: The Right to Be Forgotten*. New York: New York University Press.

Jost, John T., Pablo Barberá, Richard Bonneau, Melanie Langer, Megan Metzger, Jonathan Nagler, Joanna Sterling, and Joshua A. Tucker. 2018. "How Social Media Facilitates Political Protest: Information, Motivation, and Social Networks." *Political Psychology* 39 (S1): 85–118.

Jost, John T., Erin P. Hennes, and Howard Lavine. 2013. "'Hot' Political Cognition: Its Self-, Group-, and System-Serving Purposes." In *The Oxford Handbook of Social Cognition*, edited by Donal Carlston, 851–875. Oxford: Oxford University Press.

Jungherr, Andreas. 2014. "The Logic of Political Coverage on Twitter: Temporal Dynamics and Content." *Journal of Communication* 64 (2): 239–259.

Jungherr, Andreas. 2015. *Analyzing Political Communication with Digital Trace Data: The Role of Twitter Messages in Social Science Research*. Cham: Springer.

Jungherr, Andreas. 2016a. "Datengestützte Verfahren im Wahlkampf." *Zeitschrift Für Politikberatung* 8 (1): 3–14.

Jungherr, Andreas. 2016b. "Four Functions of Digital Tools in Election Campaigns: The German Case." *The International Journal of Press/Politics* 21 (3): 358–377.

Jungherr, Andreas. 2016c. "Twitter Use in Election Campaigns: A Systematic Literature Review." *Journal of Information Technology & Politics* 13 (1): 72–91.

Jungherr, Andreas. 2019. "Normalizing Digital Trace Data." In *Digital Discussions: How Big Data Informs Political Communication*, edited by Natalie Jomini Stroud and Shannon C. McGregor, 9–35. New York: Routledge.

Jungherr, Andreas, Harald Schoen, and Pascal Jürgens. 2016. "The Mediation of Politics through Twitter: An Analysis of Messages Posted during the Campaign for the German Federal Election 2013." *Journal of Computer-Mediated Communication* 21 (1): 50–68.

Jungherr, Andreas, Harald Schoen, Oliver Posegga, and Pascal Jürgens. 2017. "Digital Trace Data in the Study of Public Opinion: An Indicator of Attention toward Politics Rather Than Political Support." *Social Science Computer Review* 35 (3): 336–356.

Jungherr, Andreas, Matthias Mader, Harald Schoen, and Alexander Wuttke. 2018. "Context-Driven Attitude Formation: The Difference between Supporting Free Trade in the Abstract and Supporting Specific Trade Agreements." *Review of International Political Economy* 25 (2): 215–242.

Jungherr, Andreas, Oliver Posegga, and Jisun An. 2019a. "Discursive Power in Contemporary Media Systems: A Comparative Framework." *The International Journal of Press/Politics* 24 (4): 404–425.

Jungherr, Andreas, Oliver Posegga, and Jisun An. 2019b. "A Counterpublic of the Right: A Comparison of Content and Behavioral Patterns within Communities of Supporters of Donald Trump and Hillary Clinton on Reddit." Working Paper.

Jungherr, Andreas, and Pascal Jürgens. 2013. "Forecasting the Pulse: How Deviations from Regular Patterns in Online Data Can Identify Offline Phenomena." *Internet Research* 23 (5): 589–607.

Jungherr, Andreas, and Pascal Jürgens. 2014a. "Stuttgart's Black Thursday on Twitter: Mapping Political Protests with Social Media Data." In *Analyzing Social Media Data and Web Networks*, edited by Marta Cantijoch, Rachel Gibson, and Stephen Ward, 154–196. London: Palgrave Macmillan.

Jungherr, Andreas, and Pascal Jürgens. 2014b. "Through a Glass, Darkly: Tactical Support and Symbolic Association in Twitter Messages Commenting on Stuttgart 21." *Social Science Computer Review* 32 (1): 74–89.

Jungherr, Andreas, and Pascal Jürgens. 2016. "Twitter-Nutzung in den Bundestagswahlkämpfen 2009 und 2013 im Vergleich." In *Vergleichende Wahlkampfforschung*, edited by Jens Tenscher and Uta Rußmann, 155–174. Wiesbaden: Springer VS.

Jungherr, Andreas, Pascal Jürgens, and Harald Schoen. 2012. "Why the Pirate Party Won the German election of 2009 or the Trouble with Predictions: A Response to Tumasjan, A., Sprenger, T.O., Sander, P.G. & Welpe, I.M. 'Predicting Elections with Twitter: What 140 Characters Reveal About Political Sentiment'." *Social Science Computer Review* 30 (2): 229–234.

Jungherr, Andreas, Ralph Schroeder, and Sebastian Stier. 2019. "Explaining the International Surge of Political Challengers: Digital Media and the Success of Outsiders in the Usa, Germany, and China." *Social Media + Society* 5 (3): 1–12.

Jungherr, Andreas, and Yannis Theocharis. 2017. "The Empiricist's Challenge: Asking Meaningful Questions in Political Science in the Age of Big Data." *Journal of Information Technology & Politics* 14 (1): 97–109.

Jürgens, Pascal, and Birgit Stark. 2017. "The Power of Default on Reddit: A General Model to Measure the Influence of Information Intermediaries." *Policy & Internet* 9 (4): 395–419.

Jürgens, Pascal, Birgit Stark, and Melanie Magin. 2019. "Two Half-Truths Make a Whole? On Bias in Self-Reports and Tracking Data." *Social Science Computer Review*. https://doi.org/10.1177/0894439319831643.

Kahan, Dan M. 2016a. "The Politically Motivated Reasoning Paradigm, Part 1: What Politically Motivated Reasoning Is and How to Measure It." In *Emerging Trends in the Social and Behavioral Sciences*, edited by Robert A. Scott and Marlis C. Buchmann, 1–16. Hoboken, NJ: John Wiley & Sons.

Kahan, Dan M. 2016b. "The Politically Motivated Reasoning Paradigm, Part 2: Unanswered Questions." In *Emerging Trends in the Social and Behavioral Sciences*, edited by Robert A. Scott and Marlis C. Buchmann, 1–15. Hoboken, NJ: John Wiley & Sons.

Kahan, Dan M. 2017a. "Misconceptions, Misinformation, and the Logic of Identity-Protective Cognition." Cultural Cognition Project Working Paper Series, no. 164. https://papers.ssrn.com/sol3/papers.cfm?abstract_id=2973067.

Kahan, Dan M. 2017b. "On the Sources of Ordinary Science Knowledge and Extraordinary Science Ignorance." In *The Oxford Handbook of the Science of Science Communication*, edited by Kathleen Hall Jamieson, Dan M. Kahan, and Dietram A. Scheufele, 35–50. Oxford University Press.

Kahan, Dan M., Ellen Peters, Erica Cantrell Dawson, and Paul Slovic. 2017. "Motivated Numeracy and Enlightened Self-Government." *Behavioural Public Policy* 1 (1): 54–86.

Kahn, Richard, and Douglas Kellner. 2004. "New Media and Internet Activism: From the 'Battle of Seattle' to Blogging." *New Media & Society* 6 (1): 87–95.

Kahne, Joseph, Nam-Jin Lee, and Jessica T. Feezell. 2013. "The Civic and Political Significance of Online Participatory Cultures among Youth Transitioning to Adulthood." *Journal of Information Technology & Politics* 10 (1): 1–20.

Kahneman, Daniel. 2011. *Thinking, Fast and Slow*. New York: Farrar, Straus and Giroux.

Kang, Byungkyu, John O'Donovan, and Tobias Höllerer. 2012. "Modeling Topic Specific Credibility on Twitter." In *IUI'12: Proceedings of the 2012 ACM International Conference on Intelligent User Interfaces*, 179–188. New York: ACM.

Kaplan, Ethan, Jörg L. Spenkuch, and Haishan Yuan. 2018. "Natural Disasters, Moral Hazard, and Special Interests in Congress." CESifo Working Paper Series 7408.

Kapor, Mitchell. 1993. "Where Is the Digital Highway Really Heading." *Wired* 1 (3): 53–59.

Kargar, Simin, and Adrian Rauchfleisch. 2019. "State-Aligned Trolling in Iran and the Double-Edged Affordances of Instagram." *New Media & Society* 21 (7): 1506–1527.

Karpf, David. 2010a. "Macaca Moments Reconsidered: Electoral Panopticon or Netroots Mobilization?" *Journal of Information Technology & Politics* 7 (2–3): 143–162.

Karpf, David. 2010b. "Online Political Mobilization from the Advocacy Group's Perspective: Looking beyond Clicktivism." *Policy & Internet* 2 (4): 7–41.

Karpf, David. 2012a. "Social Science Research Methods in Internet Time." *Information, Communication & Society* 15 (5): 639–661.

Karpf, David. 2012b. *The MoveOn Effect: The Unexpected Transformation of American Political Advocacy*. New York: Oxford University Press.

Karpf, David. 2015. "The E-Mail-Television Advertising Funnel: Digital Disappointment in American Electoral Campaigning." Working Paper.

Karpf, David. 2016a. *Analytical Activism: Digital Listening and the New Political Strategy*. New York: Oxford University Press.

Karpf, David. 2016b. "Preparing for the Campaign Bullshit Season." *Civicist*. https://civichall.org/civicist/preparing-campaign-tech-bullshit-season/.

Karpf, David. 2017. "Will the Real Psychometric Targeters Please Stand up." *Civicist*. https://civichall.org/civicist/will-the-real-psychometric-targeters-please-stand-up/.

Katz, Elihu, and Paul F. Lazarsfeld. 1955. *Personal Influence, the Part Played by People in the Flow of Mass Communications*. Glencoe, IL: The Free Press.

Kavada, Anastasia. 2015. "Creating the Collective: Social Media, the Occupy Movement and Its Constitution as a Collective Actor." *Information, Communication & Society* 18 (8): 872–886.

Kavanagh, Chris. 2018. "Why (Almost) Everything Reported about the Cambridge Analytica Facebook 'Hacking' Controversy Is Wrong." *Medium*. https://medium.com/@CKava/why-almost-everything-reported-about-the-cambridge-analytica-facebook-hacking-controversy-is-db7f8af2d042.

Kavanaugh, Andrea L., Debbie Denise Reese, John M. Carroll, and Mary Beth Rosson. 2005. "Weak Ties in Networked Communities." *The Information Society* 21 (2): 119–131.

Keane, John. 2009. *The Life and Death of Democracy*. London: Simon & Schuster.

Keane, John. 2013. *Democracy and Media Decadence*. Cambridge, UK: Cambridge University Press.

Keller, Sallie, Stephanie Shipp, Mark Orr, Dave Higdon, Gizem Korkmaz, Aaron Schroeder, Emily Molfino, Bianica Pires, Kathryn Ziemer, and Daniel Weinberg. 2016. *Leveraging External Data Sources to Enhance Official Statistics and Products*. Blacksburg: Social; Decision Analytics Laboratory (SDAL), Biocomplexity Institute of Virginia Tech.

Kerbel, Matthew R. 2009. *Netroots: Online Progressives and the Transformation of American Politics*. Boulder, CO: Paradigm Publishers.

Khatchadourian, Raffi. 2010. "No Secrets: Julian Assange's Mission for Total Transparency." *The New Yorker*. www.newyorker.com/magazine/2010/06/07/no-secrets.

Khatchadourian, Raffi. 2017. "Julian Assange, a Man without a Country." *The New Yorker*. www.newyorker.com/magazine/2017/08/21/julian-assange-a-man-without-a-country.

Kim, Hyang-Sook, and S Shyam Sundar. 2014. "Can Online Buddies and Bandwagon Cues Enhance User Participation in Online Health Communities?" *Computers in Human Behavior* 37: 319–333.

Kim, Yonghwan, Hsuan-Ting Chen, and Homero Gil de Zúñiga. 2013. "Stumbling Upon News on the Internet: Effects of Incidental News Exposure and Relative Entertainment Use on Political Engagement." *Computers in Human Behavior* 29 (6): 2607–2614.

Kim, Young A., and Muhammad A. Ahmad. 2013. "Trust, Distrust and Lack of Confidence of Users in Online Social Media-Sharing Communities." *Knowledge-Based Systems* 37: 438–450.

Kim, Young Mie. 2009. "Issue Publics in the New Information Environment: Selectivity, Domain Specificity, and Extremity." *Communication Research* 36 (2): 254–284. https://doi.org/10.1177/0093650208330253.

Kim, Young Mie, Jordan Hsu, David Neiman, Colin Kou, Levi Bankston, Soo Yun Kim, Richard Heinrich, Robyn Baragwanath, and Garvesh Raskutti. 2018. "The Stealth Media? Groups and Targets behind Divisive Issue Campaigns on Facebook." *Political Communication* 35 (4): 515–541.

King, Gary, Jennifer Pan, and Margaret E. Roberts. 2017. "How the Chinese Government Fabricates Social Media Posts for Strategic Distraction, Not Engaged Argument." *American Political Science Review* 111 (3): 484–501.

Kioupkiolis, Alexandros, and Francisco Seoane Pérez. 2018. "Reflexive technopopulism: Podemos and the search for a new left-wing hegemony." *European Political Science* 21 (3): 1–13.

Kitschelt, Herbert. 1989. "The Internal Politics of Parties: The Law of Curvilinear Disparity Revisited." *Political Studies* 37 (3): 400–421.

Kitschelt, Herbert. 1993. "The Green Phenomenon in Western Party Systems." In *Environmental Politics in the International Arena: Movements, Parties, Organizations and Policy*, edited by Sheldon Kamieniecki, 93–112. SUNY, Albany.

Kitschelt, Herbert. 1999. "European Social Democracy Between Political Economy and Electoral Competition." In *Continuity and Change in Contemporary Capitalism*, edited by Herbert Kitschelt, Peter Lange, Gary Marks, and John D. Stephens, 317–345. Cambridge, UK: Cambridge University Press.

Klandermans, Bert, Jacquelien van Stekelenburg, Marie-Louise Damen, Dunya van Troost, and Anouk van Leeuwen. 2014. "Mobilization without Organization: The Case of Unaffiliated Demonstrators." *European Sociological Review* 30 (6): 702–716.

Klandermans, P. G. 1984. "Mobilization and Participation in Trade Union Action: An Expectancy-Value Approach." *Journal of Occupational Psychology* 57 (2): 107–120.

Knopper, Steve. 2009. *Appetite for Self-Destruction: The Spectacular Crash of the Record Industry in the Digital Age*. New York: Free Press.

Kohavi, Ron, and Roger Longbotham. 2017. "Online Controlled Experiments and A/B Testing." In *Encyclopedia of Machine Learning and Data Mining*, edited by Claude Sammut and Geoffrey I. Webb, 1–8. Boston, MA: Springer.

Konieczny, Piotr. 2009. "Governance, Organization, and Democracy on the Internet: The Iron Law and the Evolution of Wikipedia." *Sociological Forum* 24 (1): 162–192.

Korpi, Walter. 1983. *The Democratic Class Struggle*. London: Routledge.

Kovach, Bill, and Tom Rosenstiel. 1999. *Warp Speed: America in the Age of Mixed Media*. New York: The Century Foundation.

Kovic, Marko, Adrian Rauchfleisch, Marc Sele, and Christian Caspar. 2018. "Digital Astroturfing in Politics: Definition, Typology, and Countermeasures." *Studies in Communication Sciences* 18 (1): 69–85.

Kramer, Gerald H. 1971. "Short-Term Fluctuations in U.S. Voting Behavior, 1896–1964." *American Political Science Review* 65 (1): 131–143.

Kreiss, Daniel. 2011. "Open Source as Practice and Ideology: The Origin of Howard Dean's Innovations in Electoral Politics." *Journal of Information Technology & Politics* 8 (3): 367–382.

Kreiss, Daniel. 2012a. "Acting in the Public Sphere: The 2008 Obama Campaign's Strategic Use of New Media to Shape Narratives of the Presidential Race." In *Media, Movements, and Political Change*, edited by Jennifer Earl and Deana A. Rohlinger, 195–223. Bingley: Emerald Group Publishing Limited.

Kreiss, Daniel. 2012b. *Taking Our Country Back: The Crafting of Networked Politics from Howard Dean to Barack Obama.* Oxford: Oxford University Press.

Kreiss, Daniel. 2012c. "Yes We Can (Profile You)." *Stanford Law Review Online* 64: 70–74.

Kreiss, Daniel. 2015. "The Problem of Citizens: E-Democracy for Actually Existing Democracy." *Social Media + Society* 1 (2): 1–11.

Kreiss, Daniel. 2016. *Prototype Politics: Technology-Intensive Campaigning and the Data of Democracy.* New York: Oxford University Press.

Kreiss, Daniel, and Christopher Jasinski. 2016. "The Tech Industry Meets Presidential Politics: Explaining the Democratic Party's Technological Advantage in Electoral Campaigning, 2004–2012." *Political Communication* 33 (4): 544–562.

Kreiss, Daniel, and Shannon C. McGregor. 2018. "Technology Firms Shape Political Communication: The Work of Microsoft, Facebook, Twitter, and Google with Campaigns during the 2016 U.S. Presidential Cycle." *Political Communication* 35 (2): 155–177.

Kreiss, Daniel, and Shannon C. McGregor. 2019. "The 'Arbiters of What Our Voters See': Facebook and Google's Struggle with Policy, Process, and Enforcement Around Political Advertising." *Political Communication* 36 (4): 499–522.

Kreuter, Frauke, Georg-Christoph Haas, Florian Keusch, Sebastian Bähr, and Mark Trappmann. 2018. "Collecting Survey and Smartphone Sensor Data with an App: Opportunities and Challenges around Privacy and Informed Consent." *Social Science Computer Review.* https://doi.org/10.1177/0894439318816389.

Kroll, Andy. 2018. "Cloak and Data: The Real Story Behind Cambridge Analytica's Rise and Fall." *Mother Jones.* www.motherjones.com/politics/2018/03/cloak-and-data-cambridge-analytica-robert-mercer/.

Krueger, Brian S. 2002. "Assessing the Potential of Internet Political Participation in the United States: A Ressource Approach." *American Politics Research* 30 (5): 476–498.

Krugman, Herbert E., and Eugene L. Hartley. 1970. "Passive Learning from Television." *Public Opinion Quarterly* 34 (2): 184–190.

Krugman, Paul. 2011. "The Post-Truth Campaign." *The New York Times.* www.nytimes.com/2011/12/23/opinion/krugman-the-post-truth-campaign.html.

Kruschinski, Simon, and André Haller. 2017. "Restrictions on Data-Driven Political Micro-Targeting in Germany." *Internet Policy Review* 6 (4): 1–23.

Kunda, Ziva. 1990. "The Case for Motivated Reasoning." *Psychological Bulletin* 108 (3): 480–498.

Küng, Lucy. 2015. *Innovators in Digital News*. London: I. B. Tauris.

Kuran, Timur. 1995. "The Inevitability of Future Revolutionary Surprises." *American Journal of Sociology* 100 (6): 1528–1551.

Kurtz, Howard. 2018. *Media Madness: Donald Trump, the Press, and the War over the Truth*. Washington, DC: Regnery Publishing.

Kwon, K. Hazel, Shin-Il Moon, and Michael A. Stefanone. 2015. "Unspeaking on Facebook? Testing Network Effects on Self-Censorship of Political Expressions in Social Network Sites." *Quality & Quantity* 49 (4): 1417–1435.

Ladd, Jonathan M. 2012. *Why Americans Hate the Media and How It Matters*. Princeton, NJ: Princeton University Press.

Lafrance, Adrienne, and Robinson Meyer. 2015. "The Eternal Return of Buzzfeed." *The Atlantic*. www.theatlantic.com/technology/archive/2015/04/the-eternal-return-of-buzzfeed/390270/.

Lago, Ignacio, and Jose Ramón Montero. 2006. "The 2004 Election in Spain: Terrorism, Accountability, and Voting." *Taiwan Journal of Democracy* 2 (1): 13–36.

La Monica, Paul R. 2018. "Facebook Has Lost $80 Billion in Market Value Since Its Data Scandal." *CNNMoney*. http://money.cnn.com/2018/03/27/news/companies/facebook-stock-zuckerberg/index.html.

Langone, Alix. 2017. "#MeToo and Time's Up Founders Explain the Difference Between the 2 Movements – And How They're Alike." *Time*. https://time.com/5189945/whats-the-difference-between-the-metoo-and-times-up-movements/.

Lapowsky, Issie. 2016. "The Man behind Trump's Bid to Finally Take Digital Seriously." *Wired*. www.wired.com/2016/08/man-behind-trumps-bid-finally-take-digital-seriously/.

Lapowsky, Issie. 2019. "Inside the Democrats' Plan to Fix Their Crumbling Data Operation." *Wired*. www.wired.com/story/democrats-fix-crumbling-data-operation/.

Laswell, Harold. 1948. "The Structure and Function of Communication in Society." In *The Communication of Ideas*, edited by Lyman Bryson, 243–276. New York: Institute for Religious & Social Studies.

Lathrop, Daniel, and Laurel Ruma. 2010. *Open Government: Collaboration, Transparency, and Participation in Practice*. Sebastopol, CA: O'Reilly Media.

Lau, Richard R., and David P. Redlawsk. 2001. "Advantages and Disadvantages of Cognitive Heuristics in Political Decision Making." *American Journal of Political Science* 45 (4): 951–971.

Laver, Michael. 1997. *Private Desires, Political Action: An Invitation to the Politics of Rational Choice*. London: SAGE.

Lawrence, Eric, John Sides, and Henry Farrell. 2010. "Self-Segregation or Deliberation? Blog Readership, Participation, and Polarization in American Politics." *Perspectives on Politics* 8 (1): 141–157.

Lazarsfeld, Paul F., Bernard Berelson, and Hazel Gaudet. 1944. *The People's Choice: How the Voter Makes up His Mind in a Presidential Campaign*. New York: Duell, Sloan & Pearce.

Lazer, David, Alex Pentland, Lada Adamic, Sinan Aral, Albert-László Barabási, Devon Brewer, Nicholas Christakis, et al. 2009. "Computational Social Science." *Science* 323 (5915): 721–723.

Lazer, David, Matthew A. Baum, Yochai Benkler, Adam J. Berinsky, Kelly M. Greenhill, Filippo Menczer, Miriam J. Metzger, et al. 2018. "The Science of Fake News." *Science* 359 (6380): 1094–1096.

Lazer, David, Ryan Kennedy, Gary King, and Alessandro Vespignani. 2014. "The Parable of Google Flu: Traps in Big Data Analysis." *Science* 343 (6176): 1203–1205.

Leach, Darcy K. 2005. "The Iron Law of What Again? Conceptualizing Oligarchy Across Organizational Forms." *Sociological Theory* 23 (3): 312–337.

Leahy, Joe, and Andres Schipani. 2018. "How Social Media Exposed the Fractures in Brazilian Democracy." *Financial Times*. www.ft.com/content/8c08654a-c0b1-11e8-8d55-54197280d3f7.

Lederman, Josh. 2016. "Obama Campaign Machine Prepares to Support Clinton." *PBS News Hour*. www.pbs.org/newshour/politics/obama-campaign-machine-prepares-for-clintons-campaign.

Lee, Francis L. F., Hsuan-Ting Chen, and Joseph M. Chan. 2017. "Social Media Use and University Students' Participation in a Large-Scale Protest Campaign: The Case of Hong Kong's Umbrella Movement." *Telematics and Informatics* 34 (2): 457–469.

Lee, Francis L. F., and Joseph M. Chan. 2015. "Digital Media Activities and Mode of Participation in a Protest Campaign: A Study of the Umbrella Movement." *Information, Communication & Society* 19 (1): 4–22.

Lee, Francis L. F., and Joseph M. Chan. 2018. *Media and Protest Logics in the Digital Era: The Umbrella Movement in Hong Kong*. New York: Oxford University Press.

Lee, Kai-Fu. 2018. *AI Superpowers: China, Silivon Valley, and the New World Order*. Boston, MA: Houghton Mifflin Harcourt.

Leonhardt, David, and Stuart A. Thompson. 2017. "Trump's Lies." *The New York Times*. www.nytimes.com/interactive/2017/06/23/opinion/trumps-lies.html.

Lessig, Lawrence. 2004. *Free Culture: How Big Media Uses Technology and the Law to Lock down Culture and Control Creativity*. New York: The Penguin Press.

Levendusky, Matthew. 2009. *The Partisan Sort: How Liberals Became Democrats and Conservatives Became Republicans*. Chicago, IL: The University of Chicago Press.

Levin, Sam. 2017. "Did Russia Fake Black Activism on Facebook to Sow Division in the Us?" *The Guardian*. www.theguardian.com/technology/2017/sep/30/blacktivist-facebook-account-russia-us-election.

Levine, Frederick, Christopher Locke, David Searls, and David Weinberger. 2000. *The Cluetrain Manifesto: The End of Business as Usual*. Cambridge: Perseus Publishing.

Levitsky, Steven, and Daniel Ziblatt. 2018. *How Democracies Die*. New York: Crown Publishing Group.

Levy, David A. L., and Rasmus Kleis Nielsen, eds. 2010. *The Changing Business of Journalism and Its Implications for Democracy*. Oxford: Reuters Institute for the Study of Journalism.

Lewis, Paul. 2018. "'Fiction Is Outperforming Reality': How YouTube's Algorithm Distorts Truth." *The Guardian*. www.theguardian.com/technology/2018/feb/02/how-youtubes-algorithm-distorts-truth.

Liang, Fan, Vishnupriya Das, Nadiya Kostyuk, and Muzammil M. Hussain. 2018. "Constructing a Data-Driven Society: China's Social Credit System as a State Surveillance Infrastructure." *Policy & Internet* 10 (4): 415–453.

Lim, Merlyna. 2012. "Clicks, Cabs, and Coffee Houses: Social Media and Oppositional Movements in Egypt, 2004–2011." *Journal of Communication* 62 (2): 231–248.

Lin, Nan. 2008. "A Network Theory of Social Capital." In *The Handbook of Social Capital*, edited by Dario Castiglione, Jan W. van Deth, and Guglielmo Wolleb, 50–69. New York: Oxford University Press.

"List of Newspapers in the United Kingdom by Circulation." 2017. In *Wikipedia*. https://en.wikipedia.org/wiki/List_of_newspapers_in_the_United_Kingdom_by_circulation.

Little, Andrew T. 2016. "Communication Technology and Protest." *The Journal of Politics* 78 (1): 152–166.

Little, Andrew T., Joshua A. Tucker, and Tom LaGatta. 2015. "Elections, Protest, and Alternation of Power." *The Journal of Politics* 77 (4): 1142–1156.

Livingston, Steven. 2016. *Digital Affordances and Human Rights Advocacy*. SFB-Governance Working Paper Series 69. SFB 700 Governance in Areas of Limited Statehood. www.sfb-governance.de/publikationen/sfb-700-working_papers/wp69/SFB-Governance-Working-Paper-69.pdf.

Livingston, Steven, and Gregor Walter-Drop, eds. 2014. *Bits and Atoms: Information and Communication Technology in Areas of Limited Statehood*. Oxford: Oxford University Press.

Livingston, Steven, and W. Lance Bennett. 2003. "Gatekeeping, Indexing, and Live-Event News: Is Technology Altering the Construction of News?" *Political Communication* 20 (4): 363–380.

Lizza, Ryan. 2014. "Inside the Collapse of the New Republic." *The New Yorker*. www.newyorker.com/news/news-desk/inside-collapse-new-republic.

Lockett, Dee. 2017. "Time's up Has Already Raised $20 Million, Helped over 1,000 People." *Vulture*. www.vulture.com/2018/02/times-up-has-raised-usd20-million-helped-over-1-000-people.html.

Lodge, Milton, and Charles S. Taber. 2013. *The Rationalizing Voter*. Cambridge, UK: Cambridge University Press.

Lorenz, Taylor. 2019. "The Shooter's Manifesto Was Designed to Troll." *The Atlantic*. www.theatlantic.com/technology/archive/2019/03/the-shooters-manifesto-was-designed-to-troll/585058/.

Lotan, Gilad, Erhardt Graeff, Mike Ananny, Devin Gaffney, Ian Pearce, and danah boyd. 2011. "The Revolutions Were Tweeted: Information Flows During the 2011 Tunisian and Egyptian Revolutions." *International Journal of Communication* 5: 1375–1405.

Lourenço, Rui Pedro. 2015. "An Analysis of Open Government Portals: A Perspective of Transparency for Accountability." *Government Information Quarterly* 32 (3): 323–332.

Lucas, Robert E. 1976. "Econometric Policy Evaluation: A Critique." *Carnegie-Rochester Conference Series on Public Policy* 1: 19–46.

Lundby, Knut, ed. 2009. *Mediatization: Concept, Changes, Consequences*. New York: Peter Lang Publishing.

Lundry, Alexander. 2012. "Making It Personal: The Rise of Microtargeting." In *Margin of Victory: How Technologists Help Politicians Win Elections*, edited by Nathaniel G. Pearlman, 161–174. Santa Monica, CA: ABC-CLIO.

Lupia, Arthur, and Mathew D. McCubbins. 1998. *The Democratic Dilemma: Can Citizens Learn What They Need to Know?* Cambridge, UK: Cambridge University Press.

Lupia, Arthur, and John G. Matsusaka. 2004. "Direct Democracy: New Approaches to Old Questions." *Annual Review of Political Science* 7: 463–482.

Lupia, Arthur, and Gisela Sin. 2003. "Which Public Goods Are Endangered? How Evolving Communication Technologies Affect the Logic of Collective Action." *Public Choice* 117 (3/4): 315–331.

Luskin, Robert C., James S. Fishkin, and Roger Jowell. 2002. "Considered Opinions: Deliberative Polling in Britain." *British Journal of Political Science* 32 (3): 455–487.

Lusoli, Wainer, and Stephen Ward. 2004. "Digital Rank-And-File: Party Activists' Perceptions and Use of the Internet." *The British Journal of Politics and International Relations* 6 (4): 453–470.

Luttwak, Edward. 1968. *Coup d'etat: A Practical Handbook*. New York: Knopf.

Lynch, David J. 2017. "Big Tech and Amazon: Too Powerful to Break up?" *Financial Times*. www.ft.com/content/e5bf87b4-b3e5-11e7-aa26-bb002965bce8.

Maass, Wolfgang, Jeffrey Parsons, Sandeep Purao, Veda C. Storey, and Carson Woo. 2018. "Data-Driven Meets Theory-Driven Research in the Era of Big Data: Opportunities and Challenges for Information Systems Research." *Journal of the Association for Information Systems* 19 (12): 1253–1273.

McAdam, Doug. 1982. *Political Process and the Development of Black Insurgency, 1930–1970*. Chicago, IL: The University of Chicago Press.

McAdam, Doug. 1986. "Recruitment to High-Risk Activism: The Case of Freedom Summer." *American Journal of Sociology* 92 (1): 64–90.

McAdam, Doug, and Ronnelle Paulsen. 1993. "Specifying the Relationship between Social Ties and Activism." *American Journal of Sociology* 99 (3): 640–667.

McAdam, Doug, Sidney Tarrow, and Charles Tilly. 2001. *Dynamics of Contention*. Cambridge, UK: Cambridge University Press.

McCarthy, John D., and Mayer N. Zald. 1977. "Resource Mobilization and Social Movements: A Partial Theory." *American Journal of Sociology* 82 (6): 1212–1241.

McCarty, Nolan, Keith T. Poole, and Howard Rosenthal. 2016. *Polarized America: The Dance of Ideology and Unequal Riches*. 2nd ed. Cambridge, MA: MIT Press.

McChesney, Robert W., and Victor Pickard. 2017. "News Media as Political Institutions." In *The Oxford Handbook of Political Communication*, edited by Kate Kenski and Kathleen Hall Jamieson, 263–274. Oxford University Press.

McChrystal, Stanley, Tantum Collins, David Silverman, and Chris Fussell. 2015. *Team of Teams: New Rules of Engagement for a Complex World*. New York: Portfolio.

McClurg, Scott D., Casey A. Klofstad, and Anand Edward Sokhey. 2017. "Discussion Networks." In *The Oxford Handbook of Political Networks*, edited by Jennifer Nicoll Victor, Alexander H. Montgomery, and Mark Lubell, 515–536. New York: Oxford University Press.

McCormack, Thelma. 1961. "Social Theory and the Mass Media." *The Canadian Journal of Economics and Political Science* 27 (4): 479–489.

MacFarquhar, Neil. 2016. "A Powerful Russian Weapon: The Spread of False Stories." *The New York Times.* www.nytimes.com/2016/08/29/world/europe/russia-sweden-disinformation.html.

MacFarquhar, Neil. 2018. "Inside the Russian Troll Factory: Zombies and a Breakneck Pace." *The New York Times.* www.nytimes.com/2018/02/18/world/europe/russia-troll-factory.html.

McGarty, Craig, Emma F Thomas, Girish Lala, Laura GE Smith, and Ana-Maria Bliuc. 2014. "New Technologies, New Identities, and the Growth of Mass Opposition in the a Rab S Pring." *Political Psychology* 35 (6): 725–740.

McGregor, Shannon C. 2019. "Social Media as Public Opinion: How Journalists Use Social Media to Represent Public Opinion." *Journalism* 20 (8): 1070–1086.

McGregor, Shannon C., Rachel R. Mourão, Ivo Neto, Joseph D. Straubhaar, and Alan Angeluci. 2017. "Second Screening as Convergence in Brazil and the United States." *Journal of Broadcasting & Electronic Media* 61 (1): 163–181.

McKenna, Elizabeth, and Hahrie Han. 2015. *Groundbreakers: How Obama's 2.2 Million Volunteers Transformed Campaigning in America.* New York: Oxford University Press.

McLeod, Douglas, Gerald M. Kosicki, and Jack M. McLeod. 2009. "Political Communication Effects." In *Media Effects: Advances in Theory and Research*, edited by Jennings Bryant and Mary Beth Oliver, 3rd ed., 228–251. New York: Routledge.

McQuail, Denis. 1997. *Audience Analysis.* Thousand Oaks, CA: SAGE.

McQuail, Denis. 2010. *McQuail's Mass Communication Theory.* 6th ed. London: SAGE.

McQuail, Denis. 2013. *Journalism and Society.* London: SAGE.

Macy, Michael W. 1991. "Chains of Cooperation: Threshold Effects in Collective Action." *American Sociological Review* 56 (6): 730–747.

Madrigal, Alexis C. 2012. "When the Nerds Go Marching in." *The Atlantic.* www.theatlantic.com/technology/archive/2012/11/when-the-nerds-go-marching-in/265325/?single_page=true.

Magleby, David B., J. Quinn Monson, and Kelly D. Patterson, eds. 2007. *Dancing without Partners: How Candidates, Parties, and Interest Groups Interact in the Presidential Campaign.* Lanham, MD: Rowman & Littlefield.

Mair, Peter. 2002. "Populist Democracy Vs Party Democracy." In *Democracies and the Populist Challenge*, edited by Yves Mény and Yves Surel, 81–98. Basingstoke: Palgrave Macmillan.

Mair, Peter. 2013. *Ruling the Void: The Hollowing of Western Democracy.* New York: Verso.

Manucci, Luca, and Michi Amsler. 2018. "Where the Wind Blows: Five Star Movement's Populism, Direct Democracy and Ideological Flexibility." *Italian Political Science Review/Rivista Italiana Di Scienza Politica* 48 (1): 109–132.

Margetts, Helen. 2001. "The Cyber Party." Working Paper.

Margetts, Helen, Peter John, Scott Hale, and Taha Yasseri. 2015. *Political Turbulence: How Social Media Shape Collective Action.* Princeton, NJ: Princeton University Press.

Margolick, David. 2016. "Nick Denton, Peter Thiel, and the Plot to Murder Gawker." *Vanity Fair*. www.vanityfair.com/news/2016/11/nick-denton-peter-thiel-plot-to-murder-gawker.

Margolis, Michael, and David Resnick. 2000. *Politics as Usual: The Cyberspace "Revolution."* Thousand Oaks, CA: SAGE.

Marshall, Josh. 2016. "The Secret behind Trump's Comically Bad Digital Campaign?" *Talking Points Memo*. https://talkingpointsmemo.com/edblog/the-secret-behind-trump-s-comically-bad-digital-campaign.

Martínez, Antonio García. 2018a. "How Trump Conquered Facebook – Without Russian Ads." *Wired*. www.wired.com/story/how-trump-conquered-facebookwithout-russian-ads/.

Martínez, Antonio García. 2018b. "The Noisy Fallacies of Psychographic Targeting." *Wired*. www.wired.com/story/the-noisy-fallacies-of-psychographic-targeting/.

Marwick, Alice E. 2018. "Why Do People Share Fake News? A Sociotechnical Model of Media Effects." *Georgetown Law Technology Review* 2 (2): 474–512.

Marwick, Alice E., and danah boyd. 2011. "I Tweet Honestly, I Tweet Passionately: Twitter Users, Context Collapse, and the Imagined Audience." *New Media & Society* 13 (1): 114–133.

Marwick, Alice E., and Robyn Caplan. 2018. "Drinking Male Tears: Language, the Manosphere, and Networked Harassment." *Feminist Media Studies* 18 (4): 543–559.

Marwick, Alice E., and Rebecca Lewis. 2017. *Media Manipulation and Disinformation Online*. New York: Data & Society.

Marx, Gary T. 2016. *Windows into the Soul: Surveillance and Society in an Age of High Technology*. Chicago, IL: The University of Chicago Press.

Masters, Kim. 2017. "Fighting 'the Gawker Effect' in the Wake of Weinstein." *Columbia Journalism Review*. www.cjr.org/first_person/amazon-roy-price.php.

Matthes, Jörg. 2015. "Observing the 'Spiral' in the Spiral of Silence." *International Journal of Public Opinion Research* 27 (2): 155–176.

Mau, Steffen. 2019. *The Metric Society: On the Quantification of the Social*. Cambridge, UK: Polity.

May, John D. 1973. "Opinion Structure of Political Parties: The Special Law of Curvilinear Disparity." *Political Studies* 21 (2): 135–151.

Mayer, Jonathan R., and John C. Mitchell. 2012. "Third-Party Web Tracking: Policy and Technology." In *2012 IEEE Symposium on Security and Privacy*, edited by Robert Cunningham, Somesh Jha, and Wenke Lee, 413–427. New York: IEEE. https://doi.org/10.1109/SP.2012.47.

Mazzoleni, Gianpietro, and Winfried Schulz. 1999. "'Mediatization' of Politics: A Challenge for Democracy?" *Political Communication* 16 (3): 247–261.

Medina, Eden. 2011. *Cybernetic Revolutionaries: Technology and Politics in Allende's Chile*. Boston, MA: The MIT Press.

Medina, Luis Fernando. 2013. "The Analytical Foundations of Collective Action Theory: A Survey of Some Recent Developments." *Annual Review of Political Science* 16: 259–283.

Meier, Christian. 2016. "So sieht die AfD die Zukunft von ARD und ZDF." *Welt.de*. www.welt.de/kultur/medien/article153360779/So-sieht-die-AfD-die-Zukunft-von-ARD-und-ZDF.html.

Meijer, Albert J, Deirdre Curtin, and Maarten Hillebrandt. 2012. "Open Government: Connecting Vision and Voice." *International Review of Administrative Sciences* 78 (1): 10–29.

Mendelberg, Tali. 2002. "The Deliberative Citizen: Theory and Evidence." *Political Decision Making, Deliberation and Participation* 6 (1): 151–193.

Mendelberg, Tali, and John Oleske. 2000. "Race and Public Deliberation." *Political Communication* 17 (2): 169–191.

Meraz, Sharon, and Zizi A. Papacharissi. 2013. "Networked Gatekeeping and Networked Framing on #Egypt." *The International Journal of Press/Politics* 18 (2): 138–166.

Merchant, Brian. 2017. *The One Device: The Secret History of the iPhone*. New York: Little, Brown Company.

Mergel, Ines. 2015. "Opening Government: Designing Open Innovation Processes to Collaborate with External Problem Solvers." *Social Science Computer Review* 33 (5): 599–612.

Merleau-Ponty, Maurice. 1945. *Phénoménologie de La Perception*. Paris: Éditions Gallimard.

Meserve, Stephen A., and Daniel Pemstein. 2018. "Google Politics: The Political Determinants of Internet Censorship in Democracies." *Political Science Research and Methods* 6 (2): 245–263.

Messing, Solomon, and Sean J. Westwood. 2014. "Selective Exposure in the Age of Social Media: Endorsements Trump Partisan Source Affiliation When Selecting News Online." *Communication Research* 41 (8): 1042–1063.

Metaxas, Panagiotis Takis, and Samantha Finn. 2017. "The Infamous #Pizzagate Conspiracy Theory: Insight from a Twittertrails Investigation." *Wellesley College Faculty Research and Scholarship* 188: 1–5.

Metaxas, Panagiotis Takis, Samantha Finn, and Eni Mustafaraj. 2015. "Using Twitter-trails.com to Investigate Rumor Propagation." In *CSCW'15: Companion Proceedings of the 18th Acm Conference Companion on Computer Supported Cooperative Work & Social Computing*, edited by Dan Cosley, Andrea Forte, Luigina Ciolfi, and David McDonald, 69–72. New York: ACM.

Metaxas, Panagiotis Takis, and Eni Mustafaraj. 2009. "The Battle for the 2008 Us Congressional Elections on the Web." In *WebSci 2009: Proceedings of the 1st International Web Science Conference*. Athens, Greece: Web Science Trust.

Metaxas, Panagiotis Takis, and Eni Mustafaraj. 2012. "Social Media and the Elections." *Science* 338 (6106): 472–473.

Michels, Robert. 1915. *Political Parties: A Sociological Study of the Oligarchical Tendencies of Modern Democracy*. New York: Hearst's International Library Company.

Miladi, Noureddine. 2011. "Tunisia: A Media Led Revolution?" *Media Development* 58 (2): 8–12.

Min, Seong-Jae. 2007. "Online Vs. Face-to-Face Deliberation: Effects on Civic Engagement." *Journal of Computer-Mediated Communication* 12 (4): 1369–1387.

Mitchell, Amy, Jeffrey Gottfried, Michael Barthel, and Elisa Shearer. 2016. *The Modern News Consumer: News Attitudes and Practices in the Digital Era*. Washington, DC: Pew Research Center.

Mitchell, Amy, and Paul Hitlin. 2013. *Twitter Reaction to Events Often at Odds with Overall Public Opinion*. Washington, DC: Pew Research Center.

Mitchell, Amy, Jocelyn Kiley, Jeffrey Gottfried, and Emily Guskin. 2013. *The Role of News on Facebook: Common yet Incidental.* Washington, DC: Pew Research Center.

Mocanu, Delia, Luca Rossi, Qian Zhang, Marton Karsai, and Walter Quattrociocchi. 2015. "Collective Attention in the Age of (Mis)information." *Computers in Human Behavior* 51 (Part B): 1198–1204.

Mohan, Pavithra. 2015. "This Is How the Ted Cruz Campaign Could Be Mining Your Facebook Data." *Fast Company.* www.fastcompany.com/3054566/this-is-how-the-ted-cruz-campaign-could-be-mining-your-facebook-data.

Möller, Judith, Damian Trilling, Natali Helberger, and Bram van Es. 2018. "Do Not Blame It on the Algorithm: An Empirical Assessment of Multiple Recommender Systems and Their Impact on Content Diversity." *Information, Communication & Society* 21 (7): 959–977.

Molotch, Harvey, and Marilyn Lester. 1974. "News as Purposive Behavior: On the Strategic Use of Routine Events, Accidents, and Scandals." *American Sociological Review* 39 (1): 101–112.

Mondak, Jeffery J. 1993. "Public Opinion and Heuristic Processing of Source Cues." *Political Behavior* 15 (2): 167–192.

Montalvo, José G. 2011. "Voting after the Bombings: A Natural Experiment on the Effect of Terrorist Attacks on Democratic Elections." *The Review of Economics and Statistics* 93 (4): 1146–1154.

Moore, Alfred. 2018. "Anonymity, Pseudonymity, and Deliberation: Why Not Everything Should Be Connected." *Journal of Political Philosophy* 26 (2): 169–192.

Morgan, Michael, and James Shanahan. 2010. "The State of Cultivation." *Journal of Broadcasting & Electronic Media* 54 (2): 337–355.

Morozov, Evgeny. 2011. *The Net Delusion: How Not to Liberate the World.* London: Penguin Books.

Morrell, Michael E. 2005. "Deliberation, Democratic Decision-Making and Internal Political Efficacy." *Political Behavior* 27 (1): 49–69.

Mueller, Robert S. 2019. *Report on the Investigation into Russian Interference in the 2016 Presidential Election.* Washington, DC: US Department of Justice.

Mukerjee, Subhayan, Sílvia Majó-Vázquez, and Sandra González-Bailón. 2018. "Networks of Audience Overlap in the Consumption of Digital News." *Journal of Communication* 68 (1): 26–50.

Mullany, Anjali. 2015. "Platforms Decide Who Gets Heard." *NiemanLab.* www.niemanlab.org/2015/12/platforms-decide-who-gets-heard/.

Muller, Jerry Z. 2018. *The Tyranny of Metrics.* Princeton, NJ: Princeton University Press.

Munger, Kevin. 2017. "Tweetment Effects on the Tweeted: Experimentally Reducing Racist Harassment." *Political Behavior* 39 (3): 629–649.

Munger, Kevin, Richard Bonneau, Jonathan Nagler, and Joshua A. Tucker. 2018. "Elites Tweet to Get Feet Off the Streets: Measuring Regime Social Media Strategies During Protest." *Political Science Research and Methods* 46 (March): 1–20.

Murdock, Graham, and Peter Golding. 2005. "Culture, Communications and Political Economy." In *Mass Media and Society*, edited by James Curran and Michael Gurevitch, 4th ed., 60–83. New York: Hodder Arnold.

Murgia, Madhumita, Stephanie Findlay, and Andres Schipani. 2019. "India: The WhatsApp Election." *Financial Times*. www.ft.com/content/9fe88fba-6c0d-11e9-a9a5-351eeaef6d84.

Murphy, Joe, Michael W. Link, Jennifer Hunter Childs, Casey Langer Tesfaye, Elizabeth Dean, Michael Stern, Josh Pasek, Jon Cohen, Mario Callegaro, and Paul Harwood. 2014. "Social Media in Public Opinion Research: Executive Summary of the Aapor Task Force on Emerging Technologies in Public Opinion Research." *Public Opinion Quarterly* 78 (4): 788–794.

Mustafaraj, Eni, and Panagiotis Takis Metaxas. 2010. "From Obscurity to Prominence in Minutes: Political Speech and Real-Time Search." In *WebSci 2010: Proceedings of the WebSci10–Extending the Frontiers of Society on-Line*, 1–7. Raleigh, NC: Web Science Trust.

Mustafaraj, Eni, and Panagiotis Takis Metaxas. 2017. "The Fake News Spreading Plague: Was It Preventable?" In *WebSci'17: Proceedings of the 2017 ACM on Web Science Conference*, edited by Peter Fox, Deborah McGuinness, Lindsay Poirer, Paolo Boldi, and Katharina Kinder-Kurlanda, 235–239. New York: ACM.

Mustafaraj, Eni, Samantha Finn, Carolyn Whitlock, and Panagiotis Takis Metaxas. 2011. "Vocal Minority versus Silent Majority: Discovering the Opinions of the Long Tail." In *SocialCom 2011: The 3rd IEEE International Conference on Social Computing*, 103–110. Washington, DC: IEEE.

Mutz, Diana C. 2015. *In-Your-Face Politics: The Consequences of Uncivil Media*. Princeton, NJ: Princeton University Press.

Myers, David G., and Helmut Lamm. 1976. "The Group Polarization Phenomenon." *Psychological Bulletin* 83 (4): 602–627.

Nabi, Zubair. 2014. "Censorship Is Futile." *First Monday* 19 (11). https://firstmonday.org/article/view/5525/4155.

Nadeau, Richard, and Richard G Niemi. 1995. "Educated Guesses: The Process of Answering Factual Knowledge Questions in Surveys." *Public Opinion Quarterly* 59 (3): 323–346.

Nagle, Angela. 2017. *Kill All Normies: Online Culture Wars from 4chan and Tumblr to Trump and the Alt-Right*. Alresford: Zero Books.

Nahon, Karine, and Jeff Hemsley. 2013. *Going Viral*. Cambridge, UK: Polity Press.

Napoli, Philip M. 2014. "Automated Media: An Institutional Theory Perspective on Algorithmic Media Production and Consumption." *Communication Theory* 24 (3): 340–360.

Napoli, Philip M. 2015. "Social Media and the Public Interest: Governance of News Platforms in the Realm of Individual and Algorithmic Gatekeepers." *Telecommunications Policy* 39 (9): 751–760.

Napoli, Philip M., and Robyn Caplan. 2017. "When Media Companies Insist They're Not Media Companies and Why It Matters." *First Monday* 22 (5). https://firstmonday.org/ojs/index.php/fm/article/view/7051/6124.

Nardi, Bonnie A., and Vicki O'Day. 1999. *Information Ecologies: Using Technology with Heart*. Cambridge, MA: The MIT Press.

Natale, Simone, and Andrea Ballatore. 2014. "The Web Will Kill Them All: New Media, Digital Utopia, and Political Struggle in the Italian 5-Star Movement." *Media, Culture & Society* 36 (1): 105–121.

Neblo, Michael A., Kevin M. Esterling, and David Lazer. 2018. *Politics with the People: Building a Directly Representative Democracy.* New York: Cambridge University Press.

Neblo, Michael A., Kevin M. Esterling, Ryan P. Kennedy, David M.J. Lazer, and Anand E. Sokhey. 2010. "Who Wants to Deliberate – and Why?" *American Political Science Review* 104 (3): 566–583.

Nelson, Jacob L., and Harsh Taneja. 2018. "The Small, Disloyal Fake News Audience: The Role of Audience Availability in Fake News Consumption." *New Media & Society* 20 (10): 3720–3737.

Neuman, W. Russell. 1991. *The Future of the Mass Audience.* Cambridge, UK: Cambridge University Press.

Neuman, W. Russell. 2016. *The Digital Difference: Media Technology and the Theory of Communication Effects.* Cambridge, MA: Harvard University Press.

Neuman, W. Russell, Bruce Bimber, and Matthew Hindman. 2011. "The Internet and Four Dimensions of Citizenship." In *The Oxford Handbook of American Public Opinion and the Media,* edited by Robert Y. Shapiro and Lawrence R. Jacobs, 22–42. Oxford: Oxford University Press.

Neuman, W. Russell, and Lauren Guggenheim. 2011. "The Evolution of Media Effects Theory: A Six-Stage Model of Cumulative Research." *Communication Theory* 21 (2): 169–196.

The New York Times Company. 2017. *Annual Report Pursuant to Section 13 or 15(d) of the Securities Exchange Act of 1934 for the Fiscal Year Ended December 25, 2016.* Washington, DC: United States Securities Exchange Commission. http://d18rn0p25nwr6d.cloudfront.net/CIK-0000071691/37d516f5-b9da-4ca8-a50f-d70630760094.pdf.

Newell, Jim. 2016. "Listomania." *Slate.* www.slate.com/articles/news_and_politics/politics/2016/10/who_owns_donald_trump_s_list_of_supporters.html.

Newman, Nic, Richard Fletcher, Antonis Kalogeropoulos, David A. L. Levy, and Rasmus Kleis Nielsen. 2017. *Reuters Institute Digital News Report 2017.* Oxford: Reuters Institute for the Study of Journalism.

Newman, Nic, Richard Fletcher, Antonis Kalogeropoulos, David A. L. Levy, and Rasmus Kleis Nielsen. 2018. *Reuters Institute Digital News Report 2018.* Oxford: Reuters Institute for the Study of Journalism.

Newton, Casey. 2017. "Instant Recall: Facebook's Instant Articles Promised to Transform Journalism – but Now Big Publishers Are Fleeing." *The Verge.* www.theverge.com/2017/4/16/15314210/instant-articles-facebook-future-ads-video.

Nicas, Jack. 2018. "How YouTube Drives People to the Internet's Darkest Corners." *The Wall Street Journal.* www.wsj.com/articles/how-youtube-drives-viewers-to-the-internets-darkest-corners-1518020478.

Nicholls, Tom, Nabeelah Shbbir, and Rasmus Kleis Nielsen. 2016. *Digital-Born News Media in Europe.* Oxford: Reuters Institute for the Study of Journalism.

Nicholson, Stephen P. 2012. "Polarizing Cues." *American Journal of Political Science* 56 (1): 52–66.

Nickerson, David W., and Todd Rogers. 2014. "Political Campaigns and Big Data." *The Journal of Economic Perspectives* 28 (2): 51–74.

Niedermayer, Oskar. 2017. "Mitgliederentwicklung der Parteien." In *Parteien in Deutschland.* Bonn: Bundeszentrale für Politische Bildung (bpd). www.bpb.de/politik/grundfragen/parteien-in-deutschland/zahlen-und-fakten/138672/mitgliederentwicklung.

Nielsen, Rasmus Kleis. 2011. "Mundane Internet Tools, Mobilizing Practices, and the Coproduction of Citizenship in Political Campaigns." *New Media & Society* 13 (5): 755–771.

Nielsen, Rasmus Kleis. 2012a. *Ground Wars: Personalized Communication in Political Campaigns*. Princeton, NJ: Princeton University Press.

Nielsen, Rasmus Kleis. 2012b. "The Business of News." In *The Sage Handbook of Digital Journalism*, edited by Tamara Witschge, C. W. Anderson, David Domingo, and Alfred Hermida, 51–67. London: SAGE.

Nielsen, Rasmus Kleis. 2018. "Open Societies and Robust Institutions – Talking Points on How We Can Fight Disinformation." *Rasmuskleisnielsen.net*. https://rasmuskleisnielsen.net/2018/02/26/open-societies-and-robust-institutions-talking-points-on-how-we-can-fight-disinformation/.

Nielsen, Rasmus Kleis, and Sarah Anne Ganter. 2018. "Dealing with Digital Intermediaries: A Case Study of the Relations Between Publishers and Platforms." *New Media & Society* 20 (4): 1600–1617.

Nimmo, Ben. 2018. "Russia's Full Spectrum Propaganda." *Medium*. https://medium.com/dfrlab/russias-full-spectrum-propaganda-9436a246e970.

Noakes, John, and Patrick Gillham. 2007. "Police and Protester Innovation Since Seattle." *Mobilization: An International Quarterly* 12 (4): 335–340.

Noelle-Neumann, Elisabeth. 1974. "The Spiral of Silence a Theory of Public Opinion." *Journal of Communication* 24 (2): 45–51.

Norris, Pippa. 2001. *Digital Divide: Civic Engagement, Information Poverty, and the Internet Worldwide*. Cambridge, UK: Cambridge University Press.

Norris, Pippa. 2014. "Watchdog Journalism." In *The Oxford Handbook of Public Accountability*, edited by Mark Bovens, Robert E. Goodin, and Thomas Schillemans, 525–545. Oxford: Oxford University Press.

Noveck, Beth Simone. 2015. *Smart Citizens, Smarter State: The Technologies of Expertise and the Future of Governing*. Cambridge, MA: Harvard University Press.

Nyabola, Nanjala. 2018. *Digital Democracy, Analouge Politics: How the Internet Era Is Transforming Politics in Kenya*. London: Zed Books.

Nyhan, Brendan. 2017. "Why the Fact-Checking at Facebook Needs to Be Checked." *The New York Times*. www.nytimes.com/2017/10/23/upshot/why-the-fact-checking-at-facebook-needs-to-be-checked.html.

Nyhan, Brendan. 2018. "Fake News and Bots May Be Worrisome, but Their Political Power Is Overblown." *The New York Times*. www.nytimes.com/2018/02/13/upshot/fake-news-and-bots-may-be-worrisome-but-their-political-power-is-overblown.html.

Nyhan, Brendan, Jason Reifler, and Peter Ubel. 2013. "The Hazards of Correcting Myths About Health Care Reform." *Medical Care* 51 (2): 127–132.

Oakeshott, Michael. 1947. "Rationalism in Politics." *The Cambridge Journal* 1: 81–98, 145–157.

Oates, Sarah. 2013. *Revolution Stalled: The Political Limits of the Internet in the Post-Soviet Sphere*. New York: Oxford University Press.

Oh, Hyelim, Animesh Animesh, and Alain Pinsonneault. 2015. "Free Versus for-a-Fee: The Impact of a Paywall on the Pattern and Effectiveness of Word-of-Mouth via Social Media." *MIS Quarterly* 40 (1): 31–56.

Oliver, Mary Beth, Arthur A. Raney, and Jennings Bryant, eds. 2019. *Media Effects: Advances in Theory and Research*. 4th ed. New York: Routledge.

Oliver, Mary Beth, and K. Maja Krakowiak. 2009. "Individual Differences in Media Effects." In *Media Effects: Advances in Theory and Research*, edited by Jennings Bryant and Mary Beth Oliver, 3rd ed., 517–531. New York: Routledge.

Olson, Mancur. 1965. *The Logic of Collective Action: Public Goods and the Theory of Groups*. Cambridge, MA: Harvard University Press.

O'Neill, Onora. 2002. "Trust and Transparency." *In A Question of Trust*, edited by Onora O'Neill. London: BBC Reith Lectures. www.bbc.co.uk/programmes/p00gpzcz.

Onuch, Olga. 2014. "Social Networks and Social Media in Ukrainian 'Euromaidan' Protests." *Washington Post*. www.washingtonpost.com/news/monkey-cage/wp/2014/01/02/social-networks-and-social-media-in-ukrainian-euromaidan-protests-2/.

Onuch, Olga. 2015. "'Facebook Helped Me Do It': Understanding the EuroMaidan Protester 'Tool-Kit'." *Studies in Ethnicity and Nationalism* 15 (1): 170–184.

Opp, Karl-Dieter, and Christiane Gern. 1993. "Dissident Groups, Personal Networks, and Spontaneous Cooperation: The East German Revolution of 1989." *American Sociological Review* 58 (5): 659–680.

O'Reilly, Tim. 2005. "What Is Web 2.0: Design Patterns and Business Models for the Next Generation of Software." *O'Reilly Blog*. http://oreilly.com/web2/archive/what-is-web-20.html.

O'Reilly, Tim. 2009. "Gov 2.0: The Promise of Innovation." *Forbes*. www.forbes.com/2009/08/10/government-internet-software-technology-breakthroughs-oreilly.html.

O'Rourke, Simon. 2011. "Empowering Protest through Social Media." In *Proceedings of the 2nd International Cyber Resilience Conference*, 47–54. Perth, Australia: Edith Cowan University.

Osterhammel, Jürgen. 2009. *Die Verwandlung der Welt: Eine Geschichte des 19. Jahrhunderts*. Munich: C. H. Beck.

Ostrogorski, Moisei. 1902. *Democracy and the Organization of Political Parties*. New York: Macmillan.

Page, Benjamin I., and Robert Y. Shapiro. 1992. *The Rational Public: Fifty Years of Trends in Americans' Policy Preferences*. Chicago, IL: The University of Chicago Press.

Papacharissi, Zizi A. 2010. *A Private Sphere: Democracy in a Digital Age*. Cambridge, UK: Polity Press.

Papacharissi, Zizi A. 2015. *Affective Publics: Sentiment, Technology, and Politics*. New York: Oxford University Press.

Papacharissi, Zizi A., and Maria de Fatima Oliveira. 2012. "Affective News and Networked Publics: The Rhythms of News Storytelling on #Egypt." *Journal of Communication* 62 (2): 266–282.

Pariser, Eli. 2011. *The Filter Bubble: What the Internet Is Hiding from You*. New York: The Penguin Press.

Park, Chang Sup. 2013. "Does Twitter Motivate Involvement in Politics? Tweeting, Opinion Leadership, and Political Engagement." *Computers in Human Behavior* 29 (4): 1641–1648.

Parker, Geoffrey G., Marshall W. Van Alstyne, and Sangeet Paul Choudary. 2016. *Platform Revolution: How Networked Markets Are Transforming the Economy and How to Make Them Work for You*. New York: W. W. Norton & Company.

Parlapiano, Alicia, and Jasmine C. Lee. 2018. "The Propaganda Tools Used by Russians to Influence the 2016 Election." *The New York Times.* 2www.nytimes .com/interactive/2018/02/16/us/politics/russia-propaganda-election-2016.html.

Pasquale, Frank. 2011. "Restoring Transparency to Automated Authority." *Journal on Telecommunications and High Technology Law* 9 (1): 235–254.

Pasquale, Frank. 2015. *The Black Box Society: The Secret Algorithms That Control Money and Information.* Cambridge, MA: Harvard University Press.

Passy, Florence. 2003. "Social Networks Matter. But How?" In *Social Movements and Networks: Relational Approaches to Collective Action,* edited by Mario Diani and Doug McAdam, 21–48. New York: Oxford University Press.

Patel, Mayur, Jon Sotsky, Sean Gourley, and Daniel Houghton. 2013. *The Emergence of Civic Tech: Investments in a Growing Field.* Miami, FL: Knight Foundation.

Patinkin, Jason. 2017. "How to Use Facebook and Fake News to Get People to Murder Each Other." *BuzzFeed.* www.buzzfeed.com/jasonpatinkin/how-to-get-people-to-murder-each-other-through-fake-news-and.

Patterson, Thomas E. 1993. *Out of Order.* New York: Knopf.

Pearce, Katy E., and Ronald R. Rice. 2013. "Digital Divides from Access to Activities: Comparing Mobile and Personal Computer Internet Users." *Journal of Communication* 63 (4): 721–744.

Pearlman, Nathaniel G. 2012. "Bootstrapping an Enterprise: NGP and the Evolution of Campaign Software." In *Margin of Victory: How Technologists Help Politicians Win Elections,* edited by Nathaniel G. Pearlman, 189–202. Santa Monica, CA: ABC-CLIO.

Penney, Joel, and Caroline Dadas. 2014. "(Re) Tweeting in the Service of Protest: Digital Composition and Circulation in the Occupy Wall Street Movement." *New Media & Society* 16 (1): 74–90.

Pennycook, Gordon, and David G. Rand. 2019. "Lazy, Not Biased: Susceptibility to Partisan Fake News Is Better Explained by Lack of Reasoning Than by Motivated Reasoning." *Cognition* 188: 39–50.

Pentland, Alex. 2008. *Honest Signals: How They Shape Our World.* Cambridge, MA: The MIT Press.

Perez, Evan, Jim Sciutto, Jake Tapper, and Carl Bernstein. 2017. "Intel Chiefs Presented Trump with Claims of Russian Efforts to Compromise Him." CNN. http://edition.cnn.com/2017/01/10/politics/donald-trump-intelligence-report-russia/index.html.

Pérez-Nievas, Santiago, José Rama-Caamaño, and Carlos Fernández-Esquer. 2018. "New Wine in Old Bottles? The Selection of Electoral Candidates in General Elections in Podemos." In *Democratizing Candidate Selection: New Methods, Old Receipts?,* edited by Guillermo Cordero and Xavier Coller, 123–146. Cham: Palgrave Macmillan.

Perlmutter, David D. 2008. *Blogwars: The New Political Battleground.* Oxford: Oxford University Press.

Persily, Nathaniel. 2017. "The 2016 U.S. Election: Can Democracy Survive the Internet?" *Journal of Democracy* 28 (2): 63–76.

Peston, Robert. 2017. *WTF.* London: Hodder & Stoughton.

Peters, Benjamin. 2016. *How Not to Network a Nation: The Uneasy History of the Societ Internet.* Cambridge, MA: The MIT Press.

Peterson, Tim. 2016. "Facebook Organic Reach Is down 52." Marketing Land. https://
    marketingland.com/facebook-organic-reach-drop-steepens-52-publishers-pages-
    187253.
Petty, Richard E., Pablo Briñol, and Joseph R. Priester. 2009. "Mass Media Attitude
    Change: Implications of the Elaboration Likelihood Model of Persuasion." In
    Media Effects: Advances in Theory and Research, edited by Jennings Bryant
    and Mary Beth Oliver, 3rd ed., 125–164. New York: Routledge.
Pew Research Center. 2006. *Network Evening News Ratings*. Washington, DC: Pew
    Journalism & Media.
Pfeffer, Jeffrey, and Gerald R. Salancik. 2003. *The External Control of Organizations:
    A Resource Dependence Perspective*. Stanford, CA: Stanford University Press.
Phillips, Whitney. 2015. *This Is Why We Can't Have Nice Things: Mapping the
    Relationship Between Online Trolling and Mainstream Culture*. Cambridge,
    MA: The MIT Press.
Picard, Robert G. 2011. *The Economics and Financing of Media Companies*. 2nd ed.
    New York: Fordham University Press.
Pickard, Victor, and Alex T. Williams. 2014. "Salvation or Folly? The Promises and
    Perils of Digital Paywalls." *Digital Journalism* 2 (2): 195–213.
Pitkin, Hanna Fenichel. 1967. *The Concept of Representation*. Berkeley: The Univer-
    sity of California Press.
Plouffe, David. 2009. *The Audacity to Win: The Inside Story and Lessons of Barack
    Obama's Historic Victory*. New York: Viking.
Poell, Thomas, Rasha Abdulla, Bernhard Rieder, Robbert Woltering, and
    Liesbeth Zack. 2015. "Protest Leadership in the Age of Social Media." *Infor-
    mation, Communication & Society* 19 (7): 994–1014.
Poister, Theodore H., Maria P. Aristigueta, and Jeremy L. Hall. 2015. *Managing and
    Measuring Performance in Public and Nonprofit Organizations: An Integrated
    Approach*. 2nd ed. San Francisco, CA: Jossey-Bass.
Polanyi, Michael. 1958. *Personal Knowledge: Towards a Post-Critical Philosophy*.
    London: Routledge & Kegan Paul.
Polletta, Francesca, and James M. Jasper. 2001. "Collective Identity and Social Move-
    ments." *Annual Review of Sociology* 27 (1): 283–305.
Pollitt, Christopher, and Geert Bouckaert. 2017. *Public Management Reform:
    A Comparative Analysis - into the Age of Austerity*. 4th ed. Oxford: Oxford
    University Press.
Pomerantsev, Peter. 2015. "Inside the Kremlin's Hall of Mirrors." *The Guardian*. www
    .theguardian.com/news/2015/apr/09/kremlin-hall-of-mirrors-military-information-
    psychology.
Pons, Vincent. 2018. "Will a Five-Minute Discussion Change Your Mind?
    A Countrywide Experiment on Voter Choice in France." *American Economic
    Review* 108 (6): 1322–1363.
Ponsford, Dominic. 2017. "The Sun Cites Comscore Data to Say It Is Now the Number
    Two UK Newspaper Online." *Press Gazette*. www.pressgazette.co.uk/the-sun-
    overtakes-mirror-to-become-number-two-uk-national-newspaper-website-com
    score-data/.
Pool, Ithiel de Sola. 1983a. *Technologies of Freedom*. Cambridge, MA: Harvard
    University Press.

Pool, Ithiel de Sola. 1983b. "What Ferment?: A Challenge for Empirical Research." *Journal of Communication* 33 (3): 258–261.

Popken, Ben. 2017. "Russian Trolls Pushed Graphic, Racist Tweets to American Voters." NBC News. www.nbcnews.com/tech/social-media/russian-trolls-pushed-graphic-racist-tweets-american-voters-n823001.

Popken, Ben. 2018a. "Russian Trolls Went on Attack during Key Election Moments." NBC News. www.nbcnews.com/tech/social-media/russian-trolls-went-attack-during-key-election-moments-n827176.

Popken, Ben. 2018b. "Twitter Deleted 200,000 Russian Troll Tweets. Read Them Here." NBC News. www.nbcnews.com/tech/social-media/now-available-more-200-000-deleted-russian-troll-tweets-n844731.

Porter, Theodore M. 1996. *Trust in Numbers: The Pursuit of Objectivity in Science and Public Life.* Princeton, NJ: Princeton University Press.

Powers, Matthew. 2016. "The New Boots on the Ground: NGOs in the Changing Landscape of International News." *Journalism* 17 (4): 401–416.

Preece, Jenny, Blair Nonnecke, and Dorine Andrews. 2004. "The Top Five Reasons for Lurking: Improving Community Experiences for Everyone." *Computers in Human Behavior* 20 (2): 201–223.

Pressman, Matthew. 2018. *On Press: The Liberal Values That Shaped the News.* Cambridge, MA: Harvard University Press.

Preston, Jennifer. 2011. "Movement Began with Outrage and a Facebook Page That Gave It an Outlet." *New York Times.* www.nytimes.com/2011/02/06/world/middleeast/06face.html.

Priante, Anna, Michel L. Ehrenhard, Tijs van den Broek, and Ariana Need. 2018. "Identity and Collective Action via Computer-Mediated Communication: A Review and Agenda for Future Research." *New Media & Society* 20 (7): 2647–2669.

Prior, Markus. 2007. *Post-Broadcast Democracy: How Media Choice Increases Inequality in Political Involvement and Polarizes Elections.* Cambridge, UK: Cambridge University Press.

Prior, Markus. 2009. "The Immensely Inflated News Audience: Assessing Bias in Self-Reported News Exposure." *Public Opinion Quarterly* 73 (1): 130–143.

Prior, Markus. 2013. "Media and Political Polarization." *Annual Review of Political Science* 16: 101–127.

Prior, Markus. 2019. *Hooked: How Politics Captures People's Interest.* Cambridge, UK: Cambridge University Press.

Project for Excellence in Journalism. 2010. *How News Happens: The Study of the News Ecosystem of One American City.* Washington, DC: Pew Research Center.

Przeworski, Adam. 2018. *Why Bother with Elections?* Cambridge, UK: Polity.

Przeworski, Adam, Susan C. Stokes, and Bernard Manin, eds. 1999. *Democracy Accountability Representation.* Cambridge, UK: Cambridge University Press.

Purcell, Kristen, Lee Rainie, Amy Mitchell, Tom Rosenstiel, and Kenneth Olmstead. 2010. *Understanding the Participatory News Consumer.* Washington, DC: Pew Research Center.

Putnam, Robert D. 1993. *Making Democracy Work: Civic Traditions in Modern Italy.* Princeton, NJ: Princeton University Press.

Putnam, Robert D. 2000. *Bowling Alone: The Collapse and Revival of American Community.* New York: Simon & Schuster.

Qazvinian, Vahed, Emily Rosengren, Dragomir R. Radev, and Qiaozhu Mei. 2011. "Rumor Has It: Identifying Misinformation in Microblogs." In *EMNLP'11: Proceedings of the Conference on Empirical Methods in Natural Language Processing*, edited by Regina Barzilay and Mark Johnson, 1589–1599. Stroudsburg: Association for Computational Linguistics.

Qiang, Xiao. 2011. "The Battle for the Chinese Internet." *Journal of Democracy* 22 (2): 47–61.

Quinn, Kelly. 2016. "Contextual Social Capital: Linking the Contexts of Social Media Use to Its Outcomes." *Information, Communication & Society* 19 (5): 582–600.

Rainie, Lee, Janna Anderson, and Jonathan Albright. 2017. *The Future of Free Speech, Trolls, Anonymity and Fake News Online*. Washington, DC: Pew Research Center.

Rainie, Lee, Aaron Smith, Kay Lehman Schlozman, Henry Brady, and Sidney Verba. 2012. *Social Media and Political Engagement*. Washington, DC: Pew Internet & American Life Project.

Rainie, Lee, and Barry Wellman. 2012. *Networked: The New Social Operating System*. Cambridge, MA: The MIT Press.

Rains, Stephen A., Kate Kenski, Kevin Coe, and Jake Harwood. 2017. "Incivility and Political Identity on the Internet: Intergroup Factors as Predictors of Incivility in Discussions of News Online." *Journal of Computer-Mediated Communication* 22 (4): 163–178.

Rajagopalan, Megha. 2018. "This Country's Democracy Has Fallen Apart – and It Played Out to Millions on Facebook." *BuzzFeed*. www.buzzfeed.com/meghara/facebook-cambodia-democracy.

Ramirez, Edith, Julie Brill, Maureen K. Ohlhausen, Joshua D. Wright, and Terrell McSweeny. 2014. *Data Brokers: A Call for Transparency and Accountability*. Washington, DC: Federal Trade Commission.

Ratkiewicz, Jacob, Michael D. Conover, Bruno Gonçalves, Alessandro Flammini, and Filippo Menczer. 2011. "Detecting and Tracking Political Abuse in Social Media." In *ICWSM 2011: Proceedings of the 5th International AAAI Conference on Weblogs and Social Media*, edited by Nicolas Nicolovm James G. Shanahan, Lada Adamic, Ricardo Baeza-Yates, and Scott Counts, 297–304. Menlo Park, CA: Association for the Advancement of Artificial Intelligence (AAAI).

Ratkiewicz, Jacob, Michael D. Conover, Mark Meiss, Bruno Gonçalves, Snehal Patil, Alessandro Flammini, and Filippo Menczer. 2011. "Truthy: Mapping the Spread of Astroturf in Microblog Streams." In *WWW'11: Proceedings of the 20th International Conference Companion on World Wide Web*, edited by S. Sadagopan, Krithi Ramamritham, Arun Kumar, M. P. Ravindra, Elisa Bertino, and Ravi Kumar, 249–252. New York: ACM.

Rauchfleisch, Adrian, and Jonas Kaiser. 2019a. "The False Positive Problem of Automatic Bot Detection." Paper Presented at AoIR 2019: The 20th Annual Conference of the Association of Internet Researchers. Brisbane, Australia.

Rauchfleisch, Adrian, and Jonas Kaiser. 2019b. "The Road to Hell Is Paved with Good Algorithms: Filter Bubbles on YouTube in the United States and in Germany." Paper Presented at the 69th Annual Conference of the International Communication Association (ICA) in Washington, DC (USA), May 24–28.

Raymond, Eric S. 1999. *The Cathedral and the Bazaar: Musings on Linux and Open Source by an Accidental Revolutionary*. Sebastopol, CA: O'Reilly Media.

Reicher, S. 1984. "Social Influence in the Crowd: Attitudinal and Behavioural Effects of de-Individuation in Conditions of High and Low Group Salience." *British Journal of Social Psychology* 23 (4): 341–350.

Repnikova, Maria. 2017. *Media Politics in China: Improvising Power under Authoritarianism.* New York: Cambridge University Press.

Resnick, Brian. 2018. "Cambridge Analytica's 'Psychographic Microtargeting': What's Bullshit and What's Legit." *Vox.* www.vox.com/science-and-health/2018/3/23/17152564/cambridge-analytica-psychographic-microtargeting-what.

Rheingold, Howard. 1993. *The Virtual Community: Homesteading on the Electronic Frontier.* Reading, MA: Addison-Wesley.

Rheingold, Howard. 2007. *Smart Mobs: The Next Social Revolution.* New York: Basic Books.

Riedl, Rachel Beatty. 2016. "Political Parties, Regimes, and Social Cleavages." In *The Oxford Handbook of Historical Institutionalism,* edited by Orfeo Fioretos, Tulia G. Falleti, and Adam Sheingate, 223–238. New York: Oxford University Press.

Rivero, Gonzalo. 2019. "Preaching to the Choir: Ideology and Following Behaviour in Social Media." *Contemporary Social Science* 14 (1): 54–70.

Roberts, Margaret E. 2015. "Experiencing Censorship Emboldens Internet Users and Decreases Government Support in China." Working Paper.

Roberts, Margaret E. 2018. *Censored: Distraction and Diversion Inside China's Great Firewall.* Princeton, NJ: Princeton University Press.

Robertson, Ronald, David Lazer, and Christo Wilson. 2018. "Auditing Politically-Related Search Rankings and Suggestions." In *WWW'18: Proceedings of the 2018 World Wide Web Conference,* edited by Pierre-Antoine Champin, Fabien Gandon, Lionel Médini, Mounia Lalmas, and Panagiotis G. Ipeirotis, 955–965. New York: ACM.

Robinson, Laura, Shelia R. Cotten, Hiroshi Ono, Anabel Quan-Haase, Gustavo Mesch, Wenhong Chen, Jeremy Schulz, Timothy M. Hale, and Michael J. Stern. 2015. "Digital Inequalities and Why They Matter." *Information, Communication & Society* 18 (5): 569–582.

Robinson, Michal J. 1973. "Public Affairs Television and the Growth of Political Malaise: The Case of 'the Selling of the Pentagon'." *American Political Science Review* 70 (2): 409–432.

Robinson, Nick. 2017. "If Mainstream News Wants to Win Back Trust, It Cannot Silence Dissident Voices." *The Guardian.* www.theguardian.com/commentisfree/2017/sep/27/mainstream-news-win-back-trust-dissident-voices.

Rogers, Everett M. 1986. *Communication Technology: The New Media Society.* New York: Free Press.

Rogers, Everett M. 1994. *History of Communication Study: A Biographical Approach.* New York: The Free Press.

Rohlinger, Deana A., and Leslie Bunnage. 2017. "Did the Tea Party Movement Fuel the Trump-Train? The Role of Social Media in Activist Persistence and Political Change in the 21st Century." *Social Media + Society* 3 (2): 1–11.

Rooij, Eline A. de, Donald P. Green, and Alan S. Gerber. 2009. "Field Experiments on Political Behavior and Collective Action." *Annual Review of Political Science* 12: 389–395.

Rosen, Jay. 2006. "The People Formerly Known as the Audience." *PRESSthink: Ghost of Democracy in the Media Machine.* http://archive.pressthink.org/2006/06/27/ppl_frmr.html.

Rosenbaum, Paul R. 2017. *Observation and Experiments: An Introduction to Causal Inference.* Cambridge, MA: Harvard University Press.

Rosenberg, Howard, and Charles S. Feldman. 2008. *No Time to Think: The Menace of Media Speed and the 24-Hour News Cycle.* New York: Continuum.

Rosenberg, Matthew, Nicholas Confessore, and Carole Cadwalladr. 2018. "How Trump Consultants Exploited the Facebook Data of Millions." *The New York Times.* www.nytimes.com/2018/03/17/us/politics/cambridge-analytica-trump-campaign.html.

Rosoff, Matt. 2017. "Jeff Bezos Has Advice for the News Business:'Ask People to Pay. They Will Pay'." CNBC. www.cnbc.com/2017/06/21/jeff-bezos-lessons-from-washington-post-for-news-industry.html.

Rowe, Ian. 2015. "Deliberation 2.0: Comparing the Deliberative Quality of Online News User Comments Across Platforms." *Journal of Broadcasting & Electronic Media* 59 (4): 539–555.

Rozell, Mark J., Clyde Wilcox, and Michael M. Franz. 2012. *Interest Groups in American Campaigns: The New Face of Electioneering.* New York: Oxford University Press.

Rubin, Alan M. 2009. "Uses-and-Gratifications Perspective on Media Effects." In *Media Effects: Advances in Theory and Research*, edited by Jennings Bryant and Mary Beth Oliver, 3rd ed., 165–184. New York: Routledge.

Rubinstein, Ira S. 2014. "Voter Privacy in the Age of Big Data." *Wisconsin Law Review* 5: 861–936.

Ruddick, Graham, and Nadia Khomami. 2017. "Alternative News Sites Attack Nick Robinson's Claim of 'Guerrilla War' on BBC." *The Guardian.* www.theguardian.com/media/2017/sep/28/alternative-news-sites-attack-nick-robinsons-claim-of-guerilla-war-on-bbc.

Ruiz, Carlos, David Domingo, Josep Lluís Micó, Javier Díaz-Noci, Koldo Meso, and Pere Masip. 2011. "Public Sphere 2.0? The Democratic Qualities of Citizen Debates in Online Newspapers." *The International Journal of Press/Politics* 16 (4): 463–487.

Rusbridger, Alan. 2018. *Breaking News: The Remaking of Journalism and Why It Matters Now.* Edinburgh: Canongate.

Ryfe, David M. 2012. "News Institutions." In *The Sage Handbook of Digital Journalism*, edited by Tamara Witschge, C. W. Anderson, David Domingo, and Alfred Hermida, 370–382. London: SAGE.

Saatchi, Edward. 2012. "Actionable Data: Using Social Technology to Change Organizations." In *Margin of Victory: How Technologists Help Politicians Win Elections*, edited by Nathaniel G. Pearlman, 203–214. Santa Monica, CA: ABC-CLIO.

Sajuria, Javier, Jennifer vanHeerde-Hudson, David Hudson, Niheer Dasandi, and Yannis Theocharis. 2015. "Tweeting Alone? An Analysis of Bridging and Bonding Social Capital in Online Networks." *American Politics Research* 43 (4): 708–738.

Salganik, Matthew J. 2018. *Bit by Bit: Social Research in the Digital Age.* Princeton, NJ: Princeton University Press.

Sampson, Robert J., Stephen W. Raudenbush, and Felton Earls. 1997. "Neighborhoods and Violent Crime: A Multilevel Study of Collective Efficacy." *Science* 277 (5328): 918–924.

Sanovich, Sergey, Denis Stukal, and Joshua A. Tucker. 2018. "Turning the Virtual Tables: Government Strategies for Addressing Online Opposition with an Application to Russia." *Comparative Politics* 50 (3): 435–482.

Sarovic, Alexander. 2019. "Was hinter der Twitter-Sperre Cheblis steckt." *Spiegel Online.* www.spiegel.de/politik/deutschland/sawsan-chebli-und-die-twitter-sperre-maschinen-und-meinungsfreiheit-a-1265838.html.

Saunders, Clare. 2008. "Double-Edged Swords? Collective Identity and Solidarity in the Environment Movement." *The British Journal of Sociology* 59 (2): 227–253.

Sauter, Molly. 2014. *The Coming Swarm: DDOS Actions, Hacktivism, and Civil Disobedience on the Internet.* New York: Bloomsbury.

Scarrow, Susan E. 1996. *Parties and Their Members: Organizing for Victory in Britain and Germany.* Oxford: Oxford University Press.

Scarrow, Susan E. 2014. *Beyond Party Members: Changing Approaches to Partisan Mobilization.* Oxford: Oxford University Press.

Scheerder, Anique, Alexander van Deursen, and Jan van Dijk. 2017. "Determinants of Internet Skills, Uses and Outcomes: A Systematic Review of the Second- and Third-Level Digital Divide." *Telematics and Informatics* 34 (8): 1607–1624.

Scherer, Michael. 2012. "Friended: How the Obama Campaign Connected with Young Voters." *TIME: Swampland.* http://swampland.time.com/2012/11/20/friended-how-the-obama-campaign-connected-with-young-voters/.

Schieffer, Bob, and H. Andrew Schwartz. 2017. *Overload: Finding the Truth in Today's Deluge of News.* Lanham, MD: Rowman & Littlefield.

Schipani, Andres. 2018. "Fake News Threat Looms over Brazilian Election." *Financial Times.* www.ft.com/content/ea6f9b82-10e7-11e8-8cb6-b9ccc4c4dbbb.

Schlesinger, Philip. 1977. "Newsmen and Their Time-Machine." *The British Journal of Sociology* 28 (3): 336–350.

Schlozman, Kay Lehman, Sidney Verba, and Henry E. Brady. 2010. "Weapon of the Strong? Participatory Inequality and the Internet." *Perspectives on Politics* 8 (2): 487–509.

Schneier, Bruce. 2005. "Terrorists Don't Do Movie Plots." *Wired.* www.wired.com/2005/09/terrorists-dont-do-movie-plots/.

Schneier, Bruce. 2015. *Data and Goliath: The Hidden Battles to Collect Your Data and Control Your World.* New York: W. W. Norton & Company.

Schneier, Bruce. 2018. *Click Here to Kill Everybody: Security and Survival in a Hyper-Connected World.* New York: W. W. Norton & Company.

Schober, Michael F., Josh Pasek, Lauren Guggenheim, Cliff Lampe, and Frederick G. Conrad. 2016. "Social Media Analyses for Social Measurement." *Public Opinion Quarterly* 80 (1): 180–211.

Schoenbach, Klaus, and Edmund Lauf. 2002. "The 'Trap' Effect of Television and Its Competitors." *Communication Research* 29 (5): 564–583.

Schorske, Carl E. 1955. *German Social Democracy, 1905–1917: The Development of the Great Schism.* Cambridge, MA: Harvard University Press.

Schrock, Andrew. 2018. *Civic Tech: Making Technology Work for People.* Long Beach, CA: Rogue Academic Press.

Schroeder, Ralph. 2018. *Social Theory after the Internet: Media, Technology and Globalization*. London: UCL Press.

Schroepfer, Mike. 2018. "An Update on Our Plans to Restrict Data Access on Facebook." *Facebook Newsroom*. https://newsroom.fb.com/news/2018/04/restricting-data-access/.

Schudson, Michael. 1999. "What Public Journalism Knows about Journalism but Doesn't Know About 'Public'." In *The Idea of Public Journalism*, edited by Theodore L. Glasser, 118–133. New York: Guilford Press.

Schudson, Michael. 2008. "News and Democratic Society: Past, Present, and Future." *The Hedgehog Review* 10 (2): 7–21.

Schudson, Michael. 2011. *The Sociology of News*. 2nd ed. New York: W. W. Norton & Company.

Schudson, Michael. 2017. "How to Think Normatively about News and Democracy." In *The Oxford Handbook of Political Communication*, edited by Kate Kenski and Kathleen Hall Jamieson, 95–108. Oxford: Oxford University Press.

Schulz, Winfried. 1989. "Massenmedien und Realität." *Kölner Zeitschrift Für Soziologie Und Sozialpsychologie* 30 (Sonderheft): 135–149.

Schulz, Winfried. 2004. "Reconstructing Mediatization as an Analytical Concept." *European Journal of Communication* 19 (1): 87–101.

Schussman, Alan, and Jennifer Earl. 2004. "From Barricades to Firewalls? Strategic Voting and Social Movement Leadership in the Internet Age." *Sociological Inquiry* 74 (4): 439–463.

Schumann, Sandy, and Olivier Klein. 2015. "Substitute or Stepping Stone? Assessing the Impact of Low-Threshold Online Collective Actions on Offline Participation." *European Journal of Social Psychology* 45 (3): 308–322.

Schweizer, Peter. 2015. *Clinton Cash: The Untold Story of How and Why Foreign Governments and Businesses Helped Make Bill and Hillary Rich*. New York: HarperCollins.

Scola, Nancy. 2009. "Can Obama's Army Convert to a Peacetime Force? Plouffe Responds." *Tech President*. http://techpresident.com/blog-entry/can-obamas-army-convert-peacetime-force-plouffe-responds.

Scola, Nancy. 2018. "How Russia Turned the Internet against America." *Politico*. www.politico.com/story/2018/02/16/how-russia-turned-the-internet-against-america-353707.

Scott, James C. 1998. *Seeing Like a State: How Certain Schemes to Improve the Human Condition Have Failed*. New Haven, CT: Yale University Press.

Sears, David O. 1968. "The Paradox of de Facto Selective Exposure without Preferences for Supportive Information." In *Theories of Cognitive Consistency: A Sourcebook*, edited by Robert P. Abelson, Elliot Aronson, William J. McGuire, Theodore M. Newcomb, Milton J. Rosenberg, and Percy H. Tannenbaum, 777–787. Chicago, IL: Rand McNally.

Sears, David O., and Jonathan L. Freedman. 1967. "Selective Exposure to Information: A Critical Review." *Public Opinion Quarterly* 31 (2): 194–213.

Sehl, Annika, Felix M. Simon, and Ralph Schroeder. 2019. "The Populist Campaigns Against European Public Service Media: Hot Air or Existential Threat." Working Paper.

Sellers, Patrick. 2010. *Cycles of Spin: Strategic Communication in the U.S. Congress*. Cambridge, UK: Cambridge University Press.

Sen, Arijit, and Rasmus Kleis Nielsen. 2016. *Digital Journalism Start-Ups in India*. Oxford: Reuters Institute for the Study of Journalism.

Serdült, Uwe, Micha Germann, Maja Harris, Fernando Mendez, and Alicia Portenier. 2013. "Who Are the Internet Voters?" In *Electronic Government and Electronic Participation*, edited by Efthimios Tambouris, Hans Jochen Scholl, and Marijn F. W. H. A. Janssen, 27–41. Amsterdam: IOS Press.

Settle, Jaime E. 2018. *Frenemies: How Social Media Polarizes America*. New York: Cambridge University Press.

Shah, Dhavan V., Alex Hanna, Erik P. Bucy, David S. Lassen, Jack Van Thomme, Kristen Bialik, JungHwan Yang, and Jon C. W. Pevehouse. 2016. "Dual Screening During Presidential Debates: Political Nonverbals and the Volume and Valence of Online Expression." *American Behavioral Scientist* 60 (4): 1816–1843.

Shah, Dhavan V., Douglas M. McLeod, Hernando Rojas, Jaeho Cho, Michael W. Wagner, and Lewis A. Friedland. 2017. "Revising the Communication Mediation Model for a New Political Communication Ecology." *Human Communication Research* 43 (4): 491–504.

Shah, Dhavan V., Nojin Kwak, and R. Lance Holbert. 2001. "'Connecting' and 'Disconnecting' with Civic Life: Patterns of Internet Use and the Production of Social Capital." *Political Communication* 18 (2): 141–162.

Shane, Scott. 2018. "How Unwitting Americans Encountered Russian Operatives Online." *The New York Times*. www.nytimes.com/2018/02/18/us/politics/russian-operatives-facebook-twitter.html.

Shao, Chengcheng, Giovanni Luca Ciampaglia, Onur Varol, Kai-Cheng Yang, Alessandro Flammini, and Filippo Menczer. 2018. "The Spread of Low-Credibility Content by Social Bots." *Nature Communications* 9 (4787): 1–9.

Shapiro, Carl, and Hal R. Varian. 1999. *Information Rules: A Strategic Guide to the Network Economy*. Boston, MA: Harvard Business Review Press.

Shapiro, Ian. 2005. *The State of Democratic Theory*. Princeton, NJ: Princeton University Press.

Shaw, Aaron, and Benjamin M. Hill. 2014. "Laboratories of Oligarchy? How the Iron Law Extends to Peer Production." *Journal of Communication* 64 (2): 215–238.

Shear, Matthew. 2017. "The Long, Lonely Road of Chelsea Manning." *The New York Times Magazine*. www.nytimes.com/2017/06/12/magazine/the-long-lonely-road-of-chelsea-manning.html.

Shear, Michael D. 2015. "Obama's Social Media Team Tries to Widen Audience for State of the Union Address." *The New York Times*. www.nytimes.com/2015/01/20/us/politics/doing-more-than-putting-an-annual-address-into-140-characters.html.

Shehata, Adam, and Jesper Strömbäck. 2018. "Learning Political News from Social Media: Network Media Logic and Current Affairs News Learning in a High-Choice Media Environment." *Communication Research*. https://doi.org/10.1177/0093650217749354.

Sherman, Gabriel. 2009. "The Scoop Factory." *New Republic*. https://newrepublic.com/article/62885/the-scoop-factory.

Shipman, Tim. 2016. *All Out War: The Full Story of Brexit*. London: William Collins.

Shirky, Clay. 2008. *Here Comes Everybody: The Power of Organizing without Organizations*. New York: The Penguin Press.

Shirky, Clay. 2010. *Cognitive Surplus: How Technology Makes Consumers into Collaborators*. New York: The Penguin Press.

Shoemaker, Pamela J., and Akiba A. Cohen. 2006. *News Around the World: Content Practitioners and the Public*. New York: Routledge.

Shoemaker, Pamela J., and Stephen D. Reese. 2014. *Mediating the Message in the 21st Century*. 3rd ed. New York: Routledge.

Shoemaker, Pamela J., and Tim P. Vos. 2009. *Gatekeeping Theory*. New York: Routledge.

Shore, Jesse, Jiye Baek, and Chrysanthos Dellarocas. 2018. "Network Structure and Patterns of Information Diversity on Twitter." *MIS Quarterly* 42 (3): 849–872.

Siebert, Fredrick S., Theodore Peterson, and Wilbur Schramm. 1963. *Four Theories of the Press. The Authoritarian, Libertarian, Social Responsibility, and Soviet Communist Concepts of What the Press Should Be and Do*. Champaign: University of Illinois Press.

Sikdar, Sujoy, Byungkyu Kang, John O'Donovan, Tobias Höllerer, and Sibel Adah. 2013. "Understanding Information Credibility on Twitter." In *SOCIALCOM'13: Proceedings of the 2013 International Conference on Social Computing*, 19–24. Washington, DC: IEEE Computer Society.

Silver, Laura. 2019. "Misinformation and Fears about Its Impact Are Pervasive in 11 Emerging Economies." *Pew Research Center: Fact Tank – News in the Numbers*. www.pewresearch.org/fact-tank/2019/05/13/misinformation-and-fears-about-its-impact-are-pervasive-in-11-emerging-economies/.

Silverman, Craig. 2016. "How the Bizarre Conspiracy Theory behind 'Pizzagate' Was Spread." *BuzzFeed*. www.buzzfeed.com/craigsilverman/fever-swamp-election.

Silverman, Craig, and Jeremy Singer-Vine. 2016. "The True Story behind the Biggest Fake News Hit of the Election." *BuzzFeed*. www.buzzfeed.com/craigsilverman/the-strangest-fake-news-empire.

Silverman, Craig, and Tarini Parti. 2017. "This Hyperpartisan Conservative Site Is Connected to Several Pro-Trump Pacs." *BuzzFeed*. www.buzzfeed.com/craigsilverman/how-a-dc-lawyer-uses-hyperpartisan-websites-to-raise-money.

Simon, Bernd, and Bert Klandermans. 2001. "Politicized Collective Identity: A Social Psychological Analysis." *American Psychologist* 56 (4): 319–331.

Simon, Felix M. 2018. "The Big Data Panic." *Medium*. https://medium.com/@FelixSimon/cambridge-analytica-and-the-big-data-panic-5029f12e1bcb.

Simon, Felix M. 2019. "'We Power Democracy': Exploring the Promises of the Political Data Analytics Industry." *The Information Society* 35 (3): 158–169.

Simon, Herbert A. 1957. *Models of Man – Social and Rational: Mathematical Essays on Rational Human Behavior in a Social Setting*. New York: Wiley.

Simon, Julie, Theo Bass, Victoria Boelman, and Geoff Mulgan. 2017. *Digital Democracy: The Tools Transforming Political Engagement*. London: Nesta.

Singer, Peter W., and Emerson T. Brooking. 2018. *LikeWar: The Weaponization of Social Media*. Boston, MA: Eamon Dolan.

Sitkoff, Harvard. 1981. *The Struggle for Black Equality, 1954–1992*. New York: Hill & Wang.

Skoric, Marko M., Qinfeng Zhu, Debbie Goh, and Natalie Pang. 2015. "Social Media and Citizen Engagement: A Meta-Analytic Review." *New Media & Society* 18 (9): 1817–1839.

Smith, Peter C., and Andrew Street. 2005. "Measuring the Efficiency of Public Services: The Limits of Analysis." *Statistics in Society* 168 (2): 401–417.

Snider, Mike. 2017. "Trump Invokes'Fake News' at Press Conference." *USA Today.* www.usatoday.com/story/money/2017/01/11/trump-tackles-fake-news-press-con ference/96438764/.

Snow, David A., E. Burke Rochford, Jr., Steven K. Worden, and Robert D. Benford. 1986. "Frame Alignment Processes, Micromobilization, and Movement Participation." *American Sociological Review* 51 (4): 464–481.

Snow, David A., and Robert D. Benford. 1988. "Ideology, Frame Resonance, and Participant Mobilization." *International Social Movement Research* 1 (1): 197–217.

Snyder, James M., and David Strömberg. 2010. "Press Coverage and Political Accountability." *Journal of Political Economy* 118 (2): 355–408.

Solon, Olivia, and Sabrina Siddiqui. 2017. "Forget Wall Street – Silicon Valley Is the New Political Power in Washington." *The Guardian.* www.theguardian.com/tech nology/2017/sep/03/silicon-valley-politics-lobbying-washington.

Somaiya, Ravi. 2011. "In Britain, a Meeting on Limiting Social Media." *The New York Times.* www.nytimes.com/2011/08/26/world/europe/26social.html.

Soroka, Stuart, Blake Andrew, Toril Aalberg, Shanto Iyengar, James Curran, Sharon Coen, Kaori Hayashi, et al. 2013. "Auntie Knows Best? Public Broadcasters and Current Affairs Knowledge." *British Journal of Political Science* 43 (4): 719–739.

Soros, George. 2018. "The Social Media Threat to Society and Security." *Project Syndicate.* www.project-syndicate.org/commentary/social-media-security-threat-by-george-soros-2018-02.

Spaiser, Viktoria, Thomas Chadefaux, Karsten Donnay, Fabian Russmann, and Dirk Helbing. 2017. "Communication Power Struggles on Social Media: A Case Study of the 2011–12 Russian Protests." *Journal of Information Technology & Politics* 14 (2): 132–153.

Sparrow, Bartholomew H. 2006. "A Research Agenda for an Institutional Media." *Political Communication* 23 (2): 145–157.

Srinivasan, Balaji. 2013. "Software Is Reorganizing the World." *Wired.* www.wired .com/2013/11/software-is-reorganizing-the-world-and-cloud-formations-could-lead-to-physical-nations/.

Stahl, Lesley. 2017. "Secret Weapon." *60 Minutes.* www.cbsnews.com/video/secret-weapon/.

Stamm, Keith R. 1985. *Newspaper Use and Community Ties: Towards a Dynamic Theory.* Norwood, NJ: Ablex Publishing Corporation.

Stark, Birgit, Melanie Magin, and Pascal Jürgens. 2017. *Ganz meine Meinung? Informationsintermediäre und Meinungsbildung – Eine Mehrmethodenstudie am Beispiel von Facebook.* Düsseldorf: Landesanstalt für Medien Nordrhein-Westfalen (LfM).

Stasavage, David. 2004. "Open-Door or Closed-Door? Transparency in Domestic and International Bargaining." *International Organization* 58 (4): 667–704.

Steinert-Threlkeld, Zachary C. 2017. "Spontaneous Collective Action: Peripheral Mobilization during the Arab Spring." *American Political Science Review* 111 (2): 379–403.

Stelter, Brian. 2015. "Why Facebook Is Starting a New Partnership with 9 News Publishers." *CNNMoney*. http://money.cnn.com/2015/05/13/media/facebook-instant-articles-news-industry/.

Stern, Ken. 2016. "Stephen Bannon, Trump's New C.E.O., Hints at His Master Plan." *Vanity Fair*. www.vanityfair.com/news/2016/08/breitbart-stephen-bannon-donald-trump-master-plan.

Stockman, Daniela. 2013. *Media Commercialization and Authoritarian Rule in China*. Cambridge, UK: Cambridge University Press.

Stoker, Laura, and M. Kent Jennings. 2008. "Of Time and the Development of Partisan Polarization." *American Journal of Political Science* 52 (3): 619–635.

Stolberg, Sheryl Gay. 2002. "Under Fire, Lott Apologizes for His Comments at Thurmond's Party." *The New York Times*. www.nytimes.com/2002/12/10/us/under-fire-lott-apologizes-for-his-comments-at-thurmond-s-party.html.

Stone, Melissa Middleton, Mark A. Hager, and Jennifer J. Griffin. 2001. "Organizational Characteristics and Funding Environments: A Study of a Population of United Way-Affiliated Nonprofits." *Public Administration Review* 61 (3): 276–289.

Strömbäck, Jesper. 2008. "Four Phases of Mediatization: An Analysis of the Mediatization of Politics." *The International Journal of Press/Politics* 13 (3): 228–246.

Strömberg, David. 2004. "Mass Media Competition, Political Competition, and Public Policy." *The Review of Economic Studies* 71 (1): 265–284.

Strömberg, David. 2015. "Media and Politics." *Annual Review of Economics* 7 (1): 173–205.

Stromer-Galley, Jennifer. 2000. "On-Line Interaction and Why Candidates Avoid It." *Journal of Communication* 50 (4): 111–132.

Stromer-Galley, Jennifer. 2019. *Presidential Campaigning in the Internet Age*. 2nd ed. New York: Oxford University Press.

Stromer-Galley, Jennifer, and Andrea B. Baker. 2006. "Joy and Sorrow of Interactivity on the Campaign Trail: Blogs in the Primary Campaign of Howard Dean." In *The Internet Election: Perspectives on the Web in Campaign 2004*, edited by Andrew Paul Williams and John C. Tedesco, 111–131. Oxford: Rowman & Littlefield.

Stromer-Galley, Jennifer, and Alexis Wichowski. 2011. "Political Discussion Online." In *The Handbook of Internet Studies*, edited by Mia Consalvo and Charles Ess, 168–167. Hoboken, NJ: Blackwell Publishing Ltd.

Stroud, Natalie Jomini. 2011. *Niche News: The Politics of News Choice*. New York: Oxford University Press.

Stroud, Natalie Jomini. 2017. "Selective Exposure Theories." In *The Oxford Handbook of Political Communication*, edited by Kate Kenski and Kathleen Hall Jamieson, 531–548. New York: Oxford University Press.

Stroud, Natalie Jomini, Joshua M Scacco, Ashley Muddiman, and Alexander L Curry. 2014. "Changing Deliberative Norms on News Organizations' Facebook Sites." *Journal of Computer-Mediated Communication* 20 (2): 188–203.

Stukal, Denis, Sergey Sanovich, Richard Bonneau, and Joshua A. Tucker. 2017. "Detecting Bots on Russian Political Twitter." *Big Data* 5 (4): 310–324.

Su, Leona Yi-Fan, Michael A Xenos, Kathleen M. Rose, Christopher Wirz, Dietram A Scheufele, and Dominique Brossard. 2018. "Uncivil and Personal? Comparing

Patterns of Incivility in Comments on the Facebook Pages of News Outlets." *New Media & Society* 20 (10): 3678–3699.

Subramanian, Samanth. 2017. "Inside the Macedonian Fake-News Complex." *Wired.* www.wired.com/2017/02/veles-macedonia-fake-news/.

Subrahmanian, V. S., Amos Azaria, Skylar Durst, Vadim Kagan, Aram Galstyan, Kristina Lerman, Linhong Zhu, Emilio Ferrara, Alessandro Flammini, and Filippo Menczer. 2016. "The Darpa Twitter Bot Challenge." *Computer* 49 (6): 38–46.

Sullivan, Mark L. 2012. "A New Model: VAN and the Challenge of the Voter-File Interface." In *Margin of Victory: How Technologists Help Politicians Win Elections*, edited by Nathaniel G. Pearlman, 133–146. Santa Monica, CA: ABC-CLIO.

Sunstein, Cass R. 2001. *Republic.com.* Princeton, NJ: Princeton University Press.

Sunstein, Cass R. 2007. *Republic.com 2.0.* Princeton, NJ: Princeton University Press.

Sunstein, Cass R. 2017. *#Republic: Divided Democracy in the Age of Social Media.* Princeton, NJ: Princeton University Press.

Susskind, Jamie. 2018. *Future Politics: Living Together in a World Transformed by Tech.* Oxford: Oxford University Press.

Tang, Gary, and Francis L. F. Lee. 2013. "Facebook Use and Political Participation: The Impact of Exposure to Shared Political Information, Connections with Public Political Actors, and Network Structural Heterogeneity." *Social Science Computer Review* 31 (6): 763–773.

Tankersley, Jim. 2016. "Why Donald Trump's 1980s-Style Campaign Is Struggling in 2016." *The Washington Post.* www.washingtonpost.com/news/wonk/wp/2016/08/20/why-donald-trumps-1980s-style-campaign-is-struggling-in-2016/.

Tarrow, Sidney G. 2011. *Power in Movement: Social Movements and Contentious Politics.* 3rd ed. Cambridge, UK: Cambridge University Press.

Taylor, Andrew J. 1993. "Trade Unions and the Politics of Social Democratic Renewal." *West European Politics* 16 (1): 133–155.

Taylor, Frederick W. 1911. *The Principles of Scientific Management.* New York: Harper & Brothers.

Tewksbury, David, and Jason Rittberg. 2012. *News on the Internet: Information and Citizenship in the 21st Century.* Oxford: Oxford University Press.

Tewksbury, David, Andrew J. Weaver, and Brett D. Maddex. 2001. "Accidentally Informed: Incidental News Exposure on the World Wide Web." *Journalism & Mass Communication Quarterly* 78 (3): 533–554.

Theocharis, Yannis. 2015. "The Conceptualization of Digitally Networked Participation." *Social Media + Society* 1 (2): 1–14.

Theocharis, Yannis, Pablo Barberá, Zoltán Fazekas, Sebastian Adrian Popa, and Olivier Parne. 2016. "A Bad Workman Blames His Tweets: The Consequences of Citizens' Uncivil Twitter Use When Interacting with Party Candidates." *Journal of Communication* 66 (6): 1007–1031.

Theocharis, Yannis, and Will Lowe. 2016. "Does Facebook Increase Political Participation? Evidence from a Field Experiment." *Information, Communication & Society* 19 (10): 1465–1486.

Theocharis, Yannis, Will Lowe, Jan W. van Deth, and Gema García-Albacete. 2014. "Using Twitter to Mobilize Protest Action: Online Mobilization Patterns and

Action Repertoires in the Occupy Wall Street, Indignados, and Aganaktismenoi Movements." *Information, Communication & Society* 18 (2): 202–220.

Theocharis, Yannis, and Ellen Quintelier. 2016. "Stimulating Citizenship or Expanding Entertainment? The Effect of Facebook on Adolescent Participation." *New Media & Society* 18 (5): 817–836.

Theocharis, Yannis, and Jan W. van Deth. 2018a. *Political Participation in a Changing World: Conceptual and Empirical Challenges in the Study of Citizen Engagement.* New York: Routledge.

Theocharis, Yannis, and Jan W. van Deth. 2018b. "The Continuous Expansion of Citizen Participation: A New Taxonomy." *European Political Science Review* 10 (1): 139–163.

Thomas, Owen. 2007. "Peter Thiel Is Totally Gay, People." *Gawker.* http://gawker.com/335894/peter-thiel-is-totally-gay-people.

Thompson, Derek. 2017. *Hit Makers: The Science of Popularity in an Age of Distraction.* New York: Penguin Press.

Thorson, Kjerstin, and Chris Wells. 2016. "Curated Flows: A Framework for Mapping Media Exposure in the Digital Age." *Communication Theory* 26 (3): 309–328.

Tindall, David B. 2004. "Social Movement Participation over Time: An Ego-Network Approach to Micro-Mobilization." *Sociological Focus* 37 (2): 163–184.

Tirole, Jean. 2016. *Economics for the Common Good.* Princeton, NJ: Princeton University Press.

Toor, Amar. 2014. "Why a Messaging App Meant for Festivals Became Massively Popular during Hong Kong Protests." *The Verge.* www.theverge.com/2014/10/16/6981127/firechat-messaging-app-accidental-protest-app-hong-kong.

Tourangeau, Roger, Lance J. Rips, and Kenneth Rasinski. 2000. *The Psychology of Survey Response.* Cambridge, UK: Cambridge University Press.

Tourangeau, Roger, and Ting Yan. 2007. "Sensitive Questions in Surveys." *Psychological Bulletin* 133 (5): 859–883.

Tracinski, Robert. 2008. "The Problem with the Media's Palin Coverage." *Real Clear Politics.* www.realclearpolitics.com/articles/2008/09/palin_and_the_partisan_press.html.

Trippi, Joe. 2004. *The Revolution Will Not Be Televised: Democracy, the Internet, and the Overthrow of Everything.* New York: Regan Books.

Trump, Kris-Stella. 2018. "Four and a Half Reasons Not to Worry That Cambridge Analytica Skewed the 2016 Election." *The Washington Post: Monkey Cage.* www.washingtonpost.com/news/monkey-cage/wp/2018/03/23/four-and-a-half-reasons-not-to-worry-that-cambridge-analytica-skewed-the-2016-election/.

Tuchman, Gaye. 1978. *Making News: A Study in the Construction of Reality.* New York: The Free Press.

Tucker, Joshua A., Yannis Theocharis, Margaret E. Roberts, and Pablo Barberá. 2017. "From Liberation to Turmoil: Social Media and Democracy." *Journal of Democracy* 28 (4): 46–59.

Tufekci, Zeynep. 2013. "'Not This One': Social Movements, the Attention Economy, and Microcelebrity Networked Activism." *American Behavioral Scientist* 57 (7): 848–870.

Tufekci, Zeynep. 2017. *Twitter and Tear Gas: The Power and Fragility of Networked Protest.* New Haven, CT: Yale University Press.

Tufekci, Zeynep, and Christopher Wilson. 2012. "Social Media and the Decision to Participate in Political Protest: Observations from Tahrir Square." *Journal of Communication* 62 (2): 363–379.

Turner, Fred. 2006. *From Counterculture to Cyberculture: Stewart Brand, the Whole Earth Network, and the Rise of Digital Utopianism.* Chicago, IL: The University of Chicago Press.

Twitter PublicPolicy. 2018. "Update on Twitter's Review of the 2016 U.S. Election." *Twitter.* https://blog.twitter.com/official/en_us/topics/company/2018/2016-election-update.html.

Usher, Nikki. 2014. *Making News at the New York Times.* Ann Arbor: The University of Michigan Press.

Uslander, Eric M. 2002. *The Moral Foundations of Trust.* Cambridge, UK: Cambridge University Press.

Utz, Sonja. 2009. "The (Potential) Benefits of Campaigning via Social Network Sites." *Journal of Computer-Mediated Communication* 14 (2): 221–243.

Vaccari, Cristian. 2010. "'Technology Is a Commodity': The Internet in the 2008 United States Presidential Election." *Journal of Information Technology & Politics* 7 (4): 318–339.

Vaccari, Cristian. 2013. *Digital Politics in Western Democracies: A Comparative Study.* Baltimore, MD: Johns Hopkins University Press.

Vaccari, Cristian, Andrew Chadwick, and Ben O'Loughlin. 2015. "Dual Screening the Political: Media Events, Social Media, and Citizen Engagement." *Journal of Communication* 65 (6): 1041–1061.

Vaccari, Cristian, and Augusto Valeriani. 2018. "Dual Screening, Public Service Broadcasting, and Political Participation in Eight Western Democracies." *The International Journal of Press/Politics* 23 (3): 367–388.

Vaccari, Cristian, Augusto Valeriani, Pablo Barberá, Rich Bonneau, John T Jost, Jonathan Nagler, and Joshua A Tucker. 2015. "Political Expression and Action on Social Media: Exploring the Relationship Between Lower-and Higher-Threshold Political Activities among Twitter Users in Italy." *Journal of Computer-Mediated Communication* 20 (2): 221–239.

Vaidhyanathan, Siva. 2018. *Antisocial Media: How Facebook Disconnects Us and Undermines Democracy.* Oxford University Press.

Valentine, Melissa A., Daniela Retelny, Alexandra To, Negar Rahmati, Tulsee Doshi, and Michael S. Bernstein. 2017. "Flash Organizations: Crowdsourcing Complex Work by Structuring Crowds as Organizations." In *Proceedings of the 2017 Chi Conference on Human Factors in Computing Systems*, edited by Gloria Mark, Susan Fussell, Cliff Lampe, m.c. schraefel, Juan Pablo, Caroline Appert, and Daniel Wigdor, 3523–3537. New York: ACM.

Valenzuela, Sebastián. 2013. "Unpacking the Use of Social Media for Protest Behavior." *American Behavioral Scientist* 57 (7): 920–942.

Valenzuela, Sebastián, Arturo Arriagada, and Andrés Scherman. 2012. "The Social Media Basis of Youth Protest Behavior: The Case of Chile." *Journal of Communication* 62 (2): 299–314.

Valenzuela, Sebastián, Namsu Park, and Kerk F. Kee. 2009. "Is There Social Capital in a Social Network Site?: Facebook Use and College Students' Life Satisfaction, Trust, and Participation." *Journal of Computer-Mediated Communication* 14 (4): 875–901.

Valera, M., and S.A. Velastin. 2005. "Intelligent Distributed Surveillance Systems: A Review." *IEE Proceedings – Vision, Image and Signal Processing* 152 (2): 192–204.

Valeriani, Augusto, and Cristian Vaccari. 2016. "Accidental Exposure to Politics on Social Media as Online Participation Equalizer in Germany, Italy, and the United Kingdom." *New Media & Society* 18 (9): 1857–1874.

Valeriani, Augusto, and Cristian Vaccari. 2018. "Political Talk on Mobile Instant Messaging Services: A Comparative Analysis of Germany, Italy, and the UK." *Information, Communication & Society* 21 (11): 1715–1731.

Van Biezen, Ingrid, Peter Mair, and Thomas Poguntke. 2012. "Going, Going, … Gone? The Decline of Party Membership in Contemporary Europe." *European Journal of Political Research* 51 (1): 24–56.

van der Meer, Tom W. G. 2017. "Political Trust and the 'Crisis of Democracy'." In *Oxford Research Encyclopedia of Politics*, edited by William R. Thompson, 1–22. Oxford University Press. https://doi.org/10.1093/acrefore/9780190228637.013.77.

van Deursen, Alexander, and Jan van Dijk. 2014. "The Digital Divide Shifts to Differences in Usage." *New Media & Society* 16 (3): 507–526.

van Dijk, Jan. 2005. *The Deepening Divide: Inequality in the Information Society.* Thousand Oaks, CA: SAGE.

van Dijk, Jan. 2012. *The Network Society.* 3rd ed. Thousand Oaks, CA: SAGE.

van Dijk, Jan, and Alexander van Deursen. 2014. *Digital Skills: Unlocking the Information Society.* Thousand Oaks, CA: SAGE.

Van Laer, Jeroen, and Peter Van Aelst. 2010. "Internet and Social Movement Action Repertoires: Opportunities and Limitations." *Information, Communication & Society* 13 (8): 1146–1171.

Van Natta, Don, Jr. 2000. "The 2000 Campaign: The Money Game; McCain Gets Big Payoff on Web Site." *The New York Times.* www.nytimes.com/2000/02/04/us/the-2000-campaign-the-money-game-mccain-gets-big-payoff-on-web-site.html.

Varnelis, Kazys. 2008. *Networked Publics.* Cambridge, MA: MIT Press.

Varol, Onur, Emilio Ferrara, Clayton A. Davis, Filippo Menczer, and Alessandro Flammini. 2017. "Online Human-Bot Interactions: Detection, Estimation, and Characterization." In *ICWSM 2017: Proceedings of the Eleventh International AAAI Conference on Web and Social Media*, 280–289. Menlo Park, CA: Association for the Advancement of Artificial Intelligence (AAAI).

Verba, Sidney, and Norman H. Nie. 1987. *Participation in America: Political Democracy and Social Equality.* Chicago, IL: The University of Chicago Press.

Verba, Sidney, Kay Lehman Schlozman, and Henry Brady. 1995. *Voice and Equality: Civic Voluntarism in American Politics.* Cambridge, MA: Harvard University Press.

Victor, Daniel. 2018. "Advertisers Drop Laura Ingraham after She Taunts Parkland Survivor David Hogg." *The New York Times.* www.nytimes.com/2018/03/29/business/media/laura-ingraham-david-hogg.html.

Vitak, Jessica, Paul Zubea, Andrew Smock, Caleb T. Carr, Nicole Ellison, and Cliff Lampe. 2011. "It's Complicated: Facebook Users' Political Participation in the 2008 Election." *Cyberpsychology, Behavior, and Social Networking* 14 (3): 107–114.

Vraga, Emily K., Leticia Bode, Anne-Bennett Smithson, and Sonya Troller-Renfree. 2019. "Accidentally Attentive: Comparing Visual, Close-Ended, and Open-Ended

Measures of Attention on Social Media." *Computers in Human Behavior* 99: 235–244.

Vynck, Gerrit De, and Selina Wang. 2018. "Russian Bots Retweeted Trump's Twitter 470,000 Times." *Bloomberg Politics*. www.bloomberg.com/news/articles/2018-01-26/twitter-says-russian-linked-bots-retweeted-trump-470-000-times.

Wahlström, Mattias, and Magnus Wennerhag. 2014. "Alone in the Crowd: Lone Protesters in Western European Demonstrations." *International Sociology* 29 (6): 565–583.

Wallerstein, Michael. 1999. "Wage-Setting Institutions and Pay Inequality in Advanced Industrial Societies." *American Journal of Political Science* 43 (3): 649–680.

Wang, Gang, Christo Wilson, Xiaohan Zhao, Yibo Zhu, Manish Mohanlal, Haitao Zheng, and Ben Y. Zhao. 2012. "Serf and Turf: Crowdturfing for Fun and Profit." In *WWW'12: Proceedings of the 21st International Conference on World Wide Web*, edited by Alain Mille, Fabien Gandon, Jacques Misselis, Michael Rabinovich, and Steffen Staab, 679–688. New York: ACM.

Wang, Hongyu, and Fayong Shi. 2018. "Weibo Use and Political Participation: The Mechanism Explaining the Positive Effect of Weibo Use on Online Political Participation among College Students in Contemporary China." *Information, Communication & Society* 21 (4): 516–530.

Wang, Shan. 2017. "How Much News Makes It into People's Facebook Feeds? Our Experiment Suggests Not Much." *NiemanLab*. www.niemanlab.org/2017/12/how-much-news-makes-it-into-peoples-facebook-feeds-our-experiment-suggests-not-much/.

Ward, Stephen, Rachel Gibson, and Wainer Lusoli. 2003. "Online Participation and Mobilisation in Britain: Hype, Hope and Reality." *Parliamentary Affairs* 56 (4): 652–668.

Warschauer, Mark. 2003. *Technology and Social Inclusion: Rethinking the Digital Divide*. Cambridge, MA: The MIT Press.

Warzel, Charlie. 2013. "Facebook Drives Massive New Surge of Traffic to Publishers." *BuzzFeed*. www.buzzfeed.com/charliewarzel/out-of-the-blue-facebook-is-now-driving-enormous-traffic-to.

Watts, Duncan J. 2011. *Everything Is Obvious: How Common Sense Fails Us*. New York: Random House.

Watts, Duncan J., and David M. Rothschild. 2017. "Don't Blame the Election on Fake News. Blame It on the Media." *Columbia Journalism Review*. www.cjr.org/analysis/fake-news-media-election-trump.php.

Weaver, Matthew. 2018. "Facebook Scandal: I Am Being Used as Scapegoat – Academic Who Mined Data." *The Guardian*. www.theguardian.com/uk-news/2018/mar/21/facebook-row-i-am-being-used-as-scapegoat-says-academic-aleksandr-kogan-cambridge-analytica.

Weber, Lori M., Alysha Loumakis, and James Bergman. 2003. "Who Participates and Why? An Analysis of Citizens on the Internet and the Mass Public." *Social Science Computer Review* 21 (1): 26–42.

Webster, James G. 2014. *The Marketplace of Attention: How Audiences Take Shape in a Digital Age*. Boston, MA: The MIT Press.

Webster, James G., and Patricia F. Phalen. 1997. *The Mass Audience: Rediscovering the Dominant Model*. Mahwah, NJ: Lawrence Erlbaum Associates.

Webster, James G., Patricia F. Phalen, and Lawrence W. Lichty. 2014. *Ratings Analysis: Audience Measurement and Analytics*. 4th ed. New York: Routledge.

Weidmann, Nils B., and Espen Geelmuyden Rød. 2019. *The Internet and Political Protest in Autocracies*. New York: Oxford University Press.

Weidmann, Nils B., and Sebastian Schutte. 2017. "Using Night Light Emissions for the Prediction of Local Wealth." *Journal of Peace Research* 54 (2): 125–140.

Weisenthal, Joe. 2016. "Donald Trump, the First President of Our Post-Literate Age." *BloombergView*. www.bloomberg.com/view/articles/2016-11-29/donald-trump-the-first-president-of-our-post-literate-age.

Wells, Chris, Dhavan V. Shah, Jon C. Pevehouse, JungHwan Yang, Ayellet Pelled, Frederick Boehm, Josephine Lukito, Shreenita Ghosh, and Jessica L. Schmidt. 2016. "How Trump Drove Coverage to the Nomination: Hybrid Media Campaigning." *Political Communication* 33 (4): 669–676.

Wells, Chris, Katherine J. Cramer, Michael W. Wagner, German Alvarez, Lewis A. Friedland, Dhavan V. Shah, Leticia Bode, Stephanie Edgerly, Itay Gabay, and Charles Franklin. 2017. "When We Stop Talking Politics: The Maintenance and Closing of Conversation in Contentious Times." *Journal of Communication* 67 (1): 131–157.

Whibey, John P. 2019. *The Social Fact: News and Knowledge in a Networked World*. Cambridge, MA: The MIT Press.

White, Adam. 2018. "Google.gov." *The New Atlantis* 55 (Spring): 3–34.

Whiteley, Paul F. 2011. "Is the Party over? The Decline of Party Activism and Membership across the Democratic World." *Party Politics* 17 (1): 21–44.

Wiener, Norbert. 1950. *The Human Use of Human Beings: Cybernetics and Society*. Boston, MA: Houghton Mifflin.

Wiener, Norbert. 1961. *Cybernetics: Or Control and Communication in the Animal and the Machine*. 2nd ed. Cambridge, MA: The MIT Press.

Wilhelm, Anthony G. 1998. "Virtual Sounding Boards: How Deliberative Is on-Line Political Discussion?" *Information, Communication & Society* 1 (3): 313–338.

Wilhoit, Elizabeth D, and Lorraine G Kisselburgh. 2015. "Collective Action without Organization: The Material Constitution of Bike Commuters as Collective." *Organization Studies* 36 (5): 573–592.

Willer, Robb. 2009. "A Status Theory of Collective Action." In *Altruism and Prosocial Behavior in Groups*, 133–163. Bingley: Emerald Group Publishing Limited.

Williams, Bruce A., and Michael X. Delli Carpini. 2011. *After Broadcast News: Media Regimes, Democracy, and the New Information Environment*. Cambridge, UK: Cambridge University Press.

Wilson, Christopher, and Alexandra Dunn. 2011. "Digital Media in the Egyptian Revolution: Descriptive Analysis from the Tahrir Data Set." *International Journal of Communication* 5: 1248–1272.

Wired Staff. 2016. "25 Geniuses Who Are Creating the Future of Business." *Wired*. www.wired.com/2016/04/wired-nextlist-2016/.

Wlezien, Christopher. 1995. "The Public as Thermostat: Dynamics of Preferences for Spending." *American Journal of Political Science* 39 (4): 981–1000.

Wolf, Daniel de. 2013. "Crisis Management: Lessons Learnt from BP Deepwater Horizon Spill Oil." *Business Management and Strategy* 4 (1): 69–90.

Wolfinger, Raymond E, and Steven J Rosenstone. 1980. *Who Votes?* New Haven, CT: Yale University Press.

Wooldridge, Adrian. 2011. *Masters of Management: How the Business Gurus and Their Ideas Have Changed the World–for Better and for Worse.* New York: HarperCollins.

Woolf, Stuart J. 1984. "Towards the History of the Origins of Statistics: France 1789–1815." In *State and Statistics in France 1789–1815*, edited by Jean-Claude Perrot and Stuart J. Woolf, 81–194. Amsterdam, The Netherlands: Harwood Academic Publishers.

Woolf, Stuart J. 1989. "Statistics and the Modern State." *Comparative Studies in Society and History* 31 (3): 588–604.

Wright, Aaron, and Primavera De Filippi. 2015. "Decentralized Blockchain Technology and the Rise of Lex Cryptographia." *SSRN Electronic Journal.* https://ssrn.com/abstract=2580664.

Wright, Scott, and John Street. 2007. "Democracy, Deliberation and Design: The Case of Online Discussion Forums." *New Media & Society* 9 (5): 849–869.

Wu, Tim. 2016. *The Attention Merchants: The Epic Scramble to Get Inside Our Heads.* New York: Alfred A. Knopf.

Wuttke, Alexander. 2019. "Why Too Many Political Science Findings Cannot Be Trusted and What We Can Do about It: A Review of Meta-Scientific Research and a Call for Academic Reform." *PVS: Politische Vierteljahresschrift* 60 (1): 1–19.

Wuttke, Alexander, Andreas Jungherr, and Harald Schoen. 2019. "More Than Opinion Expression: Secondary Effects of Intraparty Referendums on Party Members." *Party Politics* 25 (6): 817–827.

Xenos, Michael, and Patricia Moy. 2007. "Direct and Differential Effects of the Internet on Political and Civic Engagement." *Journal of Communication* 57 (4): 704–718.

Yamamoto, Masahiro, and Matthew J. Kushin. 2014. "More Harm Than Good? Online Media Use and Political Disaffection among College Students in the 2008 Election." *Journal of Computer-Mediated Communication* 19 (3): 430–445.

Yang, Xiaofeng, Qian Yang, and Christo Wilson. 2015. "Penny for Your Thoughts: Searching for the 50 Cent Party on Sina Weibo." In *ICWSM 2015: Proceedings of the Ninth International AAAI Conference on Web and Social Media*, 694–697. Menlo Park, CA: Association for the Advancement of Artificial Intelligence (AAAI).

Young, Sally. 2009. "Sky News Australia: The Impact of Local 24-Hour News on Political Reporting in Australia." *Journalism Studies* 10 (3): 401–416.

Yu, Harlan, and David Robinson. 2012. "The New Ambiguity of 'Open Government'." *UCLA Law Review* 178 (August): 180–208.

Zaller, John R. 1992. *The Nature and Origins of Mass Opinion.* Cambridge, UK: Cambridge University Press.

Zaller, John R. 2003. "A New Standard of News Quality: Burglar Alarms for the Monitorial Citizen." *Political Communication* 20 (2): 109–130.

Zarsky, Tal Z. 2011. "Governmental Data Mining and Its Alternatives." *Penn State Law Review* 116 (2): 285–330.

Zelenkauskaite, Asta, and Brandon Niezgoda. 2017. "'Stop Kremlin Trolls:' Ideological Trolling as Calling Out, Rebuttal, and Reactions on Online News Portal

Commenting." *First Monday* 22 (5). https://firstmonday.org/ojs/index.php/fm/art
icle/view/7795.

Zhang, Yini, Dhavan Shah, Jordan Foley, Aman Abhishek, Josephine Lukito,
Jiyoun Suk, Sang Jung Kim, Zhongkai Sun, Jon Pevehouse, and
Christine Garlough. 2019. "Whose Lives Matter? Mass Shootings and Social
Media Discourses of Sympathy and Policy, 2012–2014." *Journal of Computer-
Mediated Communication* 24 (4): 182–202.

Zhuo, Xiaolin, Barry Wellman, and Justine Yu. 2011. "Egypt: The First Internet
Revolt?" *Peace Magazine* (July–September): 6–10.

Zickuhr, Kathryn. 2010. *"Generations 2010."* Washington, DC: Pew Internet & American Life Project.

Zittrain, Jonathan. 2014. "Facebook Could Decide an Election without Anyone Ever
Finding Out." *The New Republic.* https://newrepublic.com/article/117878/informa
tion-fiduciary-solution-facebook-digital-gerrymandering.

Zubayr, Camille, and Heinz Gerhard. 2017. "Tendenzen im Zuschauerverhalten."
Media Perspektiven 3: 130–144.

Zuboff, Shoshana. 2019. *The Age of Surveillance Capitalism: The Fight for a Human
Future at the New Frontier of Power.* New York: Public Affairs.

Zuckerman, Ethan. 2007. "Cute Cat Theory: The China Corollary." *...My Heart's in
Accra.* www.ethanzuckerman.com/blog/2007/12/03/cute-cat-theory-the-china-cor
ollary/.

Zukin, Cliff, and Robin Snyder. 1984. "Passive Learning: When the Media Environment Is the Message." *Public Opinion Quarterly* 48 (3): 629–638.

Index